D0205315

Black Women in the
New World Order

BLACK WOMEN IN THE NEW WORLD ORDER

Social Justice and the African American Female

WILLA MAE HEMMONS

 PRAEGER

Westport, Connecticut
London

Library of Congress Cataloging-in-Publication Data

Hemmons, Willa Mae.
    Black women in the new world order : social justice and the
African American female / Willa Mae Hemmons.
       p. cm.
    Includes bibliographical references and index.
    ISBN 0–275–95208–8 (alk. paper)
    1. Afro–American women. 2. Afro-American women—Legal status,
laws, etc. I. Title.
E185.86.H46   1996
305.48′8896073—dc20   95–34416

British Library Cataloguing in Publication Data is available.

Library of Congress Catalog Card Number: 95–34416
ISBN: 0–275–95208–8

First published in 1996

Praeger Publishers, 88 Post Road West, Westport, CT 06881
An imprint of Greenwood Publishing Group, Inc.

Printed in the United States of America

The paper used in this book complies with the
Permanent Paper Standard issued by the National
Information Standards Organization (Z39.48–1984).

10 9 8 7 6 5 4 3 2

To the One above who kept me in touch with myself and my people. In memory of my late mother and brother and of my father, who passed over during the writing of this book.

This book is dedicated to my husband, who kept me in touch with the views of another Gender; to my father and to my children, who kept me in touch with the views of other Generations; to my brothers and sisters, who kept me in touch with the views of other Social Institutions; to my dissertation advisor and continuing mentor, Dr. LaFrancis Rodgers-Rose, who kept me in touch with the views of Afrocentricity and the Ancestors; to my students, who kept me in touch with the views of the true meaning and purpose of Academia; to my clients, who kept me in touch with the views of the true meaning and purpose of the Law.

Contents

Black Women in the
New World Order

CHAPTER 1

Black Women in the New World Order: An Introduction

STATEMENT OF THE PROBLEM

This book takes a sociolegal approach in discussing the status of the African American (Anderson 1990, 2) woman[1] in what has been popularized primarily, by politicians and others, as "The New World Order."[2] It embodies the foundation of policy that, as inferred from one editorial[3] and a presidential quotation,[4] transcended U.S. governmental administrations. According to A. Ralph Epperson, in his 1990 book, *The New World Order*, the term has been around since the inception of the United States and relates not only to the country's ultimate destiny but to that of the world.[5] Epperson bases his belief that the "order" has been the rationale for the United States since its beginning on one primary point, that the Latin phrase, *Novus Ordo Seclorum*, found underneath the pyramid on the reverse side of the Great Seal of the United States and placed on the back of the U.S. dollar bill in 1935 (the year the Social Security Act was passed) by President Franklin D. Roosevelt, means *New World Order* in English.[6]

It appears that Epperson's view presumes that (1) the world's order has been somewhat deterministically defined; (2) the world's order has been defined by persons, institutions and forces that have intentionally avoided publicity—that, indeed, have been rather clandestine in the execution of their plans; and (3) planning for the world's order by these clandestine groups or, in Eppersonian terms, "secret societies"[7] has worked against the best interest of the world's "minorities" (e.g., non-White ethnic groups), women in general, and the African American woman in particular. This last presumption is not surprising inasmuch as Epperson quotes material that maintains that the implementation of the New World Order is the "providence" of Nordics, or Anglo Saxons,[8] and that that destiny is applicable only to certain chosen subcategories, such as the Freemasons.[9] Later references in this book term any group or groups purported (see Chapter 5) to be keepers of the "order" as the Orderites. In addition, a 1991 book by the Christian Coalition president Pat Robertson likewise entitled, *The New World Order*, although later somewhat repudiated by him,[10] reportedly had also conferred a conspiratorial bent on world history. The Robertson book was at variance with Epperson's as to the character of the putative "world controllers."[11]

In their edited book, *A New World Order? Global Transformations in the Late Twentieth Century* (1995), sociologists David A. Smith and József Böröcz use a world system analysis to assess the integration of European, Asian and African countries into the global economy. Most of the writers in the Smith and Böröcz book presume that the processes needed to effectuate any such integration began with the end of the Cold War and the relatively unfettered release of "free-world market forces." These forces are expedited by the fact that "U.S. corporations control large shares of the world market."[12] According to one contributing author in *A New World Order?*, the most serious threat to the successful imposition of the free market economy worldwide comes from the possible global unification of the world's workers, White, Black, Brown and Yellow.[13] With ethnic rivalries[14] more paramount than any such unification, the levers of racism, sexism and classism are left to perform their functions and leave their victims more vulnerable than ever before.

Reactions to the concept of the New World Order have been varied. For instance, at least one right wing vigilante group has openly entitled itself, "The Order," and another, its offshoot, "Order II."[15] Further, a newsletter[16] distributed by another group from the far right militia movement entitled, *The Resistor*, carried as its sub-title, "The New World Order."[17] Global, technological and economic forces which have made the "American Dream" more and more illusive for Blacks, Whites, Males, Females, working and "middle" classes have apparently evoked more scapegoating and greater disenchantment among some predominantly White, male extremist groups than among others. This result may be understood somewhat by using a typology introduced by sociologist Robert K. Merton, relative deprivation. If one has been socialized to expect to inherit the earth as opposed to serve at the pleasure of the heirs, one is probably going to be that much more disconcerted when one finds that the inheritance has already been dispersed before one can claim it. This analogy helps to explain somewhat the extreme frustration and aggravation of some White males who have bought into the conspiratorial theory of a one-government world as a source of their particular personal and collective failures.[18] Obviously, the New World Order concept means different things to different people. To both European American males and African American females, however, the term alludes to significant changes in their relative roles and statuses—for better or worse depending on their respective viewpoints and resources.

Conspiratorial theories aside,[19] in the social scientific sense, this book presumes that for several centuries at least, since the onset of New World slavery, the interests of the Afrogeneric woman have not been served by whoever was in power. The major focus, then, is the African American woman and her position as it has evolved to this point in the New World Order. Written from the viewpoint of one of some 11,000 Black women in legal practice in the United States[20], this book is basically a participant-observation research study based upon some of the author's own law cases. It is informed by social-scientific, legal and mass media materials and strives for a comprehensive, multidisciplinary view of its subject. Many of the observations are gleaned, in fact, from a content analysis of the reporting of "current" New World Order events. Such mass communications are incorporated into the assertions as illustrations of their validity. As a basically descriptive study, the book points toward further research into the many issues it presents as necessary to document more fully its tenets.

The foundation of the New World Order, from the perspective that it is also a heralded offshoot of the end of the Cold War, as developed by "world leaders" is economic and promising of auspicious consequences (Smith and Böröcz 1995). Such consequences are asserted to ensue not only for members of the "industrial nations" but also for countries thought to comprise what is known as the "Third World."[21] This latter assertion is challenged in the Smith and Böröcz work by one of their contributors, sociologist Philip McMichael. McMichael notes that during the 1980s there was a policy shift in terms of the funding of African states by the World Bank. He writes, "Initially, under the 1981 Berg Report from the World Report on development prospects in Sub-Saharan Africa, the goal of shrinking the state was justified on grounds of efficiency and reducing urban bias (Bernstein 1990, 19)."[22] McMichael goes on to explain that according to Beckman (1992, 92,99), "In the World Bank's major report of 1989 on Sub-Saharan Africa, "shrinking" the state was reinterpreted politically, as a device to release populist initiatives."[23] McMichael further cites Beckman in surmising, "In effect, this interpretation considers the World Bank's recent position as a deeper challenge to the African nation-state by legitimizing a postnationalist (globalist) mentality"[24] which means that intervention into an African country's affairs is justified by World Bank "notions of desirable development" as opposed to those of the country itself. The economic undermining of the African nation-states has repercussions for the Black woman insofar as it continues to emasculate potential global partners, alliances through which she and her global people might be able to mutually enhance their bargaining power within the context of their own countries, respectively, as well as that of the world with reference to civil rights, education, economics and their well-being in general.

SOCIOLEGAL PERSPECTIVE

Sociologist Alex Inkeles (1964, 25) provides insight into the sociological perspective[25] (using Functionalist theoretical formulations) embodied in this treatise with the observation that one assumption of sociology is that there is "order in nature." Further, he states that order can be "discovered," described, and understood similarly to the laws of nature governing other disciplines such as physics, astronomy, geology and "the order underlying the history and present structure of the earth." Inkeles states that "sociology seeks to discover, describe, and explain the order which characterizes the social life of man (*sic*)." Inkeles defines "order" by explaining that it refers to events which "occur in a more-or-less regular sequence or pattern." Inkeles (26) also points to the use of the word "order" in sociology to refer to "both regularized patterns of action and institutions that control, ameliorate, or canalize the conflict produced by persistent strains." However, he does caution that the "sociologist's concern with the *problem* of order should not lead one to assume that he (*sic*) has no interest in or responsibility for studying manifestations of disorder."

Perhaps somewhat at variance from the sociological perspective described above, the sociolegal perspective employed here will not presume that order is good. In fact, insofar as the "complex coordination of human action which every social system represents" (Inkeles 1964, 27) results in the subordination of African Americans and women in U.S. society, any purported stability, security and otherwise balance that "order" may be heralded as bringing to the national and global society will be concluded to be not *necessarily* good. Indeed, the guidance of Gunnar Myrdal will be followed insofar as he cautioned social scientists not to allow the study of facts alone to yield any conclusion about the goodness or desirability of the situation which those facts describe.[26]

Generally then, taking into consideration the aforementioned suspicion of the underlying concept of order, this work is probably most informed by the set of theoretical formulations in sociology known as *functionalism*. Functionalist theory, as used in this analysis, is based upon the presumption that the sociological tradition[27] is one in which recurring societal trends are identified[28] but, it is hoped, not idolized. This inquiry posits the notion that conflict is built into any social system where competition in everything— grades, spouses, prestige, property, wealth and power—is both expected and encouraged (see also Coser 1956; Dahrendorf 1959). As conflict is such an integral part of the society, conflict is functional in its existence.

In addition, insights from Afrocentric perspectives in the tradition pioneered by W.E.B. Du Bois (1903), Franz Fanon (1965), Carter G. Woodson (1933), St. Clair Drake and Horace R. Cayton (1945), Andrew Billingsley (1968), Robert Hill (1972), Joyce Ladner (1973), Harriette Pipes McAdoo (1981), James E. Blackwell (1975), Robert Staples (1973), Nathan and Julia Hare (1984), Elmer and Joanne Mitchell Martin (1978), Molefi Kete Asante

(1987), LaFrances Rodgers-Rose (1980), Doris Y. Wilkinson (1984), Maulana Karenga (1986; 1993), Lena Wright Myers (1980), Delores P. Aldridge (1991), Patricia Hill Collins (1991) and Haki Madhubuti (1990), among others, form the foundation for the concepts and ideas undergirding this treatise on the African American woman in U.S. society. The Afrocentric perspective is one in which the values, relationships and institutions of Afrogeneric persons are considered to transcend spatial and geographic boundaries (Asante 1987). The Afrocentric perspective is distinctive from a Eurocentric one insofar as the worldview of the former emphasizes a "We-ness" versus an "I-ness" modality (Nobles 1980). The African worldview includes group-ness, sameness and commonality as its underlying psychobehavioral modalities, according to Wade Nobles. In terms of values and customs, cooperation and collective responsibility are the fundamental foundations of Afrogeneric cultures (Nobles 1980). According to Asante, the Afrocentric perspective preceded the Eurocentric and the Asiocentric and allowed the world's first civilization, the Kemet (Egyptian) to grow and flourish. Indeed, Cheikh Anta Diop (1991) points out that the essence of Western law (338) and science (322) was appropriated by the Greeks from the Egyptian Africans (322). Hence, Diop maintains that the study of African thought provides a strong intellectual foundation for those seeking a linkage from their American to their African heritage (322). A distinctive difference, which made Greek thought identifiable as it evolved into Western thinking, was, according to Diop, the Greek creation of "atheistic materialism" (328).

Implicit in the exposure, exploration and expression of an Afrocentric ideology and lifestyle is the presumption that such will enable African Americans to enhance their survival skills and improve the quality of their lives (Warfield-Coppock 1990). Knowledge of the essence of their Afrocentric culture and being can enable African Americans to overcome their circumstances even in the face of intensified adversity (Karenga 1986). For African American women functioning in the social system of the New World Order, it is hypothesized here that an Afrocentric worldview is a prerequisite to truly overcoming systemic racial and sexual discrimination. To counteract the societal forces that seem to doom her to an inferior fate, the African American woman must try to recapture her "legacy," as described also in George G. M. James's *Stolen Legacy: Greek Philosophy Is Stolen Egyptian Philosophy* (1992).

The sociological perspective, as currently construed, looks at within-group and between-group dynamics in order to determine their effects upon the group members and group relationships,[29] respectively. In this study, group statistics are deemed to be evidence of the relative social justice each group is experiencing. This analysis adopts the proposition of Talcott Parsons (1951), one of the modern-day formulators of sociological theory, that the courts serve the same function as that served by the social institution of religion. The law has become an increasingly powerful factor in helping to determine and maintain social statuses and relationships desired by the "authorities" in U.S. society and, more and more, the global society. The religious and the legal (court) institutions, according to Parsons, helped to rationalize and make acceptable the conduct of the other social institutions: the political, the economic, the family, and later, the educational. Hence, in this book, case law from court decisions, legislation and other law-related material is included to illustrate, along with certain U.S. Bureau of the Census statistics, not only the fact of social injustice against the African American woman but also the fact of that social injustice's legitimation by the courts (see also Richard Neely's 1981 book, *How Courts Govern America*).

To make a long story short, it is proposed here that the Black woman's place in the New World Order is the same as it was in the "old world order" of the past four centuries: on, at, or near the bottom. Further, it is asserted that the values, planning, organizational structure, relationships and practices intrinsic to that sociological order are designed, absent some unintended outside intervention, to perpetuate such status for the African American woman—and, for that matter, for the African American man.

The reasons that this work addresses a fundamentally economic phenomenon from a Sociology of the Law (sociolegal) perspective rather than utilizing the Sociology of Economics (socioeconomic) treatment given by Smith and Böröcz are several. A primary one is that the legal institution, along with its corollary governmental systems such as the legislatures and the bureaucracies that administer societal policies, have been fiercely efficient in carrying out the New World Order agenda. Its swift implementation has been particularly effective through the use of the courts, welfare state and criminal justice systems as well as other administrative law bodies (agencies) as regard Black women. Overall, the ramifications of New World Order policies have had severe negative consequences demographically and racially for women and people of color. In addition, because of the growing recognition of the influence of global forces [and vice versa as far as certain U.S. "leaders" are concerned] on everyone in the United States,[30] sociologists are encouraged to consider such forces in their theory development, research, comparative study and analysis of society in order to produce more valid and reliable foundational as well as applied scholarship.[31]

One of the publicized, ostensible purposes of the New World Order is to strive to ameliorate such statistics as those which show that the average incomes of industrialized countries are six times those of "developing" countries.[32] As stated earlier, such Third World or developing countries are the ones purportedly targeted for the largesse of the New World Order.

However, conditions for the people of color in the United States (e.g., African Americans) who are of the same or similar racial origin as Third World peoples have grown worse than they were prior to the end of the

Cold War and the onset of the New World Order. It is ironic that, as this book attempts to show, the policies that have become endemic to the New World Order have worked so egregiously against the African American woman (and man). It is almost as if the true functions of the New World Order policies are to continue to expand, definitively institutionalize and further secure the economic gap between the rich and the poor both within and without the United States (cf. Frances Fox Piven and Richard A. Cloward's 1982 book, *The New Class War: Reagan's Attack on the Welfare State and Its Consequences*).

Sociology is a useful discipline from which to analyze this topic, inasmuch as "order" is one of the key underlying concepts[33] endemic to its framework as a social science (Inkeles 1964, 35-37). This analysis is also grounded in Black Studies as noted above. According to Talmadge Anderson, founding editor of the *Western Journal of Black Studies*,

As world and universal conditions change new paradigms and theoretical constructs are founded and put forth in response to new orders of social, political and economic phenomena and events. Black Studies is an academic result of inevitable changes in the American order. (Anderson 1990, 9)

Thus, this study acknowledges the fact that traditional paradigms such as sociology, political science, psychology and economics have not been able to present as comprehensive, valid and reliable a view of African Americans as they could have. This is because of a lack of inclusion of the Black Perspective and the tenets of Afrocentricity (Taylor 1990, 13) This is also due to the *order = equilibrium* presumptions implicit in much traditional social science thinking (Taylor 1990, 11–15; Kershaw 1990, 16–24). The examination of Black life here goes beyond the challenge of incorporating the perspective that order/equilibrium/harmony starting points while being good/functional for the dominant society may be bad/dysfunctional for the non-dominant sub-group(s). This analysis maintains that the order sought by those essentially in power is *not even good/harmonious for them.* The order in the vein of the New World Order wreaks havoc with the vitality, vision and even survival of those referred to by the code term "the middle classes." And, in the smaller and smaller global worldview, even the dichotomies evoked by the terms Eurocentric and Afrocentric are really too superficial to reflect the complex sets of relationships going on, today.[34] (Nevertheless, they will be used here in order to have comprehensible referent groups to explain social phenomena.)

Discrimination is an inevitable factor in the life of a Black woman, no matter from which class, geographic region or family background she originates. As is demonstrated by several of the case studies, the sociological analyses and the legal reviews, discrimination limits whatever chances and opportunities are available to her. Wherever she goes, there are ceilings.

Whether those ceilings are made of steel, wood or glass[35], they are there—inflexible, intractable, and, for the masses, impenetrable.

It should be pointed out here that this New World Order theme, which is conjectured to influence so highly the well being of the Black woman, basically has an economic impetus. Further, the contrivance of this theme seemed to coincide with the diminution of ideological formulations in dividing the peoples of the earth (e.g., the published fall of Communism in the former U.S.S.R.[36]) and the rise of divisions based more on brute territorial assertions of raw power (e.g., the post-Cold War factional differences in the former Yugoslavia[37]). It is asserted in this work that, given the relative powers of the earth's different ethnic groupings, if the world disintegrates into petty factional segments, the result will further lessen the probability that the African American woman will obtain social justice. Indeed, a "beggar-thy-neighbor" philosophy is claimed to worsen the plight of everyone who is struggling to survive on the planet.[38] Separation of goods, services and world-resource benefits by competition between the industrialized nations and the Third World, with racial origin being the pernicious determining factor, will only inhibit the growth and development of all working generations regardless of race.[39] It is incumbent upon the industrialized nations to invest not only in research and development but also in people in general, so that the quality of life is improved for everyone.[40] Further, competition alone cannot be the driving force for a New World Order if it is to be enlightened. The survival needs of people who form the basic economic units, either as consumers or as laborers, must be included in any agenda that aspires to address the long-term objectives of world justice and peace.[41]

Although the courts are presented here as the legitimizers, interpreters and ultimate enforcers (in the sense that the pen is mightier than the sword) of any world order, the stimulus for their guardianship comes from other organizations in the society. One type of organization, as previously mentioned, consists of modern approximations of the "secret society.[42]" Secret societies have reportedly existed since the beginning of human civilization.[43] They are mechanisms through which a society's young become socialized to its values (Warfield-Coppock 1990) and its values are reified so that its members can control the behaviors of the group (Diallo and Hall 1989; Piven and Cloward 1971). According to some, Eurocentric male-dominated secret societies[44] underlie the ostensible basis for most of the other controlling social institutions[45] in U.S. and global society (cf. C. Wright Mills's exposition in *The Power Elite*, 1959). Such world ordering schemes are exemplified by Victor Perlo in his book *Economics of Racism U.S.A.* when he states,

Private business profits from discrimination against Blacks, and manipulates it to aggravate divisions among working people. The top people in government often come from a milieu of the wealthy aristocracy, with an ideology of extreme racism, living in exclusive estate areas, belonging to private clubs which exclude Black people, and reflecting the ideology of caste and race superiority. (216–217)

The proposition that there is method behind the madness of the lowly status of the Black woman in the world's ordering is illustrated by statistical data from census agency reports as well as other sources and holds true for nearly all of the major social institutions set forth by Parsons. Stanford Lyman[46] does point out that the Parsonian functionalist view sees the Black Americans as coming into the American collective community very gradually. Lyman interprets Parsons[47] to explain this gradualism as caused by accidents of place, culture and collective strength. This author, of course, does not feel that the lack of social, economic and political inclusion of African Americans and women into full mainstream participation is an accident (cf. Epperson's 1990 book, *The New World Order*).

During the civil rights movement, the political atmosphere helped to offset to some degree the debilitating effects of minority status. However, as social conservatism in the United States became the predominant political persuasion, being of a race or gender that was not in power became a greater legal liability. This turn of events has had awesome consequences for all African Americans as corporations downsize, the welfare state constricts, public education is abandoned, the family as an entity is neglected and the values of insensitive individualism and ethnic territoriality become the controlling variables in the global society.

A basic premise of this book is that the courts, interpreting and reifying "the law" on behalf of the society's powers-that-be, currently are the major implementors of the New World Order. For the Black woman, the results of the implementation of this New World Order is fundamentally the same as those imagined in Aldous Huxley's *Brave New World*. The classifications of people are just as unequivocal, their functions are just as deterministic[48] and their lives are just as externally controlled. In fact, the same calculating principles of dehumanization apply, according to which individuals are treated in an impersonal and purely functional manner.

This book on the New World Order seeks to assess the motivations behind the policies endemic to the term. It also endeavors to identify the anticipated position of Afrogeneric peoples, particularly those of the female gender, once the anticipated goals have been met. Further, certain strategies are proposed here that aspire to prevent the essentially negative objectives behind the concept as they relate to African American women both nationally and locally.

Black people have a definitive choice between empowerment and elimination. As the author's criminal clients are told, they can either go to trial and fight for their exoneration or plead guilty and throw themselves on the "mercy" of the court. Of course, in the former case the odds are only one in three that they will win acquittal, but there is still something to be gained in the assertion of a fight that is for self-respect. Another factor that must be taken into account is that, if one loses, sentencing will be harsher after a trial than it would have been after a plea. Those choices are symbolic of the choices Black people have to weigh in deciding which strategy to pursue in seeking full societal participation and benefits.

The political and the economic institutions are the primary progenitors of the relatively low position of African American women; their manifestations are extrapolated onto the areas of education, family, criminal justice and social welfare, among others. Although Black women occupy more political and corporate offices than ever before in American history, the overwhelming influence of the White male political and economic establishment still significantly dictates governmental and thereby political policy in the United States[49] as well as in the other industrial countries.[50] Further, the trend of the New World Order is towards greater concentration and control by its major social institutions of their respective areas of influence and dominion.[51] The tactic of bloc voting is still the most effective tool in helping African Americans to have some voice in government. The most ominous challenge to this strategy is being wielded by the courts, which are allowing political district after district to dilute the Black vote through a phenomenon known as "redistricting" (see Chapter 2). Because of the lack of numbers of Black people, the bloc-voting tactic is essentially better as a leveraging point than as a full-blown effort to impact the tides of change. In litigation concerning political strength issues, gerrymandering to enhance the strength of the Black vote (cf. North Carolina in the *Shaw v. Reno*[52] case) is being struck down as an affront to the equal protection of White voters. Indeed, backlash in the areas of economics and education has been institutionalized by the courts.

METHODS OF STUDY

Each chapter in this book has a somewhat different style because of its subject matter and the author's attempt to capture the significance and meaning of that particular area in the most poignant and effective manner. Common to all the chapters, however, are the underlying premises based on the sociological, Afrocentric and legal perspectives described herein.

In using the sociological perspective to examine demographic and racial features of New World Order policies, it is recognized here that the African American woman is not one homogeneous entity. Sociologist Joyce Ladner indicated in an interview with the Association of Black Sociologists[53] that if she could change anything in her 1972 sociological classic on the Black woman, *Tomorrow's Tomorrow*[54], she would add an increased examination of the diversity of the Black woman's experiences. She would look at them by class, region and urban-rural differences, for instance. Nevertheless, she surmised that she did not think she would change her thesis that "there are common experiences that help to define" Black women.[55]

Although in this treatise the case-study examples used in the anecdotal illustrations that begin the discussions of the various sociolegal concepts come primarily from one geographic region, the other evidence—from U.S. Supreme Court cases, Congressional legislation, U.S. Bureau of Statistics data, and the like—is selected to document the common themes in the lives of Black women hypothesized by Ladner. The case-study examples in this work are from a range of classes used to help introduce the concept of "relative deprivation" (Merton 1954) as it relates, unfortunately, to the situation of Black women in each subject area of the book. These case-study examples are not meant, of course, to be representative of a generalizable population sample. To derive conclusions from one or two specific cases to any general population would be to commit an ecological fallacy. However, the case studies are important in that they reflect issues important to the Black woman in the world's order—new, old or imminent. The case-study examples and interviews herein are the starting points of discussion for the topical subjects and lead into the analyses of the sociological, statistical and legal factors that influence their positive (or negative) dispositions at the macroscopic societal level. In addition, case studies from the author's law practice are included as illustrative of different legal encounters experienced by Black, female clients. These case studies are used primarily as anecdotal materials and the names have been changed to protect the identity of the actual women.

The frame of reference or, more appropriately, the frames of reference utilized in this examination basically combine the aforementioned sociological perspective with data from the legal system, undergirded by an Afrocentric orientation, to provide evidence of certain sociological assumptions. As a behavioral science, sociology seeks to explain past or present human behavior as it is experienced directly or as it is embodied in "artifacts, monuments, laws, and books."[56] Laws, legislation and other legal materials are used here as supportive documentation for many of the theoretical propositions forwarded throughout this discussion, especially because these propositions are becoming so much a part of the intrinsic social fabric of the New World Order.[57]

The legal research methodology used in this treatise approximates that represented in such works as Evelyn Williams' *Inadmissible Evidence*[58] and Alan M. Dershowitz's *The Best Defense*.[59] Through the legal perspective of Williams and Dershowitz, certain insights are gained about the state of social justice in the legal system with reference to the poor, minorities and women. The legal and the social perspectives work together to demonstrate the interaction between the larger social system and its reinforcing component, the legal system. The rationale behind the approach of these authors is adopted here with the objective of increasing awareness about the status of the Black women as it evolves in the New World Order.

Excerpts from a legislative forum (of the 103rd U.S. Congressional Session) are also included in order to add insights about the policy issues and the status of Black women with reference to health issues. Materials are also exerpted from a health reform proposal written by a Black female law professor. These materials exemplify pressing concerns about how the health institution treats women and minorities.

TOPICAL OVERVIEW

In the political chapter, Barbara J. Mobley's story illuminates the struggles inherent in the achievement of African American and female political power. Her narrative gives new insight into the phrase "the enemy within." These glimpses of campaign history and hurdles should allow the reader a basis from which to determine the feasibility of minority and female political ascension in the twenty-first century. The lesson given by Representative Mobley highlights the need for group unity, grassroots campaigning and community mobilization.

The organizations that make up the economic institution in the United States are particularly adroit at ensuring a Eurocentric (specifically, Anglo-Saxon-German)[60] and predominantly male world order.[61] The courts have become the modern-day White Knights, so to speak, in the equal protection of innocent White male employees and students in the areas of the economic (job) and educational institutions (see also the discussion in *The Courts and Social Policy* by Donald L. Horowitz). Reverse discrimination has become a byword for challenges to affirmative action, a strategy developed in the 1960s (the term was used in Executive Order 10925 in which President John F. Kennedy established the President's Committee on Equal Opportunity[62]) to counter the lack of an African American presence in certain occupations and in certain courses of study at institutions of higher learning. No self-respecting public official in the New World Order would admit to supporting "quotas" or "goals." Norman C. Amaker[63] quotes U.S. Assistant Attorney General William Bradford Reynold, as early after the Civil Rights Movement as 1981, setting the stage for the Justice Department's position that it would not support "the use of quotas or any other numerical or statistical formulae designed to provide to non-victims of discrimination preferential treatment based on race, sex, national origin or religion." But also see Victor Perlo's discussion of quotas in his book *Economics of Racism* (1975, 242–243) where he relates that in the Nixon era Black political supporters were rewarded even by Republicans with the award of government contracts. The use of numbers in measuring "success in attracting and promoting women and minorities had its origins under President Richard M. Nixon."[64] Nixon's initiation of affirmative action in the fostering of embryonic minority business ventures, before it fell into emergent New World Order disrepute, transcended political party affiliation.[65]

Institutionalized as anathema in the New World Order, the two words, "quotas" and "goals," along with many choice others, were used to trash the nomination of Professor Lani Guinier to head the Civil Rights Division of the Justice Department.[66] Other pretenses, for example, "cronyism with a member of government," were used to discourage the nomination of another Black woman to a high position in the political realm.[67] The nomination of Lauri Fitz-Pegado to head the Commerce Department's U.S. and Foreign Commercial Service became rocky when "established" circles decried her friendship with U.S. Commerce Secretary Ronald H. Brown, who had his own troubles.[68] Both Fitz-Pegado and Brown were African American. The position with the U.S. and Foreign Commercial Service would have allowed Fitz-Pegado to apply skills and strategies in seventy countries in order to assist U.S. businesses in their efforts toward competition. Fitz-Pegado would have directed the 1,250 staff members of the Commercial Service. The press claimed that her prior roles in foreign-related service, in which she had fashioned imagery for such figures as Haitian leader Jean-Claude "Baby Doc" Duvalier and the daughters of an arms dealer and a Kuwaiti ambassador,[69] had compromised her ability to serve. One wonders how many other nominees have known and worked with government officials and assisted relatively minor governmental role players?

Such concerns seem to manifest two things. The first is how extensive xenophobia is in political and business arenas as the New World Order takes shape. The second is how meaningless are the personal characteristics of "intelligence" and "ambition" (Ms. Fitz-Pegado "graduated Phi Beta Kappa from Vassar College and earned a master's degree at Johns Hopkins University School of Advanced International Studies. And she has some international experience"[70]) are if the *order* of things is too intransigent to allow one access.

Vilification by the press and broadcast media has thus become the normative strategy to protest any perceived or imagined encroachments, no matter how infinitesimal, upon what has been deemed to be White male territory (cf. Aaron David Gresson III, *The Recovery of Race In America*, 1995[71] and the *Business Week* article, "White, Male & Worried," January 31, 1994, 50–55). Backlash seems predictable, especially in the field of economic remediation. There is evidence of White male disenchantment in spite of figures showing, for instance, that "while white males constitute only 43 percent of the work force, they hold 95 percent of the senior management jobs."[72] (White males would be even more disenchanted if they one day discovered that they had to live their lives as African Americans.[73])

Given the conservatism that is the hallmark of the New World Order, benevolent, philanthropical sorts such as the man (Lucien Wilbanks) depicted in author John Grisham's fictional account[74] of a White male law firm that preferred a criminal law and civil rights practice are the exception rather than the rule.

A similarly begrudging tone is found among Establishment sources speaking of atonement efforts being made in the mortgage credit area[75] for past discrimination by the federal government agency "Fannie Mae," the Federal National Mortgage Association. Fannie Mae's remedial action "targeted an additional $140 billion to minorities and other people it says have been shut out of homeownership."[76] After describing the expected ameliorative effects of the program such as (1) neighborhood stabilization, (2) "more homeownership opportunities for low-income families," (3) home-buying education for renters and (4) increased hiring of minorities and women by lenders, the article ended with the observation, "Some housing experts questioned whether lenders will have to charge higher interest rates or fees to make up for lending policies they suspect will lead to more foreclosures."[77] It is an interesting point to note here that there is evidence that the savings-and-loan debacle that has ensnared so many and cost taxpayers so much—estimated at from $200 billion[78] to $500 billion[79]—was certainly not caused by lending to low-income debtors.[80] Further, the same Congressional deregulation fervor in 1982 imperils the Glass-Steagall Act of 1934 passed to ensure against the excesses precipitating the 1929 Wall Street crash and designed to separate banking activities from those involving the marketing and sale of securities.[81]

In a similar fashion it has become the prerogative "of choice" of many corporations, impervious to any equal protection considerations, to eliminate the nonproductive and unworthy—or even to toss out the productive and worthy—in deference to shareholders and increased profit margins.[82] Profit-potential development has thus become more valued than human potential development,[83] and the former theme permeates both the educational institution and the economic one. It is a gross understatement to say that the courts have not been prone to uphold affirmative action principles in the face of the pressures of global competition and corporate takeovers. When it comes to the economic viability of a company, not many would have the temerity to argue that a race of people and a gender who have been scorned in the past should have some type of "preferential treatment." In the age of the New World Order, all people are expendable.[84] For example, in the first half of 1993, "Corporate America unveiled plans to do away with close to 255,000 jobs, 23% more than in the same period in 1992, and the largest first-half tally ever."[85] The New World Order does not seem to be, then, an age of people first, organization second.

"Choice" is the term used to try to demolish public education in favor of private school selectivity.[86] What the adoption of a choice or school-voucher program[87] would do to the education of Black women and men is a nightmare that one hopes will never materialize. As it is, the courts have backed off from the goal of true integration of education and is allowing white flight in housing and "innovative" ideas such as community or charter and magnet schools to keep the races essentially separate in the imparting of knowledge and state-supervised socialization. These practices isolate the races so that the speech patterns, the thought processes, the analytical skills, the dominant-group cultural exposure, the individual expectations and the behavior reinforcement appropriate for success in the Eurocentric—still the mainstream—society are learned only by and remain specific to primarily one racial group. Multicultural learning remains a mostly fringe objective, successfully fought by the more adamant cultural-purism fanatics, of whom there are more than one would think in the New World Order.

Regarding education, statistics for the African American female are slightly more auspicious currently than for the African American male or even for many of the Hispanic peoples who have recently migrated to the United States. Still, such relatively new obstacles as outcome-performance-competency-based tests (e.g., *Debra P. v. Turlington*[88]) are now being required in addition to the traditional high school diploma. Further, as this book seeks to point out, postgraduate (e.g., teacher, social worker, counselor, and drug rehabilitation) licensure certifications and preemployment tests that may or may not be job related help to determine the more deserving would-be professionals and employed members of society. In essence, educational achievement may not be transferable to employment in the present tight-money economy.[89] Such obstacles have been legitimized by the courts as reasonable criteria for professional and job screening, as "job related" or "a business necessity."[90] Drug tests[91] precede employment now for everything from dog catcher to postal employee to telephone installer to typist. Not since slavery have so many Black men and women had to get undressed before being put to work. Living in the New World Order, though, for White people as well as Black seems to mean that they will be subjected to untold indignities.[92] Being desperate for jobs, working people will subject themselves to many intrusions. Needless to say, pre-employment drug testing is a procedure likewise endorsed by the courts. The willingness of the public to accept such practices as standard operating procedure has led to consequences which are more and more bizarre. An example of this is seen in the experience of one lawyer. The lawyer was being investigated by an FBI agent who had him submit a footprint and then posted it as a prank according to the National Urban League's "1992 Chronology of Events" found in their 1993 edition of *The State of Black America*.

With reference to the family, although the popular mass media still depict the African American female's role in the family in primarily negative terms, Black sociologists such as Robert Hill (1972) and Harriette Pipes McAdoo (1981) have written extensive scholarly treatises designed to offset the debilitating images portrayed by such writers as Daniel Patrick Moynihan (Rainwater 1967). The "mammy," the matriarch, the welfare mother and the "Jezebel" are all images of Black women that do not promote a view of the Black family as a healthy, functional entity (Hill Collins 1991, 70–78). In the New World Order the images that grace the media are those of drug-addicted and usually teenage mothers who abandon their children in hospitals, hotels, and dope houses. The debilitating causes and effects of drug addiction are ignored in the discussion of how these chemically dependent women are too "sick" to care for themselves, let alone their babies. Rather than emphasizing the role of the society in disseminating drugs and eliminating jobs in the Black community and the lack of meaningful treatment and rehabilitation for addicted Black people, the mass media concentrate on the negative images evoked.

The discussion in this book of the criminal-justice world order scrutinizes the manner in which the buzzwords "law and order" and scare tactics are used to justify such indignities. The public seems to forget that various intrusions on privacy were first applied in criminal situations and that their use becomes gradually extrapolated to the noncriminal world. This extrapolation is more readily accepted when first used upon persons who are very similar in race, class and age to the persons defined as criminal by the media through imagery and focus. Executive search companies do not expect their clientele to be subjected to drug testing, but, when young Black men and women are the job applicants, tactics of criminal investigation are acceptable screening devices. Thus, the criminal justice world sets the tone for the way that the populace in general is to be treated. In fact, the harshness of the world of investigation has expanded so that not just one's racial opposite is fair game, but one's political adversary; even one's job competitor can be exposed to some type of debilitating exposé. The Eurocentric ideals of individual-centeredness, competition, utilitarianism and materialism (Asante 1980, 49–50; Nobles 1980, 103) have regained widespread adulation.

The essentially political nature of the criminal justice system[93] is highlighted in Chapter 8 on criminal law and procedure as they relate to the African American woman. The debilitating consequences of lack of empowerment are emphasized in the discussion of how criminalization is the ultimate result of the relationship between political power and delegitimation.

One does not have to visit a women's prison firsthand to imagine the dehumanizing effects of imprisonment. For some individuals, the sense of alienation, powerlessness and ineffectiveness that prison reputedly inflicts began long before they landed behind prison bars. For African American female inmates, in particular, a self-imprisonment prevents a great number of them from being self-actualized. It is impossible for such women to reach any goals that they might be able, with help, to set for themselves, let alone those objectives set for them by society. Further, society itself discriminates in terms of which objectives are for whom and who will reach them. This situation increases the frustration that African American women prisoners encounter as they attempt to keep or regain order in their lives.

In this political climate, contradictions emerge: at the same time that ruthless national crime laws[94] are being passed—and advocated[95]—many of the advocates themselves are or have been under investigation.[96] (Such incongruities give new credence to the folk wisdom of "people in glass houses should not throw stones."[97]) Incrimination, popularized for use among minorities and the poor, has become the most effective and efficient way to pick off one's political or economic enemies, so much so that the most highly publicized criminal prosecutions have been the ones dealing with politicians or White persons who have caused Wall Street or corporate America some grief (e.g., David Levine, Ivan Boesky, John Gotti, Michael Milken and Leona Helmsley). The New World Order would never have allowed a Black female to attain the position of a Nicholas W. Leeson, able to lose a billion dollars[98]—especially if she had not gone to college and came from the working class as he did.[99] Hope springs eternal for the young, gifted, *male* and White.

Slowly and insidiously, the contempt for individual liberties that began with its application to Blacks was adopted as a "business as usual" justice program for anyone—White, Black, Brown or Yellow—who was more or less permanently or temporarily out of power. This extrapolation of injustice from Blacks to Whites to everyone else is what is so dangerous about allowing African Americans to be discriminated against selectively. Eventually, discriminatory treatment is applied to anyone who is down on his or her luck or whom someone in power wants to be down on his or her luck. Meanwhile, the battle cry for law and order hides a multitude of sins, covering up the society's growing inability to provide an adequate, secure standard of living for its people.

Such provisions[100] as those specifying fifty-one crimes for which the death penalty is the sentence, mandatory life imprisonment for three-time recidivists, federal jurisdiction over previously state-judged offenses, a substantially greater proliferation of prisons and police and tough gun control restrictions[101] characterize the cries of politicians as they sublimate the concerns of the economy, health and social welfare to the needs of the iron fist.[102]

The two latter concerns, health and social welfare, are also areas in which the true needs of the African American female have been neglected. One health concern, woman battering, was treated in one of the aforementioned national crime bills. The battering proposal contained a provision for one billion dollars to address the problem. That provision was one of the most attacked parts of the bill. Although commentators (e.g., Paul Klein on CBS, aired February 20, 1994) could see the need for a hundred thousand more police, they could not see the need for a billion dollars to prevent battering and to provide rehabilitation for its victims, families and offenders. Likewise, the use of forty or fifty million for the prevention (at the school-age level), rehabilitation and treatment of drug addiction did not sit well with those who wanted a firmer handle on crime. However, there is strong evidence, based on reported cases and estimates of unreported cases, for the need to protect women from those with whom they live. The frustrations and anxieties of African American men are sometimes vented against those closest to them. Their relative lack of power and control leads to a system that has usually ignored any kind of abuse against African American women. Therefore, domestic violence is an important health concern that needs to be addressed along with other, sometimes more visible, medical and social ills.

The articulation of other health concerns seems to be left not just to politicians but to the insurers, to those in the medical professions and to business (employers).[103] (Senator Moynihan is still denying that the health care crisis exists and maintaining that there is instead a "social crisis."[104]) The amelioration of the fact that an inordinate number of the uninsured citizens are minorities and women may depend on whether the interests of such citizens coincide with the interests of the insurers and the doctors. Because of the way that illness has been handled in the past, discrimination is part and parcel of decisions as to who will be treated for what diseases, to what extent and at what costs. Purportedly, prevention will be an inherent part of any health plan that is adopted nationally, which means that the onus of preventive health care will be on the patient. Costs reputedly will be increased for those who have not been successful in the preventive aspect of health care. Those whose environment, lifestyle, culture and income—or lack thereof—subject them to greater health risks, will presumably bear the burden of those factors. In other words, many universal health care proposals presume that most individuals have more control over their lives and the contexts within which they live than do many African American women. Keeping this scenario in mind, the health discussion herein will basically consider the health policy choices most desirable for the African American woman.

That a lack of power can kill a person is pointed out vividly in discussions on health reform. That such reform is inevitable is agreed, given the current political and economic climate. That such reform will inure to the benefit of African Americans, women and other underserved groups is debatable. Any health reform proposal, however altruistic it seems, will face an uphill battle.[105] Both political and economic resources will need to be mobilized as methods are developed that assure that health reforms address the physical and mental health concerns of African American women. Representatives from the Black female community must be included in health reform debates to vocalize the health care needs of African American women.

Chapter 5 on social welfare gives the fundamentals of empowerment for community groups as they attempt to survive in increasingly difficult and hostile times. Although the 1960s are over, the hopes and dreams of unempowered peoples are not. Networking, group mobilization, unity and self-sacrifice are still requirements of adaptation among those traditionally deprived of the nation's resources and rewards. However, as long as the political institution prevents access to societal rewards, it must allow governmental intervention to mollify some of its most disastrous effects— hence the continuation of "the welfare state,"albeit in a much distorted, diminished and crippled form.[106]

The application of the welfare state has been one of the Black woman's more humiliating experiences. In the New World Order it does not promise to get any better. Punitive reforms in the name of cost containment[107] or budget balancing[108] are repeatedly introduced in order further to shame and/or drive her off welfare.[109] For instance, one of the well-publicized drives of some political leaders embarked on intensifying New World Order hierarchies embodied a program of substantial welfare cuts and a companion design "to erase the Federal deficit and slice up the old order."[110]

Prior to 1990 and the "official" political announcement of the onset of the New World Order, however, the federal government's budget deficit was something which was handled like a "velvet glove" with serious efforts to erase it treated as "a fool's errand."[111] And, even in 1989, with the initiation of what was termed a "downsized presidency devoid of the resources to address long neglected domestic problems," Congress was quietly asked for "$2.7 billion" in "annual tax reductions for business."[112]

Welfare, always a hot key of ethnocentric (DeFleur et al. 1971, 112–113, 505) maneuvers, has become an even more highly politicized watchword (almost on a par with "crime control") in the resurgence of the New World Order feeding frenzy. Its "reform" is one of the favorite ministrations of politicians to "win friends and influence people,"[113] that is, "voters" and "taxpayers."[114] Although the world of work, as far as the more desirable occupations, has been a highly illusory goal for the Black woman, social-welfare reformists, conservative and liberal, all agree that the solution to the "welfare problem" is to get the Black female caretaker to work. Features such as training, day care and continued health benefits are less attractive additions to the primary motivation of making the "able-bodied" welfare mother work for a living. Again, in a time of intense competition for jobs[115] of even a lowly or temporary[116] nature and when so many people are seeking so few jobs, the implementation of this formula for welfare success is yet to be seen.[117] Such assumptions overlook the fact that, increasingly, work itself is a precious commodity. In fact, in the new view of the new world, the ultimate goal for welfare is not its success but its elimination.[118] Selectively using statistical data, the outraged indignantly decry figures that indicate that "[n]early 30% of all Americans are now born to single mothers: 22% of whites and 66% of blacks." If the children of such mothers are taken away and put into state-run institutions (such as a deglamorized version of a Boy's or Girl's Town?) and if it costs so much money to create jobs at all, let alone for relatively unskilled, undereducated welfare mothers, then what will those mothers do all day? In short, where exactly is their place in the New World Order? Is a new bottom being contemplated, representing a new low in "mankind's" conceptualization?

Of course, the pharisaical upholders of "morality" and "family values" ignore analysts, such as Frances Fox Piven and Richard A. Cloward, who speak of the demoralization and social disorganization inherent in the life situation of some AFDC mothers. Piven and Cloward point out that, while the welfare state does not enable such women to maintain their self-respect, "it does keep them from starving—generally a very moral and good value objective."[119] The words of another analyst, Roger Wilkins, a legally trained social commentator, address the issue of the welfare state and the Black community. Professor Wilkins maintains that America has shifted from finding different foreign sites with labor pools (e.g., Eastern and Southern Europe), bringing workers to the United States. Instead, American capitalism uses the workers in different sites in Mexico, Indonesia, Malaysia and the Philippines.[120] Consider the role of NAFTA (The North American Free Trade Agreement).[121]

NAFTA's impact on workers (White, Black and Yellow) universally, who now are tied together in the framework of the global economy,[122] has led other commentators to entitle a discourse reviewing that trade agreement "The New World Disorder."[123] Nevertheless, as a function of the direction in which the world is heading, treaties such as NAFTA and GATT (the 124–nation General Agreement on Tariffs and Trade) are considered necessary by businesses who see such pacts as "vital to American competitiveness."[124] Hence, the goal of profits over people transcends any political boundaries or factions, as it becomes more important to appease the multinational than the multicultural interests in the world. Professor Wilkins further states that such American economic globalization and spread of the industrialization help to create situations in which, for some neighborhoods, the Black male unemployment rate is 47 percent. Wilkins also claims that such policies are reinforced by the fact that at times the executive branch of the federal government is run largely by polls[125] of the "American public," a public periodically manipulated by *some leaders* into viewing Black people with skepticism and suspicion and as unwanted potential competitors.[126]

Because of global economic forces,[127] coupled with the forces driven by racial animosity and antagonism, Blacks have thus become, as Wilkins terms it, "economically redundant." The bottom line, according to Wilkins, is that there cannot be families if there are not jobs. With one half of all welfare costs going towards administrative expenses, welfare (and crime) are enhancing the economic well-being of the middle-classes more than that of the welfare recipient who receives direct awards. Welfare's elimination (as well as the decriminalization of many "victimless" offenses such as possession of small amounts of illicit drugs, prostitution and gambling) would be more devastating—in terms of loss of jobs, capital structures, sales of equipment and supplies, and compensation for selected services (including medical and legal)— to the middle-classes than to the welfare-recipient classes (see Chapter 5). At least the latter, having been subject to more relative deprivation (Merton 1954) over the years, have been more socialized to the prospect of survival on nothing or less than nothing, especially as U.S. society has become more draconian and life more and more like one of Charles Dickens's worst poverty-stricken nightmares.[128]

Hence, as U.S. society has moved from gemeinschaft (community-like) to gesellschaft (corporate-type) (Tonnies 1940), it has relied more on ostensibly formal, contractual relationships to effectuate the desires, concerns and will of the established society. That reliance is epitomized in recourse to the law when even those formal, official relationships break down in uncertainty, ambiguity or perceived injustice. The outcome of resorting to the law is, it is hypothesized, determined in large part by the social characteristics of the parties, as modified by the political atmosphere of the times. Social characteristics such as race, gender, national origin, age and socioeconomic status are important factors in predicting the probable outcome of a case.

Sociologist James E. Conyers[129] of Indiana State University in one seminar session discussed four approaches used to remedy social injustice. He set forth a paradigm of these four major strategies, which were identified as part of the remedial effort for African American liberation. They include the civil rights movement, affirmative action, "universalistic" poverty programs and self-help. Conyers insists that all four are required to achieve meaningful results for African Americans. Consequently, they should be viewed as a single approach and combined into one basic strategy to be employed on a thoughtfully planned basis.

A theme underlying all chapters of this book is the need for African American access to the mass media.[130] Such access is essential in order to identify, articulate and disseminate common problems and issues. Mass-media outlets need to be identified through which to spread the African American woman's message of African American empowerment, awareness, self-determination and sensitivity.[131] The presence of Black women in the mass communications arena has been considered significant[132] from the time Lorraine V. Hansberry, the first Black woman playwright, presented her *Raisin in the Sun*, to electrified audiences in the 1950s. A short time earlier Gwendolyn Brooks had become the first African American to receive a Pulitzer Prize, in 1950. Terry McMillan raised the consciousness of young Black women during the 1980s and 1990s with books such as *Waiting to Exhale, Disappearing Acts* and *Mama*; Alice Walker's book *The Color Purple* was transformed into an Oscar-winning screenplay during the 1980s; Oprah Winfrey became the foremost TV talk show hostess during the 1990s;

and in 1993 Toni Morrison became the first Black American to receive the Nobel Prize in literature. By "taking over Warner's Elektra Entertainment," Wharton School graduate Sylvia M. Rhone became "the music industry's highest-ranking woman and African American."[133]

One reaction signifies, however, that mass media attacks upon African Americans are not limited to politics, economics or education. This reaction was manifest when the aforementioned Toni Morrison won the Nobel Prize in the field of literature, October 1993. It was claimed that Ms. Morrison's award had been obtained as a result of "lobbying."[134] The accuser hinted that a type of affirmative action had influenced the decision makers' selection of Morrison's book, *Jazz*. Such an influence, in the post-civil rights era,[135] would be seen to discredit the award unequivocally. This growing market for Black literature also transcends racial boundaries (e.g., about two years after this award the author noticed a copy of Morrison's book *The Bluest Eye* in the hands of a White female prospective juror being questioned in chambers as to her service on a criminal trial). Some writers and publishers feel that the writer Terry McMillan "proved that a crossover audience existed for books about black culture."[136] Hence, Morrison's selection was an affirmation of that trend.

Nevertheless, the prevailing image of Black women (and men) in the media is still negative. (For elaboration on this point, see Ella Barkley-Brown, "Mothers of Mind," in Bell-Scott and Guy-Sheftall's *Double Stitch* (1993), and Na'im Akbar's discussion in *Chains and Images of Psychological Slavery* (1984)). Of course, according to the underlying premise of this book, such imagery is functional for the predominantly Eurocentric U.S. society because it reinforces feelings of White supremacy and the appropriateness of the status quo. Similarly, the courts, claiming contrived protections under such Bill of Rights provisions as the First Amendment, rule in support of these methods of repression. For instance, the courts have endorsed all types of Ku Klux Klan behaviors ranging from public hate-mongering marches to public hate-speech displays on private property (see *R.A.V. v. St. Paul*[137]). Further, according to one report, one "neo-Nazi skinhead" organization has been instrumental in awakening that "once-moribund" movement by employing "a vast communications web, established by some 250 American and Canadian hate groups, that includes desktop publishing, shortwave radio, citizen access television, computer supported fax networks, independent video production, telephone lines, computer billboards and the Internet."[138]

As far as the mass media in the U.S. is concerned, communications as to the status of African Americans varies from that of this more intense New World Order advocacy only in form but not necessarily in substance. The mass media communicates the message of Black inferiority and lack of merit in ways that are more subtle and sophisticated than does the medium the mass communicators reprove as "crackpot." It is presumed here that

African American ownership and control of a greater proportion of all avenues of mass-media expression at all levels is crucial to African American defeat of bigotry and discrimination (Akbar 1984, 19–20; Neely 1981, 127–128). In this sense, the medium[139] is, indeed, the message. Thus far, African Americans have by no means been the messengers; rather, they have been only the subjects of the message. Further, the message—mass, medium or minuscule (yet, malicious)—has negated their humanity, ignored their contributions and distorted their images. This is why the New World Order climate, bent on eliminating African American participation in the mainstream of social institutions, is so potentially devastating. Technological advancements in areas such as cable television systems and cellular phones are moving so fast that, without affirmative action, Blacks could be forever precluded from gaining meaningful access to mass communication.[140]

The true value of affirmative action is made painfully clear when retreat by the government forestalls the willingness of private corporations to collaborate with minorities. For example, Viacom, a cable television system company, held up a sale to a group of Black-headed companies until a court ruled on whether or not it would get a "tax break valued at $400 million to $600 million"[141] authorized under affirmative action. Another deadly blow to meaningful participation by African Americans and women in the mass media was dealt when the U.S. Supreme Court via Justice Sandra Day O'Connor explicitly overruled the case *Metro Broadcasting, Inc. v. F.C.C.*.[142] In the 1990 *Metro Broadcasting* case, the Court had upheld a federal affirmative action program. The ruling in *Metro Broadcasting* was reversed by Justice O'Connor writing for the majority in *Adarand Constructors, Inc., v. Pena*.[143] Justice O'Connor equated all distinctions based on race—either for good or bad purposes—unconstitutional in *Adarand*. In other words, the federal government—as well as the states, according to Justice O'Connor's opinion in *Adarand*—is prohibited from even attempting to remedy disparities between various classes of persons if the basis of those class distinctions is race. This result freezes the status quo into place (also see Chapter 3). Thus, mass communication ownership is becoming so gigantic,[144] concentrated[145] and monolithic[146] that any relatively small business regardless of racial affiliation has a difficult time surviving. And, because the mass media is increasingly dominated and monopolized in the hands of a few,[147] not only are minority interests less likely to be represented, but those of the working and the middle classes in general are threatened as well.

Such increasing insensitivity is becoming more and more endemic to all of the major social institutions in the United States, especially the political and the economic. Such callousness in regard to the needs of the disenfranchised seems to be the hallmark of the New World Order. The educational institution provides the foundation for African American isolation and exclusion in those other arenas.[148]

SUMMARY

The institutionalization of conservativism, courted in the Reagan-Bush era and consummated in the New World Order, permeates the society's policies and practices as applied to maintain minorities and women in their subjugated positions. Such positions function to safeguard the security of those at the top. The "rugged individualism," "survival of the fittest" perspectives have solidified policies that ignore the needs of people in general and of African Americans in particular. Self-propelled, the New World Order is now indigenous to the global way of life and operates pretty much irrespective of time, place or person in ostensible power.

Profits, not people, drive the wheels of the major financial institutions of the industrialized world, where downsizing is king. With the demise of unions, civil rights, affirmative action, education and social welfare programs, the economic plight of African American women has worsened from the middle of the twentieth century to its end. Code words such as self-help and self-empowerment imply that the society through its government and law has minimal responsibility and role in ameliorating the second-class citizenship status of African American women and men in the United States. The repressive social environment of the New World Order has made the African American claim to reparations (as provided some Japanese Americans[149]) even less likely to prevail.

At National Bar Association/NAACP Lawyers Civil Rights Seminar held in July of 1995, in Minneapolis, Minnesota, the Legislative Director of the NAACP, Wade Henderson, asked a panel about reparations as a remedy for discrimination. One of the panelists replied that what he feared about reparations was that "we might get it." He went on to explain that given the finite resources in the United States, a one-time payoff to every African American man, woman and child would only be so large. Furthermore, it would mean that Whites could say to African Americans, "Okay, you are all paid up as to any damages you have." And, since discrimination is and has been ongoing, such a payment would not begin to be sufficient relief for it (but also see the Arnwine discussion in Chapter 3).

Community, national and global organization, networking, commitment, resourcefulness and perseverance (as seen in Nelson Mandela of Azania (South Africa)[150]) are keys to what is necessary to again make meaningful the words, "We shall overcome." The drugs of consumerism, carelessness, covetousness and an excessive fixation on competition to the neglect of cooperation, as well as cocaine, are powerful deterrents to freedom. Becoming aware not only of means of enslavement but also of one's enslavement is half of the solution. Even the most well-entrenched, insidious, systemic oppression over time cannot withstand consistent, conscientious and concerted refusals to succumb (see again, Mandela). However, as long as the educational institution suppresses knowledge, the political institution suppresses power and the economic system suppresses resources, it remains an uphill battle for the Black woman in the New World Order. She can win the battle if she mobilizes sufficiently to hold the society accountable to her and to her people for what they have contributed to the world's civilization and continued development.

NOTES

1. This book follows the terms of racial identification described by sociologist Talmadge Anderson in *Black Studies: Theory, Method, and Cultural Perspectives* (Pullman, Wash.: Washington State University Press, 1990) in which he states: "While 'Black' connotes the universality of African peoples or the diaspora of Blacks, 'African American' may refer technically and academically to only persons of African descent who are natives or citizens of the United States or Latin America" (p. 2). When African American is used in this book, it refers to persons who are natives or citizens of the United States and of African descent. The term Black is used here, also, to make intra-United States racial comparisons, especially when analyzing or presenting data from such sources as the U.S. Census. Also see Rohan Preston, "Battle to a [sic] Keep Black Professor Leaves Bruised Egos and Reputations: The Thickness of Skin Is Sometimes More Important Than The Color; Northwestern Loses a Tough Talent Fight to Boston University" (*The New York Times*, March 8, 1995, B8) on a racial-affiliation controversy involving a female law professor who was the "daughter of an African-Cuban mother and an Australian-Irish father," who is quoted as saying that she "does not define herself in racial terms."

2. Henry Kissinger, "The Trade Route: NAFTA a Step toward a Prosperous World Order," *Plain Dealer*, July 18, 1993, C-1, C-4, stating: "[The North American Free Trade Agreement linking the United States with Canada and Mexico in a free-trade area comprising a population of 370 million and a gross national product of $6 trillion] will represent the most creative step toward a new world order taken by any group of countries since the end of the Cold War, and the first step toward the even larger vision of a free trade zone for the entire Western Hemisphere"; Thomas E. Patterson, *Out of Order* (New York: Alfred Knopf, 1993).

3. Tom Brazitis, "And he still can't break the 'gaffe' spell," *Plain Dealer*, May 15, 1994, 2–C. Brazitis writes in that editorial, "Listening to Quayle criticize Clinton's handling of Haiti, Somalia, North Korea and Bosnia, one would think that the Bush-Quayle administration had left behind what they, indeed, promised—a new world order. For the most part Clinton has gone down the foreign policy road mapped out by his predecessors, a road that Quayle now says leads to disaster."

4. David S. Broder, "Lots of Nasty Enemies, a Few Lukewarm Defenders," *Plain Dealer*, May 15, 1994, 3–C. Broder quotes President Clinton, who, after four months in office, recited a passage from Machiavelli's "The Prince": "It must be considered that there is nothing more difficult to carry out, nor more doubtful of success, nor dangerous to handle, than to initiate a *new order of things* [italics added]. For the reformer has enemies and only lukewarm defenders."

5. A. Ralph Epperson, *The New World Order* (Tucson, Ariz.: Publius Press, 1990), xii-xxi.

6. Ibid., 144–145.

7. A. Ralph Epperson, *The Unseen Hand: An Introduction to the Conspiratorial View of History* (Tuscon, Ariz.: Publius Press, 1992) 88–89, 350.

8. Epperson, *New World Order*, 146–147.

9. Ibid., 1–9 (Chapter 1, "Tomorrow's Rulers") and 289–295 (Chapter 36, "Reagan and Bush").

10. Letter to the Editor from Gene Kapp, vice president for public relations, Christian Broadcasting Network, Virginia Beach, Va., "Robertson Rejects Anti-Semitism," *New York Times*, March 20, 1995, A14; also see Frank Rich, "Bait and Switch II: Ralph Reed Fronts Again," *New York Times*, April 6, 1995, A15; and Anthony Lewis, "The Crackpot Factor: Pat Robertson's Conspiracy Theory," *New York Times*, April 14, 1995, A11.

11. Richard Cohen, "Robertson's Crackpot Theory," *Plain Dealer*, October 23, 1994, C4; Frank Rich, "Bait and Switch," *New York Times*, March 2, 1995, A15; Frank Rich, "The Jew World Order," *New York Times*, March 9, 1995, A15; but also see Letter to the Editor from John Taylor Gatto, "Pat Robertson Gives Focus to Our Disaffection," *New York Times*, March 15, 1995, A14.

12. Cynthia Siemsen Maki and Walter L. Goldfrank, "Lessons from the Gulf Wars: Hegemonic Decline, Semiperipheral Turbulence, and the Role of the Rentier State," ed. David A. Smith and József Böröcz, *A New World Order? Global Transformations in the Late Twentieth Century* (Westport, Connecticut: Praeger, 1995): 59.

13. Andre C. Drainville, "Left Internationalism and the Politics of Resistance in the New World Order," ed. David A. Smith and József Böröcz, *A New World Order? Global Transformations in the Late Twentieth Century* (Westport, Connecticut: Praeger, 1995): 221, 222.

14. Philip McMichael, "The New Colonialism: Global Regulation and the Restructuring of the Interstate System" ed. David A. Smith and József Böröcz, *A New World Order? Global Transformations in the Late Twentieth Century* (Westport, Connecticut: Praeger, 1995): 37–39.

15. Peter Applebome, "Weapons: Increasingly, Extremism Is Heavily Armed," *New York Times*, April 30, 1995, A19.

16. See also, Keith Schneider, "The Far Right: Manual for Terrorists Extols 'Greatest Coldbloodedness,' " *New York Times*, April 29, 1995, p. A 8.

17. E.g., a copy of this newsletter was shown during the week of April 24, 1995, on the television program "Day One."

18. Timothy Egal, "In Congress: Trying to Explain Support from Paramilitary Groups," *New York Times*, May 2, 1995, A11.

19. George Johnson, "The Conspiracy That Never Ends," *New York Times*, April 30, 1995, Section 4, 5; Timothy Egan, "Men at War: Inside the World of the Paranoid," *New York Times*, April 30, 1995, Section 4, 1,5.

20. News and Views, *Journal of Blacks in Higher Education*, No. 5 (Autumn 1994), 31.

21. But see Howard W. French, "African Democracies Worry Aid Will Dry Up," *New York Times*, March 19, 1995, A1, A8, in which it is stated: "According to a recent report by the Organization for Economic Cooperation and Development, which monitors Western aid, the net flow of assistance to developing countries fell to $55.96 billion in 1993, down from $60.85 billion the year before. Aid to all of Africa accounts for about $20 billion of this total." Also see editorial, "The Payoff from the New Economic Order," *Business Week*, August 2, 1994, 94.

22. McMichael, "The New Colonialism," 45.

23. Ibid.

24. Ibid.

25. Alex Inkeles, "The Sociological Perspective," *What Is Sociology? An Introduction to the Discipline and Profession* (Englewood Cliffs, New Jersey: Prentice-Hall, Inc., 1964) 18–27.

26. Gunnar Myrdal, with the assistance of Richard Sterner and Arnold Rose, *An American Dilemma: The Negro Problem and Modern Democracy* (New York: Harper and Brothers, 1944).

27. C. Wright Mills, *The Sociological Imagination* (New York: Oxford University Press, 1959).

28. Robert K. Merton, *Social Theory and Social Structure* (Glencoe, Ill.: The Free Press, 1954); Talcott Parsons, *The Social System* (Glencoe, Ill.: The Free Press, 1951).

29. Kingsley Davis, *Human Society* (New York: Macmillan, 1957).

30. E.g., Agis Salpukas, "Quake Interrupts Worldwide Trade at Port in Kobe [Japan]: HUB's Goods Held Back; U.S. Effects May Range from McDonald's 'Happy Meals' to Ford Assembly Lines," *New York Times*, January 21, 1995, A1, A5.

31. Felice J. Levine (editor, *Footnotes*), "Scholarship in a World Order: The Executive Officer's Column—The Open Window," *Footnotes*, 23, No. 1, (January 1995): 2.

32. "Payoff from the New Economic Order."

33. E.g., Melvin L. DeFleur, William V. D'Antonio and Lois B. DeFleur, "The Science of Society: The Prescientific Origins of Sociology; The Quest for an Ideal Social Order," in *Sociology: Man In Society* (Glenview, Ill.: Scott, Foresman and Company, 1971), where it is stated: "the goal of an ideal social order continues to intrigue and elude mankind" (p. 4), and "the basis of a new science of society was clearly established during the seventeenth and eighteenth centuries, when political and social philosophers began to address themselves directly to the problem of order and conflict in society" (p. 5).

34. Ufot B. Inamete, Florida A & M University, "Profiles of Current International Problems and Their Manifestations As Electoral Issues in the United States," an unpublished paper presented at the 1995 Annual Conference of the Association of Social and Behavioral Scientists held in Tallahassee, Fla., March 8–11, 1995.

35. Judith H. Dobrzynski, "The 'Glass Ceiling': A Barrier to the Boardroom, Too," *Business Week*, November 22, 1993, 50.

36. "Gorbachev Quits as Party Head; Ends Communism's 74–Year Reign," *New York Times*, August 25, 1991, A1, A8–A11; "Declaring Death of Soviet Union, Russia and 2 Republics Form New Commonwealth," *New York Times*, December 9, 1991, A1, A4.

37. "After Weeks of Seeming Inaction, U.S. Decides to Punish Belgrade," *New York Times*, May 23, 1992, A1, A4; Douglas Jehl, "25,000 U.S. Troops to Aid U.N. Force If It Quits Bosnia: Danger to Allies Cited; Americans Would Be Ready to Rescue Peacekeepers in the Balkans if Necessary," *New York Times*, December 9, 1994, A1, A7.

38. Christopher Farrell and Michael J. Mandel with Bill Javetski and Stephen Baker, "What's Wrong?: Why the Industrialized Nations Are Stalled," *Business Week*, August 2, 1993, 54–59.

39. Karen Pennar, "The Global Economy Needs Bridges—Not Walls," *Business Week*, August 2, 1993, 60.

40. Editorial, "The Payoff from the New Economic Order," *Business Week*, August 2, 1993, 94.

41. Mike McNamee in Washington, "Robert's Rules of Reorder: The New Agenda Makes Reich's Star Shine All the Brighter," *Business Week*, January 24, 1994, 74, 76.

42. Kwame Nkrumah, *Neo-Colonialism: The Last Stage of Imperialism* (New York: International Publishers Company, 1966); William G. Domhoff, *Who Rules America?* (Englewood Cliffs, N. J.: Prentice-Hall, 1967); E. Franklin Frazier, *Black Bourgeoisie* (New York: Collier, 1962).

43. Molefi Kete Asante, *Kemet, Afrocentricity and Knowledge* (Trenton, NJ.: Africa World Press, 1990).

44. E.g., Mikhail I. Rostovtzev, *The Social and Economic History of the Hellenistic World* (Oxford: Clarendon Press, 1941); George C. Coulton, *Medieval Panorama: The English Scene from Conquest to Reformation* (New York: Meridian Books, 1957); Jakob Burckhardt, *The Civilization of the Renaissance in Italy*, 2 vols., trans. S. G. C. Middlemore (New York: Harper, 1958).

45. E.g., S. Martin Lipset, *Political Man* (New York: Doubleday, 1960) 51–54; Floyd Hunter, *Community Power Structure: A Study of Decision Makers* (Chapel Hill: University of North Carolina Press, 1953); W. Lloyd Warner and Paul A. Lunt, *The Social Life of a Modern Community* (New Haven, Conn.: Yale University Press, 1941); Daniel Bell, "Is There a Ruling Class in America?", in *The End of Ideology* (Glencoe, Ill.: Free Press, 1960), 43–67.

46. Stanford M. Lyman, *The Black American in Sociological Thought: A Failure of Perspective* (New York: Capricorn Books, 1972) 161–163.

47. Talcott Parsons, "Certain Primary Sources and Patterns of Aggression in the Social Structure of the Western World," in *Essays in Sociological Theory* (New York: Free Press, 1964), 298–322.

48. Ira Sager with Gary McWilliams and Robert D. Hof, "IBM Leans on Its Sales Force: Rarely Has So Much Pay Been Tied to Profits and Customer Satisfaction," *Business Week*, February 7, 1994, 110.

49. Michele Galen and Ann Therese Palmer, "White, Male, and Worried," *Business Week*, January 31, 1994, 50–55.

50. Richard W. Stevenson, "A 28-Year-Old Trader Bet Big and Wrecked a Venerable Firm: Briton's $29 Billion Play Stuns Financial World," *New York Times*, February 28, 1995, A1, C17. The subject "Trader" accused of having "wrecked" the 228-year-old Barings P.L.C., which had financed the Louisiana Purchase in the United States and advised on the investments of Queen Elizabeth II, was a White male. The Black woman's relative status and her corresponding lack of economic power in the world are illuminated when the probability of a 28-year-old Black woman's being in such a position is considered; see also Stevenson, "Investment House in Britain Fails After Giant Loss: Asian Markets Rattled; Barings in a Bankruptcy Filing after $750 Million Gamble by Trader in Singapore," *New York Times*, February 27, 1995, A1, C4.

51. Keith Bradsher, "White House Is Joining in Efforts to Loosen the Limits on Banking," *New York Times*, February 27, 1995, A1, C3.

52. 113 S. Ct. 2816 (1993).

53. Hayward Derrick Horton, ed., "ABS Profile: Interview with Joyce A. Ladner," *ABS Newsletter*, 21, No. 2 (Spring 1994): 3–5.

54. Joyce A. Ladner, *Tomorrow's Tomorrow* (Garden City, N.Y.: Doubleday, 1972).

55. "Joyce Ladner Interview," 4.

56. Ibid., 19.

57. Linda Himelstein, "Monkey See, Monkey Sue: Well-Publicized Settlements Are Spurring Bandwagon Lawsuits," *Business Week*, February 7, 1994, 112, 114.

58. Evelyn Williams, *Inadmissible Evidence: The Story of the African-American Trial Lawyer Who Defended the Black Liberation Army* (Brooklyn, N.Y.: Lawrence Hill Books, 1993).

59. Alan M. Dershowitz, *The Best Defense (New York: Vintage Books, 1983).*

60. Victor Perlo, *Economics of Racism U.S.A.: Roots of Black Inequality* (New York: International Publishers, 1975) 42,43.

61. Cf. Owen Ullman, "Is the Fed Facing a Political Correction?: Choosing a New Governor Will Put Its Lack of Diversity under Scrutiny," *Business Week*, January 14, 1994, 42; John A. Byrne with Chuck Hawkins, "Executive Pay: The Party Ain't Over Yet: Reform May Be in the Works But So Far, You Wouldn't Know It," *Business Week*, April 26, 1993, 56–64.

62. Lancelot B. Hewitt and Kim Adair Wilson, "Affirmative Action Can Help Create Tradition of Excellence," *New York Law Journal*, May 1, 1995, 1.

63. Norman C. Amaker, *Civil Rights and the Reagan Administration* (Washington, D.C.: Urban Institute Press, 1988), 124.

64. Steven A. Holmes, "G.O.P. Is Haunted by Past on Preference Hiring Plans," *New York Times*, March 19, 1995, A14.

65. Steven A. Holmes, "Dole Helped Ex-Aide with Program He Now Denounces," *New York Times*, March 23, 1995, A10.

66. Neil A. Lewis, "Clinton Ready to Withdraw His Rights Nominee," *New York Times*, June 3, 1993.

67. Douglas Harbrecht, "A Skilled Promoter—or Just a Ron Brown Crony?: Critics say Lauri Fitz-Pegado Shouldn't Be Part of Commerce's Export Team," *Business Week*, February 21, 1994, 34.

68. Cf. Keith Bradsher with Emily M. Bernstein, "Web of Business Connections Haunts Commerce Secretary," *New York Times*, February 28, 1995, A1, A9; Keith Bradsher, "Panel Chief Calls for Special Prosecutor on Brown: Evidence Is Reported of 16 Violations of U.S. Laws by Brown," *New York Times*, February 28, 1995, A9.

69. Harbrecht, "Skilled Promoter," 34.

70. Ibid.

71. Aaron David Gresson III, *The Recovery of Race in America* (Minneapolis, Minn.: University of Minnesota Press, 1995).

72. Steven A. Holmes, "Programs Based on Sex and Race Are Under Attack: Dole Seeks Elimination; Congressional Committee and Court Question the Validity of Affirmative Action," *New York Times*, March 16, 1995, A1, C22.

73. Cf. Gregory Howard Williams, *Life on the Color Line: The True Story of a White Boy Who Discovered He Was Black* (New York: Dutton, 1994).

74. John Grisham, *A Time to Kill* (New York: Island Books, 1989).

75. Geoffrey Smith with Mike McNamee, "There's No 'Whites Only' Sign, But: A Fed Study Finds Serious Discrimination in Bank Lending Practices," *Business Week*, October 26, 1992, 78; but also see Gary S. Becker, "The Evidence against Banks Doesn't Prove Bias," *Business Week*, April 19, 1993, 18.

76. Bill Lubinger, Miriam Hill and James King, "More Funds for Minority Loans: Fannie Mae Adds $140 Billion to Pool," *Plain Dealer*, March 16, 1994, 1–C.

77. Ibid.

78. Barbara Rudolph, "Special Report: The Savings And Loan Crisis; Finally, the Bill Has Come Due; Bush Puts Forth a Thrift-Industry Bailout Plan that Could Cost $200 Billion During the Next Three Decades, but Is It Enough to Solve the Problem?" *Time*, February 20, 1989, 68–73.

79. Editorial, "Protection for Corporate Fraud," *New York Times*, June 23, 1995, A14.

80. Amy Barret, "Talk about Doing Well by Doing Good: American Savings' Mortgages in the Inner City Are a Gold Mine," *Business Week*, December 6, 1993, 162–163; also see the *Financial Institutions Reform, Recovery and Enforcement Act of 1989* (FIRREA), Public Law 101–73, which authorized the Resolution Trust Corporation as fulfillment of part of its statutory mission, which included the disposition of assets acquired from failed savings-and-loan associations, to establish an outreach program to ensure the utilization, to the maximum extent possible, of women-owned and minority-owned businesses. The provision pursuant to the Standard Asset Management and Disposition Agreement (SAMDA) to dispose of RTC-owned assets was added to FIRREA as an attempted remedial measure to try to increase the numbers of female and minority contractors and participants involved in financial institution operations.

81. John W. Moscow, "Bigger Banks, Bigger Problems; Glass-Steagall Works. Why Deregulate?" *New York Times*, June 28, 1995, A13; but see J. Carter Beese, "Stop Choking Wall Street: It's Too Easy To Sue for Securities Fraud," *New York Times*, June 27, 1995, A15.

82. Tim Smart, "Let the Good Times Roll—and a Few More Heads: Corporate America Isn't Letting a Little Growth Stand in the Way of Layoffs," *Business Week*, January 31, 1994, 28–29.

83. Howard Gleckman, Paul Magnusson and Peter Hong, "Cold Comfort in Hot Springs: Corporate America's Elite See a Gloomy '93," *Business Week*, October 26, 1992, 30–32.

84. Haynes Johnson, *Divided We Fall: Gambling with History in the Nineties* (New York: Norton, 1994); but see book critique by Jack Patterson, "The Disturbing Drift of our Fragile Democracy," *Business Week*, May 9, 1994, 15 which notes that Johnson: "More than once, criticizes business' downsizing, with its permanent loss of jobs, without acknowledging the productivity gains that will translate into higher incomes and greater competitiveness."

85. Gene Koretz, "Downsizers Chalk Up a Record First Half," *Business Week*, July 26, 1993, 20.

86. Troy Segal, Christina Del Valle, David Greising, Rena Miller, Julia Flynn and Jane Prendergast, "Saving Our Schools: With America's Classrooms Besieged on So Many Fronts, Here's How the Private Sector Can Help," *Business Week*, September 14, 1992, 70–78.

87. Gary S. Becker, "School-Finance Reform: Don't Give Up on Vouchers," *Business Week*, December 27, 1993, 25.

88. 564 F. Supp. 177 (1983).

89. William A. Darity, Jr. and Samuel L. Meyers, "Racial Inequality into the 21st Century," *The State of Black America, 1992*, ed. Billy J. Tidwell (Washington, D.C.: National Urban League, 1992) 119–139.

90. Cf. *United States Postal Service Board of Governors v. Aikens*, 460 U.S. 711 (1983); *Texas Dept. of Community Affairs v. Burdine*, 450 U.S. 248 (1981); *Nashville Gas Company v. Satty*, 434 U.S. 136 (1977); *Dothard v. Rawlinson*, 433 U.S. 321, 329 (1977).

91. E.g., *Skinner v. Railway Labor Executives' Association*, 489 U.S. 602, 109 S.Ct. 1402, 103 L.Ed.2d 639 (1989).

92. *California v. Greenwood*, 486 U.S. 35, 108 S.Ct. 1625, 100 L.Ed.2d 30 (1988) (warrantless search of one's garbage); *Florida v. Bostick*, 111 S.Ct. 2382, 115 L.Ed.2d 389 (1991) (warrantless search on public bus); *Michigan Department of State Police v. Sitz*, 496 U.S. 444, 110 S.Ct. 2481, 110 L.Ed.2d 412 (1990) (warrantless use of highway sobriety checkpoints to stop cars); *New York v. Harris*, 495 U.S. 14, 110 S.Ct. 1640, 109 L.Ed.2d 13 (1990) (admissibility of statement pursuant to warrantless and nonconsensual entry into a suspect's home).

93. William J. Chambliss and Robert B. Seidman, *Law, Order, and Power* (Addison-Wesley, Reading, Mass., 1971), 73, 503.

94. "House Approves Get-Tough Crime Bill," *Plain Dealer*, April 22, 1994, 6–A; Sabrina Eaton, "Fisher Lauds Crime Bill Vote," *Plain Dealer*, April 22, 1994, 6–A; Paul Craig Roberts, "So You Say You're Not a Gang Member? Read On," *Business Week*, February 21, 1994, 22.

95. Katharine Q. Seelye, "Anti-Crime Bill As a Political Dispute: President and G.O.P. Define the Issue," *New York Times*, February 21, 1995, C10.

96. Cf. Lee Walczak, "How Clinton Can Keep His Head above Whitewater," *Business Week*, March 21, 1994, 41; Susan B. Garland and Gail DeGeorge, "Can Hillary Put the Pieces Back Together?: The Sharks Are Circling—So She's Hitting the Road to Spruce Up Her Image," *Business Week*, March 21, 1994, 40; Larry Margasak, "Rostenkowski Rejects Plea Deal, Faces Indictment," *Plain Dealer*, May 29, 1994, 1A; 8A.

97. Stephen Labaton, "Gingrich Dismisses His Newly Selected Historian of House: House Historian Is Dismissed in Wake of Holocaust Report," *New York Times*, January 10, 1995, A1, A8; Katharine Q. Seelye, "The Speaker—Gingrich Knew of Comment by Historian, Her Aide Says: He Denies Prior Knowledge of Statements," *New York Times*, January 11, 1995, A11.

98. Richard W. Stevenson, "Big Gambles, Lost Bets Sank a Venerable Firm: Breaking the Bank," *New York Times*, March 3, 1995, A1, C13.

99. Po Bronson, "The Young and the Reckless," *New York Times*, March 3, 1995, A15.

100. Nancy Benac, "Clinton Vows to Fight Crime Wave: Mayors Join Campaign for Tougher Gun Controls," *Plain Dealer*, December 10, 1993, 1–A, 10–A.

101. Gary Becker, "Stiffer Jail Terms Will Make Gunmen More Gun-Shy," *Business Week*, February 28, 1994, 18.

102. Gary Becker, "How to Tackle Crime?: Take a Tough, Head-On Stance," *Business Week*, November 29, 1993, 26.

103. James King, "CEO Says Clinton Fumbled Chance for Health-Care Plan," *Plain Dealer*, March 11, 1994, 1–A, 12–A.

104. Robert Kuttner, "Pat Moynihan's Blarney on Health Care," *Business Week*, February 14, 1994, 18.

105. Robert Pear, "Clinton Draws Heat on Plans for Vaccines: Lawmakers Say Administration Eyes Warehouse for Storage, Distribution," *Plain Dealer*, May 30, 1994, 1–A, 10–A.

106. Robert Pear, "Welfare Debate Will Re-Examine Core Assumptions: Pivotal Change Possible; Republicans Question the Idea That All Eligible Applicants Are Entitled to Benefits," *New York Times*, January 2, 1995, A1, A7.

107. Sabrina Eaton, "GOP Targets $17 Billion in Social Aid: Kasich Unveils Next $100 Billion in Cuts as House OK's First Round," *Plain Dealer*, March 17, 1995, 1–A, 4–A; Jerry Gray, "Republicans Push Their Plan Ahead with Budget Advances on 2 Fronts; House Gives Final Approval to Trims This Year and Moves to Pay for a Tax Cut," *New York Times*, March 17, 1995, A1, A9.

108. E.g., Michael Wines, "Republicans Postpone a Balanced-Budget Vote," *New York Times*, March 1, 1995, A1, A12; Michael Wines, "Senate Rejects Amendment on Balancing the Budget: Close Vote Is Blow to G.O.P.: Risk to Democrats; In Political Maneuver, Dole Shift Will Allow Rematch Any Time," *New York Times*, March 3, 1995, A1, A10; Joseph F. Sullivan, "A Balanced-Budget Bill Is Passed in New Jersey," *New York Times*, February 28, 1995, A11.

109. Jennifer Dixon, "Welfare Plan Would Require Unwed Moms to Live at Home," *Plain Dealer*, December 10, 1993, 1–A, 10–A; Robert Pear, "Democrats See Virtue in Shift to the Right on Welfare," *New York Times*, March 17, 1995, A9.

110. Wines, "Senate Rejects Amendment," A1.

111. Walter Shapiro, "Reaganomics with a Human Face: Bush's 'Action Agenda' has Something for Everyone—but the Bookkeepers," *Time*, February 20, 1989, 32–34.

112. "Reaganomics with a Human Face," 33.

113. Dale Carnegie, *How to Win Friends and Influence People* (New York: Pocket Books, 1936).

114. Dirk Johnson, "Voters Expect Congress to Make a Right Turn: One Issue Strikes a Raw Nerve with the Electorate: A Need to Cut Welfare," *New York Times*, January 3, 1995, A8; Susanne Schafer, "Reagan Signs Welfare Bill: Sweeping Reform Contains Work, Education Provisions," *Plain Dealer*, October 14, 1988, 1–A; Ann McFeatters, "President Seeks Advice to End Welfare Mess," *Plain Dealer*, February 3, 1993, 1–A, 7–A.

115. Michael J. Mandel, "Too Many Jobs: Is That Why the Fed Tightened?" *Business Week*, February 21, 1994.

116. Jacques Steinberg, "Jobs with No Future Draw Hundreds," *New York Times*, March 17, 1995, A12.

117. Lynn C. Burbridge, "Toward Economic Self-Sufficiency: Independence without Poverty," in *The State of Black America 1993*, 71–90.

118. "Politicians Take Up Proposal to End Welfare," *Plain Dealer*, April 22, 1994, 6–A.

119. Frances Fox Piven and Richard A. Cloward, *The New Class War: Reagan's Attack on the Welfare State and Its Consequences* (New York: Pantheon Books, 1982) , 4.

120. Roger Wilkins, The Clarence J. Robinson Professor of History and American Culture, George Mason University, "Goals for Our People" (Lecture, Cleveland State University, Cleveland, Ohio, April 25, 1994).

121. Stephen Baker in Mexico City, Geri Smith in Monterrey, and Elizabeth Weiner in Ciudad Juarez, "The Mexican Worker: Smart, Motivated, Cheap—And a Potent New Economic Force to be Reckoned With," *Business Week*, April 19, 1993, 84–87, 90–92; Douglas Harbrecht in Washington with Geri Smith and Stephen Baker in Mexico City, "NAFTA: The 'Side Agreements' Take Center Stage," *Business Week*, April 19, 1993, 92; Douglas Harbrecht, Susan B. Garland, Owen Ullmann, and Paul Magnuson in Washington with Geri Smith in Mexico City and bureau reports, "What if NAFTA Loses? The Consequences for the World Could Be Dire," November 22, 1993, 32–36; William C. Symonds in Toronto with Geri Smith in Mexico City, Stephen Baker in Pittsburgh, and bureau reports, "Border Crossings: NAFTA Would Fulfill the Promise of a Continental Market," *Business Week*, November 22, 1993; Susan B. Garland, Douglas Harbrecht, and Richard S. Dunham in Washington, "Sweet Victory: The NAFTA War Is Won. Now, Clinton Must Mend Fences," *Business Week*, November 29, 1993, 34,35.

122. E.g., Anthony DePalma, "Rates Up Sharply in Mexico: 10–Point Rise Made under U.S. Pressure," *New York Times*, February 21, 1995, C-1, C-9; Nathaniel C. Nash, "Biggest German Union Begins Strike: Workers Want a Shorter Workweek and a 6% Raise," *New York Times*, February 25, 1995, C17, C19.

123. Norma Jean and Don Freeman, "The New World Disorder," *Vibration* 2, No. 2 (January -June, 1994: 1–8), Cleveland, Ohio.

124. David E. Sanger, "Dole and Clinton Strike a Deal on World Trade Pact: Escape Clause for Congress Is a Key," *New York Times*, November 24, 1994, A1, A15.

125. E.g., Republican pollster, Bill McInturff, corroborated such a view when he stated, "They run an Administration by survey research," as quoted in Katharine Q. Seelye, "Anti-Crime Bill as a Political Dispute: President and G.O.P. Define the Issue," *New York Times*, February 21, 1995, C10; also see Todd S. Purdum, "Clinton, Using Old Hands and New, Slowly Creates a Re-election Team," *New York Times*, February 27, 1995, A10, in which it is stated, "although Stanley Greenberg remains the President's chief pollster, aides said, his work is now supplemented by that of two other top Democratic pollsters, Geoffrey Garin and Mark Mellman."

126. Cf. Stanley B. Greenberg, "Mistaking a Moment for a Mandate: The G.O.P. May Be in for a Shock," *New York Times*, March 9, 1995, A15.

127. E.g., Seth Faison, "U.S. and China Sign Accord to End Piracy of Software, Music Recordings and Film: Copyright Battle; Washington Drops Plan to Impose $1 Billion in Trade Sanctions," *New York Times*, February 27, 1995, A1, C5; Clyde Haberman, "For Mideast, A Hard Road: Historic Handshake Led to Dashed Hopes," *New York Times*, February 25, 1995, A1, A4; Sylvia Nassar, "Why Wall St. Cheers as Economy Slips," *New York Times*, February 25, 1995, A1 A26; Clyde H. Farnsworth, "U.S.-Canada Pact Ends Restrictions on Air Travel," *New York Times*, February 25, 1995, A1, A5; Eric Schmitt, "Pentagon to Seek Scaled-Back List of Base Closings: 2 Dozen Sites to Be Cut; Some Big Installations Spared in Military Cutback Plan; Cost Is Called a Factor," *New York Times*, February 25, 1995, A1, A8; Anthony DePalma, "Economy Reeling, Mexicans Prepare Tough New Steps:

Original Plan a Failure; Budget Cuts and Tax Increases Planned as Inflation Soars and a Recession Looms," *New York Times*, February 26, 1995, A1, A6; Donatella Lorch, "Marines Cover U.N.'s Pullout from Somalia," *New York Times*, February 28, 1995, A1, A7.

128. Cf. Charles Dickens, *The Works of Charles Dickens: Great Expectations; Hard Times; A Christmas Carol and Tale of Two Cities*, (Stamford, Conn.: Longmeadow Press, 1982).

129. James E. Conyers, "Approaches to Remedying Racial Injustices" (Presentation at the 59th Annual Conference of the Association of Social and Behavioral Scientists, Inc., Jackson, Miss., March 26, 1993).

130. E.g., Edmund L. Andrews, "Murdoch May Face New Woes: FCC Official Says He Was Misled in '85," *New York Times*, February 25, 1995, C17, C19. According to this article, the NAACP's New York branches, through their lawyer, David Honig [the author worked with Mr. Honig on another case], contended that "foreign bidders make it harder for minorities to buy American television stations." Also see Bill Carter, "Murdoch Defends Fox TV Network," *New York Times*, February 28, 1995, C 5; Nathaniel C. Nash, "Gore Says U.S. Plans to Open Phone and TV to Foreigners," *New York Times*, February 26, 1995, A5, in which it is explained that "the plan to open the American telephone markets did not alter current restrictions that prohibit foreign ownership of more than 25 percent of American radio and television stations."

131. But see *New York Times*, "Gingrich Denounces Editorial 'Socialists,' " March 9, 1995, A9.

132. "Black Women Firsts: Pioneers in the Struggle for Racial and Gender Equality," *Ebony*, March 1994, 44–50.

133. "Managers: The Best of New Products 1994 Entrepreneurs," *Business Week*, January 9, 1995, 101, 106.

134. Janice Harayda, "Lobbying Helped Morrison," *Plain Dealer*, October 8, 1993, 12–C.

135. Juan Williams with The Eyes on The Prize Production Team, *Eyes On The Prize: America's Civil Rights Years 1954–1965* (New York, N.Y.: Penguin Books, 1987); Victor Perlo, *Economics of Racism, USA: Roots of Black Inequality* (New York: International Publishers Company, Inc., 1975), 1.

136. Traci Grant, "Black Romance Novels Lighting Publishing Fire," *Plain Dealer*, March 23, 1995, E-7.

137. U.S. Supreme Court Case No. 90–7675 (1992).

138. Keith Schneider, "Hate Groups Use Tools of the Electronic Trade: Computers Help Spread the Message," *New York Times*, March 13, 1995, A8.

139. Sara Rimer, "New Medium for the Far Right," *New York Times*, April 27, 1995, A1, A12, which states, "In the past decade, shortwave radio, once primarily used by religious missionaries and government broadcasts like Voice of America, has become one of the most vital tools of far right extremists."

140. Edmund L. Andrews, "Court Stalls F.C.C. Program for Women and Minorities," *New York Times*, March 16, 1995, C22.

141. Steven A. Holmes, "Programs Based on Sex and Race Are under Attack: Dole Seeks Elimination—Congressional Committee and Court Question the Validity of Affirmative Action," *New York Times*, March 16, 1995, A1, C22.

142. 497 U.S. 547 (1990).

143. 63 U.S.L.W. 4523 (June 12, 1995).

144. Cf. Geraldine Fabrikant, "Walt Disney Acquiring ABC in Deal Worth $19 Billion; Entertainment Giant Born; Wall St. Stunned, Powerful Combination of Hollywood Studio and Network TV," *New York Times*, August 1, 1995, A1, C7.

145. Geraldine Fabrikant, "CBS Accepts Bid by Westinghouse; $5.4 Billion Deal; 2d Big TV Sale This Week; Industrial Giant in Pact With Last Independent Network—Rival Offers Possible," *New York Times*, August 2, 1995, A1, C6.

146. Cf. Edmund L. Andrews, "Mr. Murdoch Goes to Washington; The G.O.P. Welcome Is Warm Indeed," *New York Times*, July 23, 1995, Sec. 3: 1, 11.

147. William Glaberson, "The Press: Bought and Sold and Gray All Over," *New York Times*, July 30, 1995, Sec. 4: 1,6.

148. Theodore Cross, "What If There Was No Affirmative Action in College Admissions? A Further Refinement of Our Earlier Calculations," *Journal of Blacks in Higher Education*, No. 5 (Autumn 1994): 52–55.

149. Steven A. Holmes, "Washington Talk: Affirmative Action, Yes, Though Not Known as It," *New York Times*, March 10, 1995, A9, in which the author editorializes: "There is the Government's payment of $1.2 billion to the families of Japanese-Americans who spent World War II in internment. The payment to the Japanese also affirmed the notion of the sons paying for the sins of the fathers. Nearly one-third of those who paid taxes last year and, therefore contributed to the reparations payments, were born after World War II."

150. Bob Drogin, "Mandela Is President of S. Africa: 1st All-Race Parliament Elects 1st Black Leader," *Plain Dealer*, May 10, 1994, 1–A, 10–A; Elizabeth Weiner and Alan Fine in Johannesburg, "Walking the High Wire: Can Mandela Satisfy Townships and Business?" *Business Week*, May 2, 1994, 42–44; but also see Paul Shepard, "Cheers Mixed with Sad Memories," *Plain Dealer*, May 10, 1994, 10–A; Bill Keller, "Blast Puts a Bloody Cap on Campaign: Johannesburg Car Bomb Dims Prospect of Fear-Free Elections," *Plain Dealer*, April 25, 1994, 1–A, 8–A.

CHAPTER 2

Black Women in the Political World Order

POLITICS AS A SOCIAL INSTITUTION

The primary goal of the political institution is order (Parsons 1951). Order is achieved in a society by those in power. The political institution involves the distribution of power relationships. The political institution provides the foundation for the exercise of "legitimate" power. Legitimate power is authority. The way that authority is exercised is through the operating arm of the political institution known as government. Government in a society may be voluntarily or involuntarily imposed upon a people. The foundation for the government of the United States is its Constitution. That Constitution makes provision for a democratic form of government setting forth the principle that U.S. government is voluntarily imposed as an expression of the will of a people as opposed to a monarchical, oligarchical or some other form of government. The basic way that the people's will is expressed is through the franchise (voting). Hence, it is through the vote that the structures and personnel of government are determined either directly or indirectly. Therefore, voting and its corollary activities are extremely important as a manifestation of a people's degree of participation in their government. The extent and effectiveness of that participation also reflects the ability of people in a society to obtain access to other societal benefits. At different periods in the history of Blacks in the United States, they have had varying levels of political participation in government ranging from the days of slavery, Reconstruction, Jim Crow, Civil Rights (Walters 1988) to the genesis of the New World Order.

The following case study describes the participation of a Black woman in the political process as a governmental (state) representative during the latter period.

POLITICAL CASE STUDY: A BLACK WOMAN IN THE WORLD OF POLITICS

The author met Georgia State Representative Barbara J. Mobley in Indianapolis, Indiana, at the 84th Annual NAACP Convention. Both of us were attending the jointly sponsored NBA (National Bar Association)/NAACP Continuing Legal Education Seminar on Civil Rights for Lawyers. The seminar was held on Friday, July 9, and Saturday, July 10, 1993. When I learned that Representative Mobley was from the Atlanta, Georgia, area, I asked to interview her the next weekend, when I would be in Atlanta for a meeting of the Publications Committee for the *Journal of Social and Behavioral Sciences*, published by the Association of Social and Behavioral Scientists, Inc.

The next week, on Saturday, July 17, 1993, Representative Mobley and I met for several hours in Atlanta at the Black-owned Paschal's Motor Hotel located on Martin Luther King Drive, S.W. Representative Mobley's Georgia State Legislative District was 50 (after redistricting it became 69). When the U.S. Supreme Court struck down Georgia's redistricting plan, *Zell Miller, et al., v. Davida Johnson, et al.*[1], her district was in part of U.S. Congressional Representative Cynthia McKinney's (D) District 11, as well as those of Representative John Lewis (D), District 5, and Representative John Linden (R), District 4. The following section contains her account of her political career.

THE HISTORY, ETIOLOGY AND POLITICS OF A GRASSROOTS CAMPAIGN

I [Representative Mobley] am originally from Georgia, having been born there, but my mother moved to Tampa, Florida, when I was six months old, after her divorce from my father. I was educated in the public schools of Tampa (Hillsborough County). After graduation from high school, I attended Savannah State, where I received a B.S. in sociology in 1969. Upon completing the graduate social work program at the University of Illinois, I was awarded the M.S.W. in 1971. I worked for some time as a social worker and in various public-service capacities, when I went back to school to obtain a law degree from Southern Methodist University (SMU) in Texas.

My first professional job was as a social worker for the City of Tampa in its Community Relations Division. There I worked with the Youth Board during the early 1970s. The Youth Board grew out of the civil unrest in some of the cities. During that time in Tampa in response to such unrest, a Youth Council was established. It was nicknamed the "White Hats" because the members wore white hats, which were supposed to be symbolic of the "good guys." As an employee of the Tampa Youth Board, I was more than a counselor. The Youth Board comprised several different components. It had a business component, a culture component, a community component. I helped the youth develop businesses pursuant to the economic development thrust. We had a chicken business, which the children named "BOSS Biddy." One of the kids designed the logo for the BOSS Biddy business. In the cultural component, we assisted the students in the research of Black History, held African fashion shows and explored the origins of African civilization. Our community component actually held weekly community meetings, out of which grew effective social action. The programs were funded primarily by federal monies.

Next, I moved to Atlanta, Georgia. I was going through a divorce when I visited Atlanta for a National Delta [Sigma Theta Sorority, Incorporated] Convention. There was Barbara Jordan, who spoke magnificently. Maynard Jackson was running for mayor for the first time. I was so impressed with warmth and vivaciousness at the convention, I went home, told my mother I was moving to Atlanta and packed my bags. I came without a job. But, some of my Sorors from my Sorority were looking out for me. I was thus able to survive until I found employment.

Let me go back. A part of what helped to shape me was my maternal grandfather, Matthew Gregory, with whom I had a special relationship. My grandfather was the first president of the NAACP in Tampa. He also led the Tampa chapter of the Brotherhood of Sleeping Car Porters. When A. Philip Randolph, the national president of the porters' union, would visit Tampa, I would to sit on his lap and listen to his stories. My desire, initially, to become an attorney was born out of my admiration for an attorney named William Fordham. Attorney Fordham was the local Tampa NAACP lawyer who helped to develop the chapter's responses to discrimination and reaction to the civil rights movement. Whenever my grandfather took me along when he visited Attorney Fordham on NAACP business, I was fascinated by the walls and walls of books on his shelves. That exposure started my interest in public service. Living through such experiences as a bombing in Mims, Florida, heightened my commitment to that interest. In Mims, the home of the Regional Director of the NAACP was bombed, and my grandfather went there on Christmas Day. I remember that even though there was a lot of fear for my grandfather, he still had to go. Thus, having a childhood which was steeped in early civil rights activity gave me a sense of responsibility to the community. I saw how the Brotherhood of Sleeping Car Porters raised money to support the civil rights movement. I saw how even widely renowned entertainers such as Mahalia Jackson would use their talents to raise money for the civil rights movement.

Another aspect of my grandfather's influence is found in the example he set regarding the importance of education. Although he did not have a high school diploma, my grandfather was very active in the church, the First Baptist Church of College Hill. As a leader in the church, he was instrumental in establishing the Mary Robinson Scholarship Program.

This scholarship program was named after the deceased wife of the church's minister, Rev. J. C. Robinson. With my grandfather's urging, our church became very active in the civil rights movement, and every time he had an opportunity to speak, he would talk about education and voting. Along this line also, we lived very close to the railroad tracks. Living this close, we were able to tell the difference between the train whistles. There was one kind of whistle for a freight train, for example, and another for a passenger train. I remember when I was as young as nine years old, upon hearing the whistle of a passenger train, I would run out to see if it were one of my grandfather's. If it was, he would be at the caboose, throwing papers off the train. The papers were Pittsburgh *Couriers*. Grandfather knew that even at that age, I loved to read. He wanted to encourage me in any way he could.

The house where he, my step-grandmother, Ola, and my mother and I lived, on the second floor at 2624 1/2 29th Street Avenue in Tampa, still stands. My grandfather owned the two-story house. My family still owns the place. Currently, there are renters upstairs and renters living in two apartments downstairs. My grandfather also owned another house, which I eventually owned and is also still in the family. My mother is still a beautician and owns her own beauty shop. So, I had a historical role model of public service and entrepreneurship in my family.

How I decided to run for this office [Georgia State Representative]? I was a member of 100 Black Women, De Kalb Chapter [Georgia]. At the 1991 Annual Meeting the then state representative, Frank Redding, was the guest speaker. Frank Redding was a ten-year veteran of the position.

There are two things which I remember from his speech. One, that he was not ready to deal with any women's issues; and two, he acknowledged that should he decide not to run for another term of office, there were already some people who had been hand selected to run as his replacement.

Upon learning of his attitudes as regards those issues, I had a confrontation with him at that meeting. I had been on the board of the Council of Battered Women. One of our issues was mandatory arrest legislation. I asked him what his position was on that issue and he responded: "What is mandatory arrest?" At that meeting, it was suggested that some woman take his place. Momentum gathered from there. In addition to those concerns, there was some general dissatisfaction with the way in which our district had been represented by him. He was perceived as being a politician for the upper and middle classes—not the everyday people. The working classes did not perceive him as being their state representative.

Were White women as enthusiastic about my campaign as Black women? Although they are very supportive now, during my campaign the Georgia National Organization for Women (NOW) supported Frank Redding. The Georgia NOW said that he had voted correctly on women's issues. I had done volunteer work with the Georgia NOW the previous year to get the

Commission on Family Violence established. But, as I stated, we have [she and the Georgia NOW] made amends now and they are currently supportive. The Georgia NOW worked with me during Session on pending legislation which I had introduced.

The district for which I ran is composed of two counties, Atlanta and De Kalb. Part of my district is in Atlanta in De Kalb County. In the middle of my campaign, reapportionment changed my House District from being Number 50 to that of Number 69. The redistricting was approved by the Justice Department, as I indicated, after I had already started campaigning. Although this last reapportionment changed the diversity of my district— more Anglos were brought into my district—-the majority of my constituents are still Black. The majority of the registered voters in my district are women.

Another startling event, which occurred during the latter part of my campaign, was the surprise fact that Frank Redding was indicted in the last two weeks before the election. The allegation was that he had obtained $2,000 to change his vote on nude legislation. My predecessor, then opponent, was cursing so much during the surreptitious electronic surveillance which was made of the transaction which recorded his activity that they could not play the audio of it on daytime television. Despite this evidence, Mr. Redding's trial for this accusation resulted in a hung jury. Mr. Redding's trial came three weeks after the Rodney King verdict. There were eight Whites and four Blacks on the jury in a federal court. With the King trial so close, the four Blacks refused to enter a guilty verdict against Mr. Redding, who is a Black man. Two weeks later, before the election, U.S. Attorney Joe Whitley proclaimed that: "we will try Redding again ." So, after the primary but before the general election, Mr. Redding pled guilty. He thus had to resign his position and cannot run again for thirteen years.

With the resignation of Mr. Redding, I and my other opponent, Ms. Elizabeth Omilimi, had to have a runoff primary. Although Ms. Omilimi commonly uses her last name for general purposes, she uses the name Elizabeth Williams to emphasize the fact that she is the daughter of long-time civil rights activist Hosea Williams. Hosea Williams got Frank Redding to endorse his daughter. However, I had started my grassroots campaigning, which concentrated on door-to-door, direct contact, $2 to $5 donation-type activity back in January of 1992. My campaign manager, Richard Smiley, was very good at grassroots, door-to-door campaign organizing, so that by the April 25, 1992, filing deadline, we had covered half the district and Ms. Elizabeth Williams' campaign had not started.

In the primary, Elizabeth Williams received approximately 1,100 votes. Despite his legal woes, Frank Redding received about 900, and I received 1,735 (I remember mine precisely). Two weeks after Frank's hung jury episode, Elizabeth and I faced off in a runoff election. Interestingly enough, in the runoff, Elizabeth lost 100 votes, because she received about 1,000 votes in total and I lost ten, going from 1,735 to 1,725. Mr. Redding's supporters did not show up at the polls, evidently, because his 900 votes did not appear in the final election tally. I guess if they could not vote for him, they would rather not vote. I had no Republican opposition in the general election.

I introduced three bills as a freshman legislator. One passed and two are pending. The one which passed and became effective as of July 1, 1993, is HB 680. HB 680 is domestic violence protection, which provides for an automatic standing order against both parties. The order is served on the defendant and puts him [or her] on notice that he or she cannot do such things as remove children, harass, intimidate or alienate [get rid of] property. De Kalb County allows these remedies now, solely on the petition of a party to any domestic action. De Kalb County will now order such domestic violence remedy without a hearing during the pendency of that action. Cobb County is one of the counties where you can pray [in a legal complaint] for such remedy and it may be granted after a hearing with both parties. Coming to the legislature as a social worker and as a lawyer, I felt that parties needed to be protected from the moment that an order was filed.

Another bill which I introduced was HB 679, which involved the enforcement of the temporary protection order. We had one [temporary protection order as a legislative enactment] here in Georgia, but it was not being enforced as it should have been. There were different ways different counties were enforcing it. So, if a woman went from De Kalb County to Clayton County, the Clayton County judge would not enforce her De Kalb County order. I want to have a bill whereby every county will enforce the standing order. Now, the judges do not necessarily recognize out-of-county orders. The legislation which I proposed provided for uniform state-wide enforcement.

The third bill, HB 994, which I sponsored sought protection against sexual harassment. I knew that my colleagues in the legislature would need more time to pass that bill.

Sponsoring legislation in my first term, I learned an important lesson. Our legislative session is forty days. During the last twenty days, all proposed legislation has to go through the Rules Committee to be placed on the next day's agenda. Dealing with that committee, one thing I learned was not to have my legislation caught up in the Rules Committee. From now on, I will make certain all my bills get introduced during the first twenty days of the legislative session.

I had to go very early every morning before the Rules Committee. I had to go and beg them six consecutive times in this manner to have my legislation put on the agenda. I would get up and give a summary of my bills; the chairman asked, "What is the pleasure-do you hold it or do you let it go?" Before I was even considered, the chairman first went around the table to see if any member of the Rules Committee had any legislation he or she wanted to put on the agenda. Then, all the members were queried as to whether they had any objection to one—an outsider legislator could only propose one bill at a time—of my bills going on the agenda. Next, once the list of proposed bills was prepared, the chairman might ultimately only put the last ten, the first ten, or the odd-numbered proposed pieces of legislation on the agenda for consideration by the entire legislative body. This is the kind of archaic, arcane maneuvering through which the legislative work was accomplished. However, there was business to be taken care of, and that is what I did. My constituents had sent me to represent them, and that is what I fully intended to do despite the elusive shenanigans of the old-timers.

I am not sure if I would run again because there are some other personal accomplishments which I would like to achieve. In Georgia, a state legislator has to run every two years. Although there are no term limits in Georgia, I am for term limits because I think corruption corrupts. This is supposed to be like a part-time, civic-duty position to be held by concerned citizens. It pays $10,600 a year, but it is really a full-time job. If I were not a lawyer, it would be much more difficult for me to be a legislator. I still have $1,100 [as of July 1993] outstanding on my campaign expenses. My campaign funds were raised by donations from people of very modest circumstances. It really was a grassroots campaign.

The type of people and the type of campaign which I ran was exemplified today at the Home Depot. I went there with Representative June Hegstrom to hold Constituents Day. While there, one of my constituents, a Ms. Mosely, came up to me and told me that the first reason she had voted for me was because I came to her door and asked for her vote. Ms. Mosely then proceeded to volunteer in any way in which I might need her help in a future campaign.

Like I said, I am not sure if I want to continue in this type of public service. It consumes your entire life. Some day, I think, I would like to teach. The reason I chose Southern Methodist University School of Law in Dallas, Texas, was because I was looking for a place where I could get course work in immigration and international law. Ultimately, I would like to teach a course on International Organizations in Their Legal Settings. This is because I feel that African American students need a global perspective. They need to learn how they fit into the global economic needs and concerns.

For instance, after the African countries had achieved at least political liberation during the sixties, there was a meeting of the EEC (European Economic Community) at Lomé, Togo—the Lomé Convention. At that convention, it was the particular concern of France that these recently liberated countries be provided assistance in attaining economic self-sufficiency and international trade expertise. France was concerned that the Francophone countries in Africa not be abandoned in their embryonic efforts at trade, industrialization, technological development, financial applications, et cetera. Although the old line was that the European countries should not be paternalistic, the issue raised by France was that such previously colonialized countries could not just be left to be politically independent without guidance in economic and technological matters. The result of that convention was that the relationship between the participating African, Caribbean and Pacific countries and the EEC would be free passage, free jobs, basket currency [a combination of six currencies], et cetera. The EEC is now trying to implement the Treaty of Rome's [which created the EEC] European Currency Unit [or the ECU]. Thus far, the EEC has a long way to go in developing a full and fair partnership with the African countries.

What I feel is that African Americans could further their own economic viability by creating liaisons with their African sisters and brothers who need their various areas of financial, computer, business, chemical, engineering, medical, legal and other technological expertise. Such liaisons would provide African Americans with access to the benefits of the EEC as well. Such access, in turn, would enhance their economic and political stature in their own country of the U.S.A.

At any rate, I know I want to continue my family's tradition of public service, but at this juncture, I do not know exactly what form that pursuit will take in the future.

What impact has public office had upon my private life? It has erased it.

NEW WORLD ORDER POLITICAL IMPLICATIONS

Two primary factors emerge from Representative Mobley's interview: her strong family history of public service and entrepreneurship and her strong grassroots base in the Black community. Her family history is significant for its illustration of the importance of early socialization and education to an individual's future growth and development. She credits these variables with being responsible later for how her interest and involvement in a public service career developed. That early childhood socialization exposed her to the issues in the Black community which needed addressing. It taught her how to network in order to address those needs, and it familiarized her with strategies designed to be effective in the address of those needs. For example, her grandfather's union, the Brotherhood of Sleeping Car Porters, showed her how people of humble origins could effectuate powerful changes. Activities such as those engaged in by her grandfather are paralleled in the video presentation "Eyes on the Prize" by Juan Williams. For example, in the Eyes on the Prize program, "Fighting Back: 1957–1962,"[2] the Montgomery head of the local NAACP, E. D. Dixon, is featured during the account of the bus boycott initiated by the brave actions of Mr. Dixon's secretary, Mrs. Rosa Parks.

Mr. Dixon points out that he was also head of the Brotherhood of Sleeping Car Porters. The connection between passenger-train porters and the funding and, indeed, almost founding of the civil rights movement had probably eluded every group from the Black nationalists to the White Citizens' Councils during the 1960s. The author remembers how the strident, more radical groups during the 1960s used to make fun of those in supposedly "Uncle Tom" occupations; the latter's real story has yet to be told. Such revelations bring new meaning to the words, "They also serve who wait." No matter how much money a swaggering African American drug dealer or an arrogant corporate executive makes, it goes for naught if it is not used for liberating purposes.

Without exposure to the gentle and meek, yet courageous, freedom fighters who cleaned for and waited on the nation's "elite," it is improbable that Representative Mobley would even *be* Representative Mobley. The African American community must ensure that the generations of the future are receiving the training they will need to be effective members of the increasingly political society in which they will undoubtedly live. It is interesting that Representative Mobley had to leave the interview to be on the podium at her family reunion dinner, and it is further of some interest that the author herself was in the process of planning a family reunion which was to take place at the end of July. (Both were too early to benefit much from the August 1993 *Ebony* article entitled, "How to Plan a Family Reunion You Will Never Forget.") Such Black activities (with due regard to the momentum generated by the late Alex Haley, whose thoughts on the importance of family history on African American development were also presented in that same *Ebony* edition) could help in such training efforts as well as eventually help to increase national political awareness and networking. (Two family reunions were going on at Atlanta's Paschal's on the day of this interview, one group wearing red-and-white T-shirts and the other wearing green-and-white T-shirts. Roaming around the hotel, the author was taken for a member of both family trees during the day.) Education is crucial to the survival of the group, and more and more it appears that the family has to take the initiative in this regard—the education institution notwithstanding. As the society becomes more diverse and the various interests become more insistent and more adamant that their emerging needs be addressed, the African American community will have to become ever more sophisticated to ensure that, while Azanian (South African) Blacks rise to claim their heritage, American Blacks, through the use of obsolete methods and the toleration of continual political onslaughts on their social integrity, do not lapse into obscurity and further impotence. Further, there is increasing evidence that political efforts have to expand that of just the franchise to be more comprehensively effective (Walton 1972).

The second factor emerging from Representative Mobley's social and political history demonstrates how important a public official's constituent base is. Representative Mobley's story showed that if a candidate's base is of nefarious, mercenary origin, then those are the interests to which the "public servant" is responsive. Such clandestine roots are the reason for the ultimate political demise—at least for thirteen years—of her Black male opponent.

Since Representative Mobley's base is truly the grass roots, those most influential with reference to her political agenda and exercise of political resources are her grassroots constituency. The word "truly" is operative in that the daughter of a prominent, early civil-rights-era public figure could not ride on his coattails. Noting this is not to take anything away from Elizabeth's father, Hosea Williams, who during the late 1960s assisted the Rev. Jesse Jackson.

The author remembers when in Chicago briefly, around 1969, Hosea Williams pinch-hit for Rev. Jackson during the latter's absence one Saturday at one of the morning Operation Breadbasket sessions held at the old Haltnorth Theater. (The theater was located on a street now named after the Rev. Dr. Martin Luther King, Jr., as was the site of the Mobley interview. Some of those reverently named streets still house U.S. citizens with the highest poverty rates, the highest school-dropout rates, the highest crime rates, the highest teenage pregnancy rates, the highest mortality rates and the lowest incomes in the country.) "I am somebody!" Hosea had us proclaim over and over again until he was satisfied that, at least for that Saturday morning, we were convinced of that fact. Indeed, some of us did take with us an enhanced sense of self-worth and dignity upon our departure to the different neighborhoods of Chicago, parts of the nation and countries of the world.

Nevertheless, without doing the work that her father had done in terms of grassroots organizing, his daughter could not benefit in 1992 from the dues he had paid almost twenty-three years earlier. Representative Mobley's experience demonstrates that, despite the well-connected ties of her Black female opponent, she could prevail by doing serious early grassroots organizing and constituent development. This is also a lesson for those who wish to organize around other issues and Afrocentric concerns. A foot patrol is more effective in the Black community than numerous press releases or civic club appearances. An exception might be made for the latter, however, if such appearances are made for the intermediary purpose of making connections with popular ward and precinct leaders who can help a potential public servant (as in politician) connect with the masses. These strategies of grassroots development are sometimes the only means available to candidates such as Representative Mobley whose contributions consist of primarily $2 and $5 donations from neighborhood people.

Another important theme which comes through from Representative Mobley's interview is that for a nontraditional election, there probably has to be some disassociation from traditional organization politics. A rather exaggerated and distorted manifestation of organization politics eventually became a terminal liability for the former representative, Frank Redding. It was refreshing to talk to Representative Mobley insofar as the author found her much more candid and forthright than has been the author's experience with many northeastern and midwestern public officers. These latter politicians seem to be more dependent on and to derive a greater proportion of their political life from the traditional political parties. Whether this is good or bad for minorities and women depends really upon how much respective influence they have in those traditional political parties. Thus, it would seem that if their influence is, or has been in the immediate past, rather ineffectual, then such groups might reap significant benefit from the development of alternative or at least supplementary constituency bases. This is really what Representative Mobley's campaign epitomized—the nurturing of previously overlooked voters in her targeted area of political concern.

The importance of community ties which are not necessarily political—for example, her sorority affiliation, her membership in 100 Black Women, her grandfather's alignment with the Sleeping Car Porters—permeates Representative Mobley's discussion of her political ascension. These ties form a foundation for communication, issue formulation, strategy development, and social action that might not particularly inform or be part of a local or national political party's agenda.

Finally, it must be noted that this chapter does not directly address the conservative mood of the country institutionalized by, for one thing, the Reagan-Bush Supreme Court. For instance, in the case *Shaw v. Reno* (decided June 28, 1993, Case No. 92–357), the Supreme Court struck down efforts to develop two Black Congressional districts in North Carolina. The area had not sent a Black person to the U.S. Congress since 1901. As a result of the creation of these rather innovatively drawn Congressional districts, two African Americans went to Washington, D.C., as federal legislators. Objecting to this result, Justice Sandra Day O'Connor wrote the *Shaw* opinion, in which she was joined by Chief Justice William Rehnquist and Justices Antonin Scalia, Anthony Kennedy and Clarence Thomas. The *Shaw* decision has thus "appeared to open the way for challenges to districts that are drawn solely to promote the election of minorities."[3] Justice O'Connor's role in the dismantling of minority voting rights was apparently extrapolated from this area of law to that of affirmative action (see Chapter 3 and the discussion of the *Adarand* case). Her implementation of this role demonstrates that she is prepared to strike down either voting districts or economic opportunities if she determines that race had been a "predominant factor" in their *raison d'etre*.

The Court was even more definitive two years after *Shaw* in the afore-mentioned *Zell Miller, et al., v. Davida Johnson, et al.*[4] case in expressing its antipathy towards districts which even hinted at reflecting a purpose of minority racial representation. The *Miller* Court prohibited "racial gerry-mandering." Despite evidence produced by the state to the contrary, it found that the "appropriate" factors of compactness, continuity, respect for political subdivisions or communities of interests had been subordinated by the "predominant" factor of race in determining the district. (Although 'race-based' districts were decried in *Zell Miller*, districts reflecting a major-ity White racial category seem to be okay.) Unsurprisingly, the Congres-sional voting jurisdiction declared unconstitutional by the Court in *Zell Miller* was represented by an African American woman, Cynthia McKinney, from Georgia's Eleventh Congressional District. Further, unlike the "bi-zarre" shape which was a subject of the *Shaw* case, the shape of Repre-sentative McKinney's district was almost a square (e.g., continuity). It should also be pointed out here that although State Representative Mobley mentioned that the redistricting of her district had been "approved by the Justice Department," the *Zell Miller* Court showed a marked disdain for such "Justice Department" approval. As a counter to the increasing re-trenchment of the more blatantly New World Order Congress and Supreme Court, the legislative director of the NAACP, Wade Henderson, suggested that Black voter participation needed to be raised from the 1994 rate of 37 percent. In 1990, 39.2 percent of all Blacks who were eligible "to vote cast ballots."[5] Along the political vein also, Lani Guinier, Professor of Law at the University of Pennsylvania, stated, "The leadership vacuum from both the Supreme Court and the political institutions is creating a void."[6] The void theory will be tested again and again after the U.S. Bureau of the Census completes each census. It is then that redistricting across the country begins anew based on each decennial's population numbers. And, though the census taken for each decade will undoubtedly be different, whether or not the Supreme Court will be in terms of ideology or individuals, convictions or composition depends ultimately on the ideology or individuals, convic-tions or composition of the electorate.

In short, without a predominantly Black constituency, the grassroots efforts of State Representative Mobley would possibly be considerably less effective. A chance to develop the political awareness of African Americans is what gave Representative Mobley's grassroots methods a chance in the first place. It is much less likely that such a strategy would be successful in a predominantly White working-class community, particularly given the aforementioned current conservative mentality of the populace. Barbara R. Arnwine, executive director of the Lawyers' Committee for Civil Rights under Law, points out another important strategy in combating "the subtle and transmutative forms of racial segregation and prejudice that have evolved even as overt discrimination has receded."[7] Attorney Arnwine explains the "fundamental role that private lawyers and law firms play" in "promoting equal justice and equal opportunity in this nation."[8] Of course, the underlying thesis of this analysis, while lauding such efforts, is pessimistic about foreseeable results in the current political atmosphere. This cynicism is based upon the sociological perspective utilized here of the overall purpose of the courts and most legal activity as being essentially supportive of conservative trends. Thus, performing such a legal role as exemplified by the committed attorneys involved with the Lawyers' Committee for Civil Rights under Law or the NAACP Legal Defense and Education Fund is more the exception than the "rule of law."

Nevertheless, national as well as local linkages must first of all be identified and, if necessary, made, then monitored and maintained in order to ensure proportionate Black female representation in the country's political future. This level of organization should help in the next step recommended by Representative Mobley, that of international networking with African countries, in which one ancillary goal would be to give African Americans a start in becoming players in the global economy. This could be one of the only ways left to African Americans to develop a viable social-political-economic program in a period of intense intergroup competition and hostility. For African Americans, such extreme group xenophobia translates into increasingly sophisticated (more cosmopolitan) patterns of exclusion and neglect. The experience of the former Yugoslavia may represent a very crude example of the relative socioeconomic position of the African American in the United States during the next century. The experience of American Blacks should serve as an example to Blacks in South Africa as they obtain the franchise.[9] The right to vote cannot be taken for granted as an end that is self-perpetuating. It is a right that has to be continually monitored and very closely guarded.

SUMMARY

Hence, with economic resources having been exploited to the point almost of exhaustion, human resources have to be reexamined for their potential in a service economy. Group mobilization and community organization are no longer a luxury for African Americans. These activities are prerequisites to a fully participatory existence in the coming years. Proportionate political representation of African Americans and other groups in the nation's future will come only at a high price. The price includes the sublimation of purely individualistic, short-term objectives and a cessation of the ephemeral use of resources for hedonistic, materialistic pleasures. Such narcissism does not further the type of group interest that will ultimately elevate everyone, even nongroup members. Networking with other groups will also be necessary in order to attain universal goals that further the principles of an enlightened humanity.

Representative Mobley, along with her colleagues in the state legislature, were given the utmost challenge to achieving humane principles by the Supreme Court in the *Miller* case in balancing intra-racial versus inter-racial; partisan versus nonpartisan needs at the redrawing of Cynthia McKinney's Congressional District 11.[10]

NOTES

1. 115 S. Ct. 2475 (1995).

2. Juan Williams with the Eyes on the Prize production team, "We're Not Moving to the Back, Mr. Blake," *Eyes on the Prize: America's Civil Rights Years, 1954–1965* (New York: Penguin Group, 1987), 59–89, 69.

3. Sam Howe Verhovek, "3 Minority Districts in Texas Are Ruled Unconstitutional," *New York Times*, August 18, 1994, A16; also see Linda Greenhouse, "Court to Hear New Challenge to District Drawn for a Black," *New York Times*, December 10, 1994, A1, A7; and Dayna Cunningham (assistant counsel for the NAACP Legal Defense and Education Fund), "Insuring Access: Redistricting and Representation," *NBA, National Bar Association Magazine* 8, no. 6 (Nov./Dec. 1994): 12–14.

4. 115 S. Ct. 2475 (1995).

5. Steven A. Holmes, "End of an Era? Racial Quotas Seen Crumbling," *Plain Dealer*, July 6, 1995, A2.

6. Ibid., A 2.

7. Barbara R. Arnwine, "From the Executive Director," *Committee Report: 30th Anniversary Edition 1963–1993*, 5, nos. 5 and 6 (1994): 3, Lawyers Committee for Civil Rights under Law.

8. Ibid.

9. Gay J. McDougal, "South Africa: The Countdown to Elections," *Committee Report: 30th Anniversary Edition 1963–1993*, 5, nos. 5 and 6 (1994): 6–11, Direct Southern Africa Project, Lawyers Committee for Civil Rights under Law.

10. Kevin Sack, "Georgia Trying to Fix Race-Based Voting Districts," *New York Times*, August 15, 1995, A1, A10.

CHAPTER 3

Black Women in the Economic World Order

ECONOMICS AS A SOCIAL INSTITUTION

Economic concerns explore "the production and distribution of goods and services" (Inkeles 1964, 19). Sociologists study the role of values, the influence of prestige or custom and the origins and motivations of the participants in the productive and distributive process (19, 20). In other words, sociologists look at the values, customs (practices), structures and relationships that make up the economic institution. Contextual issues that affect this process, such as in which type of political or ideological framework it is operating, are also the domain of the sociologist.

The sociological perspective in this chapter, as in the others, basically looks at how the subject social institution—here the economic—interacts with legal supports in order to maintain the place of the Black woman. The chapter provides evidence of the book's thesis that each social institution investigated provides a similar function with regard to the Black woman. Each social institution uses the legal system to perpetuate the Black woman's subordinate status. In order to overcome the "natural" order imposed by this relationship between social institutions and the law, the Black woman has to exert extraordinary energies designed to circumvent the "normal" operation of societal processes.

It is asserted here, in the framework of this analysis, that in order to overcome, the Black woman has to mobilize sufficient internal and external forces. The power to overcome must come from within and without. This is the role of, for example, Afrocentricity. Knowledge of herself and her people, faith in herself and her people, acquisition of the requisite skills by herself and her people and the ability to apply those skills by herself and her people are prerequisite to overcoming in an essentially inimical environment (Asante 1990). However, because of the predominantly nonsupportive, historically and currently inapposite societal context of the African

American female's world, self-help may be the beginning of the answer, but it is not the end.

A Black Woman in the World of McDonald's

Twenty-three-year-old Robyn came to me angry and upset. She felt she had just been victimized by the manager-owner, another Black woman, at the McDonald's where she worked, and she wanted to throw the book at her. Robyn, who had worked at two other McDonald's restaurants, knew that what her employer had done was "not right." Robyn had three young mouths to feed, and she could not afford to be fired. Robyn's dilemma can best be expressed in her own words, which she had written up on her own initiative for me, her lawyer. Frustrated and furious, Robyn wrote the following account:

I got a phone call from the office where XXX was. She said she had a man on the phone from the bank. She said I had a $50.00 shortage of one of my envelopes dated on 1/2/93. Now she says to me to come the next day, which was Thursday, payday, to take care of it. I didn't know what to do but to go and see. When I arrive there she comes to me with several more envelopes dated back almost 2 months ago, amounting to $269.15 short. Right then I knew it was a setup, because why didn't she come to me back then when the first shortage occurred? So she made arrangements with YYY to take so much out of my checks every 2 weeks. Then I left. I had to be at work at 3:00 p.m. That same day I went in, only to find out my check was taken from the stack of checks that were there, so I asked AAA and BBB, where was my check? They said YYY took it, so I called XXX and asked her, "Where is my check?" She told me, "You'll get it later today."

So we hung up. I got frustrated, so I called her back to tell her that I don't think it's right for me to pay back money that I don't know about. I told her I'll even take a lie detector test. She said she didn't want me to. Then she said, "Tell you what—turn in my keys, bring me my uniform and you'll get your check today. I grabbed my coat and left to take the uniform to her office. When I got there she told me to stand out in the hallway for 20 minutes. When I went in she told me to put the uniform down and have a seat to sign a paper. I signed it only to get my paycheck and get out of her office. When I finished, she replied to me, "Sister, I'm pressing charges against you; I'm coming after you; pick your check up at the police station." Then I said, "You're going to keep my check?" She said, "Yes, I am." Then I walked out of her office.

I had rarely met a woman as tenacious as Robyn. She had worked in an extremely authoritarian environment, presided over by a Black woman who had forgotten her roots and was fanatically suspicious of her young Black employees. Overbearing and intimidating, she "cut them no slack" and interrogated them relentlessly about the slightest work detail.

Unfortunately, I had seen a couple of other similar reactions by women who had achieved employer status through the happenstance of affiliation rather than training, education, experience, family background or previous practice in running a small business. Businesspersons without such supports tend to be more insecure than other, more established employers. The hard-pressed employees of one such unsure employer had labeled her "Snoop Doggy Dogg" after a rap star, in honor of her inquisitorial, distrustful attitude toward them.

By the time Robyn came to me, she had visited the Welfare Department, the City Prosecutor and the Municipal Small Claims Court. She had compiled a list of each and every one of the eight assistant prosecutors and the one head prosecutor in the City Prosecutor's office. She had the numbers of the Legal Aid Society, the City's largest bar association and the office of the attorney who was the president of the local NAACP. She also had the address of the McDonald's corporate headquarters. I sent the following letter to the corporation on January 15, 1994.

Re: Robyn Doe, McDonald's Manager—October 14, 1993 until January 6, 1994

Dear Sir/Madam:
I am writing on behalf of the above young lady who worked for your corporation at the above referenced time period. The local McDonald's for which she worked was located at ABC Avenue in DEF City. It is owned by Mr. and Mrs. XXX: [address given].

During her brief period of employment Ms. Robyn Doe was subjected to continuous harassment and verbal abuse. She was called "nigger," constantly berated, treated discriminately and finally, falsely accused of having a short envelope on two separate occasions, in the amount of $269.15. Ms. Robyn Doe had worked at two other McDonald's and *never* had had this happen to her. With reference to the false accusation, she offered to take a polygraph to prove her innocence and was refused.

Currently, Ms. XXX, one of the owners, is holding Ms. Robyn Doe's check in the amount of approximately $365, unlawfully.

We would like any intervention appropriate in order to rectify this unfair situation. Thanking you in advance for your consideration, I am

Sincerely yours,

Willa M. Hemmons
Attorney-at-Law

A bright, determined young woman, Robyn pursued all of her alternative remedies to the hilt. The word *self-help* did not begin to describe her resoluteness in this matter.

For some reason, I never received any communication regarding this matter from the President of the McDonald's Corporation. This is unnerving because, as corporations go, since the 1969 boycott after which it began franchising to Blacks, McDonald's had been reputed to have the best record among corporations in that regard.[1] It also reportedly was the largest employer of Black youth in the nation. According to the Council on Economic Priorities, their training programs for young people, including many from the inner city, were "reputed to be excellent." Criminal defense attorneys also have begun to appreciate McDonald's in another sense. They have found that if they respond to a judge's inquiry about the suitability of a defendant for probation with, "She or he now has a full-time job as a salad person (or cashier or night supervisor or manager or fill in the blank) with McDonald's," their client's chances of remaining free are somewhat enhanced.

The down side of McDonald's reputation was that they had also been reputed to "provide low-pay, low prestige, and routine work."[2] McDonald's reputation notwithstanding, when Robyn came to me she was extremely distraught about losing what was an important source of income for herself and her children.

However, about two months after her visit to my law office, I ran into Robyn at the "justice" complex. That center houses the state and local trial courts, the police station, the prosecutors' offices for both city and county and the city and county jails (the latter are known as correction centers). Robyn had been accepted into the correction officers' academy, and she was in training. On her break, she asked if I had heard anything from McDonald's headquarters. After I told her I had not, she informed me of all her court dates as plaintiff, pursuing her complaints about her untimely McDonald's dismissal. In her attempts to claim her past McDonald's paychecks, she had a court date for the Small Claims Court as well as one for a hearing before the mediation officer in the city prosecutor's office. She had made a criminal complaint against the Black female McDonald's owner. Like many other such complaints it was referred to the Mediation division of the prosecutor's office so that some sort of truce could be worked out by the parties.

Robyn had kept on the offensive. It is very unusual for the employer to be charged with a crime of theft in such a situation. If Robyn had sat around and given up, she might have received a summons in which she was charged with a crime. Once the criminal justice system gets hold of a person, it tenaciously tries to keep them within its tentacles. Conviction of such a theft offense would have rendered her ineligible to become a rookie correction officer. Hence, whether or not she ever gets her McDonald's paychecks, at least her perseverance has allowed her to remain economically viable enough to earn a living for herself and her children.

Strategies such as affirmative action were developed initially to try to mitigate some of the ongoing societal dynamics that were systemically antithetical to success by minorities and women within the ordinary course of events. After strong undermining efforts by the prevailing European American power structure, African Americans lost the intensity, the focus and the unity present in the early civil rights movement. Their power to execute these strategies was diluted, and the legal institution was utilized to effectuate the exceptions that were being taken by the established European American male group.

The African American intensity, focus and unity were destined to become diluted for two reasons. First, they were the offshoots of a social movement, a social phenomenon that sooner or later either dies or becomes institutionalized into some type of manageable unit within the system. Second, the goal of the early civil rights movement was integration. That goal was successful to the extent that it coopted the most able and astute members of the social movement and their immediate offspring almost immediately. The top ten percent being integrated (Cf. W. E. B. DuBois 1903), the rest of the social group was left behind to fend for themselves.

As the integration movement was highly selective and noninclusive in many realms, it meant the purchase of a home, for those who could afford it and could negotiate complex establishment financial institutions; it meant a college education, for those who could afford it and could matriculate mazes of ivory tower thistles; promotions, for those who were college educated and had transcended racial barriers to master the art of office politics; and it meant business ownership, for those who could organize, mobilize and network in politically and economically adverse times (such as the Reagan-Bush era). Thus, after the entry of the first few millions (the Black Bourgeoisie), the door was shut tightly behind them. Leaving behind the rest of the race of Afrogeneric peoples turned out to be not such a good idea (Cruse 1967). The momentum of the movement was lost when certain of the key categories of African Americans were either incorporated into the system or eliminated through death, prison, discrediting or some other nefarious device (Wilhelm 1970). Not elevating the quality of life for all resulted in a large proportion of the race being lost from effective participation in empowerment and civil rights strategies for a significant period of time. They were claimed by drugs, crime, illiteracy, unemployment, inadequate housing and insufficient health care. Not enough viable masses were left to take up the gauntlet when needed to make concerted breakthroughs at crucial times. Ignoring the masses meant putting the Black middle class person's fate totally in the hands of his or her newfound integrated forum or forums and thereby sealing it.

A Black Woman in the World of Management

In Dorothy's senior year at an "elite" liberal arts college (there were 100 Blacks out of a student body of about 2,500), recruiters from the largest company in the world came to Career Day. The year was 1976. Unbeknownst to Dorothy, the company, in what was to become known as "telecommunications,"[3] was under a federal mandate (pursuant to a consent decree[4]) to hire minorities in management. Dorothy was hence solicited by a Midwest contingent of the Eastern Establishment. Thus, by the end of summer, Dorothy found herself employed by the "phone" company. She was employed as a Manager Level One, and as there were about nine management levels at the time, in theory there was plenty of room for promotion.

Twenty-one years of age, Dorothy happily settled into her job. As her employer was reputedly the most secure company in the world, its stock was the one most commonly sold to widows with children in order to guarantee their future. It was said that it was harder to fire someone from this utility company than a civil servant from the government. Dorothy was highly intelligent and able to grasp new concepts and acquire new skills quickly and easily. Despite her intellectual acumen and skilled competence, she possessed a laid-back, fun-loving, easygoing nature. At work, Dorothy found her clerical support staff to be adequate and her peers to be pleasant, eventually becoming almost like family to her. Over the years, her supervisors seemed pretty much to follow the line of "benign neglect" when it came to her evaluations. She was generally ranked in the middle of the pack with mediocre ratings no matter what she did.

For several years Dorothy was not unduly disturbed about her rather lackluster performance assessments. At the time, the only African American female she knew to get a promotion was a certified public accountant (CPA) with an MBA who was quietly responsible for a substantial portion of the company's budget. The other woman had to move to the Chicago office as part of her promotion, leaving behind a husband, whom she later divorced. (The woman did receive further promotions while serving in that regional office and later remarried and had a child.) None of the other Blacks, male or female, were getting promoted, and during this period Dorothy was busy doing other things.

In 1979 she married, and she had a son in 1981. It was at that time that she had her first major problem with the company. Dorothy became so engrossed with motherhood and caring for her child that she went beyond the six-month maternity leave (unpaid)[5] that the Personnel Office said was the limit set for her to get her job back. The company had just won a law-suit in which the court said the company did not have to give jobs back to women who went out on non-medical-emergency maternity leaves of six months or more. (In fact, the company's policy was relatively liberal for that day and time. Indeed, many employers with fifty or more employees[6] did not even have to give any time off before the Family and Medical Leave Act of 1993[7] was passed. Even then, they had to give only twelve weeks of unpaid leave, and then only to employees who could afford to leave their jobs for that period of time without pay. Such a provision excludes many Black women from participation because they are their families' primary means of support, at a rate much higher than for other categories of workers. Further, they earn much less relative to those in other worker categories; see discussion below.)

By leaving her job for that period of time, Dorothy had forfeited the health benefits also. Loss of benefits was not a problem as she and the child had health coverage from her husband's job. Nevertheless, Dorothy wanted to get back to work. Upon her inquiry, the personnel officer said that, as there were no openings in her old department, she would have to enter a competitive training program geared toward employment in the company's computerized billing office, on the opposite side of the county in which she lived. All through the summer Dorothy struggled to learn the ins and outs, loops and layouts of computer programming. In class all day, she went to her mother's home in the evening to pick up the baby and rest before going home to cook dinner. After dinner, she fought to stay awake long enough to study her materials and make her designs and formats. She could not get enough sleep because the baby woke in the night with chronic ear infections. At the end of the summer, Dorothy was not selected as one of the top three persons chosen for the computer jobs.

Miraculously, a job opened up in her old department, and Dorothy went back. She was back at work a month when she discovered she was pregnant again. This time Dorothy returned to work when her second son was six weeks old; at eleven years old, in the fourth grade, he still suffered from attention-deficit disorder. Her oldest son, at age twelve, in the seventh grade, was an honors student at his predominantly White suburban middle-school.

By 1987, Dorothy was working for a company that was somewhat different from the one at which she had started. As a regional component of the original, monolithic company, it was more localized and its services were more concentrated. A federal judge had broken up the original company conglomerate into "nonmonopolistic" parts,[8] which was effectuated in 1984.

As time went on, Dorothy discovered that her boss was condescending and consistently disdainful of her work products. He constantly undervalued her services and usually attributed anything worthwhile that came out of her work group to someone else. Although a White male, he was not a "WASP" (White Anglo Saxon Protestant), and he seemed to let his own insecurities get in the way of his treatment of others. When any of Dorothy's creative, innovative ideas were deemed to have value, he would try to appropriate them.

Feeling that she needed more education to escape the situation, Dorothy used the company benefit of education reimbursement to enroll in a master's degree program in her discipline. She obtained her degree at a local private university that is nationally acclaimed. As she grew professionally, she felt more and more stifled by her boss. Every day she would contemplate how she could get her work around his ever-present scrutiny, and she became more and more despondent. She felt that although her work was improving it could never be recognized—or recognized as hers.

The first PC software for creating newsletters came out, and being naturally curious as well as computer sensitized from her previous training course, Dorothy began experimenting with it. As no one else in the department was interested, she began gathering department-wide events, company charts and other personnel memorabilia and distributing that information in the form of a newsletter. The newsletter became so popular that it came to the attention of a director in another department—an Italian male. Dorothy had found an ally. Together, they schemed to get Dorothy out of her department into his. Her immediate boss never knew what hit him.

About this time, toward the end of the 1980s, corporate America was beginning its first reorganization trends. Dorothy's company was part of the action. Dorothy's company "restructured" so that her old boss, while retaining his management position, had no management employees under him. His abominable management style had been recognized by his superiors. For Dorothy, it was a wonderful coup d'etat and she was ecstatic about moving on to her next department in the company. The company's building architecture reflected somewhat the rank ordering of its personnel structure. In subtle acknowledgment of its hierarchical arrangement of the company, her new department was on a floor above her old one. In the offices above Dorothy's floor, the executives had separate elevators to use which required keys.

Dorothy's "coup" was also around the time of the first buyout offering. In a "five and five" plan, eligible employees were offered five years on their age and five years added to their time of service as early retirement incentives. Employees were eligible for full retirement after thirty years of service and at age fifty without the "five and five" buyout. They were also given generous lump-sum retirement pensions, savings plans, profit sharing, paid-up life insurance and health benefits for the rest of their lives. There was a flood of happy early retirees out the door. Everyone was pleased as punch. The surrounding community welcomed them onto its boards and advisory committees and as consultants with the enthusiasm that welcomes retiring generals after a popular war. One retiree was a fifty-two-year-old Black woman, a member of Dorothy's church who immediately rolled her funds over into another annuity plan and set up shop as a private consultant, training deprived inner-city youth. Another fifty-year-old Black female leaving the company under this first early-retirement program—the *voluntary* one—became the executive director (a part-time position) of the local Black affiliate of the area's United Way Fund.

The flood of retirement takers in that first batch of retiree buyouts did not eliminate enough workers. To increase its competitiveness[9] and profits as well as to enhance its balance sheet for shareholders, the company needed to get rid of more people. Thus, it began a pattern of practice that gained it national acclaim among its sibling companies as the ultimate in terms of employee cutbacks[10]—an achievement which had some rewards.[11]

The company sent executives in from the regional office in Chicago to orchestrate this next cut.

The old guard (which included the then president and his entourage of vice-presidents, directors, coordinators and support staff) had to go. They had resisted the new guard's program. Most of the proteges, "Golden Boys," of the old guard were sitting ducks—one or two survived, but that is another book.

The annual evaluation process took on a new meaning the next year. Supervisors sat in conference rooms, meeting to decide which employees warranted expulsion. Past evaluations were used in this effort as well as, more subtly, the personal relationships particular supervisors had with particular employees. Dorothy waited along with all the others through the days and weeks after the layoff announcement, to see if they would be handed a memo encouraging them to take an early retirement. The packages for this second round of cuts were much less attractive. A "two and two" deal was offered this time. Two years would be attributed to the employee's time of service and two years would be tacked onto the employee's age. As before, the minimum age for a full retirement offering was fifty. One forty-eight-year-old Black female accountant took it. She immediately bought a house and after a few months took on a part-time bookkeeping job. Only half as much as had been offered for the previous year was offered to those early retirees who were not yet eligible for full retirement. Nevertheless, when a supervisor approached an employee with "advice" to take early retirement, that employee was expected to take it.

Initially, the employees were filled with disbelief at the way they were being treated. The "Bellheads" were stunned in fact. After all, jobs here had been the most secure other than civil service or the military.[12] Many did not believe they would be walked out of the door. For some time, many thought that their supervisors' advice was really that—and that they still had options. As "D-Day" approached, tension around the company intensified. It appeared as if minorities and women were getting an inordinate number of advisory notices, compared with other categories of employees.[13]

About this time, Dorothy and several other Black male and female employees made appointments with me and with another lawyer at his law offices for some type of guidance. It was almost as if they needed to be reoriented to time, place and person. Some appeared indignant, some reconciled, some bewildered and some in shock. Some appeared at one meeting, some at another and some at both. They mentioned that several of their Black colleagues at the company refused to come on the grounds that it would be disloyal to the company. Although we discussed several strategies at those meetings, we could not come to an agreement as to how to proceed. Each of the employees was in a different set of circumstances, unique to himself or herself. One had just made the age and time of service requirements for full retirement. One had gotten disgusted with the process and submitted his resignation before it was solicited. He was going to set up an electrical engineering business. Surviving this layoff round, two in the group, one male and one female, were promoted during the next round of layoffs. In addition, the agreement the company required the "retiring" employee to sign to get any of the benefits contained a covenant not to sue.

The first class-action lawsuit filed against the company pursuant to this round of layoffs was filed by a group of White males on the basis of age discrimination.

One of the higher-level managers who had attended one of our meetings just could not believe that he would be walked out of the door. He had received good past evaluations. He had been active with the civic and community groups on behalf of the company in the area, helping to coordinate numerous luncheons, dinners and even special functions of the local NAACP. (That might have meant something to the old guard, but to the new one it was meaningless.) He had a good rapport with the other supervisors, his colleagues. He had two master's degrees. He was several months away from being the magic age of forty-eight that would entitle him to the "two and two" retirement program. He said he would under no circumstances take the partial retirement plan offered him.

It was later told that even as he was escorted out of the building by the security guards, he still did not believe what the company was doing to him. The statute of limitations (the period of time before which one forfeits one's cause of action) for him to file a lawsuit against the company was almost up before he could show such disloyalty. He went with a "major" White male law firm for that lawsuit. That firm assigned one of its White female associates to pursue his case and she obtained a settlement for him. In the settlement, he was allowed to go back to the company as a service representative at $30,000 a year, less than half of his previous annual salary.

Dorothy's first boss took the buyout as he was advised and went home to do consulting and stay with his wife, a school teacher, and children.

Just-retired employees, with their boxes strewn over the first floor lobby of the company building, waited for loved ones to come and get them. Hanging around the lobby, waiting to see how some of the Black employees were faring, I overheard security personnel being briefed as to how to recognize and treat full retirees, who would have their complimentary badges with them. Such retirees would be allowed to go up on their own for visits as guests. (Later, some of these "retirees" were hired back as contractors and added with other new individuals who joined the company ranks on such a basis. These new and old contract workers were both identified by their round metal button badges with the company name over the word *contractor* on them.)

The president of the company first took the buyout, then one of the vice-presidents. Then another of the vice-presidents. Then most of their immediate reportees—their division heads and directors (such as the director of one of the "relations" departments, a Black male)—took the buyout.

(I ran into this Black former director in divorce court almost a year and a half later. I knew him because he had been on the board of one of the agencies for which I had done research. He and his ex-wife were sorting out their respective fair shares from the pension plan, stock holdings and savings plan which he had accumulated over the years with the company. As he was one of the top-level managers, this amount totaled about half a million. The couple had been divorced a few months after his leaving the company, but this property division, along with the division of their suburban home, was taking much longer. With the house and other fringe benefits, which included a consulting contract for the gentleman, the couple, together twenty-five years, had almost as much to fight over as Marla Maples would get—one million dollars—should she become divorced from Donald Trump.)

The day before the walkouts were to begin, the Black male director of personnel who was to preside over the proceedings had a heart attack in his office and died. His wife was too broken up to come to the funeral and greet his work colleagues from the company.

The day after one supervisor had walked out one of her employee charges, she herself was walked out by her supervisor. One Black woman who had been extremely active in local political circles was walked out one day. The next day her supervisor called her and said there had been an awful mistake and would she please come back.

A forty-six-year-old Black woman's appendix burst a few days after she had been advised to retire. She had been with the company for twenty-four years. She had hired on right after college, had never married or had children and had moved from her hometown downstate in order to continue with the company fourteen years prior to this layoff. In critical condition for days, when she finally got to the recovery room, in which there was a phone, her supervisor called to see how she was doing and to reiterate her retirement advice. This Black woman's illness caused her to stay out almost three months after the other retirees' walkout date. Her supervisor walked her out the day she came back to work. At least she had had health coverage during her illness. With this buyout, health coverage ended six months after the employee's departure. The woman maintained her health once she got well and about a year after leaving the company called upon me to offer some nutritional supplements that she was selling for a multi-level marketing group with which she had gotten involved.

During these events, Dorothy waited anxiously as her fate was decided. As she had always received mediocre evaluations, she was considered by a lot of distant associates, not in her department, a prime candidate for an early buyout. (After walkout day, such persons greeted her in places like the elevator with, "Oh, you're still here?")

The company was up for review by the primary regulatory body. For some time it had been receiving stiff competition from usurping telecommunications upstarts.[14] It wanted to become more competitive. It wanted to drive the "Information Highway."[15] It wanted a rate increase. Originally viewed as a public utility, it wanted to cut its regulatory apron strings.[16] It wanted deregulation. It expressed this latter desire through the proposal of a plan for "alternative regulation."[17]

Prior to this proposal, the company had to submit preliminary filings with the regulatory body. These filings were to fulfill several purposes: to demonstrate how it had been accountable to consumers, to show how it had spent its money, to show how much income it had received, to show its expenses, and to show the basis for its rate increase request. The purpose of greatest salience to the company was that of demonstrating the desirability of deregulation and a more flexible financial base.

Those primarily charged directly with the responsibility of making these filings did not initially want to follow the example of another branch of the company located in another city under the regulatory body's authority. The other city had developed a comprehensive model for identifying the costs and expenses of the company. No one at Dorothy's company was seriously committed to or interested in developing such a model. Dorothy insisted that such a model was necessary in order to accomplish any of the company's deregulatory goals. (Another of her thoughts was to get rid of the company's lawyers on the basis that lawyers love laws, that is, regulations, but that idea met with even less acceptance.)

Despite, not so much the opposition, but the disinterest of her generally White male colleagues, Dorothy persisted in individually developing a comprehensive cost-allocation model. Slowly, it evolved in segments on her personal computer, eventually generating a formula which covered the cost for every nut and bolt in the company. As filing time approached, it gradually was recognized that Dorothy's model was the only game in town. Peers, supervisors and workers from other departments began coming to her for applications that they could integrate into their work on the filing. Not having had the foresight to collaborate substantially in its maturation, no one else in the company understood the model. Dorothy did not get a memo advising her to take an early retirement—that round.

Surviving a second buyout, Dorothy turned her attention to adapting her model company-wide in preparation for presentation to the regulatory body. As the months went on and the model became more complete, it gained universal acceptance around the company. Dorothy began to want, after all her years at the company (at that time, seventeen), to be promoted based upon her valuable contribution to the company. She had started rehearsing the staff who would make the presentation to the regulatory body as to what they should say and the most important points they should make. Although not selected to make the presentation herself, she was satisfied that everyone in the company knew that she was the originator and author of "the Model."

In the middle of these preparations for the regulatory body filing, the company announced a third layoff.[18] Dorothy was out of town at the regional office when this announcement was made. She was disconcerted, to say the least, when she came back and found out about it.

One of the newly hired White male vice-presidents insisted that the company follow affirmative action guidelines in its layoff selections. The next week he took the buyout. (Not to worry, he had a comparable job with another Fortune 500 company shortly thereafter.)

This third layoff was to be much more humane. From the start, *everyone* would be presumed to be without a job. To get a job, a company employee had to send his or her resume within the company to departments with posted vacancies. No one would be affirmatively fired. If at the end of this musical chairs scenario an employee had not been selected, he or she would just have to leave. A date was given at which time, if an employee did not have a job, this exit was to take place.

This time, instead of waiting tensely, everyone was scrambling around applying for jobs within the company. It was unnerving for some to have other employees applying for their jobs—and sometimes getting them. Dorothy's immediate supervisor (another man, as the enterprising Italian male who had first saved her had long ago been transferred within the company to another city) told the six persons in their division of the department that their division had been eliminated and they all should seek other jobs.

Unlike the two previous layoffs, Dorothy took this announcement more nonchalantly. She had two prior bouts with downsizing under her belt. She purported that she had the attitude that she was a highly skilled, highly educated professional who, if necessary, would take her partial, unvested pension and at age thirty-eight find work elsewhere.[19] (She could not divorce her husband until she found another job with health benefits, but fortunately they were getting along just fine.) Dorothy's optimism is somewhat belied by statistics propounded by U.S. Secretary of Labor Robert B. Reich, who is quoted as stating that: "Nearly one out of five who lost a full-time job since the start of 1991 is still without work. Among those who have landed new jobs, almost half, 47 percent, are now earning less than they did before."[20] In the same article, Secretary Reich reiterated the contention that job training and job creation were needed during what he termed "[c]onvulsive political change" in order to help offset "a spiral of downward mobility that started 15 years ago."

At any rate, Dorothy's self-professed positive, resilient attitude was buttressed by the experience of at least one other African American in the company, a male. This Black man was a residual Black nationalist (with a master's degree) who went up and complained to the new White female company president that the layoffs were occurring in a discriminatory manner and that the company was racist. His departure time was moved up a couple of days within hours of that particular interview. What was encouraging about his experience for Dorothy is that he had a new job at better pay within a week (with one of the company's competitive upstarts).

Finished, to her satisfaction, with work on the model, Dorothy began divesting herself of it. She gave bits and pieces to the accountants, some to the lawyers, some to the computer experts and others to the sales personnel in marketing. She no longer cared to hoard it in order to ensure her stay with the company. In the middle of the layoffs, she went to her boss and complained about not being promoted (promotions were being handed out concurrently with the layoffs). Theoretically, a promotion had been made more accessible since the nine levels of management that existed when Dorothy first started with the company had been reduced to Tier A, Tier B and Tier C management levels.

In fact, during the buyouts, three Blacks—two males and a female—had been promoted. One of the promoted Black males did not attend a "holiday" party held after the round of buyouts. Such attendance was usually considered mandatory, particularly after what the surviving (as well as the former) employees had just been through.[21] Evidently, the reasons for that man's retention at the company were more important than his party attendance, and he kept his position—for that buyout round.

The next December probably the least consternation among the remaining employees about layoffs was felt when they walked out all the lawyers. One reason for this is probably because the lawyers were put on an independent contractor basis to do the work they had done previously under the auspices of company employment. Selected other employees had been given that option, also—particularly those in higher management positions. Such employees had also left with significant benefit packages including extended or permanent health care coverage, multiple-hundred dollar savings plan and pension/annuity options, life insurance carryovers, etc. Employees who had been in lower level positions (a greater proportion of whom were Blacks) were not provided such severance supports. Most of the Blacks who were laid off that Dorothy knew were put out with a severance pension equal to maybe one to two years of their salary or wages.

So, even though the company claimed that its layoff program was racially proportionate, what the racially 'proportionately laid off employees left with was the difference between a lifetime pension and having to start all over in a new, probably lower-paying job—at an older age. In fact, one study reported in a news article noted that, " . . . Only 10 percent of black women over 65, and only 8 percent of Hispanic women, have any private pension income. Among black women aged 65 and over, 31 percent live in poverty, as do 22 percent of older Hispanic women; only 14 percent of older white women are poor."[22] That same article also pointed out that "for most women who get Social Security through their husbands, that benefit, equal to half their husbands' monthly check, is more than the amount they would get based on their own work record."

Hence, the majority of women who contribute to Social Security for years through their employment "receive the same benefits as they would have if they had never held a job."[23] The situation of women who have not had an opportunity to work substantially nor had a husband is also described in another chapter of this book (5).

Returning to Dorothy's immediate employment situation, she received another reprieve—this time. After another roller coaster wait, Dorothy was picked up by a director who, according to her, "had a vision." Nevertheless, Dorothy's next evaluation had her in the middle of the pack and unpromoted[24]—ending her eighteenth year as an entry level manager.[25] Employing a self-preservation behavioral mode, she spends her spare time planning her next move, waiting for the next layoff.

The new female CEO of the company called all the managers into a mass meeting and said that involuntary layoffs would be an ongoing process rather than occurring at set intervals. They were the new way of life for the company.

The staff personnel of the regulatory body writing its recommendation, totally unaware that a person such as Dorothy was its primary author, accepted the model completely. However, they had reservations about the company's rate increase request and its alternative regulation proposal. Citing the finding that the company was "overcharging its customers by about $135 million a year and should be forced to cut its rates,"[26] the regulators noted that "with falling equipment prices and massive layoffs in the industry, the cost of providing phone service is getting cheaper, not more expensive."[27]

A luta continua (the struggle continues).

One thing that this case succinctly points out is that when cutthroat policies are sanctioned by a society then throats will be cut. In this instance, all U.S. society wanted to do was to make sure that the "outsiders" were contained. The society's people were surprised that their heads rolled too when the New World Order gave the order, "Off with their heads!" The heedless thus became the headless and consequently they became "contractors" rather than "employees," thereby losing the benefits and protections they had striven so hard over the twentieth century to secure.[28] Archie Bunker is hoodwinked. Robbed by the Robber Barons who point their fingers at Willie Horton and thumb their noses at Cleopatra Jones. For what New World ordering did to the people, blue collar workers in the eighties during its pre-unannouncement days, and white collar workers in the nineties, the down side of downsizing was distrust. Similar to the way in which the Industrial Revolution shook the faith of societies as described by sociologist Emile Durkheim, downsizing created unprecedented insecurity, frustration, hopelessness and confusion among those in society accustomed to relative equanimity and confidence. Black people, the poor immigrants, women, anyone who was the least bit more vulnerable than the newly vulnerable working and middle classes, became the reason for their displacement. Another phenomenon Dorothy's tale helps to illustrate is that sometimes the Black Bourgeoisie was led far enough away from its roots to forget them.[29] Once they had forgotten, they did not know how to go home again. The Black working class was left leaderless and rudderless enough that large portions of them degenerated into a state of affairs that allowed them to become labeled "the underclass" (Glasgow 1981).

As was noted in the introduction to this book, sociologist James Conyers maintains that four strategies, (1) civil rights, (2) affirmative action, (3) poverty programs, and (4) self-help have been forwarded as remedies for the lack of parity in the U.S. society of African Americans. Civil rights involves government intervention through the legislative and judicial forums on a massive, group-wide level. Affirmative action involves the case by case intervention on an individual level; however, when rendered by a high-enough court, such rulings have wide import. Poverty programs involve the selective governmental intervention directed at the class of ethnic, gender or age minorities specifically classified as poor. Perspectives of self-help, according to Conyers inspired by such groups as the National Urban League, may not involve a comprehensive program of governmental intervention at all. Self-help as a philosophy depends upon the dissemination among the masses of the view that they are not to look to government for substantial amelioration of their social condition. If they are to be lifted out of their deprived condition at all, it is primarily up to them. It is hoped that the material in this book, facts, figures, law, and case studies will help to highlight the strengths and weaknesses of each of these strategies and reinforce Conyers' notion that a combination of the four strategies is probably the best strategy.

Particularly, taking away affirmative action at a point when it had only reached the tip of the iceberg was like pulling the rug from under a people when they had just stepped onto it and had not yet gotten their balance. Staggering for their equilibrium, African Americans have to pull back together in order to effectively articulate, activate and achieve programs designed to meet their needs, economic or otherwise. Essentially, affirmative action was a manifestation of the degree of mobilization and unity of a group. It emerged after concentrated and focused civil rights efforts. Its demise, then, is an indication of immobilization and disunity.[30] Although affirmative action may now be in disrepute, at least as far as its application to Black people is concerned,[31] African Americans now have the responsibility of devising a successor policy that can survive attacks by the society in the usual form of legal intervention. Furthermore, this responsibility also entails the formulation of strategies which take into consideration the fact that, at times, affirmative action competes strongly with crime and/or welfare as the quintessential "political chess piece."[32]

The law is now society's final recourse in terms of carrying out its policies. Economic policy will ultimately be determined by the law. This chapter thus contains social statistics, theoretical propositions and observations from the macro-sociology (U.S. Supreme Court) and micro-sociology (case studies) to illustrate how the law has influenced, by either direct or indirect intervention, various economic situations affecting the African American woman.

After years of hope, inspired by the civil rights movement, perhaps the most devastating news in terms of the employment picture for the Black single-parent family (90 percent of which are headed by women) came with the phasing out by the Reagan Administration of the Comprehensive Employment and Training Act (CETA) jobs. This cutback eliminated 340,000 jobs nationwide that could have been provided to low-income, unemployed persons.[33] CETA,[34] passed in 1973, consolidated manpower programs and moved away from training programs toward more meaningful work experience, particularly public service employment.[35] These federally funded public service jobs were intended for the unemployed, underemployed and economically disadvantaged; however, some workers had master's degrees and Ph.D's.

Other legislative enactments intended to protect the rights of workers include the National Labor Relations Act (the right to unionize),[36] Fair Labor Standards Act (the right to a minimum wage),[37] Equal Pay Act of 1963 (the right to "equal pay for equal work"),[38] Occupational Safety and Health Act (the right to work in a safe and healthy workplace)[39] and Title VII of the Civil Rights Act of 1964 and the Civil Rights Restoration Act of 1991 (the right to be free of employment discrimination on the grounds of race, color, sex or national origin).[40] Evidently, these statutes are but one testimony to the maxim, "you can't legislate morality." In spite of them, African American female family heads are still subject to great disparity in terms of median income, unemployment and poverty rates. Further, the prospects for the agencies that administer employment protections look bleak as those privileged enough to be taxpayers become more impatient with purportedly unnecessary, superfluous and/or duplicative regulatory governmental agencies. Such agencies are seen in tough economic times as inhibiting the viability and increasing the costs of free enterprise, thereby artificially sustaining society's "unfit." The thesis forwarded in this treatise is, of course, that reliance on the courts for all but the most superficial improvements does not generally prove fruitful. The economic system in the United

States is founded upon principles of self-sufficiency as well as the ideology of "rugged individualism."

If left to its own devices, the free market system advocates few governmental supports for the economically marginal. The courts, especially the federal ones, have been more effective over the decades in implementing majority rule than probably even Congress, which has to be more responsive to the needs of diverse constituencies.

Herbert Spencer, as one of the founding pioneers of sociology, is a primary theorist who set the tone for the implementation by the courts of a doctrine known as "survival of the fittest." Calling on the theory of Social Darwinism, which applied this doctrine to human society, Spencer applied physical evolutionary theory to group relationships. His propositions proved an excellent apology for the status quo. The "weak" and less mentally or physically able are presumed to be weeded out over time according to Spencerian ideology. Under such a rationalization, any educational, economic (for example, employment or entrepreneurial) strategy designed to overcome past and present discrimination-caused impairments would be deemed a windfall.

Applicable not just to the legal system's processing of discriminatory treatment claims by the courts, Spencerian dogma helps to augment caricatures of the African American woman as "Welfare Queen," "Matriarch" and the "Happy Hooker." These distortions, among others, are part and parcel of the normative formulations used by the Euro-American–dominated welfare state and criminal justice institutions to perpetuate oppressive government policies.[41]

From a sociological perspective, applying the survival of the fittest pretense, the Supreme Court by 1990 had demolished any concept of affirmative action as an effective mechanism for redressing job-related discrimination against African Americans and women. Theories forwarded by social scientists such as Robert K. Merton,[42] Jackson Toby,[43] William J. Goode[44] and Erving Goffman[45] are not normally used in legal formulations taking into consideration structural or systemic causes and effects of human behavior. When the *Brown v. Topeka Board of Education* court (see chapter 4) applied the research of Kenneth Clark to strike down school segregation, it was operating more in the exception than the rule.

From a legal perspective, strict constructionists of the U.S. Constitution assert that social science is relatively useless as a tool of legal analysis in determining the outcome of selected legal cases. The courts purport to base their frameworks of analysis on the American value of meritocracy.[46] However, even the typical meritocracy arguments have been challenged by social scientists.[47] Nevertheless, the courts have steadfastly clung to them as a way of giving credibility to and rationalizing their decisions. For the most part, however, the social system has erected enough barriers so that employment inequities are maintained by resort to the courts. Court access generally requires resolve and resources that, because of other overwhelming operative factors, a Black woman may not have, as seen in the preceding studies.

LEGAL ANALYSIS OF SPECIFIC COURT DECISIONS

Illustrative of the functionality asserted in this work to undergird the relationship between U.S. societal values and the social institutions designed to achieve those values is the drama being played out in the arena of the U.S. governmental system of checks and balances. With reference to economic issues, the drama focuses on the concept of affirmative action and involves the courts versus the U.S. Congress of the early 1990s. The controversy surrounding affirmative action as a concept whose time has come—and gone—reflects a most "deliberative" interplay involving the branches of government and the U.S. system of constitutional checks and balances.[48]

The controversy might be said to have begun with the passage of the Voting Rights Act of 1965[49] and the Civil Rights Act of 1964.[50] "The Second Reconstruction"[51] or the "Civil Rights Era" was a period of time in U.S. history when, along with the resuscitation of the civil rights-related amendments, an unprecedented number of ambitious laws and programs were introduced, directed at incorporating the intent and spirit of these amendments.

The Civil Rights Acts are invoked here to make a point. Those acts, needless to say, were products of legislative initiatives. Those legislative initiatives, prompted by the courts, had fashioned judicial remedies that, from an Afrocentric perspective, resulted in the case *Defunis v. Odegarrd*.[52] Certain remedial programs, particularly those embodying principles later labeled affirmative action, were proclaimed as presenting effective plans for eradicating discriminatory policies and practices.

When only a few years old, however, the concept began to be disparaged as discriminatory towards males and Whites. Complaints of "reverse discrimination" and "preferential treatment" began to weaken and, for many practical purposes, effectively to destroy it. The impetus for this process of debilitation was the *Defunis* opinion, which evoked an unanticipated amount of hostility after "protecting" minorities and women in the realm of higher education involving a discriminatory admissions policy. *Defunis* involved a White, male law student whose claim of reverse discrimination was denied by the Supreme Court. The backlash set off by *Defunis* fueled a reaction that signaled a dramatic retreat by the Supreme Court. That retreat was signaled by the decisions of *Bakke v. California Board of Regents*[53] and *United Steelworkers v. Weber*.[54] Taking the cue from the Supreme Court in the *Bakke* and *Weber* decisions, time after time an *innocent* European American male came forth to proclaim himself to have been treated inequitably, because of his color and/or gender. The *Bakke* and *Weber* cases helped to reassure the majoritarian classes and the male communities that all was not lost to the women and minorities. *Bakke* and *Weber* essentially redefined the characteristics of an "innocent" victim of discrimination. Together, these two cases established the term "reverse discrimination" and ironically legitimized the education/employment/economic discrimination victim as the European American male.

This backfiring turn of events asserting that European American males discriminate against themselves on the basis of race and sex was expanded upon by the U.S. Supreme Court in succeeding cases during the 1980s (see below). To try to eliminate the absurd impact of these cases, after much political haggling and after the highly publicized Hill-Thomas Senate Judiciary Committee debate in September of 1991, Congress passed an updated civil rights law.[55] This most intensive exercise of "seesaw" with the judiciary can be interpreted as seeking to determine who is the victim in discrimination cases. It is ironic also that in a struggle to preserve her rights, the African American woman herself has had little share in forming either the final outcome or the process that preceded it. While now there are two females on the Supreme Court, there are no female African Americans on that Bench. There is only one female African American out of one hundred senators (the first Black woman elected to the U.S. Senate, Carol Moseley-Braun, in 1992, and by 1995 there were seven women in all). Of forty members of the Congressional Black Caucus in 1993, nine were female African Americans.[56] There were 37 members in 1994, when all of the Blacks who ran for Congress kept their seats despite the general routing of "liberals" in that year; however, see again the *Shaw v. Reno* alert, Chapter 2. As members of the U.S. House of Representatives total 435, the eight Black women there accounted, *in 1994, for a little less than 2 percent of the House membership.*

Following the precedent, heralded by *Bakke* and *Weber*, thus the Supreme Court set aside important minority and female rulings of discrimination in six landmark cases.

Although the proposed rationale has been disputed,[57] many observers agree that the primary reason for the passage of the 1991 Civil Rights Act was to overturn decisions by the U.S. Supreme Court that inhibited the progress of women and minorities towards the achievement of equal rights. The primary legislative changes attempted to restore important affirmative action rights that had been decimated by the Supreme Court in 1989. These rights focused especially on certain key affirmative action issues.[58] For instance, one important issue involved "disparate impact" (see *Wards Cove Packing v. Antonio*[59]). The question in disparate impact is whether or not a hiring practice has a more negative consequence for minorities and women than for those who do not fit those categories. In *Wards Cove Packing*, Justice White held that statistical evidence that a high percentage of non-White workers were employed in cannery jobs and a low percentage of Whites were in noncannery positions did not make a prima facie case of disparate impact in violation of Title VII of the Civil Rights Act of 1964. The 1991 Civil

Rights Act specifically tried to remedy this result by explicitly being supportive of the use of such evidentiary data in justifying minority and female discrimination claims.

A second issue that the Act directly addressed was that of discrimination and harassment (*Patterson v. McLeon Credit Union*[60]). This question concerns the situation where an otherwise competent employee is treated inequitably, passed over for promotions and persecuted because of his or her race or sex. In *Patterson*, Justice Kennedy held that racial harassment was not a violation of 42 U.S.C. A. Sec. 1981, covering the civil right to make contracts. According to the Supreme Court, led by Justice Kennedy, Section 1981 covered only conduct at the initial formation of a contract and conduct that impairs the right to enforce contractual obligations through the legal process. However, it did decide that the Black female employee, Brenda Patterson, did not have to show that she was in fact better qualified than the person chosen for the position. The company had used the claim of a better qualified candidate as a pretext for not giving Ms. Patterson the position. *Presumably*, that result could not be reached under the 1991 Act.

Not only was racial harassment allowed by the Court in the *Patterson* case, but that case likewise upheld racial and ethnic discrimination in hiring, promotions, demotions, discharges, retaliation and other employment issues. The Court also removed the previous employer's burden of proving that exclusionary employment policies or practices were justified by business necessity in *Wards Cove*. In addition, the Court in *Wards Cove* transferred the burden of proving which exact individual employment practice produced a discriminatory effect. Again, an objective of the 1991 Act was to shift this burden back to the employer.

A third issue, represented by the case of *Martin v. Wilks*,[61] involved the reopening of old discrimination cases by male majority-group members who had not been specifically named in initial cases in which remedial action had been ordered. *Wilks* thus was the case in which the Court held that White male employees could ignore previous civil rights consent decrees. Hence, *Wilks* allows an infinite number of reverse discrimination claims by "innocent" Whites and males who were not a part of the original lawsuit. Likewise, whether or not the Supreme Court will follow the legislative intent of the 1991 Act, it attempted to reassert the concept of *res judicata* which would forestall subsequent attacks upon settled consent decrees.

Going on, in *Lorance v. AT&T Technologies*[62] the Court decided to do away with the right of minority and female employees to contest discriminatory seniority systems. Justice Scalia decided in *Lorance* that a claim of discrimination begins to run at the time of adoption of the seniority system. Thus, without the protections reiterated in the 1991 Civil Rights Act, countless numbers of subsequent female and minority applicants would not be able to challenge any discriminatory effect.

Also, following its mandate to vindicate White male rights, the Supreme Court abolished the use of discrimination as a motivating factor in employment decisions in *Price Waterhouse v. Hopkins*.[63] In *Price Waterhouse*, Justice Brennan said that once the BFOQ (Bona Fide Occupation) test was met, establishing that the disparate pay is a result of a factor other than sex, then the employer has the burden of proving that its limitation on the work is thereby gender neutral. If the employer meets that burden, then the affected employee does not have a civil rights claim. The 1991 Act would require more than just a modicum of evidence by the employer in attempting to show the gender neutrality of the job requirements.

Continuing its charge to support claims of reverse discrimination, in *Independent Federation of Flight Attendants v. Zipes*[64] attorneys' fees were disallowed for defending consent decrees between courts and employers from such attacks. Attorneys' fees were re-allowed by the Civil Rights Act of 1991. *Independent Federation of Flight Attendants*, an opinion written by Justice Scalia, discourages attorneys from engaging in the "protracted" litigation involved in many affirmative action cases. Based on the constraints of the litigants' resources as well as the urgency of their claims in many instances, it does seem reasonable that the complainants were the ones dragging out the proceedings.

Seeing the watering down of affirmative action by cases such as *Waterhouse* and others, Senators Edward M. Kennedy (D-MA), James M. Jeffords (R-VT) and thirty-eight other senators and in the U.S. House of Representatives Augustus F. Hawkins (D-CA), Hamilton Fish, Jr. (R-NY), and 158 other Representatives introduced the Civil Rights Act of 1990 (later of 1991) on February 7, 1990. This effort represented an effort to exert the beauty of the U.S. checks-and-balances system of government. It emerged as a balance to the check administered to affirmative action by the U.S. Supreme Court. A bipartisan effort, the bill ultimately passed and was even called the "Danforth Bill."

In such a fashion, Congress attempted to derail the attack on affirmative action in what obviously was a substantial distortion of Congressional legislative intent by the Supreme Court. Simply put, the legislative branch of the federal government tried to salvage some vestige of the civil rights that the judicial branch had tried to annihilate. In another benevolent move, Congress added sexual discrimination to coverage by the Civil Rights Act, a maneuver considered likely to increase the number of such legal claims filed in courts and the appropriate agencies.[65] For what it is worth, the African American woman was thus defended as part of the effort to come to the aid of women and minorities.

Further, the time for filing administrative charges with the EEOC was expanded by this legislative enactment from 180 days to two years. In addition, Congress specifically allowed discrimination victims the right to recover compensatory and punitive damages against private employers when intentional discrimination could be proven.

Moreover, Congress attempted a legislative veto of a serious setback to affirmative action that had been wrought by the Reagan-Bush Supreme Court, in which the Court had disallowed prevailing parties to recover their cost for the use of expert witnesses during litigation.[66] If parties cannot pay expert witnesses, their chances of ever becoming prevailing parties are significantly diminished.

In regard to the aforementioned cases, Congress attempted to reestablish employment rights through legislative initiative. This initiative, reinstituting protections for women's and minorities' employment rights, was signed by the Chief Executive of the administrative branch of government, President Bush, in November of 1991.

It would be nice to say that the future economic well-being of the African American woman is thus secure. However, it depends upon much more than the outcome of this "ping pong" diplomacy among the branches of government.

Unless African Americans network (even with other ethnic groups, including WASPs), mobilize as many of their ranks as can yet be responsive to such calls and continue to guard vigilantly against further erosions of their civil liberties, then such legislative action is futile. Although courts comprise one of the least democratic governmental bodies, African Americans, with whatever help Congress is willing to provide (given the "will" of some of their constituencies[67]), cannot allow the courts to continue to characterize the African American woman as the perpetrator of discrimination against "innocent" European American males.

SOCIOECONOMIC ANALYSIS OF CUMULATIVE EFFECT OF DECISIONS

Income Data

Because the formulation of the New World Order had a primarily economic impetus and focus, the data for this chapter centering around the economic ramifications of sociolegal processes are particularly illustrative of its purpose and function. Hence, the increasing denigration of affirmative action[68] comes at a time when the relative position of African Americans in the areas of education, economics and entrepreneurship is actually growing worse vis-à-vis their European American counterparts.

In other words, the reciprocal interaction of the economic institution with the legal one (see again Merton) having reinforced the status quo sought by the prevailing racial group, the African American woman is left poorer in the New World Order than her cohorts who are female European Americans or male.[69] As African Americans lose ground with respect to income, employment, education and business when compared with European Americans, they correspondingly lose legal redress to offset those losses, with the rationale being that any such losses are "color blind." Going further, the underlying presumption behind the elimination of affirmative action, then, is that the weakening of both African American economic viability and affirmative action is coincidental. Such a deduction stretches credibility beyond reasonable imagination. This conclusion is illustrated by some statistics taken particularly from the first few years that the call for a New World Order was in vogue (e.g., 1990 and 1991).

An African American female-headed household had a median income of $12,537 according to the 1990 U.S. Census.[70] Coincidental to the official proclamation of the New World Order by President Bush in 1990 as well as their implementation by the courts and the organizations intrinsic to the economic institution, the Black female's household had a median income of $12,196.[71] Both averages represent incomes significantly lower than the corresponding figures for households headed by White or Black males and White females. Both medians were substantially lower also than those reported by other households headed by persons who were living in a "traditional" family relationship, in other words, those headed by a "married-couple family" of either race.

Controlling for gender and making a comparison with those households which are headed by those of like sex but a different race indicates one type of inequity against Black females and the families they head. In 1990, a household headed by a woman of European descent had a median income of $20,867.[72] By the next New World Order year, the White female household's median income was $21,213.[73] After a year of the New World Order, the White female household's median income went up and that of the Black female household went down. At first glance, that trend would ostensibly say a little something about the role and function of the New World Order with reference to Black women.

To understand the meaning of any such trend at this point, it is also illustrative to control for race. In 1990, the African American single-male-headed household received a median income of $24,048. For him in 1991, that figure was $26,428. The New World Order, in this regard, would appear to have been a little kinder also to the Black single-male-headed household than to that of his female counterpart.

It should be noted here that the disparity between the median incomes of the Black single-male-headed household and that of the Black single-female-headed-household were even greater than those between the Black single-female-headed household and that of her White counterpart.

The median income in 1990 of the European American single-male-headed household was $32,869. The difference between his family's median income and that reported for the Black single female's family, $12,537, for that year speaks legions in terms of the European American male's need for protection against the African American female. A $20,000 discrepancy in median income for the respective family types is not an accident. It is the result of deterministic, predictable social forces that are continuously operationalized by the pertinent social institutions. That difference in median household income belies the depiction of the White male as a victim by the courts. Truly equitable courts would re-explore the configuration and dynamics of "innocence" as they relate to the economic relationships between Blacks and Whites, men and women.

Of course, again, the courts, and especially the Supreme Court, have chosen to ignore social data and to focus on particularized circumstances that can be more easily separated from their social context.

Reference to the next New World Order year, 1991, indicates another interesting variation. The family household of the White male in 1991 had a median income of $31,634, a loss of a little over $1,000 for his family. A year after the New World Order had started, the families of the Black female and the White male lost ground and those of the White female and the Black male seemed to have gained.

A more long range analysis, however, belies this snapshot income glance. In reality, the overall median Black family income "barely changed" between 1970 and 1995.[74] While, with inflation adjustment, in 1969 the median income for all Black families was $21,550, in 1993 it was "virtually unchanged." By comparison, the 1993 median income for White families was $39,310, a nine percent gain since 1969. Further, in 1993, the Black female-headed family median income, less than $12,000, was "only one-third of the income of black families headed by married couples."[75] In addition, as of 1993, one-half of all of the families headed by Black women lived in poverty as compared with 12 percent of those families which were headed by Black married couples.

Black people in the United States have worked in relatively low-skilled occupations. They (especially the males) were particularly dependent upon manufacturing for attainment of even relatively modest standards of living. Since 1979, approximately three million manufacturing jobs have been lost. In the geographic area from which most of the case studies in this work were taken, 37 percent of the factory jobs had been lost.[76] The pool of jobs available in light manufacturing industries that had employed many urban residents shrank by more than 25 percent since 1979. Adjusting for inflation, low-skilled White men in their twenties had their annual income fall by 14 percent. That of Black men in the same age range fell by 24 percent. While the annual earnings of White male school dropouts in their twenties fell by 33 percent, those of Black male dropouts fell by 50 percent.[77] The losses of these Black men are salient for Black women in their age categories because it provides great information about the rise of female-headed households in the Black community.

According to census data analyzed by the Joint Center for Political and Economic Studies, in 1992 "the median income for black males was only 72 percent of the income for white non-Hispanic males."[78] People without adequate incomes do not marry and raise families, when they barely can support themselves. Jobs with adequate incomes are crucial to the maintenance of the "married-couple family" category in the African American community.

The activation of New World Order policies appears initially also to have resulted in White male–dominated institutions "cutting off their noses to spite their faces." Such behavior is explained by Victor Perlo (1975) as indicating the need for the working classes to develop greater transracial unity. The institutions governed by the elite (Mills 1959), create policies that work against all the masses, White and Black, male and female. For instance, a New World Order–oriented Federal Reserve Board has a tendency to raise interest rates when it believes the economy is growing too fast.[79] Such a policy affects "most Americans" because it means, "Job-seekers will have a slightly harder time landing work as businesses find borrowing for expansion more expensive."[80] New World policies that result in such hardships for workers in general are intransigent once put firmly in place.[81]Interestingly, the only Federal Reserve Bank not to ask the Federal Reserve Board to raise interest rates during one such hike was the one from the region in which the economic case studies in this book were completed (although that Bank did not explain its decision,[82] it might be repeated here that 37 percent of the manufacturing jobs had been lost in that region).

Although these changes have affected all workers irrespective of race, worker advocacy organizations such as unions grew too weak to help much under New World Order policies.[83] Weakened unions representing fewer workers are related to such phenomena as "the six-percentage-point slide in the 1980s in the share of employees with company pension plans, for the seven-point decline in those with employer health plans, and for a 125-fold explosion in unlawful-discharge suits now that fewer employees have a union to stick up for them."[84] Some experts feel that unions were intentionally undermined in order to effectuate these types of negative consequences.[85] At any rate, diminished union representation, a result of New World Order policies, has led to a growth in the wage gap between those workers who are paid the highest and those receiving the lowest pay.[86] The United States has the widest such gap of any of the developed countries. In fact, the United States has the widest gap in wealth period of the western countries.[87] Further, at least one economist believes that a large gap between the haves and have-nots or between those with a high degree of education and those with a low degree does not foreshadow a society that is prosperous or stable.[88]

The reverberations of the New World Order have been somewhat mitigated for the "traditional" White married-couple family household, however. In 1990 the median income of that household type was $40,433. Its median income in 1991 was $41,584. Some might say the society rewarded the White traditional family for upholding appropriate family values. Social institution practices thus helped those who were living in a White and a married family situation upon the start of the New World Order. Still, the number of cases complaining of workplace grievances which were filed in federal courts jumped 400% between 1971 and 1991. This increase has been attributed, in part, to suits filed by white-collar workers, of whom there are many more White than Black persons.

The median income for the Black married-couple family household did not reflect as much of a bonus for being traditional as its White counterpart did. It did not receive any monetary enhancement during the first of the New World Order years for manifesting "appropriate" family values. Like the Black female-headed family, it was penalized by New World Order policies. The African American woman living in a married-couple family situation had a median household income 83.8 percent ($33,883) of that of her European American cohort in 1990.

By 1991, however, the Black married-couple family household's median income ratio was only 80.2 percent of the White married-couple family income, at $33,369. The Black married-couple household lost in the same range (about $500) as the Black female-headed household immediately after the start of the New World Order's regime, whose perks were not forthcoming for the Black family category that followed "orders" as they were for its White family prototype.

Still, the advantages of living in a married-couple family arrangement are significant for the Black woman. Overall, by residing in such a household, she improves her chances of parity with European Americans by more than 23 percent. Further, because of the corresponding reduction in income for both Black household family types, this proportion remained constant for both years of comparison.

In the single-female family classification, the ratio of Black to White median income was 60.1 in 1990 and 57.5 in 1991, reflecting the decrease in the earnings by the Black female household. Black single-male-headed households, contrarily, had median incomes which were 73.2 percent in 1990 and 83.5 percent in 1991 of that of their White counterparts, a gain of 10 percentage points by Black single male-headed households. Does the New World Order reward Black men for remaining single? That is an interesting question, which deserves further research. What it does currently indicate, however, is that the circumstances of the Black single-female-headed household are vastly different economically from those of the Black single-male-headed household.

Before too much comfort can be taken from the enhanced economic circumstances of the Black married-couple family, it should be noted that they comprise only 33.4% of all Black types of households whereas, married-couple families comprise 58.1% of all White household types.

With reference to all family household median income, the Black/White ratio was 58.8 in 1990 and 58.1 in 1991. In 1990, Black female households in a non-family situation earned a median income which was 59.2 percent of that of European American female ones. In 1991, the figure was 64.4 percent.

In a single-person situation, Black male households in 1990 had a slight advantage over their Black female counterparts insofar as their median income was 65.0 percent of that of the White one. The Black male single households' median income was 62.1 percent vis-à-vis their White counterparts in 1991.

In order to appreciate better the amount of economic damage that the Black female has done to the White male through reverse discrimination, it is useful to compare their respective family incomes more directly. Using the figures cited for the single heads of households, it can be observed that the White male's median income is almost *three* times that of his allegedly favored Black female counterpart's. As far as evidence of legally determined economic harm done to White females, using the respective family household comparisons, the median income of the White single female is more than 1 and 2/3 times that of the Black female for both observed sample years of New World Order operation. Recalling the median income levels for the Black female-headed family, we have to acknowledge that her income is approximately half that of the Black male comparison group's. Given the relative income status of the Black female-headed family, another statistic regarding her children is rather surprising. For example, one report notes that 67 percent of all recipients of AFDC are children.[89] This report, as illustrated in Table 3.1, also compared the children on AFDC of the total from their respective races in the years 1973 versus 1992:[90]

Table 3.1
AFDC Child Enrollment by Race: 1973 and 1992

1973		1992	
White	*Black*	*White*	*Black*
6.5%	42.7%	6.2%	35.1%

These figures reflect a downward trend in welfare enrollment—particularly of Blacks—despite New World publicity to the contrary (also see 1965 discussion by Ellul for background insights as to long-held views on welfare participation).

On a macroscopic level, then, statistical information comparing relative income medians provides patent evidence as to which parties are more innocent than others in terms of being victimized by the operation of the economic institution. Even applying the high court's microscopic purview, it would require a blatant disregard for the truth to ignore the situation of a significant number of discrimination complainants. To recognize their plight would be to recognize unequivocally the need for societally based remedial action. The onus of remedial action would not have to be on any one poor White victim if the societal mandates were comprehensive enough to encompass the basic economic needs of all of its members. In reality, all of society ultimately suffers when its policies, designed to crucify one segment of society, end up hurting unintended, "innocent" members of the society, that is, White males.

Employment Data

For most of the second half of the twentieth century, the African American females and males have been unemployed at almost twice as high a rate as their European American counterparts.[91] They were deemed almost a throwaway labor force category (cf. Wilhelm on *Who Needs the Negro?*, 1970). In addition, the mothers of African American children under six years of age are considerably more likely to be in the labor market than their European American cohort.

Further numerical insights concerning the operation of the economic institution can be obtained from a review of 1991 unemployment statistics for men and women aged twenty and over.[92] The unemployment rate for European American men was 5.8 percent, while the rate for male African Americans was 11.7 percent.

In the New World Order, women apparently are allowed to work more; however, taking inflation into account, they earn substantially less than their predecessors during the civil rights movement years and the decade immediately following. They have more years of education, yet they hold fewer jobs than in the past.[93] Although African American women had better luck in finding jobs than African American men, their unemployment rate of 10.2 percent was more than twice that for European American women. In short, following New World Order wisdom, Black people are currently discriminating against European Americans so successfully that the unemployment rate for African Americans is twice as high. Even in the area of government, which has traditionally employed Blacks at a higher level than Whites, one study indicated that Black Federal employees "were more than twice as likely to be dismissed than their white, Hispanic or Asian counterparts."[94] This "disparity was seen regardless of occupational category, pay level, education, agency, geographic location, age, performance rating, seniority, or attendance record."[95]

Not only is the African American woman likely to be unemployed relative to any slight gains she might make within the context of the education institution, she is *underemployed* as well. For example, the Glass

Ceiling Commission set up in 1990, headed by then Secretary of Labor Elizabeth H. Dole, analyzing 1990 census data, found the following statistics indicating minority female underrepresentation in *Middle-Management and Above Positions:*[96]

Table 3.2
U.S. Middle and Upper Management Positions by Race and Gender, 1990

	Women		Men	
	White	*Minority*	*White*	*Minority*
Work Type				
Utilities	17%	2%	75%	6%
Manufacturing	23	5	65	7
Health Services	67	7	23	3
Social Services	66	11	18	5

Although they are substantially missing from the top levels of management, White women hold 40 percent of U.S. middle management positions. Black women hold 5 percent of such positions and Black men hold "even less."[97] By comparison, White women make up 36 percent of the total workforce, irrespective of position. Black men are 10 percent of that total work force, and Black women compose 11 percent of it. Black women rarely find the mentors[98] and advocates that typify White male job-ladder progress, and, when they do, such mentorship is often spurious, shortlived, superficial and/or suspect.[99] It should also be noted that the work types in which Black women are best represented in terms of middle management positions are the lowest paying ones of social and health services, fields that White males have thus far eschewed to a large extent. These are also the areas most vulnerable to cuts and reductions by New World Order "cost containers."[100]

The statistics relating to the economic well-being of the African American woman, who has worked in the United States or its predecessor colonies for four hundred years, reflect policies that are fundamentally unfair. Without unequivocal governmental intervention these policies are not going to be relinquished voluntarily by the tightly patriarchal, ethnocentric (DeFleur 1971) private sector.[101] The African American woman has always contributed above and beyond the call of duty. For instance, one-half of those serving in the Persian Gulf were women and/or minorities. Even in this harshest of situations it "has been estimated . . . that as many as 40 percent of the 35,000 female soldiers" who served in that war were Black women.[102]

As has been pointed out earlier, the Supreme Court shuns what it labels as nonspecific reliance upon social data such as that discussed in this analysis. The Supreme Court, using what is termed a practice of following precedents,[103] has a legacy of looking only at the specific, individual[104] case or controversy before it. The Court has held aggregate, cumulative or nationwide statistics such as those previously recounted to be inapplicable for legal analysis. In an address before the Eleventh Annual Lawyers CLE Seminar given as a joint effort of the NAACP and the National Bar Association,[105] Brenda Wright, Director of the Voting Rights Project for the Lawyers' Committee for Civil Rights Under Law spoke of the usefulness of social statistics in legal reasoning. Attorney Wright reminded the audience of the famous footnote of the *Brown v. Topeka Board of Education* case in which the research of Dr. Kenneth Clark was cited in support of its thesis of the relationship between educational integration and student self-esteem. Ms. Wright went on to point out that program decisions from the Warren Court were undergirded by the research of social science. She then went on to surmise that with no such "footnotes," U.S. Supreme Court Justice O'Connor's reasoning in cases such as *Shaw v. Reno* and *Miller v. Johnson* (see Chapter 2) was "just pure conservative ideology." As such, Ms. Wright surmised that those opinions were thus "intellectually and morally bankrupt." It was this enmity towards numbers, as manifested in such fright-inspiring concepts as quotas and goals by the Bush Administration, that jeopardized the approval of the 1991 Civil Rights Bill.

Nonetheless, Supreme Court decisions have a "cumulative numerical" consequence in and of themselves. For example, as mentioned earlier, eighty-five political subdivisions had their minority set-aside legislation attacked within a year and a half of the *Croson* ruling. And, it was only a matter of days after the Supreme Court increased the stakes against federal set-aside programs on June 12, 1995 in *Adarand Constructors, Inc. v. Pena*[106] that at least one agency in the federal government, e.g., the F.C.C., reversed its affirmative action program[107] (also see Chapter 1). Likewise, a hundred pending claims representing thousands of people asserting racial or ethnic harassment were dismissed by federal courts around the country within four-and-one-half months after the Supreme Court ruled against the discrimination suit in the *Patterson* case.[108]

Because of the deep entrenchment of status quo forces, it is questionable whether or not, from the African American female perspective, the 1991 Civil Rights Act will restore coverage for racial harassment claims that had been pursued under its predecessor act until the *Patterson* decision was made by the Supreme Court.

Similarly, 1991 Civil Rights Act provisions prohibit attacks on existing consent decrees by new reverse-discrimination litigation. The limited resources of municipal governments across the nation are hard pressed to deal with such litigation. Numerous municipalities will be affected by the 1991 Civil Rights Act provisions. Reverse discrimination suits against cities that had already litigated discrimination claims brought by women and/or minorities were threatening to deplete further their coffers.

After *Martin*, Title VII litigation by parties not originally involved with consent decrees increased in cities from the Eastern Seaboard to the Great Lakes to the Pacific Ocean. Nonparty challenges to such consent decrees rebounded even in the southern communities of Gadsden, Alabama, and Albany, Georgia. To the extent such cities must utilize their financial and human resources to protect "innocent" European American males, they are unable to address imminent urban problems which plague and disproportionately affect African American female household heads. Is this another societal function for such suits?

Occupational Mobility Data

Another New World Order consequence of permitting global employment discrimination by specific court action lies in the area of occupational mobility and compensation.[109]

Only 7.2 percent of Black females occupy executive administrative and managerial positions. For Black males the occupational percentage distribution is the same in this category, which excludes the professional specialty category, as for Black females. Double this percentage of White males work in such positions. The proportion of White females who work in such managerial capacities is 12 percent.[110]

With regard to occupation as of 1991,[111] for persons more than 16 years of age, 26.9 percent of all European American males were at the managerial and professional level, while only half that proportion of African American males were at that same level. By comparison, according to 1991 figures, 18.6 percent of all African American females held managerial/professional positions. The percentage of European Americans at that occupational level was 27.2.

Black women are twice as likely to work in private household occupations as White women, and Black women are found in service occupations slightly more than one and a half times the rate that White women are.[112] In addition, these broad occupational categories are deceiving because the "pay and conditions of work vary widely among occupations" and because Blacks "were underrepresented in the most desirable occupations and overrepresented in the least desirable occupations."[113]

Poverty Data

Unsurprisingly, Black Americans are three times more likely to be poor than White Americans. The Black/White inequality index is 2.9 for poverty. The inequality index for the Black female-headed household compared to its White female-headed counterpart is 1.7. This means that for every European American female-headed household that lives in poverty, 1.7 African American female-headed households are poor.

Again, demonstrating her predilection for "reverse discrimination,"[114] Black American female-headed households had the highest percentage of family types below poverty level, 48.1 percent.[115] White American female-headed households were in poverty at a rate slightly more than one half (26.8 percent) that of Black female-headed households. Of the "innocent" White American males who were single and headed households, 9.9 percent were below the poverty demarcation point. That point was reached by 20.6 percent of all Black American single-male-headed households.

Twelve and six-tenths percent of African American married-couple families met the poverty criteria. The comparable poverty statistic for European American married-couple families was 5.1 percent. These figures are more telling when the fact is taken into consideration that 43.8 percent of *all* African American families are headed by a female compared with 12.9 percent of *all* European American families. African American families are headed by a female at a rate of more than three and one half times that of European American families.

A further revealing statistic is the fact that 51.2 percent of all African American children live with their mothers, while 16.2 percent of all European American children live alone with their mothers and have no fathers present.[116]

A look at where families reside also provides knowledge about the quality of family life for different household types. The above discussion about pressures upon metropolitan resources becomes even more salient when it is observed that 40.8 percent of all African American households live in central cities that are parts of large metropolitan areas. Sixteen and two-tenths percent of European American households live inside the central cities of such metropolitan areas.

Hence, as more "innocent" European American males file law claims of reverse discrimination against the cities attempting to institute affirmative action programs, the fewer resources those cities will have to address such concerns as drugs, crime, safety, environment, health, education, social services, community development and numerous other urban issues that hold the Black woman hostage to a New World Order that uses her as a scapegoat in assessing blame for urban ills.

LEGAL SIGNIFICANCE OF INCOME AND EMPLOYMENT

Despite the legislative counteractive efforts in passing the Civil Rights Restoration Act of 1991, at some point in the future the Supreme Court, in a maneuver purportedly denied employers, may use the legal fiction of "legislative intent" to undo the Congressional endeavor.[117] Ominously, as relates to this concern, during the Senate debate, Senator Dole alleged in the Congressional Record that the act was compatible with *Wards Cove*.

Additional insights as to Supreme Court views on African American women and the "innocent" may be garnered from Supreme Court Justice Clarence Thomas, who prior to ascending the bench is quoted as stating in 1983, as Chairman of the EEOC, that while he did not know exactly the difference between a goal and a quota, he preferred to side with the idea of "individual rights." According to Mr. Thomas, use of his interpretation of the idea of individual rights is ultimately what is going to be the safe haven for "*all* [italics added] groups in this society."[118] The all-inclusiveness of that statement is brought to question by the experience of a Black female lawyer. The attorney was part of a group from the Black Women Lawyers Division of the National Bar Association that was being sworn into practice before the Supreme Court in May 1995. Justice Ginsberg was in the process of explaining her decision in the housing discrimination case of *City of Edmonds v. Oxford House, Inc.*[119] The lawyer said that she will never forget how during that explanation, Justice Thomas looked down from the bench over at her group and sneered contemptuously.

The Clarence Thomas phenomenon demonstrates two points. The first is that it is an inaccurate definition of the concept of Afrocentricity to expand that term to include "any expression by a person of African descent" (see Molefi Kete Asante's *The Afrocentric Idea*, 1987, or Frantz Fanon's *The Wretched of the Earth*, 1965). This point is also illustrated in a book by journalists Jane Mayer and Jill Abramson, *Strange Justice: The Selling of Clarence Thomas.*[120] In *Strange Justice*, Mayer and Abramson relate how supporters of the affirmative action opponent Thomas, when he was on the presidential short list for the Supreme Court nomination, used his "Blackness" to help initially neutralize possible opposition from African American leaders so that he could be appointed a justice.[121] Afrogenesis, in and of itself, may have little ostensible impact upon men or women who have been incorporated into the structural components of an oppressive system and whose perceived livelihood depends upon that system. As long as an Afrogeneric person feels the need to engage within the context of a systemically oppressive structure in order to survive, then skin color has minimal impact upon decision outcomes. In other words, the ethnic or racial affinity of those being oppressed has little to no bearing upon the decision-making process of an ethnically or racially similar oppressor.

The second point is that even with the passage of the 1991 Civil Rights Act, these remarks do not bode well for future decisions regarding affirmative action and protection of "innocent" European American males from African American females, as the Supreme Court has been striking down "unreasonable," "unjust" and ill-conceived legislation ever since it assumed that authority in the *Marbury v. Madison* case of 1803.

The aforementioned goal imputed here to Congress received a major setback in a 1993 decision of the Supreme Court in the case of a Black male named Melvin Hicks.[122] As background, it must be pointed out here that in a 1973 case, *McDonnell Douglas Corp. v. Green*,[123] the Supreme Court ruled that a plaintiff must first establish a prima facie case of racial discrimination in order to prevail in an affirmative action claim. Such a prima facie case could be established by the showing of four requirements. In the *Hicks* case, as was done in *McDonnell*, the Plaintiff showed that (1) he was Black, (2) he was qualified for the position, (3) he was demoted and ultimately discharged and (4) the position remained open and was ultimately filled by a White man.[124] The *Hicks* case was appealed from the Eighth U.S. Circuit Court of Appeals.

Chief Justice William Rehnquist and Justices Sandra Day O'Connor, Anthony Kennedy and Clarence Thomas joined Justice Antonin Scalia in disallowing relief from job bias in which it was found that the employers had falsified the reasons for dismissal. Mr. Hicks had made a prima facie case of racial discrimination as set forth in *McDonnell*. His cause of action under Title VII of the Civil Rights Act of 1964 was not supported even though it was brought out in evidence that the employer had lied about Mr. Hicks's firing. Even though Plaintiff Hicks had alleged racial discrimination in his lawsuit, the Supreme Court remanded it to the Eighth Circuit for a consideration as to whether or not he had been dismissed based on personality differences or based specifically on racial differences.

Such a decision reflects what the constituency on the Supreme Court felt was its charge in the New World Order. The *Hicks* Court was led by a Chief Justice (William Rehnquist) who is essentially a strict constructionist. A strict constructionist of the Constitution supposedly takes the view that if a fundamental right is not specifically enumerated in the Constitution, it should not be implied to be there by judicial interpretation or otherwise, as by legislation. As of 1994, the Black member of the Court had voted nearly 100 percent of the time with its most ideologically conservative member, the author of the *Hicks* case, Justice Antonin Scalia.

It should be indicated at this point that Supreme Court Justice Ruth Bader Ginsburg and Justice Thomas were on the D.C. Circuit Court of Appeals at the same time. Incredulous as it might seem based on their inapposite legal ideologies (Ginsburg is characterized as a liberal on many issues (cf. the *Edmonds* case), and Thomas as predominantly conservative), the majority of the time on the D.C. Circuit they voted together. That voting pattern is undoubtedly a thing of the past, given Justice Thomas's proclivity to align himself almost 100 percent of the time with Justice Antonin Scalia, who abhors affirmative action. An interesting alliance on affirmative action seems to be that of Justice Ginsburg and Justice Sandra Day O'Connor, the two female members of the Supreme Court bench. That alliance remains a dream for affirmative action proponents.

Thus, the Civil Rights Act of 1991 may be insufficient given the Rehnquist Court.[125, 126] African American socioeconomic improvement may not be rapidly forthcoming, at least not through the vehicle of affirmative action.

The decisions of the New World Order Courts,[127] however, should not be surprising. Essentially, courts maintain the status quo in a society (Parsons, 1951), reflecting power relationships that currently exist in the society and are sought by the, by definition, powerful. It is not reasonable to believe that, without facing some form of countervailing power, a societal institution can be counted on to make decisions that would result in substantial changes in the ordering of the hierarchies present in the social structure.

This is not to say that providing adequate legal and economic remedies to African American women would in any way diminish those really available to European American males in the New World Order. It is becoming clearer and clearer that as resources become less available, those in the highest realms of power and privilege develop contrivances geared so that they can get more, while those, Black or White, in the lower ranges, receive less.[128] This trend, with the assistance as this examination contends of the legal system, is accentuated for the Black woman.[129] It might be that the average, working-class European-American male is "innocent" (cf. Lani Guinier's discussion in her 1989 *Harvard Civil Rights–Civil Liberties Law Review* article, "Keeping the Faith: Black Voters in the Post-Reagan Era"). But the essence of the problem is the question of relative culpability and relative opportunity. The true power elite has put some of the working class in the position of claiming "reverse discrimination," fighting over bread crumbs, while those at the highest echelons continue to "eat cake." As long as this situation exists, antipathy towards affirmative action will be exacerbated. The only way to counter such attitudes would be to unify sufficiently and to develop a truly educated populace capable of making sophisticated observations, assessments and conclusions.

The only problem with this solution is that, as in the legal institution, the education institution is in the hands of the power elite—and the saga continues.

ENTREPRENEURSHIP

Hovering over such embryonic entrepreneurial efforts, no matter how self-reliant at this point however, is the *Croson* case described below. *Croson* threatens to undo the gains of many small, Black businesses and prevent the initiation of others. As in other affirmative action efforts in the area of education and employment, the courts are being used to protect innocent White male entrepreneurs from the slightest bit of encroachment. The rationale used to effectuate this contrary result is so ominous that it bears examination.

Undoubtedly one reason Black females are deemed economically insignificant in the larger scheme of things, that is, the New World Order, is that entrepreneurship in the Black community is only a minuscule fraction of that in the larger society.[130] Using figures from data provided by the Bureau of the Census,[131] Swinton (1993) calculated the total Black receipts to have been $22.8 billion in 1991. Hence, it seems as if the lowest of the top ten corporations made twice as much in sales as all the Black firms combined in the United States.

In a small effort to help remedy this discrepancy, local, state and federal governments instituted programs designed to enhance "Black Capitalism."[132] Since the program's inception in the early 1970s, it has had relatively limited success. Over the years, however, a few Black entrepreneurs were able to scratch out a living. One of these was a female construction contractor who came to the author to help develop a joint venture arrangement with a "majority" corporation. The following is the author's work product pursuant to that effort.

A Black Woman in the World of Entrepreneurship

Rose was a housewife who went back to school to learn the business and technical end of construction contracting after her children were in college. She had always been very handy with things and became even handier after her husband became disabled.

Rose's mother died when she was three years old, and she had been raised by her aunt. Married right out of high school, Rose had immediately started her family and had not had an opportunity to go to college. She obtained her construction and business education by taking classes, seminars and workshops offered by the most convenient two-year and four-year colleges, city and state equal opportunity programs and private training enterprises set up to familiarize women and minorities with commercial skills. The city's affirmative action officer at the time was aggressive in seeking out promising new minority businesses and constantly held seminars to which the community at large would be invited through notices in the major and Black news publications. (He was a Black Republican whose Baptist church could not hold the 2,000 people who showed up at his funeral.) Rose would faithfully attend even the early morning breakfast seminars designed to accommodate working people. Her first customers were the homes and shops of neighbors and friends but she eventually branched out to try for government work. At first Rose started out bidding for very small jobs. She had attended bidding workshops at the community college. As she was working out of her home[133] and her overhead was low, after several unsuccessful bids she finally landed an "itty-bitty" (her words) contract to repair sidewalks in a designated neighborhood in the inner city. Rose industriously multiplied that contract into others. Her business grew. Rose was the first woman I knew to own a "4 X 4" (truck) motor vehicle as her regular mode of transportation. She ran about town conducting her business in her 4-wheel-drive truck before they became popular as a regular household recreational vehicle.

Her crew consisted of her husband's brothers and her sons. It was good that so many different family members were involved especially because they were of various political persuasions which helped to sustain the company during changing political times.[134]

Her crew also included some potential drawbacks though which consisted of some "recently rehabilitated" cousins and long time family acquaintances. These workers sometimes proved so intermittently reliable that she always had to plan for the eventuality that one of them would take a brief hiatus from his duties. She always had to have backup personnel to make up for those eventualities.

Eventually, however, Rose was able to attain enough continuity in her job contracts that she could provide sufficient stability to attract the caliber of employees needed for the bigger construction opportunities. However, for some time she was "robbing Peter to pay Paul" and relying on any loans or financing available from small business,[135] women and minority set-aside programs to fund her[136] as even a sub-sub-contractor on city and state projects.

Her biggest accomplishment, businesswise, was the qualification of her company as a federal 8(A) contractor. As Rose became known as an honest, dependable, reliable and forthright businessperson, she gained the respect of large contractors working on the major building projects in the area. As was the practice among the MBE or FBE (Minority Business Enterprises or Female Business Enterprises), she regularly dealt with one principal contractor on most projects up for bid. Thus, if that company won a major contract, she would have been included in the bid as the minority partner and therefore she would be on that project, also. Fortunately, her majority contractor partner won participation on two of the projects that were promoted as having revitalized the city. By the time those two projects were well on their way, Rose was well on her way to becoming a regional player.

Her success set the stage for her being called by a Maryland contractor requesting her to join him in a joint venture for bidding on a very large federal contract that would be done in Rose's state. Rose called me to review the joint venture agreement he had sent to her. Because I got the message that due to the relative contributions of the parties and the specialized technical nature of the project, there was very little room for negotiation by a minority contractor and because, comparatively speaking, Rose had so much to gain in terms of nationwide recognition and financial remuneration, I had very few changes. The changes I did propose, which were sent in a letter of October 11, 1993, included a change in the composition of the management committee, to include more of Rose's company members; the registration of the company's Fictitious Name Certificate with the county;

the principal place and official address to be that of Rose's company (she had purchased a building by that time), which was in the same state as the federal project; the issuance of quarterly reports for review rather than annual reports; the definition of net profits to include *all* income that came into either company by virtue of the proposed venture; a binding arbitration requirement; the maintenance of separate books of accounting for each respective company as well as the one book for the joint venture itself; a prohibition against any withdrawal of capital from the joint venture without the written consent of both parties; the deletion of the provision terminating the joint venture upon a determination of insolvency by the majority company; and the requirement that Rose's state be the jurisdiction whose laws would determine any disputes which might arise.

My recommendation was sent back to the majority company contractor, and the bid submitted by the joint venture of that company and Rose's.

Despite all the work and time Rose and her people put into the preparation of the bid as well as its corollary groundwork requirements, she did not get the bid. Something happened, however, that was almost as disappointing to Rose as not winning the contract. Two other major contractors along with their minority partners had bid for the subject federal project. Both of those minority partners were headed by males.

The federal government had chosen one of the other major/minor joint venture firms to do the project. However, the minority contractor of the other joint venture firm that was not chosen sent a letter filing a dispute with the government. The government then reviewed the joint venture firm it had originally selected and, upon reconsideration, denied that firm the contract and then chose that of the letter writer for the award of the project. Although Rose was disheartened by the background surrounding that news, her overall attitude was, "You win some, you lose some."

In summation it should be noted that this FBE/MBE client now employs up to one hundred persons at various times throughout the year. However, upon receiving an award last year, she noted that for six years after she first started her business, the banks made her deal solely with cash. The 1977 Community Reinvestment Act requires banks to only report loans by race and gender which are made for home mortgages. Small business loans and those applied for by consumers have no such requirement. Banks operate pursuant to only a *voluntary* request—if that—to report lending rates to minority groups and women.[137] Nevertheless, Rose's company survived because of a feature that Henderson (1993) notes about Black businesses. Following the sociological approach, Henderson (100) notes that such enterprises are a group phenomenon, held together by a network of kin, peer and community support systems. This was certainly true in this FBE/MBE's situation, where brothers, sisters, spouses, in-laws and children banded together to work relentlessly to make a go of the business.

Rose's company, our entrepreneurial case study, was able to bid for federal contracts as an FBE/MBE because it was certified as an 8A company. In other words, it had been able to self-certify its status as a small business and as a socially and economically disadvantaged small business. Pursuant to the Small Business Act,[138] the term "small business" means a business qualifying as a small business concern under Section 3 of the Small Business Act. The term "disadvantaged small business" means a small business that is:

At least 51 per centum owned by one or more socially and economically disadvantaged individuals, or in the case of any publicly owned business, at least 51 per centum of the stock of the business is owned by one or more socially disadvantaged individuals, and

Whose management and daily business operations are controlled by one or more such individuals. Socially and economically disadvantaged individuals include Black Americans, Hispanic Americans, Asian Pacific Americans, and other minorities or any other individual found to be disadvantaged by the Small Business Administration pursuant to Section 8(a) of the Small Business Act.

Such 8(a) companies are not eligible forever, as they are limited to a nine-year term, after which time 8(a) status is terminated.

Actually, the first federal intervention on behalf of civil rights since the Reconstruction was the Executive Order 8802 of President Franklin D. Roosevelt signed in 1941 that prohibited discrimination by federal defense contractors.[139] In 1965, Congress enacted legislation that imposed an affirmative action requirement as a condition of government contracts or grants.[140] Further, in the case *Fullilove v. Klutznick*,[141] the Supreme Court upheld a congressionally enacted 10 percent set-aside for minority enterprise. Six justices in *Fullilove* agreed that there must be a finding by a competent body of past constitutional or statutory violations. However, in 1989, with regard to the area of entrepreneurship, the highest court in the land was as supportive as it had previously been of affirmative action. It struck down some minority business programs that had been protectors of struggling minority concerns, as in the case *City of Richmond v. J. A. Croson Co..*[142] By 1990, because of the rulings given in *Croson*, 85 of the country's 236 jurisdictions with minority set-aside programs were being subjected to legal attack by White male contractors.

Justice Sandra Day O'Connor wrote the deciding parts of the opinion in *Croson*. It was paradoxical that in her opinion she relied on the *Slaughter House Cases*.[143] She stated that the Court in *Slaughter House* noted that the Civil War Amendments gave "additional powers" to the federal government as well as putting "additional restraints upon those of the States."[144]

In actuality, the author of the *Slaughter House Cases* opinion, Justice Miller, viewed the intent of the Fourteenth (Equal Protection) Amendment and its sisters as essentially applicable to African Americans. This perspective on the Fourteenth Amendment was evident when he stated in that opinion that "We doubt very much whether any action of a State not directed by way of discrimination against the negroes as a class, or on account of race will ever be held to come within the purview of this provision."[145] Nevertheless, Justice O'Connor maintained that the city of Richmond's affirmative action plan "denies certain citizens the opportunity to compete for a fixed percentage of public contracts based solely upon their race."[146] Since the plan called for a 30 percent set aside for minorities, Justice O'Connor was obviously objecting to the fact that "certain citizens" could only compete for the 70 percent of the bidding opportunities that were left to open competition. In the "innocent" citizens behalf, Justice O'Connor wrote that, "[t]o whatever racial group these citizens belong, their 'personal rights' to be treated with equal dignity and respect are implicated by a rigid rule erecting race as the sole criterion in an aspect of public decisionmaking."[147] Going on, Justice O'Connor berated the fact that "[i]t is sheer speculation how many minority firms there would be in Richmond absent past societal discrimination."[148]

Justice O'Connor also discounted the five predicate facts on which the District Court had relied in making its decision that there was adequate basis for a 30 percent "quota." The facts she minimized[149] were: (1) the ordinance declared itself to be remedial; (2) several proponents of the measure stated there had been past discrimination in the construction industry; (3) minority business received 0.67 percent of the principal contracts from the city while minorities constituted 50 percent of the city's population; (4) there were very few minority contractors in the local and state contractors' association; and (5) in 1977 Congress had made a determination that the effects of past discrimination had stifled minority participation in the contracting industry, nationally (The Public Works Employment Act of 1977[150]).

Evaluating the legal efficacy of these facts at the Supreme Court level, Justice O'Connor stated: "There is nothing approaching a prima facie case of a constitutional or statutory violation by *anyone* in the Richmond construction industry."[151] According to Justice O'Connor, none of the District Court "findings," either singly or together, provided a "strong basis in evidence for its conclusion that remedial action was necessary."[152] Thus, since the city of Richmond had failed to identify the need for remedial action in the awarding of its public construction contracts, it had discriminated against the innocent White contractors on the basis of the Equal Protection Clause of the Fourteenth Amendment.[153]

With that, Justice Miller probably turned over in his grave. Justice Thurgood Marshall, in a dissent joined by William J. Brennan and Harry A. Blackmun, pointed out that "Whatever the Framers of the 14th Amendment had in mind in 1868, it certainly was not that"[citation omitted].[154] Justice

Marshall bewailed the fact that the majority in the *Croson* case had decided to "trivialize the continuing impact of government acceptance or use of private institutions or structures once wrought by discrimination."[155] Justice Marshall explained that when the government directs its contracting funds to a "white-dominated community of established contractors whose racial homogeneity is the product of private discrimination,"[156] it not only stamps its "imprimatur" on the practices which cause that result, it likewise "provides a measurable boost to those economic entities that have thrived within it, while denying important economic benefits to those entities which, but for prior discrimination, might well be better qualified to receive valuable government contracts."[157]

Justice Marshall felt that the *Croson* majority had created a "daunting standard" upon the states and localities contemplating racially based remedial measures to eliminate "the present effects of prior discrimination and prevent its perpetuation."[158] He further lamented the fact that Richmond had been thus inhibited in fulfilling two powerful interests in setting aside a portion of public contracts for minority-owned enterprises. One was the city's interest in eradicating the effects of past racial discrimination, of course. The second was that of preventing the city's own spending decisions from "reinforcing and perpetuating the exclusionary effects of past discrimination."[159]

Writing for the *NBA, National Bar Association Magazine*, John A. Turner, Jr., and Courtney M. Billups (Director of Special Projects and Chief of Investigations and Research for the Minority Business Enterprise Legal Defense and Education Fund, Inc., respectively), explain "Why MBE Programs Are Important."[160] In that explanation they described, for instance, how the skilled construction trades went from being over 80 percent Black during slavery days to 1.6 percent by 1930. Turner and Billups state that this decrease is attributable to the fact that the construction trades were "converted by law and practice into 'white only' industries." Thus crippled, minority entrepreneurship after slavery denied "minority workers almost all opportunities to prosper during the industrial boom of the 19th century" and the "institutionalization of discriminatory barriers in the marketplace had catastrophic effects on minority businesses" that "are still with us today."[161]

Further, in their analysis of the impact of *Richmond v. Croson*,[162] the authors relate how in 1993, the Supreme Court *Northeastern Chapter Associated General Contractors v. City of Jacksonville*[163] decision to give "standing to a group of contractors who had not even bid on a city contract but simply stated that they were able to bid," along with *Croson*, has "contributed to an increased number of legal challenges to MBE/WBE programs nationwide."[164]

Currently, cities and states that actually want to overcome *Croson* have to do things such as hire a professional business research firm to specifically document the "wrongdoers" (conduct a disparity study),[165] identify the exact subclass of persons within the minority group that has been discriminated against, provide opportunities for subcontracting, joint ventures, partnerships and the like between majority and minority firms (see above FBE/MBE case study), have jurisdiction-wide bidding and specification workshops/educational seminars, maintain viable equal opportunity and affirmative action offices with personnel who do extensive outreach, small business training and community networking and provide flexible financial arrangement access and availability services; however, this list is not at all exhaustive.

The *Croson* case dealt with state and local contractors. Supreme Court Justice Sandra Day O'Connor was assigned to write the federal version of a *"Croson-type"* decision which would be applicable to federal contracting. Thus, Justice O'Connor got the awesome task of giving a more definitive TKO to affirmative action for federal minority contractors in the form of the previously cited case known as *Adarand vs. Pena*.[166] Adarand, a White contractor, challenged a bid from a Hispanic-owned business which had been made on a Central Federal Lands Highway Division (CFLHD), Department of Transportation project. Mr. Pena had been certified pursuant to the above described Small Business Act as disadvantaged. The majority contractor was a company named Mountain Gravel. The prime contract which Mountain Gravel had with the CFLHD provided that the former would obtain more compensation if it hired "socially and economically disadvantaged individuals." Adarand Constructors, Inc. was not so certified and Mountain Gravel selected Mr. Pena as its guardrail subcontractor. As with *Croson*, *Adarand* means that minority businesses at the federal level are even more seriously handicapped as they attempt to build their experience, skills and capacity to compete with non-minorities with no past historical impediments to participation in the entrepreneurial world of contracting. Turning the tables of minority protection, Justice O'Connor proclaimed that *any* racially based classification, regardless of its history or purpose, required the strictest scrutiny by the court. Since even before the days of *Bakke*, the "strict scrutiny" test essentially meant that the classification could not stand up under any circumstances.

The debate among legal scholars presently is, Does it really mean that now the tables have been turned and racial classifications originally intended to protect those with a history of discrimination are likewise to be subjected to the same tests as those without such a history? Notwithstanding that debate, it is pretty clear that Justice O'Connor in *Adarand* interpreted protection to mean a preference. It is not very debatable that she unequivocally intended to knock out the racially prescribed remedies the federal small business statute provided for those who had been successfully precluded from business opportunities due to their race or their gender. Without the redress provided in the federal 8(a) structure, Blacks are effectively locked out of the federal bidding process. Even though such support was for a limited period, in a time of New World Order retreat from affirmative action,[167] there is no leeway to allow outgroups to become producers and suppliers rather than merely clients and consumers. Locked out of trades since slavery when Black people prevailed in those areas, affirmative action helped to overcome the "isms" of racism, sexism and nepotism that precluded their reentry as skilled contractors.

The perspective underlying the movement to terminate affirmative action presumes that thirty years of affirmative action are sufficient to remedy four hundred years of institutionalized negative action. European Americans had a four-hundred-year head start on achieving economic equanimity. Any closing of the gap is more imagination than reality as measured by most economic indicators selected for comparison. The "They're taking our jobs" mentality continues to cloud rational assessment of this issue.[168] Such thinking overshadows the fact that the discrimination that affirmative action addresses is *structural*, not individual (Harrington, 1986). But even as African American economic achievement in the United States continues to erode, the attacks on affirmative action intensify.[169] The time in which Black people are judged "by the content of their character" has not yet arrived, and African Americans as a people are even further from "the Promised Land," relatively speaking, than they were in 1968 when Rev. Dr. Martin Luther King, Jr., was killed.

Critics of affirmative action also overlook its largely symbolic impact.[170] Most cases of discrimination, as indicated by the low economic status of African Americans, were never filed; those that were filed pursuant to its statutes and regulations either never reached the official agency complaint stage or did not result in any redress.[171] Further, the courts are refusing to remedy the inequities experienced by an entire people in the case-by-case, individual-by-individual strategy of the justice system: Did this particular European American do anything personally to injure that particular African American such that the former should be denied his "natural" right to the job, contract, and so on. The courts are making the burden of a plaintiff so great and the liability of an individual employer or government entity so low that the plaintiff's success is rendered almost impossible.

The cases signaling the death knell of affirmative action in entrepreneurship by the state, local and federal governments also very probably herald the essential end of most meaningful Black business in the United States. This is true even though the potential of the Black buying market is reported to be enormous.[172] The African American population is the largest ethnic group in the nation, and it is growing at twice the rate of Whites.[173] Further, for the foreseeable future, the median age of Blacks "will continue to hover in the 18–25 range that many mass marketers covet."[174] One worry that Black entrepreneurs have when they consider tapping into Black markets is "being preempted by established white firms."[175] There are several reasons why this might be a legitimate concern. One reason is that although a Black business network may be labeled "powerful" monetarily, such participating ventures come nowhere near the financial status of any of the Fortune 500 firms.[176]

Another reason for trepidation by Black entrepreneurs is illustrated by the situation of a Wall Street entrepreneur planning a foray into the South African market. That entrepreneur got such bad reviews from the financial institutions charged with protecting the public (such as the Securities and Exchange Commission) and the private (such as the investor consultation firms) that his peanut-size efforts probably will be nipped in the bud.[177] This negative result might be circumvented, and he might still be able to explore the imminent Azanian (South African) market, if the Black entrepreneur gets the message and opens up his endeavor to a share of ownership and control by "established" financial entities. White Fortune 500 investing firms that are traded on Wall Street seem to be allowed much more flexibility. For example, one Fortune 500 firm[178] ultimately settling a lawsuit involving 30 million investors (one of them was this author who invested $10,000 in a limited partnership)[179] received much more encouragement when there was evidence that the sales personnel were playing fast and loose with their fiduciary responsibility.[180] Even the SEC itself,[181] other "reputable" security organizations[182] and financial advisors from certain investing firms who are contemptuous of "Brother Man's" brokerage firms have had their share of problems, too.[183] However, neither the firms nor their partners were drummed out of the business entirely and made penniless for their particular peccadillos.[184] And, in the future, investing firms and public corporations will probably be even more shielded from John/Jane Q. public-type attacks.[185]

Entrepreneurship in the Black community among African American women has in a bootstrap way been more the rule than the exception. Babysitting, hairdressing, manicuring, sewing, singing, cleaning, cooking, baking and other forms of arts and crafts are businesses in which the Black woman has engaged almost since the beginning of civilization (Asante 1990). From her African homeland to her involuntary landing upon American shores, the Black woman's ingenuity, creativity, perseverance and fortitude have made her the survival backbone, together with her mate, of her family and her community (Rose 1980).

The Black woman's resiliency and entrepreneurial legacy notwithstanding, she is not currently destined to be a major player in the New World Order from a globally economic point of view. Absent the field of entertainment or other forms of mass communications, the chances are slim for the rise of another Madame C. J. Walker, who became the first self-made Black woman millionaire in the early twentieth century. The New World Order has become too tightly exclusionary for such an anomaly to slip past the strictly guarded watch of the protective financial agencies now in place.

One does not see many ventures owned or operated (as CEO or otherwise) by the Black woman on any list of the 1000 most valuable companies in the United States (see "The *Business Week* 1000").[186] For instance, the top ten in market value included (in billions of dollars): (1) General Motors, $132.4; (2) Exxon, $104.1; (3) Ford, $100.1; (4) AT&T, 64.9; (5) IBM, $64.5; (6) General Electric, $62.2; (7) Mobil, $57.2; (8) Wal-Mart, $55.5; (9) Sears, $52.3; and (10) Philip Morris, $50.1.

Of the twenty-five executives "to watch" for that (1993) year, twenty-two were White males, one was an Asian male and the other two were White females. In the presentation by the Black press of those Fortune 500 business presidents who were Black, four of the twenty-six were African American women.[187] (The varied contexts of the units of measurement as well as the low number of subjects make it impossible to make any generalizations or extrapolations based upon that data.)

At the 70th Annual National Bar Association (NBA) Conference,[188] Shirley J. Wilcher, deputy assistant secretary in the Office of Federal Contract Compliance, a U.S. Department of Labor Agency, stated that the OFCCP had 60 percent of the staff in 1995 that it had in 1980. The OFCCP is the office charged with "Making EEO and Affirmative Action Work." One of its directives includes the enforcement of Executive Order 11246. Executive Order 11246, as amended: "[P]rohibits federal contractors and subcontractors and federally-assisted construction contractors and subcontractors from discriminating in employment decisions on the basis of race, color, sex, religion, or national origin. The order also requires that employers take affirmative action to ensure that all employment decisions are made in a non-discriminatory manner."[189] Those covered include "contractors and subcontractors who do over $10,000 in government business in one year." For instance, in 1994 approximately $161 billion awards were made to federal contractors. According to Ms. Wilcher, the 4000 reviews a year which the OFFCP conducts in its ten regions, as well as its other activities, will not be affected by the U.S. Supreme Court decision in *Adarand* because it does not involve quotas. Therefore, the OFCCP would continue to enforce Executive Order 11246. The Executive Order does not require the hiring of women and minorities. What it requires, Ms. Wilcher maintained, is the development of a reasonably attainable pool of qualified individuals. It just increases the pool. As previously implied, then, what is perhaps more potentially devastating than *Adarand* is the Congressional budget ax slicing away at the OFCCP's personnel and resources.[190] The National Bar Association has long been a continued major forum for civil rights lawyers and leaders. The American Bar Association elected Roberta Cooper Ramo, a woman president, 117 years and two months after *Adarand*. Ms. Ramo supported a resolution passed by the ABA's policy-making Board of Governors that endorsed the use of affirmative action as a legal and voluntary remedy for racial and sexual discrimination.[191]

Following Ms. Wilcher at that NBA session podium, Barbara Arnwine, executive director of Lawyers Committee for Civil Rights Under Law, described the tax during slavery days for freeing slaves. She stated that it was used to help poor Whites. Ms. Arnwine posited this example to illustrate the way in which even, at the onset of African American life in the United States, *helping* Blacks was somehow twisted around to mean that one was *hindering* Whites. That was why, Ms. Arnwine explained, the Reconstruction idea of providing the newly freed slaves with 40 acres and a mule was so soundly defeated. In fact, that idea was the precursor of the reparations movement. And, according to Attorney Arnwine, affirmative action was a weak response to the reparations debate in the late 1960s. Hence, Congressional Representative John Conyers continued to introduce a Reparations Bill year after year. Affirmative action was an antidote to discrimination. A discrimination strategy, Ms. Arnwine elaborated, used to find some kind of counterweight and give some kind of inclusion of people who are not there.

The attack on affirmative action is caused by the fact that the country has undergone a serious economic revolution and become largely a service-based economy. *Every* worker found himself or herself displaced. In this context, the one constant is the fact that since slavery, Blacks have only owned 1 to 2 percent of the wealth of the country. A five percent federal set-aside for socially and economically disadvantaged contractors is relatively inconsequential when the fact is taken into consideration that the rest of the billions and billions of dollars contracted by the federal government go to majority firms. In addition, the disadvantaged firms are using majority suppliers and subcontractors. So, the whole fight of affirmative action is whether Blacks can rise to an economic power, Ms. Arnwine surmised. That is why she proclaimed that it was no surprise that the number one target of affirmative action was the minority set-asides. Also, minorities and women are scapegoats in the efforts by majority business to keep its market share in the face of it going to places like China and Mexico. As with the budget cuts mentioned above, again Congressional action poses a serious threat to minority set-asides. In the Senate, Robert Dole introduced Senate Bill 1085, the "Equal Opportunity Act of 1995." Representative Charles T. Canady introduced a corollary of the same name as Dole's bill in the House, H.R. 2128 (Canady's bill was joined by an amendment of Representative Gary Franks, who is Black[192]). Arnwine pointed out that if that legislation were ever to be enacted, it would:

"[B]ar the federal government from entering into consent decrees or other court orders providing for affirmative action where necessary to remedy proven discrimination against minorities or women"; and

"[P]rohibit recruitment and outreach to minorities or women to produce an applicant pool that reflects the actual availability of minorities and women qualified to participate."

Without the economic power threatened by such legislation, Ms. Arn-wine maintained that African Americans will not have the ability to have an effective exercise of power in any realm.

Along these lines, at a subsequent conference session, Loretta King, deputy assistant attorney general, Civil Rights Division, U.S. Department of Justice, stated that in an attempt to undermine the original principles of achieving the right to vote, the U.S. Supreme Court in the 1995 *Miller v. Johnson* case (see Chapter 2) had applied its affirmative action reasoning to voting rights cases. The Court's 1990 rulings represented the first time affirmative action-type theories had been applied to cases filed pursuant to the Voting Rights Act of 1965 which had the goal of preventing obstacles to the Black franchise in the United States. Such misapplication likewise interfered with the ability of minorities to achieve full parity in the interplay between political and economic societal dynamics.

It has been posited that a way for the Black woman to overcome con-straints in the employment realm posed by such blocks as glass ceilings is to pursue entrepreneurship.[193] Still, from a practical standpoint the legal and business supports necessary for a successful entrepreneurial venture for most Black women do not seem readily forthcoming as can be seen from the foregoing discussion. Given these obstacles to success of any African American venture, Black business in general will very probably continue to remain at side show status in the three-ring circus of U.S. and worldwide business economics.

The experience of the OFCCP has been repeated in other agencies. For instance, the aforementioned Equal Employment Opportunity Commis-sion (EEOC), "the agency that Congress created to enforce civil rights laws in the workplace,"[194] had "about 100,000 unresolved cases at the end of last year [1994], double the backlog of just two years ago."[195] According to its chairman, Gilbert F. Casellas, the big problem in addressing that backlog was "a woefully inadequate budget."[196]

Without affirmative action and its effective enforcement, the African American woman will not be brought closer to parity within the nation's educational, employment and entrepreneurial institutions. Absent such intervention, she will most probably remain in her subordinate position with reference to other groups. Thus, as the New World Order marches on towards fruition, the Black woman will be able to rely upon such agencies for redress to a lesser and lesser degree. At the same 1995 NBA Convention referenced above, in a later session, Anthony W. Robinson, President of the Minority Business Legal Defense and Education Fund, Inc. of Washington, D.C., exhorted lawyers to be social engineers in the vein led by Charles Hamilton Houston [former Howard Law School Dean]. This was necessary, he felt, because *Adarand* had scuttled Black access to money, market and management opportunities.

By whatever economic route the Black woman seeks to provide food, clothing and shelter for her family, she will probably have less expendable income in the near future. Thus, it may be assumed that she will have to depend more on credit for her survival. Let us now look at how she fares with reference to that system.

CREDIT ISSUES

A major problem with credit issues in the New World Order is that it has implications that reach far beyond a specific debtor-creditor relationship itself. For example, one Black female lawyer who worked as a lobbyist for the insurance industry happened to mention to the author that she had just written a letter of recommendation for a young Black woman seeking admission to the practice of law. The young woman, who was in her mid-twenties, had graduated with good grades and successfully passed the state's bar exam but had been refused admission on the basis of her credit report containing disparaging information from her teen years. It was deemed to say something about her veracity and moral character. Thus, the consequences of one's credit report are extending into realms of life unheralded prior to the New World Order. Who are the persons most likely to be unable to pay their bills?

The piece of legislation which most directly protects the American consumer is the Equal Credit Opportunity Act (ECOA).[197] That act went into effect on October 28, 1975, and at that time prohibited discrimination based on sex or marital status. In March 1977, coverage was extended to prohibit discrimination based on race, color, national origin, age, receipt of public assistance, or good faith exercise of rights, under the Consumer Protection Act.[198] Relief available under the ECOA includes actual damages, punitive damages up to $10,000, equitable and declaratory relief, attorney's fees and costs. There is federal jurisdiction regardless of the amount in controversy, and the act covers applications for mortgages and other forms of credit with respect to housing.[199] The act prohibits discrimination with respect to any aspect of a credit transaction on any of the prohibited bases and discrimination because all or part of an applicant's income is derived from public assistance.

Within thirty days, a creditor must notify an applicant of action taken in rejecting a credit application, along with either a specific statement as to the reason such adverse action was taken or a statement advising the applicant that he or she has a right to receive a specific statement of reasons for the adverse action. The Federal Trade Commission is the major enforcement agency for violations under this act even though the Federal Reserve Board has promulgated regulations under ECOA. Anyone who believes that he or she has been subjected to credit discrimination may file an administrative complaint with the FTC. Many states, in addition, have their own administrative agencies which regulate credit discrimination. Further, a person may file a private civil action, within two years of the time of the occurrence of the discriminatory act, with the federal district court having jurisdiction over the parties. These "official" protections notwithstanding, many female-headed families are discriminated against in creditworthiness decisions because of their lack of knowledge of these resources. Further, because Black women have lower incomes and thereby have a greater need "to borrow a lot of money," they are more vulnerable to creditors with higher interest rates.[200] And, even when credit is extended to them, many Black single-parent families get into financial difficulty maintaining it at an "appropriate" level because of their finite, limited resources. Hence, they are subjected to such embarrassments as repossession, cognovit notes, judgment liens, foreclosures, bank account attachments and garnishments.

The intricate, abstruse way in which these debt collection techniques are structured leaves the average debtor very little recourse against them. Many debtors who cannot pay a $200 debt can afford to pay an attorney $300 to defend them in the collection process. The Legal Services Corporation[201] has been of some assistance in credit matters to debtors but, because of severe cutbacks in their own resources, can only reach a very few individuals.

Changes in the bankruptcy and other federal debt resolution codes[202] have provided some relief to the debtor who is overwhelmed by the formidable debt collection processes. Under these reforms, a debtor can retain somewhat more of his or her equity in such assets as a house, a car, household furnishings and personal items. For instance, 1994 amendments to the Bankruptcy Code allow a "debtor the right to cure a home mortgage default at least up to the point of an actual foreclosure sale."[203] While totally (under bankruptcy) liquidating most debts except for such notables as alimony, tax obligations, government-insured student loans and a few others, the stigma of having gone bankrupt or been in trusteeship is still there. The report of a bankruptcy can stay on one's credit report for up to ten years. Any financial activity that a debtor has stays on the credit report for up to seven years. Many Black Americans are reluctant to pursue remedies under bankruptcy because they already have enough strikes against them.

It is, for most insolvents (including the Black woman), a humiliating process. Many are bewildered and frightened by intimidating creditors who make mockery of them and use nefarious collection techniques after having charged what should be outlawed as usurious rates of interest. Most consumers have never heard of a Fair Debt Collection Practices Act and are unaware of any legal remedies for which they might be eligible.

In the past, credit-rating institutions (credit bureaus) have been notorious for their errors.[204] It has been suggested that one should check one's record "once a year for accuracy and completeness." The numbers given to make this check and to ask for a copy of one's report are those of the national credit bureaus, TRW (800 682–7654); Equifax (800 685-1111); or Trans Union (216 779–7200).[205] Debts which are in controversy should be disputed. This can be done by writing each of these three major credit reporting companies. The addresses for these respective companies are:

Equifax Credit Information Services, P.O. Box 740256, Atlanta, Georgia 30374

TRW Credit Data, 7261 Engle Road, Middleburg Hts., Ohio 44130

Trans Union Corporation, 555 W. Adams St., Chicago, Illinois 60661

One can get an annual copy of one's credit report which is complimentary by calling 1–800–392–1122. In addition to the aforementioned phone numbers, one can call Trans Union Corporation between the hours of 8:15 a.m. and 4:15 p.m. at 1–800–851–2674 for one's credit information. Besides its (404) 885-8000 number, Equifax has regional affiliates which can be reached toll free as well. For instance, if one is within the Ohio area region, one can call 1–800–738–7609. Of course, these numbers are subject to change and should be updated as one needs them.

Further, a debtor should make sure that any corrected information is sent to as many local and national credit bureaus as can be identified because they are all independent entities that may or may not pick up each other's information. Finally, one should be careful about how many inquiries are made regarding one's credit (pursuant to credit applications or for any reason) because each time an inquiry is made, it is noted on that report. So, one can be denied credit because there are too many inquiries on one's credit report. Hence, if Benjamin Franklin were to have lived in the Twenty-First Century, he undoubtedly would have had to have added credit-related issues to his list of sure things (besides death and taxes[206]).

HOUSING ISSUES

Housing Case Study

The particulars of this particular case are best represented by a letter which I wrote to the head of the public housing authority that administers the Greater Cleveland area, on July 20, 1993, as follows:

Dear Ms. Freeman:

You probably do not remember me but we have met on several public occasions—one here at the University and one at a Small Business Luncheon. At those times, I was impressed with your sensitivity, concern and genuine interest in the welfare of the CMHA tenants.

In that vein, I am writing on behalf of a person, the above referenced Ms. Terry Jones, whom I have known since she was a little girl. Her mother works in the University's ABC Department and I have watched her grow from an inquisitive, precocious youngster to a warm, intelligent, accomplished, civic-minded, responsible citizen, admirable woman and aspiring physician. I know Ms. Jones to be a person full of integrity, honest beyond reproach and as a deserving a young mother as there ever was.

Ms. Jones was married at nineteen and has four children, two boys and two girls, ranging in age from fifteen to ten years of age. Her youngest daughter, LaTanya, received nine awards—more than any other student—at her graduation from DEF Elementary School in GHI Heights this past June. LaTanya obtained the highest scholastic average of any of the June 1993 ABC graduating class. LaTanya will be featured in this month's JKL Children's Hospital publication as an exceptional asthmatic child who is living a full life despite her illness. Ms. Jones's other children have likewise been noted as outstanding in their various schools and activities. For instance, her fifteen-year-old son, Estaban, is active in his church, works with the elderly and is currently involved with the Inroads Program. Rhadhia, her fourteen-year-old daughter, has been on the Merit Roll the entire first year at GHI Heights High School. In addition, she is on the basketball and the track teams at the High School. Rhadhia further tutors her classmates in algebra. And, Markus is in the GHI Heights Community Basketball team. He has been Reader of the Month at his elementary school and takes Karate at GHI Heights' High School. As you can tell, the children's activities have been based in the GHI Heights community where they live—as participants in the CMHA Section 8 program until terminated, May 1993.

The children get these accomplishments honestly. Theresa herself has just started assisting me as a tutor for the MNO program at the University. She received her baccalaureate degree from PQR College in 1991. Currently, she attends a podiatric medicine college in the pursuit of her dream of becoming a podiatrist (foot doctor).

This background probably gives you some insight as to why I feel it is so important that I write this letter hoping to rectify a grievous decision made by someone in your organization.

In explanation, I must first point out that Theresa's daughter LaTanya has asthma. In December of 1991, Theresa applied for SSI benefits for LaTanya. In February of 1992, LaTanya began receiving presumptive SSI payments. As you can see from the attached Social Security form, Theresa was advised *not* to report such payments as they were only temporary. In August of 1992, the state doctor finally approved LaTanya for permanent disability benefits, also attached. After the receipt of that approval, Theresa called the CMHA office to advise them of the income change. However, Mr. STU, a CMHA attorney, at a hearing in which Theresa was not represented, disbelieved her and terminated nevertheless. This finding was reconfirmed at subsequent CMHA appeal levels.

At this point, I would like to personally vouch for the honesty of Ms. Jones. As I have noted earlier, I have known her for thirteen years and presently rely on her heavily in helping me to orient forty-two inner-city youth to the University in the MNO program. She is one of the most reliable tutors I have ever had. The students assigned to her have overcome the odds and made remarkable adjustments to college life. She stands as a highly esteemed and dedicated role model for her own children, the MNO students and the community in which she resides. And, she has been and is a beacon of light in the effort of individuals to overcome circumstances of poverty, hardship and deprivation in their attempts to enter the American mainstream.

Please give Ms. Theresa Jones another opportunity to participate in the CMHA Section 8 program. As an attorney, I have represented other clients in other social welfare programs who have asserted such a notification to their agencies. I *know* that if Theresa Jones said she did something, she did it.

Thank you for your time and attention to this matter.

[Ms. Theresa Jones (a pseudonym, of course) was reinstated in the Section 8 program.]

Housing Discussion

Besides the provision of food, shelter is perhaps the most onerous burden shouldered by the Black single-parent family head. Housing becomes increasingly problematic the more children one has.[207] Even without the difficulties in mortgage procurement (see Chapter 1), more Blacks have been renters than have been homeowners, as demonstrated by the fact that only 43.46 percent of all Blacks have equity in a home. Among European Americans, 66.72 percent own their homes.[208] By predominantly being renters, Blacks have been subject to wealth-protecting state laws that favor the landlord over the tenant. Although these state laws vary, they usually depict some variant of this protective scheme with reference to rental property.

At the federal level, the Fair Housing Act, Title VIII of the Civil Rights Act of 1968, as amended,[209] prohibits discrimination in the sale or rental of housing or the provision of services relating to housing, on the basis of race, color, religion, sex or national origin. This prohibition extends to financial services. In spite of the strong language of this statute, housing remains one of the most segregated areas of American life. Even when Blacks do "escape" to the suburbs, as one in three now do, they still do not escape many vestiges of discrimination. Such vestiges follow them in such forms as racial steering, lower valuation of their houses upon resale and yet higher suburban taxes than are paid for comparable housing by Whites.[210] Further, Blacks are rejected for mortgage loans at a rate that is more than twice that for Whites. Mortgage lenders including banks, credit unions, savings institutions and others turned down 33.4 percent of the applications which were made by Blacks for mortgages. Whites were turned down for mortgage loans at a rate of 16.4 percent. The mortgage rejection rate for Hispanics who "may be of any race" was 24.6 percent. In addition, these differences are not totally explained by income differentials.[211]

Black children who are residing with a single parent are particularly likely to grow up in an entirely segregated environment. Having two incomes in one family makes a crucial difference among Black people themselves inasmuch as it enables a family to move to the perhaps more integrated suburbs. A federal district court is the effective forum for relief under the Fair Housing Act. The Department of Housing and Urban

Development (HUD) cannot order a respondent to cease its discriminatory practices. Nor can it award a complainant any damages.[212] Conversely, a court can grant any relief it deems appropriate, including temporary or permanent injunctive relief, actual damages, and punitive damages not to exceed $1,000. In addition, a court, if it sees fit, can award a plaintiff the costs of his or her action as well as reasonable attorney's fees.[213] The Housing and Community Development Act of 1974[214] resulted in the consolidation of a number of federal categorical programs into one block grant program that decentralized the planning and implementation of activities funded through Community Development monies. Its stated purposes included:

The elimination and prevention of slums and blighting conditions, primarily for persons of low and moderate income (families whose income is less than 80% of the median income of the SMSA);

The conservation and expansion of the nation's housing resources, principally for persons of low and moderate income;

The expansion of the quality and quantity of community services, principally for persons of low and moderate income;

The spatial deconcentration of income groups throughout communities.[215]

Despite these laws and recent ameliorative housing and landlord/tenant legislation passed by some states,[216] the conditions in which many Black inner-city single-parent families live are deplorable. Although the courts have approved the use of "checkers" (White couples follow up when Black couples are denied housing to show differential treatment) in housing discrimination cases,[217] it is still very difficult for a tenant to be able to get a judgment against a large commercial landlord that orders such a landlord to pay a fine. Recalling their societal function, it is not surprising that courts seem to be sympathetic with the argument that a piece of property is not worth putting an "excessive" amount of money into if it is located in an undesirable area—"undesirable" in the sense that the tenants are unmotivated and unambitious, that is, undeserving.

A Black female single parent has exacerbated problems in obtaining adequate housing for her children, as she usually has less income to procure decent living quarters. Despite the federal and state laws, it has been the private public-service law firms and nonprofit agencies who generally have taken the responsibility to react against housing discrimination on the basis of race and/or sex. They use such methods as sending out checkers, demanding tenant's rights, lobbying for housing code legislation and enforcement, and bringing class-action suits in court (when the courts allow them).[218]

Because of discrimination in this area, many Black single-parent families live in the public housing authorized by the aforementioned Housing and Community Development Act, otherwise known as "subsidized housing."

One of the first things that the Reagan administration did when it came into office was to increase the amount of the supplement paid by the poor from 25 percent of their income to 30 percent. Thus, the Black female-headed family living in subsidized housing now has to pay a higher percentage of its already limited income for substandard housing, often in a physically deteriorating area with subhuman conditions, leaving the family with even less money for other living requirements.

Such second-class housing conditions, unfortunately, will be present for a longer period of time in public housing units than planned because, after years of unhampered spending, largely on defense-related items, a primary concern now is "the deficit." The concern with the budgetary deficit has been a major pretext for the cutbacks in the funds necessary for public-housing renovation[219] and repair and new building. The initial public housing modernization program approved by Congress was a comprehensive effort toward the goal of ensuring that all public housing projects (1) met minimum health and safety standards, (2) were made more energy efficient, and (3) were rendered less costly to operate.[220]

Obviously, as the initial plan was not funded, it will be a long time before many public housing units meet minimum health and safety standards and are made more energy efficient and less costly to operate. Although these reformulations made the construction industry rather unhappy, the biggest losers were those who have had to live in substandard housing.

The subject of housing cannot be ended without making note of the role of the banking and insurance establishments. In the New World Order, those financial organizations developed policies and regulations that helped to make discrimination even more intractable in the housing area. African Americans are so low on the current creditworthiness determination totem poll that even in periods of relatively generous lending practices, they are missed.[221] The term that describes the more blatant bank, realtor and insurance practices that target certain areas for discriminatory treatment is *redlining*. The *Atlanta Journal Constitution* carried a series that documented its persistence entitled "The Color of Money" in May 1988. The African American woman and her family, even with all the aforementioned housing and credit reforms to the contrary, must still live in densely populated, segregated, substandard and polluted (see Chapter 7) environments—her New World Order.

SUMMARY

Thus, the ability of Blacks and women to obtain the goods and services endemic to the economic institution have been made more problematic as the United States moved closer to a service economy as opposed to a primarily manufacturing one. This economic deprivation has also been fueled by a reaction to global economic forces, set off in large part by the multinationals themselves, which in a word is reactionary. That reactionary stance is manifested in the retreat of affirmative action efforts which had been at least ideally approved by legal authority during the civil rights era. Unfortunately, as for substantive improvement in the overall economic status of women and minorities, affirmative action efforts had not been able to get much past the level of the *ideal*. The New World Order has removed even the tolerance of equal opportunity ideals.

NOTES

1. Steven D. Lydenberg, Alice Tepper Marlin, Sean O'Brien Strub and the Council on Economic Priorities, *Rating America's Corporate Conscience: A Provocative Guide to the Companies behind the Products You Buy Every Day* (Reading, Mass.: Addison-Wesley, 1986).

2. Ibid., 147.

3. Steve A. Granata, "Telecommunication Reform: The History and Conditions Leading to Political Action," *The George Washington University Journal of Public Administration: Policy Perspectives*, 2, 1 (Spring 1995): 53-62.

4. U.S. Congress, House, Committee on Education and Labor, Subcommittee on Employment Opportunities, *Oversight Hearings on Equal Employment Opportunity*, 97th Cong., 1st sess, 1981, pt. 1, pp. 219, 221, Statement of Economist Bernard Anderson.

5. See, for example, also *General Electric*, 429 U.S. 125 (1976).

6. 29 U.S.C.S. Sec. 2611(2)(A)(1)(ii).

7. Pub. L. 103–3; 29 U.S.C.S. Sec. 2612(c), 29 C.F.R. Sec. 825.206.

8. *United States v. American Telephone and Telegraph Company*, 552 F. Supp. 131 (1982); 460 U.S. 1001, 103 S.Ct. 1240 (Modification of Final Judgment).

9. Cf. Mark Landler, "Plan for a Bell's Long-Distance Service: A Justice Department Proposal Faces Criticism," *New York Times*, April 4, 1995, C4.

10. Edmund L. Andrews, "Ameritech Forcefully Stays Home: One Baby Bell Still Emphasizes Phones," *New York Times*, November 22, 1994, C1–C16, in which appeared as a caption, "Ameritech in Fighting Trim: By Cutting Jobs and Costs, Ameritech Has Prepared Itself Better Than Most Other Bell Companies to Meet Mounting Competition. And Its Stock has been the Top Performer Among the Bells This Year."

11. Edmund L. Andrews, "U.S. May Let a Baby Bell Widen Reach," *New York Times*, December 9, 1994, C1, C6.

12. Gene Koretz, "Defense Cuts Could Wound the Economy for a Decade," *Business Week*, October 5, 1992, 30; see also, for example, "Pentagon Seeking 140 Reduction in Reserve Forces; Every State Would Be Hit; Congress Criticizes Cuts, Which Would Take Place over the Next 2 Fiscal Years," *New York Times*, March 27, 1992, A1, A10.

13. Billy J. Tidwell, "African Americans and the 21st Century Labor Market: Improving the Fit," in *The State of Black America 1993* (New York: National Urban League, 1993): 35-57, 51, 52.

14. Peter Coy and Robert D. Hof with James E. Ellis, "The Baby Bells' Painful Adolescence: Competition and New Technologies Are Crowding Them at Every Turn," *Business Week*, October 5, 1992, 124–134.

15. Gerald W. Brock, *Telecommunications Policy for the Information Age* (Cambridge, Mass.: Harvard University Press, 1994).

16. Cf. Katharine Q. Seelye, "Bill to Decontrol Phones and Cable Ties up the House: 2d Night of Wrangling, G.O.P.'s Tactics Are Criticized by Democrats as a Clinton Veto Threat Remains," *New York Times*, August 4, 1995, A1, C4; and Mark Lander, "House Passes Bill Curtailing Rules on Phones and TV: Networks Losers; Vote Is 305 to 117–Chips to Let Parents Screen Programs," *New York Times*, August 5, 1995, A1, A18.

17. Advertisement, "Notice of Application of the Ohio Bell Telephone Company for Alternative Regulation," *Plain Dealer*, January 19, 1994, 7–A.

18. Marcus Gleisser, "Ameritech to Cut Up to 1,500 Jobs: Involuntary Release Program Will Include Benefits," *Plain Dealer*, August 31, 1993, 1–D.

19. But see Louis Uchitelle, "The Rise of the Losing Class: Different Incomes, Different Educations, Different Jobs, But the Same Anxiety," *New York Times*, November 20, 1994, 4: 1, 5, which includes the quote (p. 5): "In the new order, managers are not the enemy. 'We deal with the boss by ousting the Congressman.' "

20. Catherine S. Manegold, "Labor Secretary Urges Cuts In 'Corporate Welfare' Too," *New York Times*, November 23, 1994, A11.

21. See also, Nathan McCall, *Makes Me Wanna Holler: A Young Black Man in America* (New York: Random House, 1994) 254–255.

22. Tamar Lewin, "Income Gap Between Sexes Found to Widen in Retirement," *New York Times*, April 26, 1995, A15. This article also notes from this study by the Older Women's League that, "the mean private pension for women is $3,940 annually, compared with $7,468 for men" as well as the fact that the average monthly Social Security benefit for women is $538, "compared with an average of $858 for men." The article points out with reference to its report of the widening income gap between retired men and women that, "Social Security benefits and most private pensions are based on the number of years that a person is employed and the yearly earnings."

23. Ibid

24. Peter T. Kilborn, "Women and Minorities Still Face 'Glass Ceiling': White Men's Fears Are Barrier, Report Says," *New York Times*, March 16, 1995, C22.

25. Judith H. Dobryznski, "Some Action, Little Talk," *New York Times*, April 20, 1995, C1.

26. Vindu P. Goel, "Phone Company Charges Too Much, State Study Shows," *Plain Dealer*, March 2, 1994, 1–A, 10–A.

27. Ibid.

28. David Cay Johnston, "Workers Paid as Contractors: A Widespread Abuse is Cited," *New York Times*, August 16, 1995, A1, C4.

29. Frantz Fanon, *The Wretched of the Earth* (New York: Grove Press, 1965), 152, 153.

30. William H. Honan, "Regents [California] Prepare for Storm on Affirmative Action; A Black Developer [Ward Connerly] Says Preferences Devalue Black Achievements," *New York Times*, July 19, 1995, A 13.

31. Steven A. Holmes, "Defending Affirmative Action, Liberals Try to Place the Debate's Focus on Women: Serving Notice to President Clinton About a Review," *New York Times*, March 2, 1995, A 11. A New York Times/CBS News Poll reported in the article ". . . found 43 percent agreeing that women should receive preferences in hiring and promotion where there had been bias against women in the past. But when asked whether preference should be given to blacks in cases where there had been racial discrimination, only 33 percent said yes." Also see, Steven A. Holmes, "Preference Plans May Escape Move for Major Change: G.O.P. Putting off a Ban: Affirmative Action Programs Also Escape Revision after Study by White House," *New York Times*, July 19, 1995, A1, C18.

32. Steven A. Holmes, "U.S. Issues New, Strict Tests for Affirmative Action Plans," *New York Times*, June 29, 1995, A1, A7.

33. Gary R. Clark, *Plain Dealer*, March 7, 1981.

34. 29 U.S.C. Sec. 801, et seq.

35. *The American Economy* (Washington, D.C.: President (Carter's) Commission for a National Agenda for the Eighties, 1980) 39.

36. 29 U.S.C., Sec. 151–69.

37. 29 U.S.C., Sec. 201–19.

38. 29 U.S.C., 206(d).

39. 29 U.S.C., 651–78.

40. 42 U.S.C., Sec. 2000(e) et seq.

41. Cf. Maya Angelou "They Went Home," "Momma Welfare Roll," "Avec Merci Mother," in *Poems* (New York: Bantam Books, 1986), 4, 139, 185.

42. Robert K. Merton, *Social Theory and Social Structure* (New York: Free Press, 1954). Sociologist Merton was also the first sociologist to receive the highest United States award for basic research, the National Medal of Science. *Footnotes*, 22, no. 8 (October, 1994).

43. Toby, Jackson, "Some Variables in Role Conflict Analysis," *Social Forces* 30 (1952): 323–327.

44. William J. Goode, "A Theory of Role Strain", *American Sociological Review* 25 (August, 1960): 483–496.

45. Erving Goffman, *Stigma: Notes on the Management of Spoiled Identity*, (Englewood Cliffs, N.J.: Prentice-Hall, 1963).

46. *San Antonio Independent School District v. Rodriguez*, 411 U.S. 1 (1973).

47. W. E. B. DuBois, *The Autobiography of W.E.B. Du Bois* (New York: International Publishers 1969); C. Wright Mills, *The Power Elite* (New York: Oxford University Press, 1959); Lawrence J. Peter, *The Peter Principle* (New York: William Morrow, 1969).

48. Todd S. Purdum, "President Gives Fervent Support To Fighting Bias; Says Minorities Need Aid; Affirmative Action Should Be Repaired, Not Eliminated, Clinton Tells Group," *New York Times*, July 20, 1995, A1, A10; Editorial, "Defending Affirmative Action," *New York Times*, July 20, 1995, A12.

49. 42 U.S.C. Sec. 1973 et seq.

50. 42 U.S.C. Sec. 2000 et seq.

51. Alton Hornsby, Jr. *Chronology of African American History* (Detroit, Mich.: Gale Research, 1991), xxxiii.

52. 416 U.S. 312 (1974).

53. 132 Cal. Rptr. 680(176); 98 S.Ct. 2733 (1978).

54. 443 U.S. 193; 99 S.Ct. 2721 (1979).

55. Civil Rights Restoration Act of 1991, 42 U.S.C. 1981 as amended; 42 U.S.C. 2000e as amended.

56. Beginning in 1993, the Black female members of the U.S. House of Representatives included Corrine Brown, 3rd District, Fla.; Eva M. Clayton, 1st District, N.C.; Barbara Rose-Collins, 15th District, Mich.; Cardiss Collins, 7th District, Ill.; Eddie Bernice Johnson, 30th District, Texas; Cynthia McKinney, 11th District, Ga.; Carrie P. Meek, 17th District, Fla.; Maxine Waters, 35th District, Calif.

57. *New York Times*, "With Rights Act Comes Fight to Clarify Congress's Intent," November 18, 1991, A1, C10.

58. *New York Times*, "Senate Democrats Back Compromise on Civil Rights Bill: Bush Takes Major Credit, President Insists the Measure Bolsters Workers' Equality without Using Quotas," October 26, 1991, A1, A8.

59. 490 U.S. 642 (1989).

60. 109 S. Ct. 2363 (1989).

61. 109 S. Ct. 2180 (1989).

62. 109 S. Ct. 2761 (1989).

63. 109 S.Ct. 1775 (1989).

64. 109 S.Ct. 2732 (1989).

65. *New York Times*, "Rash of Suits Seen after Rights Act: Many Charges of Sexual Bias are Expected to be Filed," November 30, 1991, A1, A16.

66. Lawyers' Committee for Civil Rights Under Law, "Civil Rights in 1989–1990: Overview, Annual Report," 1989–1990, (Washington, D.C.) 5-19.

67. Christopher Farrell, Michael Mandel, Joseph Weber, Michele Galen and Gary McWilliams, "The Economic Crisis of Urban America," *Business Week*, May 18, 1992, 38–41, quotation on 40.

68. B. Drummond Ayres, Jr., "Conservatives Forge New Strategy to Challenge Affirmative Action," *New York Times*, February 16, 1995, A1, A11.

69. U.S. Department of Commerce, Bureau of the Census, *Poverty in the United States: 1991* (Washington, D.C.: GPO, August 1992), Tables 2 and 3.

70. U.S. Department of Commerce, Bureau of the Census, *Money Income of Households, Families, and Persons in the United States: 1990* (Washington, D.C.: GPO, September, 1991), Table 1.

71. U.S. Department of Commerce, Bureau of the Census, *Money Income of Households, Families, and Persons in the United States, 1991* (Washington, D.C.: GPO, August 1992), Table 1.

72. U.S. Department of Commerce, Bureau of the Census, *Money Income of Households, Families, and Persons in the United States, 1990* (Washington, D.C.: GPO, September, 1991), Table 1.

73. U.S. Department of Commerce, Bureau of the Census, *Money Income of Households, Families, and Persons in the United States, 1991* (Washington, D.C.: GPO, August 1992), Table 1.

74. Joye Mercer, "Political TrendLetter: Blacks Lag in Income, But Graduation Rates Increase," *Focus: The Monthly Magazine of the Joint Center for Political and Economic Studies* 23, 4 (April 1995).

75. Ibid.

76. Christopher Farrell and Michael Mandel in New York, Michael Schroeder in Pittsburgh, Joseph Weber in Philadelphia, Michele Galen in New York, Gary McWilliams in Boston, and bureau reports, "The Economic Crisis of Urban America," *Business Week*, May 18, 1992, 38–43.

77. Ibid.

78. Mercer, "Political TrendLetter: Blacks Lag in Income, But Graduation Rates Increase".

79. Christopher Farrell with Michael Mandel in New York, and bureau reports, "Why Are We So Afraid Of Growth?: Conventional Wisdom Doesn't Hold Anymore," *Business Week*, May 16, 1994, 62-65, 68, 69, 72.

80. Miriam Hill, "Credit Card, Car Loans to Cost More: But Fed's Interest Rate Hike Shouldn't Affect Mortgages," *Plain Dealer*, May 18, 1994, 1–A, 12–A.

81. "Clinton Nominees May Shift Fed Policy: New Members Could Ease Hard Line on Rates," April 23, 1994, 1–C.

82. Hill, "Credit Card, Car Loans to Cost More," 1–A. "The Federal Reserve Bank of Cleveland was the only one of 12 district banks that didn't ask the Fed's board of governors in Washington, D.C. to raise the discount rate by 0.5%." The Cleveland Fed would not explain its decision.

83. Aaron Bernstein in New York, with bureau reports, "Why America Needs Unions But Not the Kind It Has Now," *Business Week*, May 23, 1994, 70, 71, 74, 78, 82.

84. Ibid, 70.

85. Frances Fox Piven and Richard A. Cloward, *The New Class War: Reagan's Attack on the Welfare State and Its Consequences* (New York: Pantheon Books, 1982).

86. Tom Diemer and Sandra Livingston, "Report Finds Wage Gap Growing," *Plain Dealer*, June 3, 1994, 1–C.

87. Keith Bradsher, "Gap in Wealth in U.S. Called Widest in West," *New York Times*, April 17, 1995, A1, C4, points out, "Even class societies like Britain, which inherited large differences in income and wealth over centuries going back to their feudal pasts, now have greater economic equality than the United States, according to the latest economic and statistical research, much of which is to be published soon."

88. Diemer and Livingston, "Wage Gap Growing," June 3, 1994.

89. Rosenbaum, "Welfare: Who Gets It? How Much Does It Cost?" *New York Times*, March 23, 1995, p. A 11.

90. Ibid.

91. Bureau of Labor Statistics, *Employment and Earnings, 1991* (Washington, D.C.: GPO, January, 1991), Table 5; and, Bureau of Labor Statistics, Employment and Earnings, 1991, (Washington, D.C., October, 1991), Table A-44.

92. Bureau of Labor Statistics, *Handbook of Labor Statistics* (Washington, D.C.: GPO, June 1985), 69, 71–73; Bureau of Labor Statistics, *Employment and Earnings, 1991* (Washington, D.C.: GPO, January, 1991), Table 5; and, Bureau of Labor

Statistics, *Employment and Earnings, 1991* (Washington, D.C., October, 1991), Table A-44.

93. Farrell et al., "The Economic Crisis of Urban America."

94. Karen De Witt, "Study Sees High Rate of Dismissal for Black Government Workers," *New York Times*, April 20, 1995, A15.

95. Ibid.

96. Kilborn, "Women and Minorities Still Face 'Glass Ceiling': White Men's Fears Are Barrier, Report Says," data from pie chart, "The Manager Class."

97. Editorial, "Shattering the Ceiling," *New York Times*, March 17, 1995, A14.

98. Cf. Diana B. Henriques, "Ties That Bind: His Directors, Her Charity: Did Joining the Agees' Cause Make It Hard to Say No in the Board Room?" *New York Times*, March 21, 1995, C1, C4.

99. E.g., William Celis 3d, "Dean's Note Indicates Anita Hill Will Quit," *New York Times*, March 17, 1995, A 6. (Speaking at the 70th Annual National Bar Association, August 4, 1995 at Baltimore, Maryland, Ms. Hill indicated she was returning to her law school teaching position in Oklahoma.)

100. Robert Pear, "2 House Panels Clear Bills to Revamp Welfare Laws: The Idea That the Poor Have a Right to Aid Comes under G.O.P. Attack," *New York Times*, March 9, 1995, A9; Eric Schmitt, "School Lunch Bill Leaves Out Military Children: The Fine Print—A Periodic Look Behind the Law," *New York Times*, March 9, 1995, A9; Michael Wines, "Republicans in Senate Set Budget Cuts," *New York Times*, March 11, 1995, A8; Robert Pear, "Shalala Says Welfare Bill Is Improper," *New York Times*, March 11, 1995, A8; Sabrina Eaton, "GOP Targets $17 Billion in Social Aid: Kasich Unveils Next $100 Billion in Cuts as House OK's First Round," *Plain Dealer*, March 17, 1995, A1, A4; Jerry Gray, "Republicans Push Their Plan Ahead With Budget Advances On 2 Fronts; House Gives Final Approval to Trims This Year and Moves to Pay for a Tax Cut," *New York Times*, March 17, 1995, A1, A9.

101. Peter T. Kilborn, "White Males and the Manager Class: Report Finds Prejudices Block Progress of Women and Minorities—Why Most Senior Executives Are Still White and Male," *New York Times*, March 17, 1995, A7.

102. Laura B. Randolph, "The Untold Story of Black Women in The Gulf War: African-Americans Helped Redefine the Role of Females in the Armed Forces," *Ebony*, September 1991, 100–107.

103. However, Supreme Court Justice Scalia has described himself as a "textualist," eschewing the U.S. court interpretive practice institutionalized in the 1803 *Marbury v. Madison* case and desiring an approach that does not include "a guarantee of any substantive rights." Reported by Linda Greenhouse, "At the Bar: Justice Scalia, Cheerfully, Tells What's Behind Following the Letter of the Law," *New York Times*, March 17, 1995, B12.

104. Linda Greenhouse, "Justices Limit Government Appeals on Behalf of Individuals: Policy Alone, the Court Says, Doesn't Bring Legal Standing," *New York Times*, March 22, 1995.

105. "Celebrating Our Legacy—A Vision for the 21st Century: Academia and Civil Rights Organizations Coalescing to Navigate the Road to Racial Justice," July 6–8, 1995, Marriott City Center, Minneapolis, Minnesota, Co-Sponsored by the NAACP and the National Bar Association.

106. 63 U.S.L.W. 4523 (June 12, 1995).

107. Steven A. Holmes, "Government Acts to Set Its Policy on Race Programs: Response to High Court—Direction from Justice Deptartment Is Due, but Some Agencies Are Moving with Haste," June 24, 1995, A1, A7.

108. Barbara Arnwine, "From the Executive Director," 5. *Committee Report: 30th Anniversary Edition 1963–1993*, Lawyers Committee for Civil Rights Under Law. 5, nos. 5 and 6 (1994): 5.

109. Peter T. Kilborn, "Take This Job—Up from Welfare: It's Harder and Harder; The Big American Leap into the Middle Class Is Not Made on $225 a Week," *New York Times*, April 16, 1995, Sec. 4; 1, 4.

110. U.S. Department of Labor, Bureau of Labor Statistics, *Employment and Earnings, January 1992* (Washington, D.C.: GPO, 1992), Table 21.

111. U.S. Department of Labor, Bureau of Labor Statistics, *Employment and Earnings, January, 1991* (Washington, D.C.: GPO, 1991), Table 21, 184.

112. Ibid.

113. David H. Swinton, "The Economic Status of African Americans during the Reagan-Bush Era: Withered Opportunities, Limited Outcomes, and Uncertain Outlook," in *The State of Black America 1993* (New York: National Urban League, 1993), 135–200, 191.

114. David G. Savage, "High Court Lets Stand Reverse Bias Rulings," *Plain Dealer*, April 18, 1995, A1, A6; Linda Greenhouse, "Ruling That Bias Plan Is Unfair Stands: Justices Won't Review Ruling on Program to Promote More Blacks," *New York Times*, April 18, 1995, C23, noting the rulings in the cases of *Arrington v. Wilks*, No. 94–1397 and *Martin v. Wilks*, No. 94–1422.

115. U.S. Department of Commerce, Bureau of the Census, *Current Population Survey*, (Washington, D.C.: GPO, March 1990).

116. Ibid.

117. *New York Times*, "With Rights Act Comes Fight to Clarify Congress's Intent," November 18, 1991.

118. *Plain Dealer*, "Abortion Foes Yes, Quotas No: Rights Panel Shifted Under Thomas," July 14, 1991, 1A, 18A.

119. 115 S.Ct. 1776 (Decided May 15, 1995).

120. Jane Mayer and Jill Abramson, *Strange Justice: The Selling of Clarence Thomas* (Boston/New York: Houghton Mifflin Company, 1994).

121. Ibid., 170–186.

122. *St. Mary's Honor Center et al. v. Hicks*, 61 USLW 4782; 113 S.Ct. 2742 (decided June 25, 1993). It was noted in the case that the *McDonnell Douglas* framework is fully applicable to racial-discrimination-in-employment claims under 42 U.S.C. Sec. 1983 and 42 U.S.C. Sec. 1981.

123. 411 U.S. 792 (1973).

124. *Hicks*, 113 S. Ct. 2742, at 2747.

125. Linda Greenhouse, "Gavel Rousers-Farewell to the Old Order in the Court: The Right Goes Activist and the Center Is a Void," *New York Times*, July 2, 1995, Sec. 4; 1, 4.

126. David J. Garrow, "On Race, It's Thomas v. an Old Ideal," *New York Times*, July 2, 1995, Sec. 4; 1, 5.

127. Linda Greenhouse, "Warren E. Burger Is Dead at 87; Was Chief Justice for 17 Years: Nixon Appointee Eased Supreme Court Away From Liberal Era," *New*

York Times, June 26, 1995, A1, A4; *New York Times,* "A New Order Reigns On the Highest Court," July 2, 1995, A1.

128. *New York Times,* "Income Data Show Years of Erosion for U.S. Workers," September 7, 1992, A1, 20; Michael Harrington, *The New American Poverty* (New York: Penguin Books, 1985).

129. John E. Jacob, *The State of Black America, 1992* (New York: The National Urban League, 1992).

130. Lenneal J. Henderson, "Empowerment through Enterprise: African-American Business Development," in *State of Black America 1993* (New York: National Urban League, 1993) 91–108; Swinton, "The Economic Status of African Americans," 173; U.S. Department of Commerce, Bureau of the Census, *Money Income of Households, Families, and Persons in the United States: 1991* (Washington, D.C.: GPO, August 1992), Table 34.

131. Swinton, 141; U.S. Department of Commerce, Bureau of the Census *Survey of Minority-Owned Businesses: Black* (Washington, D.C.: GPO, 1987), and U.S. Department of Commerce, Bureau of the Census, *The Statistical Abstracts of the United States, 1990* (Washington, D.C.: GPO, Table 859) 521.

132. Victor Perlo, "Black Capitalism" in *Economics of Racism USA* (New York: International Publishers, 1975), 179–195.

133. But see Raymond Hernandez, "Easing the Way for Home Businesses," *New York Times,* March 20, 1995, A 13.

134. Cf. Jerry Gray, "G.O.P. Courts the Black Candidates: Getting Ready to Win More Votes Among Minorities in 1996," *New York Times,* March 13, 1994, A9; but also see Steven A. Holmes, "Dole Helped Ex-Aide With Program He Now Denounces: Foes Say Dole's Stands on Minority Contracts Shift with Political Winds," *New York Times,* March 23, 1995, A10.

135. Cf. Jonathan Gaw, "SBA Lending Soars in Cleveland Area," *Plain Dealer,* March 25, 1995, C1.

136. Jennifer Winkler, "The Small Business Administration's 8(a) Program: An Historical Perspective on Affirmative Action," *George Washington University Journal of Public Administration: Policy Perspectives,* 2, no. 1 (Spring 1995): 17-29.

137. Also see Robert D. Hershey Jr., "U.S. Regulators Drop a Proposal Aimed at Bias in Banks' Lending," *New York Times,* April 19, 1995, A1, C2.

138. 15 U.S.C., Section 632 (and Rules and Regulations promulgated pursuant thereto).

139. Rick Hampton, "'They Could Only Break Our Hearts,'" *Plain Dealer,* August 13, 1965, C1.

140. 42 U.S.C.A. Sec. 2000e note (1965).

141. 448 U.S. 448; 100 S.Ct. 2758 (1980).

142. 109 S.Ct. 706 (1989).

143. *Slaughter House Cases* of 1872, *The Butchers' Benevolent Assc. of New Orleans v. The Crescent City Live Stock Landing and Slaughter House Company,* 83 U.S. (16 Wall.) 36, 21 L.Ed. 394 at p. 410 (1873).

144. 109 S. Ct. 706, 721 at 720, citing *The Slaughter House Cases,* 16 Wall. at 68.

145. 83 U.S. (16 Wall.) 36, 21 L.Ed. 394 at p. 410 (1873).

146. 109 S.Ct. at 721.

147. Ibid.

148. 109 S.Ct. at 724.

149. 109 S.Ct. at 725.

150. Pub. L. 95 - 28, 91 Stat. 116, 42 U.S.C. Sec. 6701 et seq. (Act).

151. 109 S.Ct. at 725.

152. Ibid.

153. 109 S.Ct. at 731.

154. 109 S.Ct. at 754.

155. 109 S.Ct. at 745.

156. Ibid.

157. Ibid.

158. 109 S.Ct. at 754.

159. Ibid. at 744.

160. John A. Turner Jr. and Courtney M. Billups, "Minority Business Development Strategies: A Mosaic Formula," *NBA, National Bar Association Magazine* 8, no. 6 (November December 1994): 16-19.

161. Ibid.

162. 488 U.S. 479, 102 L.Ed. 2d 854, 109 S.Ct.706 (1989).

163. 113 S.Ct. 2297 (1993).

164. Ibid., 17. Also see, John A. Turner, Esq. "Supreme Court to Review *Adarand v. Pena*," *NBA National Bar Association Magazine* 8, no. 6 (November/December, 1995): 15.

165. Turner and Billups, "Minority Business Development Strategies," at 17.

166. Ibid., 63 U.S.L.W. (June 12, 1995); Sharon Dukes, "Michael Rogers: Taking the Minority Business Development Agency in the Right Direction," *NBA, National Bar Association Magazine* 9, no. 1 (January/February, 1995): 20, 21 and 22.

167. Steven A. Holmes, "Clinton to Review Federal Affirmative Action Programs," *New York Times*, February 25, 1995, A9; Steven A. Holmes, "Review of Affirmative Action Gains Support: Three Liberals Agree to Reconsider Federal Preferences Extended by Race and Sex," *New York Times*, February 27, 1995, A10. The three liberals were stated in the article to be:
"Willie L. Brown Jr. the Speaker of the California Assembly; Senator Daniel Patrick Moynihan of New York, and representative Kweisi Mfume of Maryland, the former head of the Black Congressional Caucus"; also Todd S. Purdum, "Defending Hiring Preferences, Clinton Details Plan to Review Them," *New York Times*, March 24, 1995, A11.

168. James G. Thomson, letter to the editor, "Don't Blame All White Men," *New York Times*, March 21, 1995, A14.

169. E.g., Steven A. Holmes, "Pentagon Seeks to End Preference Program: At First, Success, but Later, Criticism for a Pilot Affirmative-Action Plan," *New York Times*, May 1, 1995, A12.

170. Bob Herbert, "In America—The Wrong Target: Affirmative-Action Isn't Anti-White," *New York Times*, April 5, 1995, A17.

171. Peter T. Kilborn, "A Family Spirals Downward in Waiting for Agency to Act," *New York Times*, February 11, 1995, A1, A7.

172. Maria Mallory with Stephanie Anderson Forest, "Waking Up to a Major Market: The 1990 Census has Spotlighted the Power of Black Consumers," *Business Week*, March 23, 1992, 70–73.

173. Ibid.

174. Ibid.

175. Ibid., 73.

176. Elizabeth Lesly with Maria Mallory, "Inside the Black Business Network: A Far-Flung Web of Entrepreneurs and Executives Is Driving African American Economic Growth," *Business Week*, November 29, 1993, 70–81.

177. William Glasgall with Michael Schroeder and Alan Fine, "Is This Any Way to Invest in South Africa?: Steve Goodwin's Mutual Fund Hopes to Raise $125 Million. But It's Off to a Rocky Start," *Business Week*, February 28, 1994, 90–92.

178. Chuck Hawkins with Leah Nathans Spiro, "Pru Securities Isn't Secure Yet, Investigations of Its Limited-Partnership Deals Are Nowhere Near Over," *Business Week*, September 7, 1992, 82–84.

179. Chuck Hawkins with Leah Nathans Spiro, "Pru Securities: A Final Deal May Be Elusive: States Are Not Yet Behind the SEC's Proposed Settlement," *BusinessWeek*, August 2, 1993, 76.

180. Larry Light, "How Much Prudence Is Good for Prudential?" *Business Week*, July 13, 1992, 124–126. Also see Stephanie Anderson Forest and Zachara Schiller with Phillip L. Zweig, "Small Towns, Big Losses: Did a Texas Brokerage Mislead Ohio Officials about High-Risk Mortgage-Backed Securities?" *Business Week*, December 6, 1993, 158–162.

181. Linda Himelstein and Michael Schroeder, "The SEC Resolves to Bow Out: Battered by the Courts, It Won't Give Advice on Proxy Proposals," *Business Week*, November 20, 1993, 124.

182. Gary Weiss, "The Big Bad Big Board: Academic Critics Charge That the NYSE Hoards Data and Plays Dirty," *Business Week*, April 26, 1993, 80, 81.

183. Leah Nathans Spiro, "The $1 Billion Kiss-Off: Will Lehman Be Able to Make It on Its Own?" *Business Week*, February 7, 1994, 106.

184. *Bloomberg Business News*, "Moody's Downgrades Its Rating for Debt of Lehman Brothers," *New York Times*, March 22, 1995, C2; also see Harris Collingwood, "Salomon: The SEC Points Its Finger," *Business Week*, December 14, 1992, 46; Leah Nathans Spiro, in New York, "Make It $40 Million: That's What Ex-CEO Gutfreund Claims Salomon Owes Him," *Business Week*, January 24, 1994, 85.

185. Jerry Gray, "Effort to Weaken Lawsuit Bill Defeated: Senate G.O.P. Protects Measure to Discourage Claims by Investors," *New York Times*, June 27, 1995, A11; Jane Fritsch, "The Grass Roots, Just a Free Phone Call Away: Special Pleaders—The Lobbyist's Art," *New York Times*, June 23, 1995, A1, A11.

186. *Business Week*, "The *Business Week* 1000: America's Most Valuable Companies," January 1993 (Special Bonus Issue).

187. Lynn Norment, "Black Presidents in Fortune 500 Companies," *Ebony*, January, 1994, 100–108.

188. National Bar Association—70th Annual Convention, "Economic and Political Empowerment: Justice for *Our* Time!" Hyatt Regency Baltimore, Baltimore, Maryland, July 30–August 5, 1995.

189. U.S. Department of Labor, Robert Reich, Secretary, *OFCPP: Making EEO and Affirmative Action Work*, Washington, D.C., September 1993, 4.

190. Steven A. Holmes, "Once-Tough Chief of Affirmative Action Agency Is Forced to Change Tack," *New York Times*, August 6, 1995, A 13.

191. "Woman Heads Bar Association," *New York Times* August 11, 1995, A13.

192. Steven A. Holmes, "2 Black G.O.P. Lawmakers [Gary A. Franks, R-Connecticut and J.C. Watts, R-Oklahoma] in House Differ Slightly on Affirmative Action," *New York Times*, August 6, 1995, A13.

193. Jonathan Gaw, "Cracking the Glass Ceiling," *Plain Dealer*, April 23, 1994, 1–C. The article notes that "Many women and minorities find it easier to build their own corporations than to break glass ceilings elsewhere, local business leaders told the commission."

194. Kilborn, "A Family Spirals Downward in Waiting for Agency to Act," *New York Times*, February 11, 1995.

195. Ibid., A1.

196. Ibid.

197. 15 U.S.C. Sec. 1691 et seq.; *Credit: A Workshop Guide*, National Commission on the Observance of International Women's Year, Washington, D.C., 1977.

198. Title VIII of the Consumer Credit Protection Act.

199. *Laufman v. Oakley Building and Loan Co.*, 408 F. Supp. 489 (S.D.Ohio 1976); see also 12 CFR Part 202.

200. Saul Hansell, "Merchants of Debt: This Credit Card Is Tailored to *You*," *New York Times*, July 2, 1995, Sec. 3, 1, 12.

201. Created by the Legal Services Corporation Act of 1974 (42 U.S.C. 2996 Sec. 100 a.2.

202. The Bankruptcy Reform Act of 1978, Title 11, U.S.C. Ch. 1–7; Chapter 13 of the Bankruptcy Code.

203. Gloria Jean Liddell, "The New and Improved Bankruptcy Act of 1994," *NBA, National Bar Association Magazine*, 9, no. 1 (January/February 1995): 8, 9, 10, 11, 24 (Although the author also states: "However, in view of the intense lobbying on the part of the financial industry and after a review of the provisions that were passed, it does appear the scales were more heavily tipped in favor of the industry" at 24; also see P.L. 103–394 (1994).

204. E.g., *New York Times*, "Equifax in Settlement With F.T.C. on Credit Reporting," February 9, 1995, C2.

205. *Business Week*, "Credit-Rating Agencies Rate a Bit of Credit," February 14, 1994, 122.

206. David Cay Johnston, "I.R.S. Is Preparing a Tough Audit for Groups of Unwary Taxpayers," *New York Times*, July 19, 1995, A1, C6.

207. Catherine S. Manegold, "Housing Secretary Proposes Reshaping HUD to Save It: Rent Vouchers in Place of Public Housing," *New York Times*, March 21, 1995, A11.

208. David H. Swinton, "The Economic Status of African Americans: Limited Ownership and Persistent Inequality," *State of Black America 1992* (New York: The National Urban League, 1992): 61–117.

209. 42 U.S.C. 3601, et seq.

210. Diana Jean Schemo, "Suburban Taxes Are Higher for Blacks, Analysis Shows," *New York Times*, August 17, 1994, A1, A13.

211. *New York Times*, "Minority Applicants Gain on Mortgages," July 19, 1995, C6.

212. 42 U.S.C. 3610.

213. 42 U.S.C. 3612.

214. 42 U.S.C. 5301 et seq. as amended in 1977 and 1978.

215. Ibid.

216. Cf. Ohio Revised Code, Section 5321 et seq.

217. *Havens Realty Corp. v. Coleman*, 455 U.S. 363 (1982).

218. *U.S. v. City of Parma*, 494 F. Supp. 1049 (N.D. Ohio 1973).

219. But see Shawn G. Kennedy, "New Look in Housing: Refurbishing S.R.O.'s," *New York Times*, March 28, 1995, A13.

220. Ibid.

221. Keith Bradsher, "Bank Regulators Taking Close Look at Lending Risks: Reviews by a New Panel; Comptroller Urges Caution; Large Banks May Be Asked to Change Loan Policies," *New York Times*, April 9, 1995, A1, A13.

CHAPTER 4

Black Women in the World Order
of Education

EDUCATION AS A SOCIAL INSTITUTION

The court order embodied in the 1954 *Brown v. Topeka Board of Education*[1]
decision requiring that segregated schools be integrated "with all deliberate
speed", has lost its urgency over the decades. At the public school level,
students are almost as segregated racially as they were when the decision
was rendered. At the college levels, the rationale behind the *Brown* decision
has been distorted to try to destroy historically Black colleges and universities (HBCUs) that have traditionally had the most successful rate of
graduation for African Americans.

The sabotage of the HBCU started, in part, because of its mission in
assisting Blacks to get an education in the face of poverty, unequal preparation and discrimination. Many HBCUs can trace their origin to the
Freedman's Bureau which was instrumental in establishing Black colleges
such as Atlanta University, Fisk University, Hampton Institute and Howard
University.[2] As the discussion below illustrates, given the continued segregated state (*Brown* notwithstanding) of the public schools, two thirds of
which attended by African Americans are predominantly Black, it is not
inconsistent to advocate integration for the public schools and continued
existence as a countervailing education mechanism for the Black college.

Taking the logic of *Brown* to its most illogical extreme, the continuation
of the Black college now appears to depend greatly on the outcome of
interpretations of a case known as *Jake Ayers, et al. v. Kirk Fordice, Governor
of Mississippi, et al.*[3] At the trial court level in 1987, using between them
seventy-one witnesses and producing 56,700 pages of exhibits, both sides
presented evidence on educational issues such as admissions standards,
faculty and administrative staff recruitment, program duplication, on-cam-
pus discrimination, institutional funding disparities, satellite campuses,
and the like.[4]

Writing the decision in *Ayers,* Justice Byron White stated that a state that had a dual university system for Blacks and Whites had an "affirmative duty" to dismantle that system and eradicate state-attributable policies and practices that continue segregation. The remand to the trial federal court for the implementation of the *Ayers* decision could thus be ominous for the continued existence of not just the Mississippi Black colleges, but all state-supported Black colleges, which means forty-two other public Black colleges in seventeen states.[5] In addition, the *Ayers* case could jeopardize significant governmental support for some essentially private Black colleges.

In the case of Mississippi, the Supreme Court charged the lower-court judge in making any necessary subsequent findings and/or remedial measures to determine whether or not the maintenance of eight institutions of higher learning was "educationally justifiable." Educational justifiability is a concept that has to be looked at very carefully in terms of the "societal" goals and purposes of education (see the functionalist formulations of Talcott Parsons).

Addressing a conference session entitled "The Role of Historical Black Colleges in the 21st Century,"[6] Dr. Mary Benjamin maintained first of all that many advances of Blacks are due to the mass movement of the sixties, whereby Blacks gained ground toward the goals of equal employment and political savvy. The current distribution of any power and advancement won by Blacks can be traced back to the sixties when there was a coming together of people over the issues.

Dr. Benjamin describes the goals and purposes fulfilled by Black colleges and universities as crucial sources of Black empowerment. HBCUs were closely intertwined with the sixties' processes of empowerment through extensive involvement in the civil rights movement. As an example she cited the lunch counter sit-ins by the college students from North Carolina A & T, in which their chancellor was supportive. Further, she recalled that when a tired Black woman [there is now a Rosa Parks Boulevard in Detroit, Michigan, her transplanted home] sparked the Montgomery Bus Boycott, the engineer of that movement, Dr. Martin Luther King, Jr., came from Morehouse College in Atlanta.

The author, attending spring commencement exercises of two twenty-one-year-olds, her daughter and a niece, at their respective HBCUs, observed that both of the persons giving the commencement addresses were alumni of the two institutions. One was a federal appellate court judge,[7] and the other was the state's Secretary of Health and Human Resources.[8] Such examples prove Dr. Benjamin and others correct when they say that "black colleges fill crucial needs—role models, remedial instruction, nurturing environments."[9] In addition, the commencements of both institutions of higher learning demonstrated a patriotism and loyalty supportive of the country's values as their respective University Choirs sang Peter

Wilhousky's arrangement of "The Battle Hymn of The Republic."[10] Both addresses emphasized themes of hard work, self-sufficiency, perseverance, sharing and accountability to the Black college and the Black community. That Spring, General Colin L. Powell gave a similar address extolling those themes at Howard University.[11]

Dr. Benjamin proclaims that students at Black colleges were given an orientation and a set of values. Students carried with them an orientation of sharing and understanding of the community. That orientation allowed them to come back and make a difference, and Black college students became resident role models. Black colleges were key socializing agents. Economic stability and advancement were enhanced by and for those who walked through the doors of the Black college.

Now, Dr. Benjamin remonstrates, some Black students put on three-piece suits and drive down to the Black community to be role models for an hour or so before they hurry back to their suburban homes. During the sixties, Dr. Benjamin noted, little children saw people making it with college degrees, even if they ended up at the post office. Despite the lack of opportunities for many Black college graduates, the leaders were out there providing hope, right in the community. This outreach (from inside) led to *intraracial* diversity. Little children saw hope, in a socioeconomically integrated society. Black college students had a psychological attachment to the Black community. Dr. Benjamin decries the fact that now Blacks drive to inner-city churches, where their luxury cars are in parking lots surrounded by fences, but the educationally prepared leadership potential is absent.

Dr. Benjamin listed five ways in which Black colleges could continue to fulfill goals directed at serving the Black community and thereby obtaining full and equal treatment. The first is in the preservation and the transmission of the Black heritage. The second is through the education and socialization of leaders as change agents. The third is by providing advocacy for causes crucial to the Black community—speaking out when others are afraid and serving as a worker for people. Establishing a data base sensitive to Blacks that helps develop responsive policy and shape needed services is a fourth way that Black colleges can serve the Black community. The fifth, but not necessarily the final, way in which Black colleges can help Blacks is by serving as an institutional catalyst for the Black community—remaining on the cutting edge of informational and networking services necessary for the enlightenment and awareness of Blacks.

Dr. Benjamin summarized her lecture with the admonition that in order for the Black community to remain viable, we must ensure that the Black college remains viable. The two are interdependent and should provide mutual support.

To Justice Clarence Thomas's credit (whatever his reasoning may have been, e.g., continued segregation à la Justice Scalia), his concurrence in the *Ayers* case at least appeared to be concerned with the continued viability of the Black college. Justice Thomas agreed with the Court that the state did not have an obligation to dismantle a dual system of higher education just by the adoption of race-neutral policies. Agreeing that that was the appropriate standard to apply in the higher education context, Justice Thomas stated that he wrote separately to emphasize that because the standard "does not compel the elimination of all observed racial imbalance, it portends neither the destruction of the historically black colleges nor the severing of those institutions from their distinctive histories and traditions."[12] In addition, Justice Thomas said that although he agreed that a state was "not constitutionally *required* to maintain its historically black institutions as such . . . I do not understand our opinion to hold that a state is forbidden from doing so."[13]

Justice Thomas's consideration for Black colleges stemming from their unique purposes seems to have support from other levels of the federal government. For example, Congress approved a loan waiver allowing Black colleges who have a higher student default waiver than earlier mandated to retain their eligibility to participate in the federal student loan program.[14]

Despite such supportive gestures, the institution of education has a long way to go before racial equity in education can be achieved.[15] Despite the fact that the Black college is still so important to the Black community as well as the Black student, it is grossly underfunded compared to White institutions of higher learning both public and private,[16] a primary reason the *Ayers* case was brought in the first place with regard to Mississippi's public college financing structure. Further, as is illustrated below, even with increases in educational achievement such increases do not automatically translate into economic parity for Black women.

For instance, although Black women have been somewhat more successful in attaining baccalaureate degrees than Black men,[17] their incomes are still significantly lower, despite their higher levels of education. In fact, White males without a college degree earn more than Black females with one.[18] And, although the percentage of poor family heads who hold high school diplomas had risen from about 37 percent in 1979 to over 50 percent in 1990, the percentage of such family heads who held no job decreased from approximately 58 percent to 55 percent during that eleven year period.[19] Thus, although diplomas among the poor are going up, that increase is not positively affecting the unemployment rate.

If secondary and elementary schools have failed, it is because Blacks lost that part of the curriculum that told them about themselves. In their edited work, Allen, Epps and Haniff write that Black colleges are particularly strong in the dimension of the psychosocial development of Black students.[20]

The Black Church and the HBCU "are it." The Black Church is in the middle of the Black Community standing as a citadel and thus its mission has to include education and service to the Black community; further, that mission is sacred. As is pointed out by Sociologist Patricia Hill-Collins (1991, 147), the mission of education for African American communities serves as a "powerful symbol" of crucial connections between "self, change, and empowerment." Hill-Collins also describes how African American women such as Anna Julia Cooper (*A Voice from the South*, 1892), Mary McLeod Bethune (Bethune-Cookman College), Nannie Burroughs (Black women's education advocate) and Johnetta Cole (first Spellman College president who was a Black woman) were instrumental in the evolution of education as a rallying point for community development in the Black community (1991, 147). Also, according to Hill-Collins, education provided not just the technical skills related to African American employability, but in and of itself, education was an expression of the "political activism" that could be used to "uplift" Black people.

As African Americans have pinned most of their hopes on obtaining a higher standard of living upon education, the demise of educational opportunities and financial aid is a loss of crisis proportions. Fortunately, the federal government's Department of Education refrained from outlawing racially based scholarships. In fact, it even put a notice in the Federal Register on February 23, 1994, specifically permitting "a college to award financial aid based on race or national origin as part of affirmative action to remedy the effects of its past discrimination without waiting for a finding to be made by the Office for Civil Rights (OCR), a court, or a legislative body, if the college has a strong basis in evidence of discrimination justifying the use race-targeted scholarships."[21] Although the Office of Education endorsed not waiting for the courts in using race-targeted scholarships given the appropriate circumstances, the courts, specifically, the Fourth Circuit of the U.S. Court of Appeals, proceeded expeditiously to demolish the use of such scholarships at the University of Maryland at College Park on October 27, 1994.[22] (The Supreme Court declined to address the issue on May 22, 1995, after the state of Maryland appealed to it in order to continue its use of the racially based scholarship. Thus the Fourth Circuit decision stands—if not the law of the land, at least the law of the Fourth Circuit's states).[23] This sad scenario signifies that New World Order courts will take up the cause célèbre of educational exclusion where another potential arm of the New World Order leaves off.

In such manner, minority education programs aimed at crosscultural awareness, curriculum enrichment, ethnic heritage observance, esteem building, environmental compensation, academic amelioration and community involvement are being stripped of any African American thrust or focus. Further, the reaffirmation of a convoluted version of White maleness by some is likewise threatening the "political correctness" of minority and women's issues.[24] These conditions thus obviate the purpose for which the Black political activists struggled and fought. That purpose, to acknowledge and recognize previously ignored African American contributions as well as to facilitate African American access to high-quality, mainstream educational subject matter and processes has been thereby trivialized and averted. That is why there is renewed interest in sustaining and (re)developing educational institutions and programs owned and operated by African Americans even at the pre-college level. For instance, Black boarding schools are felt by some to offer "learning, discipline, community and safety to all-black student bodies at a time many black parents are often desperate for all four."[25]

Parsonian theory (Parsons 1951) predicts that the general U.S. education institution (among others) fulfills the function of pattern maintenance. As it is presently being implemented by the courts, the patterns which, with the help of education, will be maintained are those of exclusion and isolation. The wisdom and knowledge and ability to think analytically purportedly imparted by education will be the private domain of the favored few. Public education in urban African American communities has been reduced to a warehousing function in which armed guards patrol the hallways and students live in fear. Unlike what many might attribute the source of that fear to, that fear is more accurately traced to the hopelessness and despair of entering a jobless, moneyless, dead-end world without the prospects of the bright future painted for others who are not Blacks.

The prospects for upward mobility through education are probably brighter for an Azanian (South African) youth than for an African American one. If one is conscientious, prompt, courteous, studious and committed to getting an education while enrolled in the public schools of the inner city, one might be able to land a low-level job as a clerk, janitor or laborer. If one does not have those attributes, one will not be able to land a job at all. Moody, introverted, noncommunicative European Americans might be tolerated (as youngsters too much so at times[26]); if employers are questioned, the reply probably would be made that such employees might be jerks, but they have needed job skills. An African American jerk would be hard pressed to be retained on a job, skill or no skill. Hence, Black "jerks" and "geniuses" have recourse to illicit forms of gainful activity, taking the negative consequences of such conduct as occupational hazards (see Chapters 6 and 8 on family and on crime).

African Americans, not having the benefit of anything but babysitting, car-wash or cleaning experience to supplement their impaired educational background, will be unable to compete in New World Order occupational, professional and entrepreneurial settings. The actual knowledge integral to the education experience may not even be as important as the fact that relative deprivation, as described by sociologist Robert K. Merton, which has become incorporated into Black education, would not lead Blacks to expect a higher level of existence. The goals set forth in their education experience would be limited ones, designated to keep them satisfied at performing low-level service and manufacturing jobs at best.

African Americans are sufficiently separated from their European American age cohorts to eliminate significant exposure to life enhancing educational and economic opportunities. For example, when the author's oldest daughter was a high school senior, she went to a financial aid seminar. The daughter of one of the European-American fathers present was still only in the ninth grade. This type of preparation for the future is missing from the lives of many African American children, who are not being single-mindedly prepared to rule the world, new or old.

Indeed, the socialization of African American females, dominance conjectures to the contrary, does not for the most part include becoming equipped for world leadership. Subservience and obsequiousness are more prevalent in the young African American girl's training. Conformity and obedience are the foundational values emphasized from the time an African American female enters kindergarten. "Works well with others," "Obeys the rules of the school" and "Is neat and clean" (evaluative criteria from the author's kindergarten report card) are working- and middle-class prerequisites that one's failure to perform can cause one to flunk kindergarten. Even on the "performance-based tests" included now in many ninth-grade curricula, "civic deportment and responsibility" are requirements to be passed along with English and math (the implementation of "outcome-based education" is mandated for any school district that receives state or federal dollars under Goals 2000[27] or H.R. 1804). Ingenuity, creativity, innovation, independence, autonomy and individual self-motivation are characteristics that seem to be valued only in elite private schools or suburban schools servicing the upper and upper-middle classes. Yet, they are the same qualities sought in the highest-level managers, directors, vice-presidents, presidents and chairmen(*sic*) of the board for corporate leadership. A Black woman who has these qualities has them usually in spite of her education and life experiences rather than because of them.

Further, the United States has developed class-related speech dichotomies as functional for a person's categorization, as in the days of Professor Henry Higgins and Eliza Doolittle of "My Fair Lady" fame. The "Black Speak" of the inner-city public school is repugnant to employment counselors and job interviewers, who selectively screen applicants for just such attributes. A young Black woman who has not learned to emulate the predominant group's speech patterns during the course of her education will find herself at a disadvantage when seeking one of the higher paying jobs. Again, schools in which most of the day has been spent fighting despair, hopelessness, drug trafficking and gangs with only the weapons of financial neglect, substandard structures, inadequate educational materials, out-of-date technological equipment, underpaid teachers, authoritarian administrators and overly politicized boards will not have taught a little

Black girl about the subtleties and dualities of language. Therefore, she will not be able to adapt her speech to whatever variation of U.S. societal culture she finds herself in. The education institution will thus have failed her but not necessarily the society for which it is functioning. The pattern maintenance of the established society is being continued, because the African American female has been prepared to remain on the bottom. Through this type of societal servicing, the education institution is performing its designated function. Those trained for leadership roles are the children of those already on top, and the status quo is preserved.

This chapter also presents evidence that education is inextricably tied to economics.[28] A University of Michigan study that matched children by income, race, family type and mother's education found that income was the greatest determinant of a child's I.Q. (Intelligence Quotient).[29] The findings led a Yale University psychologist to conclude that such an identified gap between the I.Q.'s of low income and high income children was one of "many compelling reasons" why policies are needed "to end childhood poverty." (At the time of this study, the poverty line was determined by the Bureau of the Census to include, for example, a family of four with an income of less than $13,924.[30]) As far as school-district policy is concerned, poverty is an accepted and court-approved distinction between students in different districts.[31] This being the case, it is unsurprising when a 70,000 student school district, 70 percent Black, reeling from the loss of half its students in a thirty year period, the loss of 93,000 manufacturing jobs in a fifteen year period, the loss of a viable property economic base during that same period and the loss of hope from its constituency also suffers the loss of its autonomy to a takeover by the state.[32] Such vulnerability made the district much more vulnerable to New World Order educational experimentation such as privatization and voucher plans.[33] Under such conditions, the obtaining and maintenance by students of acceptable performance scores would seem to be the *performance* of a miracle. In addition, when students respond to such conditions with weapons[34] that are congruent to their "Wild, Wild West" neighborhoods, which have been spawned by the adult Dillingers of the New World Order, they are further banned for the year or forever to alternative schools with others of their ilk.[35]

Of course, the very definition, assessment and use of I.Q. and other standardized tests have been challenged as being racially biased[36] against Blacks.[37] Asa Hilliard, dean of San Francisco State University, helped to mount an objection, albeit unsuccessful, to the way I.Q. tests were used to disproportionately place Black children in EMR (educably mentally retarded) classes.[38] It has further been asserted that the higher average poverty rate of Black children makes it easier to place them disproportionately in EMR classes with impunity.[39] Purported differences in I.Q. scores between African Americans and European Americans also have been used to rationalize a "benign neglect" policy perspective with regard to the former group in the education institution[40] (also see Chapter 5). Sociologists have refuted assertions that inherent genetic inferiority in I.Q. means that nothing can be done to increase the education levels of Blacks in the United States.[41]

There are indications that there are other wide-ranging ramifications of I.Q. and testing. For instance, the Los Angeles chapter of Mensa (an organization for people whose I.Q.'s are in the top 2 percent range of the population) ran into difficulty when its newsletter published articles that advocated euthanasia for "defective" people.[42] The use of testing for the "merit-based" placement of individuals in educational and employment settings is challenged by the fact that in some instances such test results are patently ignored.[43] For instance, it has been pointed out that the children of European American alumni ("legacies") are chosen above Asians with higher average S.A.T. scores at highly ranked colleges and universities.[44] This phenomenon renders proclamations of institutional meritocracy, in education or elsewhere, hypocritical. The conclusive decisions based upon standardized testing such as I.Q. and S.A.T. scores are shown to be even more spurious by findings such as that "statistical studies have established that [S.A.T.] test scores are calibrated to income and ZIP codes; students coming from families with incomes of over $50,000 will perform on the average of 25 percent better than students coming from families with incomes of $12,000."[45] These figures lead one to conclude that standardized testing is both formulated and focused towards certain desired student groups. When it unintentionally supports the selection of student groupings (e.g., Asians) who are not so highly valued, the test is conveniently eliminated.

The impact of racism on education generally makes elusive a supportive educational climate for African American students at any level. Forty years after the 1954 *Brown* decision, its detractors were still complaining about everything from its use of "racial classifications" to avoid the segregation that had existed since the 1896 *Plessy v. Ferguson* decision to the fact that the "court waxed sociological, citing such data as the preference of some black children for white dolls" [and] "the effects of segregation on children's abilities to learn."[46] On the other hand, it was also reported that "40 years after the Brown decision, two-thirds of black students attend predominantly minority schools."[47] Complicating the issue is the fact that the African American students who are the first to integrate an educational setting whether at the public school[48] or college[49] level, are subjected many times to the most dehumanizing harassment.[50] In *Goss v. Lopez*,[51] an Ohio case, the Supreme Court provides guidelines surrounding school suspensions of Black children from school for the same infractions for which White children were not suspended. Thus, there are indications that even the goal of integration poses dilemmas for African Americans.

African American educators have noted the need to address intransigent problems with integrated educational settings (Hale, 1982; Kunjufu, 1984), and there are movements to develop educational organizations that foster Afrocentricity (see Warfield-Coppock's book, *Adolescent Rites of Passage,* 1990). Along the lines of supportive educational processes for African American youth, activities such as those of the author's sorority's, "Teen Lift"[52] program are found in some sectors of the Black community. Such programs are designed to supplement the educational curriculums found in the public schools in order to assist young African Americans make the transition to the adult world.

Still, as long as education remains a public function essentially monopolized by the government, the government controls "the medium and the message" for most practical purposes. However, there is a rise of "community or charter" schools, which are run by management teams of teachers, parents and community activists but are funded by the government, in several states.[53] Community schools are funded by the state in an amount equal to the per-pupil funding formula in whichever school district the community school is located. Community schools require that the pupils be residents of the same school district as the community school. There are ostensibly no admission requirements, and all residents would theoretically be eligible to attend on a first come, first served basis. The charter or community school would have to meet basic state educational goals in order to continue, or it is supposed to be disbanded. Otherwise, the management team controls the school's budget and develops its curriculum.

The main fear concerning such schools is that they would primarily end up in the hands of those who are better-off and that fear, given U.S. educational history, is probably well founded. The temptation to privatize the public school through the use of private contractors is too much for a profit-driven society to resist if left to its own devices.[54]

Nevertheless, the idea might be a mechanism through which perspectives such as Afrocentricity could be institutionalized to a greater extent within the curriculum, climate and character of the public school. The adoption of the community school concept in Afrocentric neighborhoods would require a high degree of organization and mobilization of residents for fruition (see Chapter 2). Such organization would require a degree of political sophistication, resolve and ingenuity reminiscent of the sixties. Still, the situation is so desperate in some African American neighborhoods, which currently resemble abandoned ghost towns of the Old West after rampages by Doc Holiday, Wyatt Earp and Billy the Kid, that some such neighborhoods might be tempted to try to effectuate that goal. The business community, which currently holds the key to many school systems, is likewise so highly politicized, organized and sophisticated that the chances of success for the creation of truly Afrocentric charter schools are remote, however. The proponents of a *mainstream* "Western Civilization" education at all levels of schooling are significantly more wealthy and powerful as they attempt to support their curricular agendas.[55] On the other hand, funding for public[56] as well as higher[57] education for African Americans in inner-city schools is minuscule when compared to the averages for European Americans who generally are in wealthier school districts.

Achievement of the Afrocentric educational goal would thus be a formidable goal to achieve inasmuch as community advocates are so easily coopted, criminalized or otherwise discredited. The forces of the New World Order are extremely intolerant of items not on its agenda and move swiftly and surely to eliminate annoying diversions.

The current governmental monopoly of education means that any lack of opportunities[58] and hardships which are caused by the government in providing education to Blacks and others must be overcome. The imminent predominance of such technological developments from the information highway[59] to biotechnology[60] to micromachines[61] to fiber optics[62] to pharmaceuticals[63] to robotics[64] to aeronautics[65] to electronics[66] or engineering[67] and even an emerging phenomenon known as "edutainment"[68] also means that African Americans cannot educate their children for twenty-first-century life in isolated forums. It means that, given the public school's past track record, they cannot rely upon the government to educate their children for the future without holding it strictly accountable. It further means that an educational climate must be fostered that will ensure that African American female students are encouraged and supported in their enrollment in the algebra, geometry, calculus, statistics, biology, geography, geology, chemistry, physics, computer, astronomy, engineering and economics classes required to master the knowledge necessary to the mastery of the aforementioned developing technologies. Further, the quality of instruction in these subjects, as well as in the fundamental ones of reading, writing, arithmetic, social studies and history, must not be compromised.

The achievement of such an academic climate, one which instructs as well as provides a respect for the African American student's heritage and humanity, is problematic because of the institutional racism inherent in the educational system. Another factor looming on the horizon is that posed by private educational ventures such as those headed by Christopher Whittle, a media entrepreneur who secured Benno C. Schmidt, Jr., a former president of Yale University, as head of the project.[69] In one projection concerning "the movement for charter schools, public schools operated autonomously at the school level," Mr. Whittle speculated that "[i]n 20 or 30 years it would not surprise me if 30 percent of U.S. schools had some relationship with a private provider."[70]

Because of the discriminatory treatment received by Black students in the past which is even manifested in their primarily segregated school settings, performance measures are less valid (accurate) and reliable for them than they are for White students; performance measures are less predictive of their future ability; and, whatever their performance measures, discrimination in other social institutions (for example, the workforce) inhibits their achievement in those forums, resulting in lower average incomes, unemployment and an inferior standard of living. In fact, it is almost a question of what comes first, the chicken or the egg. "Standardized" tests are done at the very beginning of a child's educational experience, before any meaningful educational intervention (except in Head Start, which serves only a fraction of the eligible preschool children) has been attempted to counter the debilitating effects of poverty, racism and discrimination. These tests of family, socioeconomic and cultural background are then used to place children in an essentially irreversible, "self-fulfilling" educational prophecy known as ability tracking.[71] Such tracks assure that even in an integrated setting, students are separated by family, socioeconomic and cultural (e.g., ethnic) background.

According to sociologist Talcott Parsons, the social institution of education evolved to supplant the family as a primary socialization agent. Originally, the social institution of the family provided the society with pattern maintenance as well as tension management. It was the former function of pattern maintenance that the social institution of education expropriated from the family. Much of this usurpation of the family's role had to do with the rapidly developing technological changes attendant to the Industrial Revolution. The knowledge, training and values specific to the predominantly rural family ethos quickly became outdated as far as usefulness to "the Modern Age" was concerned. The schools became the repositories of not only the new technology but also the new values needed to fuel allegiance and loyalty to the new age.[72] The schools also became the main sanctuary for the pattern maintenance of class and social position continuation. U.S. parents did not have to preselect mates and proper associates for their children. Through school tracking, living in the appropriate neighborhoods limiting school access or having sufficient funds to send their offspring to private schools did that for them. One way or another, the schools generally found ways to restrict the circles in which students interacted, developed relationships and perceived each other. In this manner, usually, the status quo was maintained.

Probably because of their infinitesimal numbers and the judges' sentimental reminiscence of "America's pioneering history," the Supreme Court in 1972 allowed the Amish, and only the Amish, to take their children out of the public schools after the eighth grade (*Wisconsin v. Yoder*).[73] This was to permit the Amish to preserve their culture as well as to prevent the irreversible contamination of their children by modern ways of living, thinking and doing. Although the Ohio Supreme Court has reversed convictions of parents for sending their children to a "non-accredited" school,[74] no other group, Black or White, has been allowed such educational autonomy from the public school system. Of course, the financially well-to-do have the alternative of private schools, so far without the subsidy of the voucher program whereby the government would subsidize such choices. According to some, including an opinion rendered by the Wisconsin Supreme Court,[75] a voucher program would use public monies to support private schools.[76] One educator observed, for instance, that "none of this does anything to address the massive needs of African-American children, most of whom will continue to be educated in public schools for the foreseeable future."[77]

Some voucher proposals give first choice to students already in private schools, then to their siblings and lastly to the children currently in public schools; it does not stretch the imagination to wonder who they are. Other proposals advocating vouchers provide that the amount of reimbursement would be made on a percentage basis in which all children would ostensibly have the same percentage. This means, for instance, that if all children were given 45 percent of whatever their respective school districts spent on education, then the child whose school district spent $4,500 per pupil and the one whose district spent $14,500 would be getting decidedly different results, which would retain the initial disparity inherent in their respective schools' funding. Vouchers and privatization would thus further deprive African American and poor children of an education. The issue is exacerbated by the fact that the United States ranks eighteenth among industrialized nations in terms of the incom gap between rich and poor children.[78] Further, the same "quality control" issues in the current race/class contextual situation in the U.S. pervade voucher supported schools as public ones.[79] And, it has been asserted that any payments to private schools with religious affiliations deprive taxpayers of First Amendment rights protected by the U.S. Constitution.[80]

Few public schools permit extensive presentation of the celebration of African American heritage conceptualized as "Afrocentricity" by Maulauna Karenga and Jacob Carruthers.[81] Even fewer incorporate Afrocentricity concepts while concurrently preserving the type of educational format that would enable students to compete with non-Black students in terms of preparation for technological advances in the New World Order.

African American males and females are forced to learn to take their subservient places in the New World Order as communicated explicitly to them by their continued geographically segregated (*Milliken v. Bradley*)[82] and financially inferior (*San Antonio Independent School District v. Rodriguez*)[83] schools. The *San Antonio* case assured the situation in which school funding could be based upon a community's revenue from property taxes. Hence, the wealth of the property owners in the various state subdivisions (counties, cities, towns and villages) determines the per-pupil funding of the respective school districts. Further, increases are dependent upon "school levies," and residents are asked to vote for or against their passage. Needless to say, in communities in which voters are loath to increase their property taxes or in which many voters do not have school-age children or in which many voters are tenants whose rent would be raised if property taxes go up and therefore vote such levies down, the results can be disastrous.[84] Because voters in more affluent districts may also be better able to afford property tax hikes as well as more sympathetic to educational funding and thus more supportive of rate increase requests, such situations as school levy failures tend to exacerbate already huge differences in per-pupil funding formulas. Even within the same county, per-pupil funding differences between school districts are as large as ten thousand dollars.

Thus, present systems of public education rely upon the same selective access economic bases as other areas.[85] Such schools generally lack even the remnant of technologically updated equipment needed to familiarize and acclimate Black children to the scientific foundations of the New World Order. Although there are questions about the value of increased school financing[86] to student performance as well as about the type of financing public schools should receive,[87] the financing of public education has surfaced as a critical equal-protection issue as relates to the poor and minorities.[88] This is particularly true in light of the fact that intradistrict remedies to disparate student treatment and educational quality are strictly limited to intradistrict resources and student populations no matter how restrictive they might be, economically and/or racially *Missouri v. Jenkins*.[89]

EDUCATIONAL REORDERING FOR THE BLACK WOMAN

An initial step in pursuing equal education for the African American woman is to become aware of the issues that interface with her ability as a student to learn in as supportive an environment as possible. As the foregoing shows, this is almost an impossible mission in the face of the segregation, disparate funding, disproportionate discipline, hostile climate, (non) standardized testing measurements and unequal resource access that hamper the ability of Black children to achieve an education.

These problems must be surmounted before a Black female student can be expected to adjust, interact and have a successful school experience. Further, once this objective is attained, the next is to have her education be as meaningful as that of others of different races and gender. The Black woman's education, in other words, should be as predictive of other economic, employment, health and political well being as it is for males and Whites.

Until this outcome is reached, the Black woman's status in the New World Order is preordained, and the social institution of education is fulfilling the objective of maintaining the status quo. In short, as long as the Black female-headed family is the poorest on average of any U.S. family type, her children will continue to be those assessed as most poorly endowed intellectually and thereby precluded from participation in the rewards of educational achievement, that is, economic prosperity. The elimination or substantial decrease of poverty among the Black woman's family would have an inverse effect upon her children's IQ evaluation, standardized test assessment and the bottom line of grades. When poverty goes down, IQ's and academic success go up. The amelioration of the Black female-headed family's socioeconomic status would result in an increase in its educational position.

SUMMARY

The achievement of that objective is further impeded by U.S. society's refusal to allow Black children to be educated with White children at the primary and secondary school level.[90] As long as this refusal exists, functioning to keep disparate the preparation of Blacks for a highly technological, literary and intellectually sophisticated world, then the Black college is needed to help ameliorate some of the devastating consequences of educational discrimination that work to inhibit learning and educational achievement. The Black college is needed because as long as glass and fiberglass ceilings exist to restrict the actualization of the education, skills, experience and talents of the Black woman in existing employment environments, then realization may have to be sought through creating new ones.[91] It is through the Black college (Hemmons 1982) that the Black woman (with the Black man) currently develops the most self-confidence and self-assurance to make such a transition.[92]

Further, it must be recognized that the need for education is a lifelong continuing effort.[93] For example, although the author took French as a second language in high school and college, after ten years of law practice she had to take a ten-week intensive Spanish course in order to get a greater appreciation of the culture and perspectives of her Hispanic students and clients (primarily Puerto Rican). The incorporation into one's life of ongoing reeducation initiatives is particularly crucial in light of the fact that human expendability has become part of the fabric of U.S. corporate planning (but see the worker-training/apprenticeship models of Europe[94]). The constant downsizing, merging and takeovers of the multinationals are creating global generations of throwaway people.

Finally, a New World Order that invests in research and development and does not invest in its human resources, as in education[95] or meaningful retraining, is doomed to failure. The only new order that will be achieved will be a disorder, a disorder that will fragmentize, delegitimize and eventually capsize the global society, making the world unlivable not only for the Black woman but for all "mankind," that is, humankind.

NOTES

1. 347 U.S. 483 (1954); *Bolling v. Sharpe*, 347 U.S. 497 (1954).

2. Alton Hornsby, Jr., *Chronology of African-American History: Significant Events and People from 1619 to the Present* (Detroit, Mich.: Gale Research, 1991), 38.

3. 112 S.Ct. 2727 (1992).

4. 112 S.Ct. 2727 at 2734.

5. John Ritter and Tom Watson, "Desegregation Takes a Twist: Mississippi Wants to Shut Black Schools," *USA Today*, May 9, 1994, 3A; also see Ronald Smothers, "Mississippi Mellows on Campus Bias Case," *New York Times*, March 13, 1995, A6, which states: "There are 38 historically black, publicly financed universities or colleges in the 19 states that once had segregated higher education systems." In addition, it is noted that with the uniform admission standard order, "an estimated 1,500 black high school graduates" would be "ineligible for unconditional admission to any of the state's eight universities." Further, an NAACP Legal Defense and Education Fund lawyer, Janell Byrd, is quoted as saying, "But in the long run this [Judge Bigger's] ruling doesn't seem to connect to the harm of lack of access for blacks to quality higher education that it was supposed to address."

6. Dr. Mary Benjamin, vice-chancellor for academic affairs, University of Arkansasin–Pine Bluff, "The Role of Historical Black Colleges in the 21st Century" (Speech delivered at the Association of Social and Behavioral Scientists' 59th Annual Conference, March 23-26, 1994. Other panelists were Dr. Dorothy Cowser Yancy, then interim president and currently president, Johnson C. Smith University; Dr. Dora Washington, vice-president for academic affairs, Jackson State University; Dr. Bettye Parker Smith, vice-president, academic affairs, Tougaloo College; but their comments are not included here.)

7. The Honorable Joseph W. Hatchett, United States Circuit Judge, United States Court of Appeals for the Eleventh Circuit, Commencement Address, Florida Agricultural and Mechanical University—established 1887, Tallahassee, Saturday, April 30, 1994 at 6 P.M., Tallahassee/Leon County Civic Center.

8. The Honorable Kay Coles James, Secretary of Health and Human Resources, State of Virginia, Commencement Address, The 124th Annual Commencement, Hampton University—established 1868, Hampton, Virginia, Sunday Morning, May 8, 1994 at 10 A.M., University Convocation Center.

9. Ritter and Watson, "Desegregation Takes a Twist," *USA Today*, 3 A (a quote from James Appleberry, President of the American Association of State Colleges and Universities). U.S. District Judge Neal Biggers is the trial court judge in the *Ayers* case.

10. 1994 Commencement Exercises, FAMU, 2 and 1994 Commencement Excercises, Hampton, 3.

11. David S. Broder, "America: 'Its Faults Are Yours to Fix, Not to Curse,' " *Plain Dealer*, May 29, 1994, 3–C.

12. 112 S.Ct. 2727 at 2744.

13. 112 S.Ct. 2727 at 2746.

14. "Black Colleges Given Student Loan Waiver," *Plain Dealer*, April 16, 1994, 5–A.

15. Cf. Judge Neal Biggers, Jr., requiring one set of admission standards in the eight subject Mississippi universities (five White, three Black), as reported by Ronald D. Smothers, "Judge Rejects Part of Mississippi Plan to Desegregate Colleges: Eight Universities Are Ordered to Establish One Set of Admission Standards," *New York Times*, March 9, 1995, B8.

16. Theodore Cross and Robert Bruce Slater, "The Financial Footings of the Black Colleges," *Journal of Blacks in Higher Education* no. 6 (Winter 1994/1995): 76–79.

17. "Minority College Rates Unveiled: Fewer Hispanics, Blacks Graduate," *Plain Dealer*, February 28, 1994, 5–A.

18. David Swinton, "The Economic Status of African Americans," *State of Black America 1993*, (New York, Urban League, 1993), 146, 147.

19. Christopher Farrell and Michael Mandel in New York, Michael Schroeder in Pittsburgh, Joseph Weber in Philadelphia, Michele Galen in New York, Gary Mc Williams in Boston, and bureau reports, "The Economic Crisis of Urban America," *Business Week*, May 18, 1992, 38–43, 41.

20. Walter P. Allen, Edgar G. Epps and Nesha Z. Haniff, *College in Black and White: African American Students in Predominantly White and in Historically Black Public Universities* (Albany, New York: State University of New York Press, 1991), 6.

21. Department of Education, "Nondiscrimination in Federally Assisted Programs: Title 6 of the Civil Rights Act of 1964; Notice of Final Policy Guidance," *Federal Register* 59, no. 36 (February 23, 1994): 8756–8764.

22. *Podbersky v. Kirwan*, 38 F. 3d 147 (4th Cir. 1994).

23. E.g., Maryland, Virginia, North Carolina, South Carolina and Florida.

24. Davidson Goldin, "A Law Center Wages Fight Against Political Correctness, Mostly on College Campuses," *New York Times*, August 13, 1995, A 14.

25. Peter Applebome, "Black Boarding Schools Filling a Growing Need," *New York Times*, September 21, 1994, A1, B12.

26. Charles M. Sennott, "Rash of Parent Killings Reported," *Plain Dealer*, March 15, 1995, A10; "Skinheads Won't Fight Extradition for Trial," *New York Times* March 9, 1995, A9.

27. Mary Beth Lane, "School Board Approves Goals 2000," *Plain Dealer*, March 15, 1995, B5.

28. Marilyn Elias, "Poverty Impairs Children's IQ's," *USA Today*, March 9, 1994, 1–D; Editorial, "Yale and Mr. Bass's $20 Million Gift," *New York Times*, March 18, 1995, A14; Rick Bragg, "All She [Oseola McCarty, a washer-woman] Has, $150,000, Is Going to a University," *New York Times*, August 13, 1995, A1, A11.

29. Elias, "Poverty Impairs IQ's," 1–D.

30. Ibid.

31. Cf. *Rodriguez v. San Antonio Independent School District*, 337 F. Supp. 280 (WD Tex. 1971).

32. Dirk Johnson, "State Will Try to Shore up Cleveland's Shaky Schools: Judge Addresses 'Crisis' of Cash and Culture," *New York Times*, March 14, 1995, A8.

33. Thomas Suddes (Mary Beth Lane Contributing Author), "Voinovich's Voucher Plan May Be Limited to Cleveland," *Plain Dealer*, March 17, 1995, A1, A12.

34. Editorial, "Disciplining Dangerous Students," *New York Times*, March 18, 1995, A14.

35. Maria Newman, "Weapons at School: Box Cutters Escape Detection," *New York Times*, March 10, 1995, A1, A6; Maria Newman, "Disciplinary Schools Planned for Students Carrying Weapons: Cortines Proposal Is Aimed at Growing Violence," *New York Times*, March 8, 1995, A1, B12.

36. Kofi Lomotey, *Going to School: The African-American Experience* (Albany, New York: State University of New York Press, 1990).

37. Cf. *Johnson v. San Francisco Unified School District*, 339 F. Supp. 315 (1971).

38. Ibid.

39. Rogers Elliott, *Litigating Intelligence: IQ Tests, Special Education, and Social Science in the Courtroom* (Dover, Massachusetts: Auburn House Publishing Company, 1987).

40. (Reprinted from *The London Observer*), "Charles Murray: White America's Deadly Seducer," *Journal of Blacks in Higher Education* no. 6 (Winter 1994, 1995): 72, 73; News and Views, "Hernstein, Murray, and the Long Tradition of Racism in Academic Robes," *Journal of Blacks in Higher Education* no. 5. (Autumn 1994, Number 5): 9.

41. "Sociologists Square Off on The Bell Curve," *Footnotes* (March 1995) 23, no. 3: 1.

42. "I.Q. Group Ousts Editor Over Euthanasia Articles," *New York Times*, January 14, 1995, A9.

43. E.g., Jacques Steinberg, "Well-Connected Civil Servant Survives Many a Test," *New York Times*, January 11, 1995, A16.

44. Stanley Fish, "Affirmative Action and the SAT," *Journal of Blacks in Higher Education* no. 4 (Winter, 1993, 1994): 83; Theodore Cross and Robert Bruce Slater, "Alumni Children Admissions Preferences at Risk: The Strange Irony of How the Academic Achievements of Asians May Rescue Affirmative Action for Blacks," *Journal of Blacks in Higher Education* no. 6 (Winter 1994/1995): 87–90.

45. Fish, "Affirmative Action and the SAT."

46. George F. Will, "Court Was Right with the Wrong Reasoning," *Plain Dealer*, May 15, 1994, 7–C.

47. Patrice M. Jones, "How Far Have We Come? 40 Years After the Brown Decision, Two-thirds of Black Students Attend Predominantly Minority Schools," *Plain Dealer*, May 16, 1994, 1–A, 5–A.

48. Juan Williams, *Eyes on the Prize: America's Civil Rights Years 1954-1965* (New York: Penguin Books, 1987), 108–119; Nathan McCall, *Makes Me Wanna Holler: A Young Black Man in America* (New York: Random House, 1994), 17–20.

49. Williams, *Eyes on the Prize*, 213–218.

50. Desiree F. Hicks, "Heights System Showed Bias in Discipline, Report Says," *Plain Dealer*, 1993, 1–A, 5–A.

51. 419 U.S. 565, 95 S.Ct. 729 (1975).

52. "Visions of Black Pearls: Reflections of Our Heritage; Teen Lift Debutante Cotillion" (Delta Sigma Theta Sorority, Greater Cleveland Alumnae Chapter: Landerhaven, Mayfield Hts., Ohio, March 5, 1994).

53. Thomas Suddes, "Charter Schools Called Effective: Hearings to Put 'Idea on Table,' " *Plain Dealer*, May 27, 1994, 1–B.

54. Peter Applebome, "$30 Million in Financing Is Secured for For-Profit Whittle Schools Venture," *New York Times*, March 15, 1995, A6.

55. Jacques Steinberg, "Yale Returns $20 Million to an Unhappy Patron: Harvard Gets $70 Million Gift," *New York Times*, March 15, 1995, A1, B6.

56. William Celis 3d, "Deepest U.S. Cuts Since '81 Are Proposed for Education: Urban Schools May Be Especially Hard Hit," *New York Times*, March 18, 1995, A6.

57. Cross and Slater, "The Financial Footings of the Black Colleges."

58. Norman Parish, "Lack of Education, Segregation, Racism Fuel Unemployment," *Plain Dealer*, May 1, 1991, 1–A, 5–A.

59. John Carey and Mark Lewyn in Washington, with Ronald Grover in Los Angeles, Bart Ziegler in New York, Joseph Weber in Philadelphia and bureau reports, "Yield Signs on the Infor Interstate: As Regulations Take Shape, It Seems Everyone Must Give a Bit," *Business Week*, January 24, 1994, 88–90; Robert D. Hof in Santa Clara, Calif., with Gary McWilliams in Boston and Peter Burrows in Dallas, "Intel Steers the PC onto the Info Highway: Jazzy Communications Add-ons Could Spur Intel Chip Sales," *Business Week*, January 31, 1994; John Carey, "Big Brother Could Hobble High Tech," *Business Week*, March 21, 1994, 37; Kathy Rebello in San Francisco, with Paul Eng in New York and bureau reports, "Digital Pioneers: Blazing a Trail on the Interactive Frontier," *Business Week*, May 2, 1994, 96–99, 102, 103.

60. James E. Ellis in St. Louis, "Can Biotech Put Bread on Third World Tables?" *Business Week*, December 14, 1992, 100; Joan O'C. Hamilton in San Francisco, with James E. Ellis in Chicago, "A Storm Is Breaking Down on the Farm: The Fight Over Gene-Spliced Food Is About to Explode as a Rot-Resistant Tomato Goes on Sale Next Year," *Business Week*, December 14, 1992, 98–101; Mary Beth Regan in Chevy Chase, Md., "A Research Behemoth Gets Even Bigger: Hughes Medical Adds the Equivalent of a University Department," *Business Week*, February 21, 1994, 56.

61. Peter Coy in Fort Lauderdale, Fla., with John Carey in Washington, Neil Gross in Tokyo, and bureau reports, "Mighty Mites Hit It Big: Micromachines Go from Gee-Whiz to Whiz-bam in Practical Uses," April 26, 1993, 92–94.

62. William D. Marbach, "Using Fiber Optics to Watch Pistons Fly Up and Down," *Business Week*, April 26, 1993, 95.

63. Joseph Weber in Philadelphia, with Sunita Wadekar Bhargava in New York, "Drugmakers Get a Taste of Their Own Medicine: The Balance of Power Tips, Letting Big Buyers Dictate Terms," *Business Week*, April 26, 1993, 104, 106; David Greising in Indianapolis, "Randall Tobias Takes a Pruning Hook to Lilly: The New CEO Means to Spin off Six Units and Focus on Pharmaceuticals," *Business Week*, January 31, 1994, 32.

64. John W. Verity in New York, with Richard Brandt in San Francisco, "Robo-Software Reports for Duty: Powerful New Programs Automate Routine—and Complex—Tasks," *Business Week*, February 14, 1994, 110, 113.

65. Eric Schine in Calabasas, Calif., "Lockheed Sticks to Its Guns: Acquiring GD's Fighter Division Defies Typical Peacetime Strategy," *Business Week*, April 26, 1993, 100-102; Eric Schine in Palmdale, Calif., "Out at the Skunk Works, the Sweet Smell of Success," *Business Week*, April 26, 1993, 101; Richard S. Dunham in Los Angeles, "A Different Kind of Launch for McDonnell: A New Program Is Catapulting Women into the Political Arena," *Business Week*, August 2, 1993, 66, 70.

66. David Woodruff in Detroit, with Mary Beth Regan in Washington, "Is It Too Soon to Jump-Start Electric Cars? More States Are Mandating Them, But Critics Say Better Alternatives Exist," March 21, 1994, 36; John Carey in Washing-

ton, with David Woodruff in Detroit and Peter Coy in New York, "Where's the Juice? A Good Battery Is Hard to Find," *Business Week*, May 30, 1994, 110.

67. Gary McWilliams, "Coming off the Drawing Board: Better Engineers? Curriculums Shift So Industry Gets the Sort of Graduates It Needs," *Business Week*, August 2, 1993, 70, 71; David Woodruff in Sacramento, with Larry Armstrong in Los Angeles, John Carey in Washington, and bureau reports, "Electric Cars: Will They Work? And Who Will Buy Them?" *Business Week*, May 30, 1994, 104–107, 110, 111, 114.

68. Larry Armstrong in Los Angeles with Dori Jones Yang in Bellevue, Washington, Alice Cuneo in San Francisco, and bureau reports, "The Learning Revolution: Technology Is Reshaping Education—At Home and at School," *Business Week*, February 28, 1994, 80–88; Larry Armstrong, "Riding the Educational-Software Wave," *Business Week*, February 28, 1994, 84, 85; John W. Verity, "The Next Step: Reengineer the Classroom," *Business Week*, February 28, 1994, 88.

69. Applebome, "$30 Milliion in Financing Is Secured for For-Profit Whittle Schools Venture."

70. Ibid.

71. Desiree F. Hicks, "Grouping divides: Ability 'Tracks' in Schools Spur Controversy,' " *Plain Dealer*, May 29, 1994, 1B, 4B; Desiree F. Hicks, "Heights Schools Face Bias Probe," *Plain Dealer*, June 8, 1994, 1B, 12B.

72. *Prince v. Commonwealth of Massachusetts*, 321 U.S. 158 (1944); *Pierce v. Society of the Sisters of the Holy Names of Jesus and Mary*, 268 U.S. 510 (1925).

73. 406 U.S. 205 (1972).

74. *Nagle v. Olin*, 64 Ohio St. 2d 341, 415 N.E. 279 (1980).

75. Peter Applebome, "Milwaukee Is Forcing the Debate on Vouchers for Church Schools," *New York Times*, September 1, 1995, A1, A8.

76. "Voinovich's Voucher Plan May Be Limited to Cleveland," *Plain Dealer*, March 17, 1995, A1, A12.

77. Applebome, "Milwaukee Is Forcing the Debate on Vouchers," A8 quoting Walter Farrell, education professor at the University of Wisconsin at Milwaukee.

78. Keith Bradsher, "Low Ranking for Poor American Children: U.S. Youth Among Worst Off in Study of 18 Industrialized Children," *New York Times*, August 14, 1995, A7. The article compares "a family of four that includes children and that is poorer than 10 percent of the households in the country and more affluent than 10 percent of the households."

79. Kimberly J. McLarin, "In Test of School-Voucher Idea, the Sky's Not Falling but Neither Is Manna," *New York Times*, April 19, 1995, B8.

80. Scott Stephens, "School Vouchers Unconstitutional, ACLU Contends," *Plain Dealer*, March 30, 1995, B4.

81. Maulana Karenga and Jacob H. Carruthers, *Kemet and the African Worldview (Los Angeles: University of Sankore Press, 1986).*

82. 418 U.S. 717 (1974).

83. 411 U.S. 1 (1973).

84. Evelyn Theiss, "Schools Told to Cut All Sports: Rejection of Levy Blamed in Call for 1,070 Layoffs in Cleveland," *Plain Dealer*, May 19, 1994, 1A, 14A.

85. Cf. *Serrano v. Priest*, 487 P. 2d 1241 (Cal. 1971); *Robinson v. Cahill*, 306 A. 2d 65 (N.J. 1973).

86. W. E. Sparkman, "School Finance Challenges in State Courts," *The Impacts of Litigation and Legislation on Public School Finance: Adequacy, Equity and Excellence,* ed., J.K. Underwood and D.A. Verstegen (New York: Harper & Row, 1990); Stephanie Anderson Forest in Dallas, with bureau reports, "True or False: More Money Buys Better Schools: As the U.S. Education System Continues to Flunk, the Debate Over Funding Methods Intensifies," *Business Week,* August 2, 1993, 62, 63; Ron Stodghill II, in South Collaway and Osage Counties, Mo., "A Tale of Two School Districts: In Missouri, a Poor Area's Students Outperform Richer Neighbors," *Business Week,* August 2, 1993, 63-65.

87. A. R. Odden and L. O. Picus, *School Finance: A Policy Perspective* (New York: McGraw-Hill, 1992).

88. *Rodriguez v. Los Angeles Unified School District,* No. C611358 (Los Angeles County Sup. Ct., filed Aug. 6, 1986), consent decree (May 5, 1992); *Abbot v. Burke,* 119 N.J. 287, 575 A.2d 359 (1990); *Edgewood Independent School District v. Kirby,* 777 S.W. 2d 391 (Tex.1989); *Alabama Coalition for Equity v. Hunt,* No. CV-90–883–2 (Cir. Ct. of Montgomery County, Ala., decided March 31, 1993); *Committee for Educational Equality v. State of Missouri,* No. CV 190–137–1000 (Cir. Ct. of Cole County, Mo., decided January 15, 1993); *Helena Elementary School District No. 1 v. State,* 236 Mont. 44, 769 P. 2d 684 (1989), modified, 236 Mont. 60, 784 P. 2d 412 (1990).

89. 63 U.S.L.W. 4486 (June 12, 1995).

90. Cf. *Riddick v. School Board of Norfolk,* 784 F.2d. 521 (4th Cir. 1986).

91. Jonathan Gaw, "Cracking the Glass Ceiling," *Plain Dealer,* April 23, 1994, 1–C.

92. Willa Hemmons, "From the Halls of Hough and Halsted: A Comparison of Black and White Campuses," *Journal of Black Studies* (Spring, 1982).

93. Mike McNamee in Washington, "Robert's Rules of Reorder: The New Agenda Makes Reich's Star Shine All the Brighter," *Business Week,* January 24, 1994, 74, 75.

94. Bill Javetski, "These Days, Europe's Safety Net Looks More Like a Noose," *Business Week,* January 24, 1994, 78.

95. Editorial, "The Payoff from the New Economic Order," *Business Week,* August 2, 1993, p. 94.

CHAPTER 5

Black Women in the World Order of Social Welfare

SOCIAL WELFARE AS A SOCIAL INSTITUTION

The New World Order mandate has not been and probably will not be kind to "the Welfare State"[1] in the foreseeable future.[2] Not only in the United States but also globally the poor are facing an increasingly hostile world-wide climate.[3] The African American woman, largely because of the political, economic and educational conditions described in previous chapters, is especially hard hit by the rise of anti–welfare state forces. To much of society, even though governmental largesse generally extends to many,[4] the word "welfare" has been made to correspond to the word "Black." Further, the word is no longer used as it is in the Preamble to the U.S. Constitution (1789):

"We the people of the United States, in Order to form a more perfect Union, establish Justice, insure domestic Tranquility, provide for the common defence, promote the general Welfare, and secure the Blessings of Liberty to ourselves and our Posterity, do ordain and establish this Constitution for the United States of America."

It has been forgotten that the "general Welfare" includes taxpayer monies going for such amenities as freeways, hiking trails, parks, zoos, public universities, sport stadiums, museums, libraries and entertainment/civic centers which inure largely to the benefit of the middle and upper classes. As pointed out in an earlier law review article written by this author with a colleague,[5]

The conviction of the AFDC mother is arbitrary and capricious. It has no more relationship to legitimate governmental goals than would convictions of persons in other "welfare" categories which the government has seen fit to create in order to supplement the resources which such persons need to exist in American society.[6]

That summary was made in recognition of the fact that AFDC[7] recipients (Aid to Families with Dependent Children) were disproportionately prosecuted when compared with other welfare beneficiaries such as those receiving income from Social Security,[8] Supplemental Security Income[9] and Medicare.[10]

WELFARE CASE STUDY: RECIPIENT REPERCUSSIONS

Patricia was a tall, big-boned woman who was forty years old and had a daughter who had just turned twenty-one. She lived with her daughter, who was her only child. In addition, Patricia's mother stayed with them. Her mother was a double amputee, suffering from diabetes and from severe heart problems, arthritis and hypertension. The three of them stayed in a house that needed a lot of work in a near city suburb that had become 95 percent Black. Patricia had finished high school in that community when it was more "integrated" and the family had lived there ever since. Patricia had the sole responsibility of caring for her mother. Although she received some help from her daughter, most of the time the latter was away attending a community college. Patricia had had several jobs. At the time we met, she held a job as a custodial worker for thirty to forty hours a week at the city-owned power plant. Before that, she had held a job cleaning and maintaining the city's sports stadium, and prior to that she had worked in a restaurant and then in a cafeteria.

Patricia's legal problems derived from those jobs. The statute of limitations for noncapital felony criminal cases is six years. In welfare-fraud cases, then, the state has six years in which to prosecute such offenses. Consequently, many welfare fraud cases that come before the county (state) court are five and a half years old, which means that a lot of records are lost or discarded by the defendants by the time they are indicted. Further, with the constant changeover in caseworkers at the welfare department, tracing what actually happened can be problematic.

Patricia was charged with welfare fraud and trafficking in food stamps. The first month's transgression listed in the indictment was alleged to have occurred almost six years before the indictment was issued. The first charge in her indictment read as follows:

Count 1. The Jurors of the Grand Jury of the State of Ohio, within and for the body of the County aforesaid, on their oaths, IN THE NAME AND BY THE AUTHORITY OF THE STATE OF OHIO, Do find and present, that the above named Defendant(s), on or about the date of the offense set forth above, in the County of Cuyahoga, unlawfully and knowingly and by deception obtained or exerted control over warrants and money with the purpose to deprive the owner, Cuyahoga County Department of Human Services, of said property or services.

The value of said property or services being $5,000.00 or more.

Count 2 of her indictment, for trafficking in food stamps, read that she:

unlawfully did knowingly possess, buy, sell, use, alter, accept or transfer food stamp coupons in a manner not authorized by the "Food Stamp Act of 1977", 91 Stat. 958, 7 U.S.C.A. 2011 as amended. The face value of the food stamp coupons involved in the violation being $500.00 or more.

Due to the amount involved in Count 1 (over $5,000), Patricia faced a Felony 3 punishable by one to two years in prison. In addition, the Food Stamp charge carried the same penalty. The unlawfulness alleged in the indictment encompassed an allegation that she had received monies and food stamps for which she was ineligible.

Despite an appearance that to some would have been overbearing, Patricia spoke with a tiny, "feminine" voice. Bemoaning her possible fate, Patricia broke down in tears constantly. She insisted she had informed her caseworker of her employment.

The time period covered in Patricia's indictment included three years during which, it was alleged, she had worked while concurrently receiving welfare. Welfare recipient caretakers have to report to their caseworkers for an eligibility update every six months, when recipients are required to report any changes in their incomes. Every time Patricia went in to see her caseworker, she brought to her all of her pay stubs from her respective employers. Patricia maintained that the caseworker had even photocopied them. At the time of her first interview with me, Patricia brought with her almost two hundred paystubs. When I took them, seeking exculpatory action, to the assistant county prosecutor who was handling the case (although he and I generally had a pretty good rapport), he shrugged them off and did not want to look through the two hundred.

The essence of the problem lay in the type of employment Patricia had. She was on an as-needed basis with all her employers in her capacity as a part-time laborer at their various cafeterias, restaurants, stadiums and power plants. She never knew beforehand the number of hours for which she would be called. Each week she worked a different number of hours, and, unlike some welfare recipient-workers, she did not receive any funds under the table, that is, in which the employee is paid in cash with no Social Security or local, state or federal taxes being taken out of the wages. Patricia's employers were primarily government agencies. A computerized state system compares the Social Security numbers of employees with the Social Security numbers of welfare recipients. Before the six-year statute of limitations for prosecution of a noncapital felony is up, any parallel Social Security numbers appearing in both the wage database and the welfare one are identified and sent to the appropriate auditing or fraud-detection state agency division. Further investigation is then done to see if the wages have been disclosed by the recipient. It is almost a foolproof system of welfare-fraud detection if the wages of an earner have been reported to the state.

The reason it is *almost* foolproof and not fully foolproof involves the human factor. Although Patricia claimed she dutifully showed her paystubs to her case worker, she had no evidence of that assertion other than her own word. When she informed me of her disclosure, as per usual, I asked her the name of her caseworker. As have other clients in the same predicament, she looked at me as if in a fog. She couldn't remember from six years ago who her caseworker had been, and plus, they were always changing.

Patricia asked me some important questions. Slightly paraphrased, they were: Why didn't she [the caseworker] document my paystubs? Why didn't they call me to come in for the investigation to give me a chance to pay them before indicting me? Why didn't the welfare worker reduce my welfare payments according to what they should have been after she saw my paystubs? Why do you have to treat me like a criminal?

These questions were punctuated throughout all of Patricia's interviews with me by her tears. "I don't want to make no excuses, if they sent it to me, I cashed it." "I don't mind paying it back." "Why they want me to go to jail?" "You come here, girlfriend [me], and check this out." "I don't understand this."

At a loss, I showed her a copy of the code book section containing the charges reflected in her indictment, again. Patricia just went on: "I'm showing you my paystubs, why would you constantly send me a whole check rather than cut me off or break my check down?" "I wasn't working full time." "I was working 30 to 32 hours—if I was working 40 hours, it was holiday season." "I was making $4.00 an hour, then it went to $4.25." "Why the Welfare wouldn't send me a notice to come in and discuss it rather than . . .?" "The little bit—the little few dollars—that I was getting—I showed them all my paystubs." "When I showed them, they told me that I was still eligible for welfare." "I have copies of the copies they took of my paystubs." "They didn't have to do this." "They just. . . ."

During one pre-trial [at which plea bargaining occurs], the assistant prosecutor showed me that Patricia had checked "no" in the box following the question on the welfare update sheet that asked, "Have you, your husband or your children received any earnings from work? Please sign yes or no." Patricia had signed no.

I left the inner court chambers and went back out to the courtroom where Patricia was waiting for the determination of her future. I told her the new development in our discovery process and asked her about her signature.

Patricia replied, "Yes, I checked the box." I asked her why she had done that, and she responded that she thought the question meant no other income than what she was showing to the caseworker. She still insisted, "I ain't hiding nothing from them." In other words, Patricia said she had thought that the caseworker's computation had incorporated the monies from the paystubs.

Unfortunately, the caseworker had not. Even worse, there was no way to prove Patricia's contention that the caseworker had been shown the paystubs. Moreover, the way the law operates presently, the burden is on Patricia (or was when she had a minor child) to know the appropriate computational formula for her welfare disbursement. Such a burden is especially onerous given the complexity of the rules and regulations underlying the computation of each family's welfare award.

Since it was up to me to compute, after the fact, Patricia's chances for success at trial, I presented her with her options. The cards were stacked against us.

The assistant prosecutor was an amiable sort and, even though practices surrounding the diversion program were currently changing, offered that option to us. The diversion program was supposed to be limited to cases under $5,000. However, it had been the practice to allow defendants with amounts over that $5,000 figure to pay down to it and then get on diversion. Including Patricia's food stamp charge, the amount of her alleged fraud was $6,331. The assistant prosecutor said he would allow Patricia to get on the program if she would pay $1,332 up front to the welfare department. Patricia was up to $5.50 an hour in her present employment. With her mother's prescriptions only partially covered by Medicaid and with her daughter's community college tuition, there was no way she could come up with the money.

The assistant prosecutor then said he would reduce the charges to a felony of the fourth degree (F-4). A Felony 4 covers theft cases ranging in amount from $300 to $5,000. Pleading to the lowered charge in no way diminished her responsibility to pay back the entire $6,331. The reduced charge was offered pursuant to a legal fiction by which if she failed to complete probation, by virtue of not putting the court to the test of a full-blown trial, she would face the lowered Felony 4 penalty of six months to a year to a year and a half. If Patricia reneged on her welfare restitution payments, she would face the penalty pursuant to a Felony 4 crime as opposed to a Felony 3 one. That was the price the state paid for not having to put its proof on trial in front of twelve of Patricia's peers.

After pleading guilty to the Felony 4 with the full restitution stipulation, Patricia was referred to the county probation department for consideration as a candidate for probation. A defendant is allowed to be on probation for up to five years. If the penalty calls for more or if restitution cannot be made within the five years, the defendant is supposed to go to prison, at the discretion of the court. If a defendant's restitution is not paid, by the time his or her original probation is scheduled to be terminated, the probation can be extended until it is paid, up to the maximum of five years. At her sentencing hearing about a month after entering her guilty plea, Patricia was placed on probation for one year.

It is also interesting to note that, although unavailable to Patricia, with the influx of drug indictments in the eighties and nineties, diversion became more available to those accused of relief fraud.

The Basis of Welfare

The case study in this chapter illustrates the type of legal dilemma in which a Black woman can find herself when she tries to supplement the inadequate income derived from the AFDC program with wages that still will leave her below the federally determined poverty line. The issue of who the AFDC recipient is has a lot to do with the heightened prosecution.

Welfare fraud is a crime that was not found at common law. Of course, during common-law times in Medieval England there were debtors' prisons and dungeons for the poor—possibly the next step in the New World Order reordering process. Common-law crimes generally required criminal intent for completion. Welfare fraud is a creation of the legislature and, regardless of intent, is an act-only crime. The calculation by a welfare worker of the slightest overpayment makes its recipient a criminal. That the crime of welfare fraud is strictly a matter of statutory construction was upheld in the case of *U.S. v. Marvin, cert denied*, 1983.

The requirement that AFDC be awarded to a financially eligible single caretaker has been interpreted to mean a single parent or other relative or to families with a physically disabled father. Although it is a federal program, it is paid for through a matching-funds mandate in combination with the states. The states have a great deal of decision-making power, under the concept of federalism or respect for states' rights, to determine how much a family with a given number of dependents will receive. Differences between states became even greater as the Reagan administration (Piven and Cloward 1982) prepared for life under the New World Order. Funding became more arbitrary and discretionary irrespective of predetermined adequate-living-standard formulas. Funds were awarded on a more punitive level, as each state saw fit. Differences in AFDC expenditures already varied widely from state to state according to each state's fiscal capacity as well as its welfare philosophy.[11]

Pains are generally taken to make sure that recipients do not live comfortably on AFDC. For example, in 1992, the state of Ohio provided only 47 percent of the state-determined need standard to recipients. Further, in April of that year, almost half of all of the General Assistance recipients were purged from the welfare rolls with the admonition to come back in six months for a reassessment.

The morality aspect of AFDC has historical implications (Glueck 1952). Originally, AFDC was intended to be provided for "morally upstanding" widows whose households were "wholesome home." Such strictures were eliminated by the Eisenhower administration by 1960. An Eisenhower administration study reported that AFDC provided financial assistance for "homeless, dependent, and neglected children—found not where a parent is dead or physically incapacitated, but also in families where there is desertion, divorce, or indeed where there was no marriage."[12]

Unsurprisingly, alleged morality concerns still permeate AFDC rules and regulations. As the various welfare reforms discussed here indicate, morality rears its head particularly where the target is most vulnerable, as with the Black teenage welfare mother.[13] A minor lacking the franchise (Horowitz, 1995), she is almost as vulnerable as the immigrant in the United States[14] when it comes to her welfare being protected by some politicians. What is ironic is that despite the antipathy generated towards the welfare mother who is under 18 years of age, she represents only 1.2 percent of all AFDC mothers.[15] In addition, as reported by the Joint Center for Political and Economic Studies, "90 percent of black teenagers between 15 and 17 are childless, as are 75 percent of black 18- and 19-year-olds."[16]

Moral micro-management of the lives of the poor is also found in regard to living situations. Even though it has been legally overturned in the *King v. Smith* decision,[17] the "Man in the House" rule has been revitalized. In its new form, it presumes any man present in an AFDC household stands in the shoes of stepfather and has a legal responsibility towards that household's children. Such a presumption makes easier a finding of failure of disclosure or welfare fraud and facilitates benefit terminations. Towards such ends, there is a tendency for courts to find the existence of common-law marriages or substitute fathers, when a man is present in the household. Although AFDC rules impute an obligation to a stepfather to support a child living in his home, the common law (judicial precedents) and statutes in domestic relations, family and juvenile law generally do not.

Thus, AFDC law encourages formerly intact families to separate in order to receive benefits when economic conditions change.[18] President Carter's Panel on Government and the Advancement of Social Justice found that "a Minnesota mother of three could receive AFDC, Medicaid, and food stamps until her income reached $8,000 a year. A Minnesota father who remained with his family and worked full-time at a low wage disqualified his family for aid, regardless of need."[19]

Under New World Order "orders," men who become unemployed without any compensation must generally leave the home in order for their children to receive AFDC, a move that should be avoided. Further, much heralded "Child-Support Crackdowns" have limited success getting "blood from turnips."[20] Major changes in AFDC following a preliminary

New World Order mandate intended to get at the elusive father or father figure that were adopted by many states included the following:

1. Counting the income of a child's stepparent as a source of support in determining the child's AFDC eligibility benefits.

2. Counting a family's earned income tax credit (EITC) on a current basis in determining the monthly AFDC benefit to better reflect the family's actual, current need for assistance.

3. Limiting deductible child care costs and standardizing other work-related expenses (which offset earned income in determining AFDC benefits) and reforming other earned income disregards.

4. Requiring states to determine a family's AFDC eligibility and benefits based on previous actual income and circumstances.

5. Prohibiting AFDC payments below $10/month to simplify and reduce the costs of administration for marginal cases that may be on and off the rolls from month to month.[21]

Former President Reagan made these "reforms" specific to the Child Support Enforcement Program (CSEP). It became more incumbent upon states to pass these rules because the CSEP financed 75 percent of a state's costs of enforcing and collecting child support from liable missing parents. The CSEP changes included:

1. Charging an applicant fee in non-AFDC cases to reimburse CSE costs of states and the federal government, which have no direct stake in such cases and do not otherwise share in such collections.

2. Financing incentive payments out of the state, as well as the federal share of collections.

3. Extending CSE activities to include the collection of alimony.

4. Mandating that the Internal Revenue Service intercept federal income tax returns to collect child support arrearages from liable absent parents where a court judgment has already been obtained.[22]

The reason for the disparate prosecution of AFDC recipients and Social Security beneficiaries can be found in the fear that decision makers in the political institution have of the voting power of the latter.[23] The relative reluctance to touch Social Security or Medicare is normally present despite the fact that "The great middle-class entitlements, Social Security and Medicare, which pay benefits regardless of financial need, dwarf the programs for low-income people." [24]

For example, the federal government reportedly spent in 1994 more than four times the amount on Social Security and Medicare ($47.5 billion) than on Aid to Families with Dependent Children, food stamps and Medicaid ($12.5 billion). The states' share of the cash benefits purportedly received by the fourteen million people on welfare was $10.3 billion.[25] Although two thirds of the recipients of AFDC are children, figures such as that 55 percent of them (5.3 million out of a total of approximately 9.7 million) "were born out of wedlock"[26] are often used rather sophomorically to enhance efforts to increase state regulatory control over the lives of their mothers and caretakers.[27] These efforts are rather thinly disguised attempts to punish the allegedly immoral, indolent (93 percent for many reasons do not work) and illegitimate behavior of the oft-reviled "welfare mother." As a manifestation of both states' rights and state resources, the "average monthly benefit for a family of three ranges from $120 in Mississippi to $950 in Alaska, with a national median of $365."[28] The work and wedlock issues supposedly underlie competing movements among the states to enact increasingly draconian measures.

Hence, another regulatory punishment for being poor presumes a scenario in which lack of work or education is assumed to be a choice:

Low-income women should not stay home at taxpayer expense while working-class mothers must help support their families. Health and Human Services Secretary Donna E. Shalala said yesterday in comments on welfare-to-work requirements. . . . The Clinton administration is beginning work on overhauling the welfare system that serves a record 5 million families. Shalala's comments on work requirements for welfare mothers, including those at home with infants and toddlers, were the first indication of how stringent the reforms might be.[29]

Such bipartisan mandates for the poor arise even though they run counter to past experiences as well as past "experiments."[30] For example, as one news article relates:

Most Americans believe that people who can work ought to. And getting people to work costs money. The difficulty is that jobs are scarce in the inner cities and rural communities where welfare beneficiaries generally live. Many people on welfare are uneducated and have few skills. Job-training programs are expensive and often fruitless.[31]

The work issue is inextricably tied to larger issues of discrimination in the education and economic institutions. Social Security is a benefit which inures to those who have had the opportunity to work outside the home as an employee in U.S. society. To provide this benefit, the federal government spends one-fifth of its budget.[32] The greater the work opportunity level one has been able to achieve, the greater the amount of the Social Security benefit providing for one's welfare one can expect to collect at retirement. Hence, "[in] 1990, families with income above $100,000 received more than $8 billion in Social Security benefits."[33] This is all well and good, but how can people structurally deprived of employment put away rainy day/retirement funds? They increasingly are left to the varying whims of their state and local communities—as well as the employment plans of the private sector. It should also be pointed out here that, unlike AFDC, there is no thought that Social Security be left to such state-level speculation.

New World Order Reforms in Welfare

As an example of the states' preference for federally unfettered block grants to states for "welfare" distribution, Massachusetts legislators developed a law that was renowned for the fact that it "would give their state one of the most restrictive welfare systems in the country."[34]

The legislative objectives of this "welfare overhaul" require "a third of the state's able-bodied welfare recipients to find work after 60 days, eliminate any increase in payments to mothers who have more children while on welfare and end payments altogether for beneficiaries who have been receiving assistance for two years."[35]

With such legislation, Massachusetts sought to be the first state to enact all three of the most draconian measures thus far applied in one form or another by the various states. Although twelve or so states have enacted versions of the two-year limitation feature,[36] Arkansas, Georgia and New Jersey led the way in eliminating more benefits to "after acquired" "welfare" children.[37] In addition, the Massachusetts legislation requires that "teen-aged mothers live at home, or in a group home, and finish high school in order to receive benefits."[38]

Thus, welfare alternates with crime control as a topic for politicians to showcase the fierceness of public anger[39] against the poor, the Black and the otherwise out of power.[40] The political gloss imposed upon the welfare question does not even approach being in the nature of *subtle*.[41] Anxious to show how tough they are, political leaders want to "waiver" the welfare poor out of existence. Waivers are sought by states when they want to experiment with some "innovative" idea about how to address welfare in their jurisdiction. The Department of Health and Human Services has to approve any changes in the primary welfare program, a federally funded, state-administered collaboration, that includes Aid to Families with Dependent Children, by granting the applicant state a waiver. The innovations presented by Massachusetts are prime examples of such state creativity.

These efforts reflect a desire on the part of the states for independence, which even before the Civil War reflected a balance of federalism (states' rights) and federal supremacy as a crucial consideration in the formulation of the United States itself. Many states, while desiring federal monies, want as few strings attached to that support as possible. For instance, the use of the unfettered block grants or "categorical grants for narrow purposes" given to a state for the disposition of any obligation, as perceived by it, to the poor would give it much more flexibility in fulfilling that obligation, while involving a "fundamental change in the Federal-state relationship."[42]

The amount of federal direct aid received by a given state varies from state to state.[43] For instance, in 1992, 58 percent of Alabama's budget came from the federal government. Mississippi received 39 percent of its budget from the "feds," Tennessee 36 percent and California and Louisiana 33 percent. On the other hand, 20 percent of Florida's, Washington's, Maryland's, Wisconsin's and Minnesota's budgets, came from the federal government; 21 percent of Illinois' and Massachusetts', 23 percent of Nebraska's, Utah's and Ohio's, 26 percent of Pennsylvania's and Kentucky's, 27 percent of New York's and Michigan's, and 28 percent of Arkansas's and Georgia's state budgets came in direct aid from the federal government.[44] It is precisely due to such varying formulas that the crusade to base state welfare distributions upon block grants is a legislative nightmare.[45]

The movement to cut welfare drastically is a convenient ploy in demonstrating fiscal austerity since belt tightening has made increased prison building counterproductive for even the most conservative of governors.[46] However, get-tough welfare measures will probably always be secondary to get-tough crime control measures "rooted more in punishment (Piven and Cloward, 1971) than in prevention,"[47] such as prison building and long sentences to symbolize how devoted to law and order a politician is.[48]

Despite widely publicized cost-containment drives, politicians of whatever political party have found the politically correct Social Security "to be a volatile issue"[49] and any reduction has reportedly been "off the table," with Congress loathe to consider "changing the entitlement status of Medicare."[50] (Although, depending upon how far right the nation drifts in its course towards the New World Order, even those sacrosanct icons have become susceptible to review.[51]) Any New World re-ordering of overall social welfare will affect the middle class much less harshly than the poor, with one important exception. This exception relates to the fact that one half of the administrative costs of AFDC goes toward compensation for social workers, investigators, accountants, capital expenditures and supplies, as well as to other service personnel in the form of medical, training, counseling, resource, child care, employment and consultant professionals, not to mention the impact that the reordering of social welfare priorities has upon farmers,[52] supermarkets and, of course, lawyers.[53] Probably the greatest safety net for the poor is provided by welfare links and general social well-being connections that are interwoven with the fate of the middle class.[54]

Sophisticated code words, thinly disguising the underlying intent, have been developed to target those more likely to be of a racial or socio-economic outgroup, however. For instance, the two-year welfare limitation, modeled after the Massachusetts law, passed by Virginia's legislature prevailed "[i]n a vote along racial lines." Furthermore, according to state officials, two thirds "of those people [of the 74,000 Virginians who receive AFDC assistance] are black."[55] Moreover, the coded rationale for such targeting is grounded in assertions (implicit or explicit) of outgroup moral and/or genetic inferiority.[56] The middle class seems to be willing to tolerate numerous sacrifices inflicted by the policies of their "democratically" chosen representatives, jeopardizing their "health, safety, welfare and morals" in order to ensure order—at least of the race relations variety—in the New World.

Hence, the "intellectual" wisdom of the day rationalizes the intended persecution of the poor and downtrodden. Rather than the conventional wisdom of a Charles Dickens, a Louisa May Alcott, a Zora Neale Hurston, an Ernest Hemingway, a Langston Hughes, a Maya Angelou or a Norman Mailer, the "Counter Counterculture"[57] wisdom of the New World Order, particularly as augmented by the New World Orderites, fuels the political crusades that justify its tyrannies. Such wisdom seeks not just to institutionalize the Black woman's position in society but, indeed, to celebrate the lowliness of that position. The New World Order celebrants, the Orderites—not just any WASPs—are unremitting in their efforts to take advantage of their less fortunate European Americans' disillusionment about the lack of quality in their lives.

As used here, Orderites are viewed as those (1) whose group is currently in power in the United States; (2) who directly have a strong vested interest in keeping their group in power; and (3) who currently have the right, responsibility and resources to keep their group in power. Black women, while they may not be a specific target, are an easily expendable casualty in the New World Order elite's opportunism, in preparation for "a conservative opportunity society."[58] Rather unabashedly arrogant, understandably so given the success of most of their ventures, the Orderites seem to make it a plus to have the status of being White and not on welfare—at least not the stigmatized version.[59] On the other hand, these Orderites seldom miss an opportunity to magnify caricatures of African Americans either in featured crime (males) or welfare (females) media series. Mass-produced pictures of desperate Black males and despondent Black females, both caught up in their downtrodden, dependent states, help to feed the frenzy explaining what is *really* wrong with America. The irony is that they *really* do represent what *really* is wrong with America—xenophobia gone haywire, otherwise known as racism, classism, sexism and ageism.

Further, since young welfare mothers so stigmatized are not seen as a viable electorate nor as having the right type of allies,[60] they are that much easier to scapegoat.[61] Stripped of their humanity, as they are not the intended beneficiaries of New World Order largesse as are the Orderites,[62] they are more or less dispensable (see also Harrington 1986).

The dehumanization process for persons who sooner or later end up on welfare really begins at birth for all living native-born Americans. The dehumanization process is the denial of humanity and is one of the primary purposes of the U.S. concept of race in the first place. This process is completed by consistent reinforcements from mass communication vehicles. Given these pervasive, persistent, persuasive, permissive and sanctimoniously pious messages, the middle class is adequately desensitized and becomes obdurate towards the welfare populace. The working and middle classes do not readily recognize that the overall policies that victimize the welfare mother embody the same callousness and inhumanity that will come back to haunt them in other areas.[63]

This phenomenon is similar to the massive support for the disassemblage of Constitutional protections, derided as "technicalities" by the same middle-class people who then wonder why the federal government, as the quintessential Big Brother, has the temerity to propose "Clipper Chip"[64] devices that give it the capacity to invade the privacy of their computers. The same middle class might also wonder to whom "revenue-short states" and consumer database companies are selling their personal information collected through such New World technological processes as "caller ID," automatic number identification (ANI) and driver's license data (vision, height, weight, name and address).[65] Computer crooks are not the only ones the middle class has to worry will make "Cyberspace" violations of their privacy. It is shameful that their governments—federal, state and local—may be as inconsiderate of their Internet confidentiality as a Kevin Mitnick.[66]

These personal intrusion dynamics, originally sanctioned to "fight crime," make more salient than ever the issue of "For Whom the Bell Tolls," increasingly more important than "for whom the bell curves." Less well publicized than the contempt and disdain fostered for the "have nots" is the goal of the New World Order to ultimately end up with two major social classes, rather than the three widely heralded as the hallmark of democracy. Like Huck Finn's father, many of the would-be middle-class-constituency will end up with little more than their "Whiteness" to comfort them through the meaner and leaner days of the New World Order. Enter the Black woman, whose situation is manipulated to divert attention away from more powerful alien forces undermining the quality of life for most people in the New World Order. Such a climate helps to foster a "We" and "They" mentality developed to divide further and more completely conquer. As life gets tougher under the strains of the global economy and shifting technological bases, the image of the Black woman emerges as a convenient decoy to assuage wounded feelings derived from losses in income, job security, material wealth, health care, educational access, political power and overall sense of well-being.

Welfare's elimination has been touted as the ultimate in reform.[67] While its elimination is awaited, whatever welfare (AFDC) regulations can make the recipient's life more uncomfortable have been embraced. Austere measures toward that end include "family caps"[68] (the denial of additional benefits to women who have more children while on welfare) and two-year time limits on receiving benefits.[69] In such vengefulness against the downtrodden, the victims of oppression and discrimination are disciplined for the condition of being in poverty (see Ryan's *Blaming the Victim*, 1972).

In defending the movement to eliminate welfare as an entitlement program, one legislator, Representative John L. Mica of Florida, commented, "with our current handout, non-work welfare system, we've upset the natural *order* [italics added]."[70] It is not hard to figure out whether or not a return to "the natural order" in the New World will significantly increase the standard of living for most African, European or Hispanic Americans.

Hence, in the search for a scapegoat for a perceived stagnation in the economy,[71] morale, and malaise in the quality of life in general, a whole generation of Simon Legrees has been created and maintained.[72] Failure to acknowledge the systemic nature of the diminished standard of living in the United States keeps the onus also on the African American male, helping to undermine and tear apart the relationship of the African American couple. Black men and women are kept at each other's throats rather than at each other's command as mutual and reciprocal resources (see also Chapter 6). Such policies are particularly ominous for Black children, 60 percent of whom live in single-parent families, headed by women that have the lowest average income of any family type (see Chapter 3).

Remarks attributed to Supreme Court Justice Clarence Thomas illustrate not only how highly politicized welfare is but also how much of a stigmatizing force it is (West 1993). Justice Thomas is described as using his sister, Emma Mae, as an example of the welfare mother.[73]

This example indicates how emotional a subject the racially tinged nature of welfare (approximately 40 percent[74] of the families receiving AFDC are Black) is for many who have been programmed to take it as a personal affront. Justice Thomas's views on welfare were likewise vented in the *Anderson v. Edwards* case,[75] in which Mrs. Verna Edwards was denied compensation for two separate sets of sibling grandchildren at the level of two separate families. She, her granddaughter and her grandneice were reformulated into a single AU (AFDC "assistance unit") so that their monthly award was reduced from $901 per month to $694 per month. Such extended family living units are found much more frequently among Black and Hispanic peoples. Justice Thomas's perspective easily provides the legal underpinnings for judicial opinion which treats welfare as a privilege rather than a right without any due process protection against termination in contradiction to such cases as *Goldberg v. Kelly*.[76] Justice Thomas's ruling is also an example of how such judicial decisions have a long-term cumulative, societal effect even though they are ostensibly made on an individual basis. The aggregate result of Thomas's opinion in the *Anderson* case would be a reduction in welfare "costs."

Unfortunately, most citizens do not see that the cost of denying access for African Americans and Hispanics to quality education and meaningful job opportunities is the cost being borne by welfare. In fact, the allocation of costs in such a manner gives some the same ego-boosting feeling of superiority manifested in Justice Thomas's comparison of himself with his sister, as opposed to other, more-affluent relatives.[77] Mark Twain described similar feelings when he presented the attitude of Huck Finn's degenerate father toward Blacks. Many Whites, bereft of other forms of dignity, job security and social supports can at least be left with the feeling that they are better than those on welfare. Indeed, this important function for welfare helps to keep such persons from seriously confronting inequities in the society.

The provision of work for Black men and women would be a huge help in reuniting and strengthening the family,[78] as unemployment is a primary cause of family break-up. However, as indicated in unemployment and income statistics in Chapter 3, if those in power can select employees of their own racial and ethnic background rather than others, absent affirmative action, they will. The *Anderson* case undermined the view of welfare being a right given certain eligibility circumstances as had been enunciated in *Goldberg*. In the New World Order, work is more a privilege than a right.

Employment is probably the greatest (nonaffectional) incentive to the type of matrimony recognized in the nation's courts. Although the Family Support Act of 1988[79] greatly expanded the requirements for the collection and distribution of child support from the "absent parent" (90 percent of whom are fathers) and created specific national procedures for the establishment of paternity,[80] such policies will be useless when applied to men without work.[81]

One thing that the act did do to help families stay together was to allow benefits for two-parent families.[82] Still, the requirement of a wedding certificate precludes many de facto families from taking advantage of this program. Thus, the "man in the house" rule penalizes the type of unofficial family relationships that have evolved in correlation with the increased economic instability inherent in New World Order policies. Now, more Black children are born out of wedlock than in wedlock. To require fathers to leave the house in order for their children to receive support is to effectively deprive the children of the companionship of their fathers.

Recently, for instance, the author represented a young woman resisting visitation attemped by the unmarried father as related to their 20-month-old son. The mother had us subpoena four witnesses on her behalf. The father had smoked marijuana in the past, put a beer bottle up to the baby's mouth and gotten her and another woman pregnant at the same time. Reinforcing that issue, the referee insisted that the right of the child to his father's companionship and care (he was already paying $390 per month in child support) was independent of those allegations. The referee then ordered a regular schedule of visitation for the father.

A major problem with the work requirement for primary caretakers (90 percent of the time who are the mothers) is its lack of feasibility at a time when jobs have become such a precious commodity.[83] In addition, it is unlikely that Americans will tolerate creation of employment safety nets for such a despised and maligned segment of the population. Such a system would be too akin to "the European welfare state" in which government takes an active role in ensuring the positive fate of the worker[84] (this is probably also why, except for Ireland, the income gap between rich and poor children in the European countries is less than that of the United States—again, see Chapter 4). While U.S. corporate interests favor the more authoritarian regimes for investment purposes, there appears little evidence, even in the time of the New World Order, that the social democracy of Western Europe is seriously in abatement (Piven and Cloward 1982, 148).

Whom would former welfare recipients-turned-workers displace, other than the children[85] in precarious child-care situations? Recalling the precariousness of the work situation for many described in Chapter 3, the masses (rank and file) in the United States have already been put on notice that they are largely expendable at the whim of New World Order potentates. No employment now is too lowly for desperate job seekers. Since the onset of the New World Order, part-time jobs with few or no benefits and near the minimum wage level are in the majority of those being created. Given the fact that the Black female-headed family type makes up about 40 percent of all families receiving AFDC, in the U.S., welfare discussions have decidedly racial implications. Such a racially charged issue is undoubtedly a primary reason welfare instigates such animosity from "innocent" taxpayers. Any governmental administration, particularly one whose policies are heavily influenced by the goals of the New World Order, is under tremendous pressure to decrease welfare assistance and the number of welfare recipients. Actually, corporate America would not allow too much interference by big government in terms of meaningful workfare, as such an income-maintenance program would "by protecting the subsistence of working people, intrude upon and constrain the dynamics of the labor market" (Piven and Cloward 1982, 147). In fact, it is not only corporate America which has reservations about workfare. With regard to the expansion of workfare in New York, one news article reported, "Municipal unions, battered by large work force cuts (17,000 in the Giuliani administration alone), may see workfare as a threat."[86] The report goes on to state that the municipal unions maintain that workfare recipients "take jobs from city workers."

If many welfare mothers could enter the workforce and thereby make enough to afford adequate child care, and with sufficient health-care coverage and retirement benefits, they would gladly get off public assistance.

But otherwise, who will care for the infants and children left at home? In an era of fiscal restraint it is not likely that enough orphanages or public institutions could be built to accommodate all 10 million children now on AFDC. The closest this country comes to a national child-care system is the child-care credit parents may receive on their income tax. Although child care is supposed to be provided as a transitional measure for a limited time in some workfare measures, the paycheck of the average new jobholder will be insufficient to cover average weekly child-care expenses. According to the conference report on the Family Support Act of 1988,[87] the act was "to replace the existing AFDC program with a new Family Support Program which emphasizes work, child support, and need-based family support supplements, and assist needy children and parents under the new program to obtain the education, training and employment needed to avoid long-term welfare dependence." A professor of economics at the University of Michigan, Greg J. Duncan, is quoted by the *New York Times* as rejecting the claim that there is an increase in the proportion of children who are dependent upon welfare.[88] In comparing the number of welfare dependents of the Great Society 1970s with the New World Order age twenty years later, Professor Duncan's data showed no greater dependency in the latter period than in the former.[89]

The essence of the problem with welfare really lies with two societal features. One is its politicization, and the other is its purported drain on the taxpayers. The former feature is exemplified in politicians' campaign strategies developed with the knowledge that there "are few votes to be had in defending welfare recipients."[90] Underlying the second feature is the racial association made by many "taxpayers" when they hear the word "welfare." Because of such racial undercurrents, a bank failure costing taxpayers 2.5 billion dollars gets much less fanfare than the relatively modest amounts the government spends on the welfare of its citizens. Savings-and-loan insolvencies, just one of which cost taxpayers almost 2 billion dollars alone,[91] do not appear to generate the intense resentment good citizens feel toward one Black welfare mother. The huge deficits in the budget caused by defense expenditures made near the close of the Cold War are chalked up as unwise investments, whereas welfare expenditures, a fraction of the former, evoke much more hostility. (The former got much better press.) Taxpayers would rather support defense contractors than welfare mothers, both of whom hold the key to investment in the nation's most valuable resource, human beings.

An important point in this chapter is that the welfare state acts in a diversionary fashion to characterize Whites and males as victims of poor Blacks and females who intentionally misappropriate the valuable tax dollars of the former. As pointed out by Piven and Cloward (1982, 159–160), the welfare-state programs help to "stabilize and stimulate capitalist growth while also legitimating a class society." Further, favored members of the New World Order elite are dealt with much more leniently when they commit fraud against the private sector, even though the cost to the public may ultimately be just as substantial, if not more so.[92] The public, however, because of the messages from mass communications, seems to tolerate the duplicity of a New World Order leader's misappropriating millions of dollars much better than the duplicity of a poor woman's misappropriating food stamps in order to buy insulin or soap. A caretaker recipient of AFDC who gets a scholarship for college tuition and does not report it as income has committed fraud in some states.

Even the intensity of budget balancing efforts varies with the political motivations and focus of the policy makers. As mentioned Chapter 1, prior to the New World Order's official announcement, budget deficit reduction efforts were done in a cavalier, almost offhand, style.[93] Only when such efforts were to be used against the poor, women and minorities, were they activated with a vengeance.

Culpability, then, is a matter of person and perspective with reference to the welfare state. Who is more blameworthy, illegal-alien babysitters who have been denied their Social Security benefits or their employers (for example, Zoe Baird and Kimba M. Wood, both nominated to the highest law enforcement position in the land)?[94] African American single-parent females making the average income for their group would be less likely to have such a child care problem. (Former Surgeon General Jocelyn Elders' nomination challenge survived because her husband bore the responsibility of paying the social security taxes for the care of her mother-in-law.)

Facing inordinate child care and survival problems, the Black woman has been subjected to such horrific social conditions of racism and gender discrimination that she has not had access to the broader job market.[95] Given these conditions, however, the Black woman has done a remarkable job of surviving, as was indicated in sociologist Lena Wright Myers' 1980 book, *Black Women, Do They Cope Better?*. Black women have used innovative strategies to deal with their inordinately stressful lives (McAdoo 1985). Some, however, have fallen victim to the "victimless" offenses of welfare fraud, drugs or prostitution. Such cases have been highlighted in the news, helping to perpetuate and reinforce negative images of the Black woman, images that help to justify the secondary status of the Black woman in the New World Order. Because of the unequal distribution of income in the United States, as enforced by the courts and reinforced by the mass media, an inordinate number of Black single-parent families receive AFDC. As previously mentioned, about 14.1 million persons receive AFDC. Of those, 17.3 percent (5.55 million) of all Blacks and 10.8 percent (2.7 million) of all Hispanics receive welfare. Conversely, 2.7 percent (5.85 million) of all Whites are on the "dole."[96]

From Roosevelt's New Deal to Reagan's New World, membership in certain racial and socio-economic groupings has shaped the ability to receive certain governmental benefits. As a prototypical New World Order scheme, the "Contract with America" initiative contains ten major sets of legislative objective tenets[97]:

1. The Fiscal Responsibility Act: Balanced-budget constitutional amendment; presidential line-item veto.

2. The Taking Back Our Streets Act: Anti-crime package including warrantless home searches, longer prison terms, prison construction, quicker deportation of alien offenders, fewer state prison appeal rights and, for crimes involving victims, full restitution requirements.

3. The Personal Responsibility Act: Prohibits welfare to minor mothers, denies increased AFDC for additional children while on welfare, cuts spending for welfare programs, two-years-and-out provision with work requirements and mandatory five-year limitation on cumulative AFDC and work program participation.

4. The Family Reinforcement Act: Intensified child support enforcement, tax incentives for child adoption, broadened rights of parents in their children's education (such as vouchers), stronger child pornography laws and tax credit for elderly dependent care.

5. The American Dream Restoration Act: A $500 per child tax credit, begin repeal of the marriage tax penalty, expansion of I.R.A. (American Dream) savings accounts.

6. The National Security Restoration Act: Prevent use of U.S. troops under U.N. command, restoration of national security funding, develop system to defend United States against ballistic missile attack and establish bipartisan commission on military readiness and worldwide U.S. credibility.

7. The Senior Citizens Fairness Act: Raise Social Security earnings limit, repeal 1994 tax hikes on Social Security benefits subject to income tax and provide tax incentives for private long-term care insurance.

8. The Job Creation and Wage Enhancement Act: Small business incentives, reduce capital gains tax and indexation, neutral cost recovery, risk assessment/cost-benefit analysis, strengthen the Regulatory Flexibility Act and unfunded mandate reform.

9. The Common Sense Legal Reform Act: Make lawsuit losers pay winners' legal fees in certain federal court cases, place reasonable limits on punitive damages and reform product liability laws to reduce litigation.

10. The Citizen Legislature Act: Constitutional amendment to limit terms (to 12 years) for members of Congress (coincidently, in its 1994–95 term, the Supreme Court ruled Congressional term limits unconstitutional in the *U.S. Term Limits, Inc. v. Thornton* case[98]).

Like the social institutions of Orwellian fame[99] (Orwell's Hall of Justice, for example), these New World Order policy prescriptions for social reengineering[100] misspoke their true intent. Challenging the welfare component of the Contract with America, one member of Congress from Harlem,

Representative Charles B. Rangel, characterized the debate as the difference between being governed "by conscience" and being governed "by contract."[101]

According to a brochure distributed by the Black Community Crusade for Children (BCCC), an initiative coordinated by the Children's Defense Fund,[102] welfare provisions derived from the full implementation of the original Contract with America would:

1. Make as many as 5 million to 6 million additional children destitute by permanently denying them public assistance benefits.

2. Make millions of additional children hungry by reducing funds for school meals, food stamps, and WIC.

3. Slash child investments for decades to come by amending the U.S. Constitution to require a balanced federal budget.

4. Repeal at least $4 billion in crucial after-school and summer programs and other violence prevention initiatives.

5. Bankrupt the federal government through sweeping new tax give-aways to the wealthy.

6. Accelerate the trend of helping the well-to-do elderly at the expense of poor and near-poor children.

7. Mock family values by authorizing increased housing discrimination against families with children and allowing landlords to evict or increase rents for hundreds of thousands of children and their families.

8. Create hundreds of thousands—even millions—of new "orphans" by taking poor children from their parents and placing them in government-operated orphanages.

9. Leave a $4.3 trillion debt on our children and deny them the basic investments they need to grow up and get educated and become productive citizens.

10. Eliminate virtually all services and aid to *legal* immigrants, many of whom are children.

Even modified, the Contract has dire implications.[103] While the focus of the BCCC brochure is upon children, women in general and Black women in particular as a disproportionate *underclass* (Marable 1983) are targeted, as they are still the primary caretakers and custodians of children who are poor and near-poor.[104] For instance, when Congressional (House of Representatives) proponents of welfare cutbacks and state control wanted to demonstrate in visual imagery a success point in their efforts, they featured a Black woman in a photograph happily checking off welfare reform from their agenda.[105]

Child Care

The United States resembles an "emerging" nation more than a "developed" one when it comes to providing such humane necessities as universal health care, quality public education, work opportunities, housing and child care. It should even do better, given the abundance of crops it produces in providing nutritious food for everyone. But all these necessities (even education because of the way it is financed) are at the mercy of the marketplace.

There is no national program for child care, other than the federal government's allowance of tax credits for eligible child care expenses. A few private corporations started "family leave" initiatives before the passage of the Congress's legislation of that benefit, but the closest the federal government has come to providing child care nationally is in connection with the AFDC program.

Significantly for Black women, particularly those who are poor, unsubsidized child care is an extremely expensive proposition. In many areas, adequate child care costs as much as a woman's entire salary or wages. When the author's children were preschool age, she discussed the issue with an African American schoolteacher who had three children of the same age. Although this mother's income was above average (for women), she described how she had just signed her entire paycheck over to her babysitter.

The government will not infringe upon the "right to privacy" of the family by interfering in this area. Even related benefits such as school lunch programs have been decreased.

Under the Reagan administration even the limited deductible child-care costs used to help determine eligibility for AFDC were decreased. In addition, although Title XX of the Social Security Act, implemented in 1974, provided $2.5 billion dollars to the states to provide a variety of social services, including child care, to low-income residents, including those who are poor but do not qualify for public assistance, in following their own "laboratory" versions of the New World Order directive, most states decided to discontinue many such benefits.

Social Security—From the New Deal to the New World

The Social Security Act, passed in 1935, governs both AFDC and the more "respectable" program Social Security. Both programs were created to address the needs of vulnerable populations. Social Security addresses the income needs of persons who were fortunate enough to work, and AFDC addresses the income needs of persons who were unfortunate enough to be born into families in which a person was not fortunate enough to work.[106]

Although covered under the same legislative rubic, Social Security is not as stigmatizing as AFDC, probably because the receipt of AFDC originally meant that there was not a man in the house (but see the 1968 *King v. Smith* case again). Another reason may be that one who has worked and grown old is more "deserving" than one who has not worked or who belongs to a family where the need arose before a breadwinner could grow old and is thereby "undeserving." The distinction translates at an administrative level as a difference between the deserving and the undeserving poor or, in other terms, the certification of the "truly needy."

For many Black women now who are single parents, this value judgment translates into a policy that it is more deserving to have been married and to have lost the support of a spouse through death than it is to be alone through desertion, divorce or through not having been married. The latter circumstance, coupled with joblessness and no other income, would almost surely mean a Black female single parent would have to obtain AFDC and its accompanying stigmatic baggage (Rank, 1994).

When describing Social Security to the public, President Roosevelt in the 1930s avoided the words "welfare" and "social insurance." Similarly, the "deserving poor" were eligible to receive unemployment compensation. In short, the only respectable way to receive governmental aid was to belong to the deserving-poor category of being too old, too young, too blind or too permanently disabled to care for oneself. It was also somewhat tolerable to be temporarily separated from one's employment through "no fault of one's own."[107] Even now, in the days of untempered layoffs due to downsizing and cost-cutting,[108] if one is laid off for long, one's competency, skill and worth become susceptible to doubt. President Roosevelt's initial social welfare reservations notwithstanding, there were some fundamental protections it represented. In addressing Congress in 1941, President Roosevelt talked about freedoms "everywhere in the world." The first two freedoms related to the First Amendment (Speech and Religion). And then Roosevelt went on to state:

" . . . The third is freedom from want—which, translated into world terms, means economic understandings which will secure to every nation a healthy, peacetime life for its inhabitants—everywhere in the world."[109]

Social Security itself is inadequate as a public assistance mechanism. In fact, the middle-class only begins to have reservations about the orders of the Orderites (such as budget balancing) when Social Security is threatened.[110] Otherwise, as long as the Orderites, using their code words, promise to keep the "racial scales balanced," they pretty much have carte blanche.

Social Security does not effectively reach people in the labor force who have part-time employment, as more and more people do. It does not reach people who are kept from entry into the labor force. (The initial purpose of Social Security it may be recalled was to insure against loss of income.) Further, the program has severe funding problems because it relies upon employer-employee contributions. Benefit levels have increased at a faster rate than payroll taxes. The government uses the fund for general revenue purposes, resulting in intermittent shortages in the fund used to pay benefits.

Such a situation does not bode well for the time when the postwar generation, the baby boomers,[111] reaches Social Security age after 2010. Unless funding alternatives are found, the shortage will be critical, partially because there will probably be only three workers, if that, for every retiree by the time the baby boomers reach retirement age.

Last, the Social Security program was developed with many antiquated social conventions of the 1930s, such as divorced women receiving fewer benefits than did married women.[112] However, a change made in 1979 reduced the number of years a man or woman had to be married in order to receive his or her spouse's Social Security benefits, from 20 to 10 years. The New World Order administrations of Presidents Reagan and Bush would have eliminated altogether the benefits for dependent spouses, had it not been for Congress. As it is, whether one is a Social Security beneficiary or an AFDC recipient, one's future does not look that secure.

Another victim of New World Order social engineering was the adult student. This add-on has been eliminated. Prior to this Social Security cut, family heads whose spouse was deceased or disabled could call upon Social Security for assistance with college tuition for their offspring. With this modification, college will be an impossibility for many Black children who are in that situation, as well as for many White children. Their situation has been made worse because many college financial-aid programs have been drastically reduced. In addition, the funding in most states for public institutions of higher learning has been substantially cut. People have to make it through college "on their own," which means, as the American Council on Education Vice President Terry W. Hartle notes, "when college tuition goes up, enrollment among low- and middle-income students falls, and for those students a very important form of social and economic opportunity disappears."[113]

Single heads of family who wish to obtain additional training for themselves may not be able to do so because of these financial aid reductions. The lack of educational access described in Chapter 4 is hence exacerbated by the cuts, which deny the knowledge, skills and training crucial for most Black women to escape poverty. Though the New World Order education policies may thus work a further hardship upon the poor Black woman, middle-income students and their families do not escape unscathed. Their hopes, dreams and aspirations for a better life or just to live in "the manner to which they were accustomed" are sharply diminished by reductions in the availability of a higher education.

Further, if one is disabled, as a disproportionate number of Black women are, by hypertension, heart disease, diabetes, sickle cell anemia, tuberculosis, AIDS, or any of the other illnesses that beset Blacks to a relatively higher degree, then lowered government benefits pose a true hardship. Twenty-five percent of the approximately 43 million Americans in the United States who do not have health insurance are Black (see Chapter 7). If one is the sole caretaker for one's children and stricken by disease while under fifty-five years of age, the chances of being eligible for disability benefits under present Social Security guidelines have decreased (The author did have a forty-two-year-old Black female client with an inoperable brain tumor whom, at the hearing, the state doctor gave less than two years to live that the administrative judge ruled was eligible.) In 1992, Legal Services revealed that 50 percent of all claims which had been denied by the Social Security Administration at the administrative level were reversed when appealed at the appellate court level. A New World Order maxim had tried to cut domestic spending by systematically denying legitimate Social Security claims clandestinely and thereby avoiding political fallout from the aging U.S. electorate.

It has become harder and harder to prove that one is not able to engage in any "substantial gainful activity."[114] In other words, if one can engage in any work which exists in the national economy, one is not eligible to receive disability payments from the Social Security Administration. For all practical purposes, if one has been able to walk into a Social Security Administration office, and sit long enough to fill out the disability application, one probably has enough "residual functional capacity"[115] to be denied disability payments. The standards are even tougher for disability payments to those who have had insufficient employment to be eligible for Social Security benefits (SSD-General Assistance).

SUMMARY

Another name for "Black Woman in the World of Welfare" could be derived from Lewis Carroll's *Alice in Wonderland*.[116] Carroll's constructions, the Cheshire Cat, the Mad Hatter, the Queen of Hearts, the Mock Turtle and the March Hare, seem like characters that might be found today in social welfare policy development and implementation. As grotesque as the logic of Carroll's concocted creatures was, its eccentricities pale in the face of emerging ideas about what to do with poor people in the New World Order. These ideas become ever more strange when the image of the young Black unmarried mother is evoked as the scapegoat designed to fuel these sadistic inspirations.[117]

This country has not seen children on the streets scrambling for food and shelter for a long time. It is ironic that the first state to pass the most comprehensive welfare-retreat "reforms," Massachusetts, was also the first state to pass a child labor law, in 1836. The first federal child labor law was not passed by the Congress until 1916, but it was the Fair Labor Standards Act of 1938 that did the most to promote national child labor reform. To be perfectly fair, candid and consistent with its welfare policy direction, the government should now repeal such laws, to let the children and their mothers "compete" fully (and legitimately) in the open economic market for goods and services. To prevent them from participating in the labor market and yet to deprive them of food, clothing, shelter and medical care is to hamstring their increasingly laborious survival efforts. To keep such child labor laws on the books while trying to repeal the "welfare state" is even more duplicitous.

Reacting to the retreat of welfare programs under the progenitor of the New World Order movement, former President Reagan, C. W. Joe of the University of Chicago's Center for the Study of Welfare Policy stated:

President Reagan's proposals to reduce federal spending for . . . public assistance programs have two critical flaws: they strip low-income families of their already meager resources, while inflation continues to erode the value of their incomes, and they shift significant fiscal burdens onto states and localities whose budgets are already in the red.[118]

This statement remains true for most of the welfare reform measures subsequently proposed.

Of course these changes have the greatest impact upon single-parent families. Further, as almost half of all African American children under eighteen will spend some time in a single-parent family,[119] they will suffer the most from such regulations. In addition, such punitive regulations continue to hamper the ability of those on welfare to survive and ultimately to get off welfare because they reinforce a condition of hopelessness and helplessness, even while the myths which maintain their brutal treatment are torn down.[120]

Welfare policies are greatly influenced by the increased poverty of Black women, particularly those who head single-parent households. The poverty rate in 1990 for Black female-headed households was 50.6 percent,[121] while the poverty rate for the White female-headed family was 29.8 percent. The overall poverty rates for Black and White persons in 1990 were 31.9 percent and 10.7 percent, respectively, which means that women become significantly poorer when heading a family and thus have a significantly greater need for welfare.

To make a long story short, women are punished for having children and being without a spouse, a situation that speaks strangely of public policy given the fact that 50 percent of all marriages fail and that an increasing number of women do not have spouses when they have children.

One concludes from this discussion that Black women in the New World Order of welfare reform face ever more horrendous ordeals. There were few social and legal resources for the Black woman and her family in the past, and it looks as if there will be even fewer in the future. From a functional standpoint, however, the welfare system is doing what it is supposed to do. It is keeping the Black woman secure enough to be insecure, maintained enough to be marginal and hopeful enough to be constantly disappointed.

That this discussion of decreased benefits has highlighted administrations from one political party does not mean that the deficits of the social welfare system are entirely the fault of that party. The dehumanization systemic to the welfare system transcends any given political party. Further, it is interesting to note that one of the most far-reaching and positive welfare-reform proposals came from former President Richard M. Nixon of the same party as the Reagan/Bush administrations. During the Nixon administration, credited with creating the Environmental Protection Agency and the Occupational Safety and Health Administration, beginning racial quotas and set asides and instituting wage and price controls, Nixon proposed a guaranteed annual income.[122] If the poverty line, as figured by the federal government, was calculated to be $13,924, and a family's gross income was $12,924, then the government would send $1,000 to that family to make up the difference.

The most threatening (to some) problem created by this solution to poverty is that it virtually eliminates the huge social-welfare bureaucracy wherein one half of all welfare costs is directly attributable to administrative expenses. Indeed, like the criminal justice system, the welfare system provides employment and respectability to throngs of the middle classes, some of whom are Black. Also, gone would be the intimidation, the moral judgments and the stigma of "being on welfare." Gone too would be the political football aspect of government's role in parceling out welfare benefits. Hence, Nixon's guaranteed annual income proposal did not pass; it has as much chance of success in the future as it did when he was president. What might have a chance is the use of less intrusive methods meant to prevent and monitor any welfare fraud. The intrinsic criminalization of any legally defined welfare transgressions of those attempting to live on less than half the amount documented to constitute a decent standard of living is simply not fair. Technology, which has computerized the monitoring of welfare recipients to an extensive degree, perhaps could assist in developing the less-intrusive methods that should be employed (such as plastic benefit cards[123]). Whatever amenities are added to the system, it will be assured by society that welfare will not be a bed of roses. Like prison, it is supposed to inflict hardship, suffering and shame.

This is not to say that the Black female-headed family will not survive, for it has always risen to the occasion in times of adversity. What the blatant impositions of deprivation through the legal system point out is simply that Black people cannot put their faith in the source of their oppression.

However, when one talks of relying on Black community resources, one has to be selective (Piven and Cloward 1980). African Americans indisputably have a rich cultural heritage, one that gives them the ability to withstand continuous onslaughts to their dignity, humanity and self-esteem. Still, when a car is being repossessed, a family evicted, a worker laid off, many times the Black community has to stand by helplessly. This helplessness is what must be addressed through economic, political, and cultural reawakening and mobilization.

NOTES

1. Katharine Q. Seelye, "Republicans Plan Ambitious Agenda in Next Congress: Grueling Schedule Set: G.O.P. Says It Will 'Transform the Process of Governing, and Work 20 Hour Days; G.O.P. Sets 'New Order' for Congress," *New York Times*, November 15, 1994, A1, A12. For example, the article notes that "Mr. [Newt] Gingrich would not address questions on the substance of his plans. But later, his spokesman, Tony Blankley, was asked how the pro-family policy for members of Congress squared with Mr. Gingrich's proposed changes for the welfare system, which include removing children from parents who are on welfare and putting them in orphanages. 'We think the current system is hideously destroying the families who are currently serviced by the welfare system,' Mr. Blankley said."

2. Robert Pear, "G.O.P. Proposal Would Overhaul Welfare System: Spending Would Be Cut—-Recipients Would No Longer Have a Legally Enforceable Right to Get Benefits," *New York Times*, November 22, 1994, A1, A12; Richard L. Berke, "G.O.P. Governors Caution Congress on Social Agenda: Split on School Prayer; Leaders Told Federal Budget Cannot Be Cut at Expense of State Governments," *New York Times*, November 21, 1994, A1, A14; Jason DeParle, "House G.O.P. Would Replace Scores of Programs for the Poor: Money Would Be Cut and Sent to States as Grants," *New York Times*, December 9, 1994, A1, A10.

3. Barbara Crossette, "U.N. Planning Ambitious, and Risky, Conference on Poverty," *New York Times*, January 23, 1995, A5.

4. Catherine S. Manegold, "Labor Secretary Urges Cuts in 'Corporate Welfare' Too," *New York Times*, November 23, 1994, A11.

5. Robert W. Collin and Willa M. Hemmons, "Equal Protection Problems with Welfare Fraud Prosecution," *Loyola Law Review* 33, no. 1 (1987): 17–49.

6. Ibid., 48.

7. 42 U.S.C. Secs. 601–678 (1982 & Supp. III 1985); see also C.F.R. Sec. 201–282 (1986).

8. Social Security Act. 42 U.S.C. Secs. 401–431 (1982 & Supp. III 1985); see also 20 C.F.R. Sec. 404 (1986).

9. Supplemental Security Income, 42 U.S.C. Secs. 1381–1383c (1982 & Supp. III 1985).

10. Medicare, 42 U.S.C. Secs. 1395-1395xx (Social Security Act, Title XVIII); Medicaid, 42 U.S.C. Secs. 1396–1396p (Title XIX).

11. Henry A. Coleman, "Interagency and Intergovernmental Coordination: New Demands for Domestic Policy Initiatives," ed. John Jacob, *State of Black America* (New York: National Urban League, 1992): 249–263.

12. *Government and the Advancement of Social Justice—Health, Welfare, Education and Civil Rights in the Eighties*, President's Commission [Carter's] for a National Agenda for the Eighties, Washington, D.C., 1980, 57–64.

13. Sharon Elise, "Teenaged Mothers: A Sense of Self," *African American Single Mothers: Understanding Their Lives and Families*, ed. Bette J. Dickerson (Thousand Oaks, Calif.: Sage Series on Race and Ethnic Relations, 10, 1995): 62.

14. Robert Pear, "House Backs Bill Undoing Decades of Welfare Policy: Control for the States; Measure to Cut $69 Billion in 5 Years, Goes to Senate; Changes Are Expected," *New York Times*, March 25, 1995, A1, A9, relating that in House bill of the 104th Congress, "Most legal aliens would be made ineligible for cash assistance food stamps, Medicaid, Supplemental Security, Income and social services financed under Title XX of the Social Security Act," A9; also see, Sam Howe Verhovek, "Legal Immigrants Seek Citizenship in Record Numbers: Fear Cutoff of Benefits; They Feel Stigmatized, Citing Initiatives in Congress and California to Deny Aid," *New York Times*, April 2, 1995, A1, A13.

15. David E. Rosenbaum, "Notebook-Welfare: Who Gets It? How Much Does It Cost?" *New York Times*, March 23, 1995, A11 (citing 1992 data from the Department of Health and Human Services).

16. Joye Mercer, "Political TrendLetter: Blacks Lag in Income, but Graduation Rates Increase," *Focus: The Monthly Magazine of the Joint Center for Political and Economic Studies* 23, no. 4 (April 1995).

17. *King v. Smith*, 393 U.S. 309 (1968).

18. *Government and the Advancement of Social Justice*, 64.

19. Ibid., 66.

20. Rick Bragg, "Child-Support Crackdown Shows Success and Limits," *New York Times*, April 14, 1995, A1, A9.

21. *America's New Beginning*, The White House, Office of the Press Secretary, February 18, 1981 (a press release).

22. Ibid., 1–13.

23. E.g., Adam Clymer, "Gingrich Sees Need to Delay Bid to Review Old-Age Plan," *New York Times*, January 3, 1995, A8; Michael Wines, "G.O.P. in Senate Hoping for Cuts of $450 Billion: Proposal Covers 5 Years; Slashes in Spending Are Likely for Every Benefit Program Except Social Security," *New York Times*, January 4, 1995, A1, A10.

24. Robert Pear, "Welfare Debate Will Re-Examine Core Assumptions: Pivotal Change Possible; Republicans Question the Idea That All Eligible Applicants Are Entitled to Benefits," *New York Times*, January 2, 1995, A1, A7.

25. Robert Pear, "Meeting Narrows Discord on Change in Welfare Policy: No Consensus Reached; Disagreements Still Remain on Role of States in Shaping Their Own Programs," *New York Times*, January 29, 1995, A1, A9.

26. Ibid.

27. Robert Pear, "Governors Propose a Limit To Federal Control of Welfare," *New York Times*, January 28, 1995, A1, A7.

28. Pear, "Meeting Narrows Discord."

29. Jennifer Dixon, "Welfare Moms Should Work, Too, Shalala Says" *Plain Dealer*, June 4, 1993, 1–A, 12–A.

30. Celia W. Dugger, "Often-Cited Workfare Effort Provides Cautionary Lessons," *New York Times*, November 25, 1994, A1, A12; Judith Havemann, "CBO Estimates That All 50 States Will Fail Welfare Plan's Work Rates," *Plain Dealer*, March 23, 1995, A11.

31. David E. Rosenbaum, "The Welfare Enigma: Fight Against Poverty Is Hindered by Contradictions and Convolutions," *New York Times*, February 10, 1995, A11.

32. David S. Cloud, "Kidding on Social Security?: According to the 1994 Social Security Board of Trustees Report, The Trust Funds Will Not Run Dry Until 2036," *Plain Dealer*, March 27, 1995, B9.

33. Ibid.

34. Michael Cooper, "Tighter Welfare in Massachusetts: State Moves Toward System Among Most Restrictive," *New York Times*, February 4, 1995, A1, A6.

35. Ibid.

36. Michael Cooper, "Massachusetts Governor Signs Bill Overhauling Welfare," *New York Times*, February 11, 1995, A6 that lists "'Caps on Benefits Relating to Family Size': Arkansas, Georgia, Indiana, New Jersey, Wisconsin—'Time Limits or Work Requirements': Colorado, Connecticut, Florida, Georgia, Indiana, Iowa, Michigan, South Carolina, South Dakota, Vermont, Wisconsin."

37. Cooper, "Tighter Welfare in Massachusetts."

38. "Massachusetts Lawmakers Pass Welfare Restrictions," *New York Times*, February 10, 1995, A11.

39. Cf. Fox Butterfield, "California's Courts Clogging Under Its 'Three Strikes' Law," *New York Times*, March 23, 1995, A1, A9.

40. Robert Pear, "Governors Deadlocked on Replacing Welfare Programs With Grants to States," *New York Times*, January 31, 1995, A8.

41. Richard L. Berke, "Dole and Gramm Clash on Revising Laws on Welfare: Sharp Split in the G.O.P.; Doubts About Passage of Bill to Give States More Power Over Aid for the Poor," *New York Times*, July 16, 1995, A1, A10.

42. David E. Rosenbaum, "Governors' Frustration Fuels Effort on Welfare Financing," *New York Times*, March 21, 1995, A1, A4; also see, Robert Pear, "House Takes Up Legislation to Dismantle Social Programs," *New York Times*, March 22, 1995, A12.

43. David E. Rosenbaum, "Budget Amendment May Be Short of Enough States for Ratification," *New York Times*, January 23, 1995, A1, A8.

44. Ibid.

45. Robin Toner, "Drive for Block Grants Pitting State Against State," *New York Times*, June 28, 1995, A1, A8.

46. E.g., Joseph B. Treaster, "'It's Pataki, Sounding Like Cuomo': Drug Wars, Cont.; The Liberals' Unlikely Ally," *New York Times*, February 5, 1995, E3; Editorial, "Unclogging the State Prisons," *New York Times*, January 31, 1995, A10; Kevin Sack, "Pataki Asks Deep Cuts in Welfare," *New York Times*, January 31, 1995, A12; and, Ian Fisher, "Pataki Plan Would Cut Aid for Poor," *New York Times*, February 3, 1995, A16.

47. Katharine Q. Seelye, "House Overturns a Crime Provision for Adding Police: Bill Faces Clinton Veto; Local Governments Would Get Discretion Over

Spending of Anti-Crime Money," *New York Times*, February 15, 1995, A1, A7; Katharine Q. Seelye, "2 Anti-Crime Bills Cleared by House by Large Margins: New Money for Prisons; Strong Bipartisan Support for Getting Tough on Convicts, Including Longer Terms," *New York Times*, February 11, 1995, A1, A8; Douglas Jehl, "Clinton Promises to Veto Measure on Crime Policies: Confrontation Course; President Says Hiring of More Police Officers Should Not Be a Political Football," *New York Times*, February 12, 1995, A1, A13.

48. Seelye, "2 Anti-Crime Bills Cleared by House by large Margins."

49.   Clymer, "Gingrich Sees Need to Delay Bid to Review Old Age Plan," A7.

50. Ibid.

51. Robin Toner, "Gingrich Promises a Hard Look At How to Streamline Medicare: Health Programs Become Target for Cost Cutters," *New York Times*, January 31, 1995, A1, A8; Robin Toner, "G.O.P. Moves Health Debate To Medicare," *New York Times*, February 12, 1995, A1, A14; Associated Press, "GOP Votes Down Attempt to Exempt Social Security," *Plain Dealer*, February 15, 1995, 14–A.

52. Robert Pear, "Lump-Sum Grants for Nutrition Aid Proposed by G.O.P.: Food Stamps Unaffected; Programs for School Lunches and Assistance to Children Would Be Overhauled," *New York Times*, February 18, 1995, A1, A7; but also see, Robert Pear, "G.O.P. Leaders in House Agree on Alternative to Food Stamps," *New York Times*, March 2, 1995, A1, A13; Robert Pear, "G.O.P. Leaders Halt Abolition of Food Stamps: First Setback for Plan to Shift Programs," *New York Times*, February 25, 1995, A1, A7. In that article it was stated that: "The lawmakers from farm states demanded that the Government retain the food stamp program as the ultimate national safety net for poor people" A1; Peter L. Vielbig, President, School Lunch Computer Services, Letter to the Editor, "Think of School Lunch Program as Business," *New York Times*, March 2, 1995, A14.

53. Stephen Labaton, "G.O.P. Preparing Bill to Overhaul Negligence Law: More Federal Control; House Measure Offers Greater Protection to Businesses in Product Liability Cases," *New York Times*, February 19, 1995, A1, A15; Neil A. Lewis, "First of 3 Bills on Legal System Is Passed in House: Seeks To Settle Lawsuits; Anecdotes of Rampant Abuse Help Overcome Opposition from Consumer Groups," *New York Times*, March 8, 1995, A1, A12; Neil A. Lewis, "House Passes Bill That Would Limit Suits of Investors: Raises Fraud Threshold; Losing Plaintiffs Would Have to Pay Defendants' Costs if Case Is Held Frivolous," *New York Times*, March 9, 1995, A1, A8; Neil A. Lewis, "House Passes New Standards Limiting Awards in Civil Suits," *New York Times*, March 11, 1995, A1, A7; Diane McWhorter, "In Praise of Greedy Lawyers," *New York Times*, March 28, 1995, A15.

54. "Budget Measure Is Delayed Again in Angry Senate: Vote Now Set for Today; With Amendment's Advocates Still One Senator Shy, Each Side Blames the Other," *New York Times*, March 2, 1995, pp. A1, A12 which noted that "as a practical political matter, the focus had shifted from the Constitution to the ability of each party to stand up for the 40 million older Americans and the throng of lobbyists who say they know what the elderly want. [T]he rallying cry of Democrats, is that the amendment allows Congress to tap vast surpluses in the Social Security trust fund, some $650 billion by 2002, to pay down annual budget deficits" A12; Mary Anne Sharkey, "After Election, Mandate Is a Nuisance," *Plain Dealer*, March 15, 1995, B11; Linda Greenhouse, "Judicial Conference Rejects More

Secrecy in Civil Court: Plan to Make Records Easier to Seal Dies," *New York Times*, March 15, 1995, A12; and, Editorial, *New York Times*, "Injustice for Consumers," March 8, 1995, A14.

55. "Virginia Votes 2–Year Limit on Welfare," *New York Times*, February 27, 1995, A9.

56. Jonathan Tilove, "In the Shadow of the 'Bell Curve,' " *Plain Dealer*, February 5, 1995, C1, C4; also see Editorial, "A Second Chance at Rutgers," *New York Times*, February 8, 1995, A10, which commented "The discredited notion of racial genetic inferiority breeds anguish and discord wherever it arises. [A]n example is Rutgers University where the school's president, Francis L. Lawrence is fighting for his career after asserting during a faculty meeting that disadvantaged students lacked "genetic, hereditary background" to score well on college admissions tests. Mr. Lawrence apologized—Mr. Lawrence still deserves a chance to save his presidency." Also see Doreen Carvajal, "Protests Divide Rutgers Campus: President Repeats Apology but Refuses to Quit Post," *New York Times*, February 9, 1995, A1, A11; also see, Richard J. Herrnstein and Charles Murray, *The Bell Curve* (New York: Free Press, 1994).

57. James Atlas, "The Counter Counterculture: They Grew Up Railing Against the Liberal Establishment. Now They're an Establishment Themselves— Conservative, Connected and Comfortably Elite," *New York Times Magazine*, February 12, 1995, 32–39, 54, 61–63.

58. Newt Gingrich, "Beyond the 100 Days," *New York Times*, February 22, 1995, A15.

59. E.g., Editorial, "Overprotecting Corporations," *New York Times*, February 22, 1995, A14.

60. John H. Cushman Jr., "Lobbyists Helped the G.O.P. in Revising Clean Water Act," *New York Times*, March 22, 1995, A1, C19; Stephen Engelberg, "Business Leaves the Lobby and Sits at Congress's Table," *New York Times*, March 31, 1995, A1, A11; but see also, Stephen Engelberg, "Conflict of Interest Is Cited in Regulatory Bill Lobbying," *New York Times*, April 5, 1995, A13; Stephen Engelberg, "100 Days of Dreams Come True for Lobbyists," *New York Times*, April 14, 1995; Richard L. Berke, "One Change Is Not in the Contract," *New York Times*, April 9, 1995, Sec. 4, 3.

61. Robert Pear, "G.O.P. Advancing Plan to Remake Welfare System: Some in Party Object; Critics Attack Moves to Cut Aid to Unwed Teen-Age Mothers and Aliens," *New York Times*, February 10, 1995, A1, A11.

62. Stephen Moore, "How to Slash Corporate Welfare," *New York Times*, April 5, 1995, A17.

63. Cf. Jerry Gray, "Vote Is Set on Repeal of Wage Law," *New York Times*, March 29, 1995, A12 describing the efforts to repeal the Davis-Bacon Act of 1931 that "guarantees workers on Federal construction jobs the prevailing wage." The article quotes Senator Ted Kennedy: " 'This is another assault on working families,' said Mr. Kennedy, citing Republican opposition to an increase in the minimum wage and a bill that would have barred the replacement of striking workers. 'This is antiworkers ideology run amok.' "

64. Whitfield Diffie - Yes and Stewart A. Baker - No, "Does the Clipper Chip Give the Government Too Much Control Over Citizens' Privacy?" in Taking Sides:

Clashing Views on Controversial Legal Issues, Sixth Edition, M. Ethan Katsh (Guilford, Conn.: The Dushkin Publishing Group, Inc., 1995), 324-339.

65. Andrew J. Glass, "Every Phone Call Brings a New Assault on Americans' Privacy," *Plain Dealer*, February 5, 1995, C3.

66. Peter H. Lewis, "Security Is Lost in Cyberspace," *New York Times*, February 22, 1995, C1.

67. See again from Chapter 1, "Politicians Take Up Proposal to End Welfare," *Plain Dealer*, April 22, 1994, 6–A.

68. Melinda Henneberger, "State Aid Is Capped, but to What Effect?: Rethinking Welfare; Deterring New Births," *New York Times*, April 11, 1995, A1, A3; Mireya Navarro, "Threat of a Benefits Cutoff: Will It Deter Pregnancies?: Rethinking Welfare; Teen-Age Mothers," *New York Times*, April 17, 1995, A1, A9.

69. "Clinton Set to OK Welfare Family Cap," *Plain Dealer*, May 26, 1994, 7–A.

70. Robert Pear, "House Backs Bill Undoing Decades of Welfare Policy," *New York Times*, March 25, 1995, A1, A9.

71. David E. Sanger, "Outlook 1995: A Lingering Unease Despite Strong Growth," *New York Times*, January 3, 1995, C1; C3.

72. Louis Uchitelle, "The Rise of the Losing Class," *New York Times*, November 20, 1994, Sec .4, 1, 5.

73. Cornel West, "The Pitfalls of Racial Reasoning," *Race Matters* (Boston: Beacon, 1993): 23–30; also see Linda Greenhouse, "High Court Upholds Definition of 'Family' That Cuts Some Welfare Payments," *New York Times*, March 23, 1995, A11, describing the case of *Anderson v. Edwards*, U.S. Supreme Court Case No. 93–1883 written by Justice Clarence Thomas.

74. Isabel Wilkerson, "An Intimate Look at Welfare: Women Who've Been There," *New York Times*, February 17, 1995, A1, A8. According to this article, of the 14.3 million people on welfare, more than 10 million are children; and of the women who are on welfare, 38.8 percent are Black, 38.1 percent are White, 17.4 percent are Hispanic, 2.8 percent are Asian, 1.3 percent are Indian, and 1.6 percent are other or unknown. In addition, the article states that,

"37% of recipients will be on welfare less than 2 years
19% will be on 2 to 4 years
20% will be on 4.1 to 8 years
25% will be on more than 8 years" A8.

According to sources (e.g., the House Ways and Means Committee 1994 Green Book, using statistics from 1993); and David E. Rosenbaum, "Welfare: Who Gets It? How Much Does It Cost?" *New York Times*, March 23, 1995, A11, 38.9 percent of all welfare recipients are White, 37.2 percent are Black and 17.8 percent are Hispanic. The article further points out that the odds that a White adult going on AFDC will be there 10 years later are 1 in 5 and those for such a Black adult are 1 in 3.

75. 115 S.Ct. 1291 (1995).

76. 397 U.S. 254 (1970).

77. E.g., Joan Lowy, "Thomas's Wife Breaks Tradition, Works for GOP," *Plain Dealer*, February 2, 1995, A3; also see, "Careers At a Glance," *Plain Dealer*, February 2, 1995, A3.

78. Mickey Kaus, "The G.O.P's Welfare Squeeze: What Happened to Workfare?" *New York Times*, April 6, 1995, A15 points out, "Putting half the current caseload in workfare would cost about $15 billion a year."

79. 100th Congress 2d Session, Report 100–998, Subtitle A, Secs. 101–104, September 28, 1988.

80. 100th Congress 2d Session, Report 100–998, Subtitle B, Secs. 111, 112; Subtitle C, Secs. 121–129, September 28, 1988.

81. E.g., Douglas Jehl, "Clinton to Issue Order Enforcing Support Duties of U.S. Workers," *New York Times*, February 27, 1995, A10. For instance, this article reports that "President Clinton will sign an executive order intended to help states track down members of the military and other Federal *workers* [italics added] who do not pay child support or have avoided efforts to establish their paternity."

82. 100th Congress 2d Session, Report 100–998, Title IV, Sec. 401, September 28, 1988.

83. Mike McNamee in Washington, "Robert's Rules of Reorder: The New Agenda Makes Reich's Star Shine All the Brighter," *Business Week*, January 24, 1994, 74,75.

84. Bill Javetski, "These Days, Europe's Safety Net Looks More Like a Noose," *Business Week*, January 24, 1994.

85. Celia W. Dugger, "Displaced by the Welfare Wars," *New York Times*, February 26, 1995, Sec. 4, 1, 4.

86. Douglas Martin, "New York Workfare Expansion Fuels Debate," *New York Times*, September 1, 1995, A1.

87. 100th Congress 2d Session, Report 100–998, September 28, 1988.

88. Robert Pear, "Focusing on Welfare: Bush Plays Private Acts of Decency Against the Government as a Helper," *New York Times*, May 11, 1991, A5.

89. Ibid.

90. Ibid.

91. Linda Himelstein in New York, with Gail DeGeorge in Miami, "The Mud on a Fancy Law Firm: Paul, Weiss Could Pay a Bundle to Settle S & L Scandal Charges," *Business Week*, August 16, 1993, 91, 92.

92. Peter Marks, "Dealer's Plea in G.M. Fraud May Be Bargain of His Life," *New York Times*, January 20, 1995, A1, C18.

93. Walter Shapiro, "Reaganomics with A Human Face: Bush's 'Action Agenda' Has Something for Everyone—But the Bookkeepers," *Time*, February 20, 1989, 32–34.

94. Catherine S. Manegold, "After 2 Failed Nominations, Many Women Are Seething," *New York Times*, February 7, 1993, A1, A16; and Robert D. McFadden, "Backers Say Wood Gave Full Account of Employing Alien," *New York Times*, February 7, 1993, A1, A16.

95. Robert Pear, "Democrats Call Republicans Too Lenient on Welfare: Seek More Emphasis on Jobs for the Poor," *New York Times*, February 11, 1995, 6.

96. George Raymond Tyndall, Letter to the Editor, "Looking at Statistics," *New York Times*, February 17, 1995, A14.

97. David E. Rosenbaum, "Congressional Memo: G.O.P.'s Contract Gaining, But Some Obstacles Remain," *New York Times*, February 13, 1995, A1, A10; also see, Jeffrey L. Katz and David Hosanasky, "Provisions of the House Welfare Bill," *Plain Dealer*, March 23, 1995, A10.

98. 115 S.Ct. 1842 (1995).

99. Peter H. Stone, "Double-think on Capitol Hill," *Plain Dealer*, February 19, 1995, C1, C4.

100. Pear, "House Backs Bill Undoing Decades of Welfare Policy."

101. Robin Toner, "A Day of Anger as Republicans Are Put on the Defensive," *New York Times*, March 23, 1995, A11.

102. *Protecting Children in Shifting Political Winds: An Action Guide*, Children's Defense Fund—The Black Community Crusade for Children (25 E Street, N.W., Washington, D.C. 20001, 1–800–ASK-BCCC, undated—received by author, February 11, 1995).

103. Robert Pear, "Heeding Criticisms, Republicans Alter Some Parts of Welfare Overhaul Plan," *New York Times*, March 1, 1995, A13.

104. Jerry Gray, "Critics Say G.O.P. Cuts Put Unfair Burden on the Needy: The Contract with America Is Moving from the Abstract to the Concrete," *New York Times*, February 28, 1995, A11.

105. Photo by Stephen Crowley, *New York Times*, March 25, 1995, A9.

106. 42 U.S.C. Sec. 601, et seq., as amended.

107. *Government and the Advancement of Social Justice.*

108. "Armco Inc. Plans More Layoffs in Cost-Cutting," *Plain Dealer*, April 23, 1994, 1–C.

109. Clint O'Connor, "The Born Leader: Fireside Chats and Inaugural Eloquence," *Plain Dealer*, April 9, 1995, C1, C3.

110. Richard L. Berke, "Poll Finds Public Doubts Key Parts of G.O.P.'s Agenda: A Split Over Priorities; Survey Says Congress Should Stress Issues Like Crime, Jobs and Health Care," *New York Times*, February 28, 1995, A1, A11.

111. Laura Zinn, Christopher Power, Dori Jones Yang, Alice Z. Cunco, David Ross, "Move Over, Boomers: The Busters Are Here—And They're Angry," *Business Week*, December 14, 1992, 74–82; Trip Gabriel, "A Generation's Heritage: After the Boom, a Boomlet," *New York Times*, February 12, 1995, A1, A15.

112. Zinn, et al., "Move Over, Boomers: The Busters Are Here," 59.

113. William H. Honan, "State Universities Reshaped in the Era of Budget Cutting," *New York Times*, February 22, 1995, A1, A13.

114. 20 C.F.R. Sec. 404.1572; 20 C.F.R. Sec. 416.972 (rev.).

115. 20 C.F.R. Sec. 404.1505 (1980).

116. Edward Guilano, ed., *The Complete Illustrated Works of Lewis Carroll* (England: Crown, 1982). Lewis Carroll's pen name or pseudonym was Charles Lutwidge Dodgson (1832–1898).

117. Christopher D. Lamb, Staff Attorney, Center on Social Welfare Policy and Law, Letter to the Editor, "Welfare Ban Punishes Young Unwed Mothers," *New York Times*, February 22, 1995, A14.

118. *Plain Dealer*, March 20, 1981.

119. Felicity Barringer, "Rich-Poor Gulf Widens Among Blacks," *New York Times*, September 25, 1992, A7.

120. Cheryl Townsend Gilkes, "From Slavery to Social Welfare: Racism and the Control of Black Women," and Bettylou Valentine, "Women on Welfare: Public Policy and Institutional Racism," *Class, Race and Sex: The Dynamics of Control*, ed. Amy Swerdlow and Hanna Lessinger (Boston: G.K. Hall, 1981): 288–300; Gene Koretz, "Do Bigger Welfare Checks Mean More Kids? Not Really," *Business Week*, January 31, 1994.

121. U.S. Dept. of Commerce, Bureau of the Census, *Poverty in the United States* (Washington, D.C.: GPO, 1991), Tables 2 and 3.

122. George F. Will, "His Tenacity Finally Drew Grudging Respect," *Plain Dealer*, April 24, 1994, 2–C.

123. "Plastic Could Be in Cards for Needy: Benefits Via ATM by 1999?" *Plain Dealer*, June 1, 1994, 1–A.

CHAPTER 6

Black Women and the World's Ordering of "Family"

FAMILY AS A SOCIAL INSTITUTION

Social institutions are functionally related and develop dependent and interactive dynamics according to sociologist Talcott Parsons (1951). Using this framework of analysis, it can be determined that the manner in which the economic and political systems interact with the family system operates to preserve predominantly held values in the society. This is true even though such majoritarian values operate to the detriment of Black women and their families. The New World Order policies have only served to solidify and magnify the pathologies imputed to the Black family from the mid–1960's (as in the 1965 [Daniel] Moynihan Report) or before. The New World Order represents a socially disorganizing phenomenon similar to that described by sociologist Emile Durkheim in the Nineteenth Century that occurred with the onset of the Industrial Revolution. The New World Order's impact upon the Black family has been particularly disruptive and devastating by virtue of its corollary baggage (variables) of political disenfranchisement, confirmed educational isolation, increased economic impoverishment, health care fragmentation and intensified criminal prosecution.

It must be noted here, too, that these pathologies are societal, not familial or specifically generated by the Black family. They are generated by the forces set off by those in charge of the achievement of New World Order goals and objectives.

From a Parsonian perspective, the values of the society that were behind the implementation of these pathologies have been manifested through the officialdom of the legal system, which, in turn is a manifestation of what Parsons identifies as the ways the functions of the "religious" institution are expressed. Those functions include the fostering of solidarity, "brotherhood," and unity within the society. In performing such a religious function, the legal system rationalizes and justifies the existing economic and political order. In much the same manner as the criminal justice system provides propriety and esteem enhancement for law-abiding citizens, the legal system provides a sense of self-respect and propriety for those who have been able to maintain a normal family life.

In defining the Black family as broken, dysfunctional, disoriented, dilettante, abusive[1] and neglectful,[2] the legal system is reinforcing such adjectives about the Black woman, because she is so often the head of that much maligned entity. The definitions superimposed upon the Black family by the legal system are often the result of contrived, impressionistic, misleading images. For instance, Andrew Billingsley cites statistics in his book *Climbing Jacob's Ladder: The Enduring Legacy of African-American Families* (1992, 159) to show that Black families have a lower incidence of child abuse than their White counterparts.

In other words, the legal system's negative pronouncements and declarations about the Black family help to promote a feeling of unity, solidarity, patriotism, altruism and brotherhood among the non-Black families. Less encumbered by negative societal "baggage" than the Black family, non-Black families have been able to acquire a higher standard of living, manifest fewer of the pathologies that bring one into such stigmatizing systems as welfare and criminal justice and therefore have more protections from arbitrary governmental intrusions into their privacy.

The unification function of the legal system with reference to its family decision-making power is important because, in endorsing such attitudes, the society thereby accepts the existing order and context in which the family operates as a just and fair one. The declarations of the legal system as they are imposed upon the individual help to control and direct the behavior of all members of all families. The community is looking on to see what are the boundaries of family interaction that will be tolerated by the courts. It is also looking on to see if its own will is being upheld.

One problem with this scenario and the Black family is that the court is applying a Eurocentric value system. For another, the Black family, is held to the same degree of responsibility and accountability as European Americans while being denied the resources, supports and attributes that help a family to meet those obligations. White, middle-class values and beliefs might be appropriate when applied to a strictly nuclear European American family, but not when applied to an African American family extended family ties that transcend the framework of a mommy, daddy, child trilogy. The legal system forces a foreign ideology upon the Black extended family, which has been extolled as being one of the strengths of the Black family by researchers knowledgeable of and sensitive to the needs of African Americans (Robert Staples, 1973; Joyce Ladner, 1973; Harriette Pipes McAdoo, 1981; Robert Hill, 1972; 1993.) Legal edicts of this sort work to the detriment of efforts to build and fortify the Black family against the "unusual" circumstances in which it finds itself. For instance, when courts find that a grandmother and a child make up two different families in violation of a city's single-family housing laws it is putting salt in a wound that already has had a hard time healing. Or, when courts will not allow two sisters to live together and raise their children in the same household unit, again they are preventing alternative solutions from remedying socioeconomic problems. From the Parsonian functionalist perspective, what has served to maintain the jurisprudence and social structure of the Eurocentric society serves to dismantle and undermine the responses of the African American families to institutional racism and discrimination. Eventually, even for changing, Eurocentric people of the working classes, who are also fraught with the ravages of the New World Order, faith in the procedures and the product of the legal system will be shaken and its values and principles will no longer be accepted as incontrovertible.

The legal system may be deemed to be in part a political institution directed by a group of elites who administer the "order." C. Wright Mills (1959) termed such a group the "Power Elite" and described various sectors of U.S. society as directed by the different rulers. These sets of "powers" who controlled different aspects included the military-industrial complex (economic), the educational and the political institution. The family is controlled by these external forces, which ultimately direct and frame the outcome of many personal decisions, such as when and where to reside, when and where to worship, when and where to eat and, even, when and where to have children. "How" might be reasonably added to these "whens and wheres" in many instances. For example, Billingsley talks about the formation of the Cleveland "ghetto" as an offshoot of the socioeconomic-political forces operating upon the Black family which had similar results in Philadelphia, Cincinnati and many other major urban centers (1992, 124, 125).

The resolution of controversy about "family values," though, is decided by the legal system, which is a direct arm of the political institution and a repository of the unifying value system that is part and parcel of the religious institution. It is perhaps ironic that most family/domestic relations/children's courts are termed in jurisprudence as courts of "equity." Courts of equity were supposed to have superior legal authority in situations where the formal law was insufficient to effectuate justice. Courts of equity were developed during the Middle Ages as a response to a perceived lack of normal legal remedies under law available to community recourse. For all practical purposes, family values and family conflicts are still defined and decided by members of the power elite who come from European American, middle-class backgrounds. More galling to some is that, even though divorce courts service mainly those who are generally felt to be middle-class (Bernard, 1966) participants (i.e., those who have "sanctified" their union through matrimony), it is not unknown that the upper classes who administer family court doctrine often impose standards not adhered to by the members of the inner circle themselves. Hence, members of the working and middle classes often are held to a stricter code of behavior than are the upper-class elites.

The purported "lower" classes thus have not been incorporated into the structured marital-ceremony process to the extent that the middle classes have, for various reasons. Therefore, the resolution of their family dilemmas that have come to official attention lies with the juvenile and criminal courts. These courts tend to be more paternalistic and punitive than even the traditional divorce courts frequently formulating remedies that are even more foreign to families' true needs.

Robert Merton (1965) has developed theoretical formulations that assert that social institutions have mutually reciprocal functions. Further, these functions primarily are developed in the best interests of those who have power rather than in the best interests of any children who might be part of any legal family controversies. Thus, such ruling legal administrators have been effective in maintaining the status quo and preserving the unequal status of the African American family. The current inequities experienced by the African American family are just as intractable and effective as when they were first reported by the likes of W.E.B. Du Bois (1903) or Carter G. Woodson (1933) or Jessie Bernard (1966). These societal inequities wreak havoc upon the ability of a Black man and wife to stay together as illustrated in the following case study of "Shirley."

Black Family Case Study: Divorce Involving Children

Shirley met her husband when he was a coach of her women's softball team. They both loved sports and grew closer together while pursuing their mutual interests. Her husband helped Shirley when she became an assistant coach of her nine-year-old daughter's softball team. Her daughter was from a previous relationship, but Shirley's husband treated her like his own after they were married.

Shirley was an executive secretary for a quasi-governmental agency. Although she had finished high school, she had not gone to college. Shirley's husband was a college graduate. When she met him he had a promising job at a bank and made extra money on weekends and evenings coaching and refereeing basketball games.

They bought a house together, using his credit rating. Several years before their marriage Shirley had pled guilty to welfare fraud with regard to confusion as to the appropriate level of benefits for her daughter. Several months after their marriage, Shirley became pregnant. She gave birth to a baby boy. Both parents were ecstatic. Shirley's husband had a daughter, born to another woman a year prior to his marriage to Shirley. This was the first son for either of them.

Things were going along well until Shirley's husband lost his job at the bank. Shirley later told me that he was too "arrogant." He could not get along with his co-workers. He became abusive towards her, and he would argue so that Shirley could not reason with him. They got behind on their bills, including their house note. Her husband would fight her one minute and the next minute he would cry and beg her to forgive him. During those times, she would pretend to forgive him and wait until morning, then gather her things together and move with the children over to her mother's house. This made him frantic because he was "horrified" at the thought of being separated from his son. This happened a couple of times. Each time he promised the abuse would stop so that she would come home and bring his son back with her. So, she came back.

One night, however, he strangled Shirley so badly that she was left with a permanent irritation in her throat.[3] Shirley left that night in her nightgown and slippers, after he went to sleep, grabbing the children up with her. The next week her girlfriend gave her my number and she came to see me about obtaining a divorce.[4] She was still staying at her mother's with her children, her sister and her sister's children. It was a little crowded. She had put her daughter into the new school district. Her son was three years old at the time and was cared for by a day-care center, for which she paid $75 a week.

We started talking quite frequently because of all her attendant problems. Several other clients in similar situations also called me a lot. Some even began calling me "Ma," which was a little disconcerting because several were in their mid-thirties (Shirley was thirty-five when she contacted me). However, as divorce is such a traumatic event, I let the clients call me whatever and pretty much whenever they wanted. One thirty-four-year-old divorce client, whose mother had died when she was a teenager, even got me a beeper. This client would call much more than Shirley, sometimes even two or three times a day. "Hey Ma," she would begin the conversation, before going on to tell me what "he" was doing next. "He" had been escorted out of the house by the police during one of his tirades and was ordered by the court to stay away from the premises. However, he would come back occasionally. Several husbands would trespass in such manner. They would come back to get their toolbox, or their stereo, or their child, or for one last tag at their estranged wives. That tag could be for violent purposes, or it might just as likely be to try to resume connubial relations. Sometimes they were successful in the latter objective, and I would get a call to drop the case. Sometimes it would stay dropped, but as often as not it would have to be picked up again. Even after a divorce, sometimes a couple would get back together. Although one woman in her mid-thirties did not go back to her husband, she did defend the marriage a couple of years later. She said, "My marriage would have been alright if he had not hit me in the head with his gun that time and kept messing around with them drugs."

In an other instance, one twenty-seven-year-old went back and forth three times until her husband gave her a sexually transmitted disease, which was almost the final straw; she forgave him. A year later, as she told me, she woke up one Saturday at 4:30 in the morning. Something told her to go to a nearby motel, where she saw her husband's car. She knocked and knocked at the corresponding room, but there was no answer. She then drove her car around the corner and parked it, ran back and took her husband's car to her brother's house. They then drove back and got her car. Because she had gone to school with "the car thieves," she knew where they took the products of their larceny. She and her brother took her husband's car to the place where her former miscreant classmates had dropped off their stolen cars and left it there. She and her brother then retrieved her car, and she stayed with a girlfriend Saturday and Sunday nights. Monday evening, she came to my office and had me draw up the papers to file for her divorce the next morning and arrange for police protection so that she could go back home. (On Sunday, her husband had come to her college, where she was in an intensive weekend education program, seeking his car, and she had told him where to find it. She told him it was alright when she last saw it.)

Another issue regarding Shirley's divorce was whether or not she could handle the six-hundred-dollar house note by herself. She replied that as she had shouldered all the bills when he was fired, she could do it again. I informed her that this burden would be permanent, and she replied that she had had plenty of time to reflect on the pros and cons.

Given the ambivalence of many divorce clients who wish to drop a suit, I usually wait a little while and call back to check before going through the legal paperwork of dismissing a divorce. Some of the couples who tried again were successful in their reconciliations. Another young woman with a son who went back to her attorney husband after he ended an affair with his nineteen-year-old secretary has lived more or less "happily ever after." The attorney has even forgiven me for filing her divorce against him.

Shirley manifested no such indecision this time. Moreover, as she was at her mother's, she had some protection from unannounced doorstep visits. During Shirley's divorce proceedings, though, she had become so financially strapped that she had fallen behind in her restitution payments to the welfare department, payments ordered by the criminal division of the general county common pleas court as a condition of probation for her welfare-fraud conviction. Her probation officer had reported her violation and her judge was reputedly one of the toughest in the county system. I had her borrow money from her mother and presented it to the court on the date of Shirley's Probation Violation Hearing. She was shaken because, in the case immediately preceding ours, a welfare-fraud probationer had violated probation, her probation was terminated, and she was sent to the women's reformatory for the imposition of her original sentence. That woman's mother cried but she had no money to give to the defendant for restitution.

Our case was called and Shirley and I went before the stern, awesome-appearing judge. As Shirley had shown her five hundred dollar money order to her probation officer minutes before the hearing, she was given another opportunity to maintain her probationary status.

Shirley was concerned because she did not want to lose the house while her divorce was in process. Although her husband had been receiving paychecks through temporary employment as a substitute teacher, she had been primarily responsible for the mortgage. Because she now had to contribute to her mother's household, it had become financially burdensome to try to keep up both places. She felt her husband would intentionally let the house go into foreclosure unless she went back to him, as he was pressuring her to do. He was not giving her any money to help with her son's support while she was staying at her mother's. (As it turned out, he did not make any payments the year that Shirley was out of the house and HUD did begin foreclosure procedures. With a great deal of cajoling, HUD[5] finally let Shirley refinance the house, although it meant that her mortgage went up an additional $100 per month.)

Nevertheless, Shirley did not want to go back to her husband because she did not want him to beat her up again. Although I generally try to get couples to go to counseling before filing for divorce, this situation seemed so rife with immediate concerns that I agreed to file on Shirley's behalf for a divorce right away.

I told Shirley what she would have to bring to the next interview in order to fill out the "Domestic Relations Court Child Support Computation—Sole Residential Parent or Shared Parenting Order" form. That form requires computing the respective averages of three years' income of both the father and the mother. Taxes and court-ordered support paid for other children as well as adjustments being allowed for minor children born to either parent who are living with such parent are taken into consideration. This form is completed so that each parent's proportionate contribution to the household can be computed. The resulting fractions determine each parent's share of the child support award. The computation form is used in conjunction with the "Basic Child Support Schedule" in order to determine what the total child support award should be. The total award varies, depending upon the gross combined income of the couple and the number of children of the marriage. The amount can differ from what is thus computed only with signatures indicating consent by both father and mother.

Shirley was concerned because much of her husband's income was derived from his coaching and weekend stints as a referee. As she maintained, he did not report those funds for tax purposes, the computation would underestimate his portion of the family income. I told her we would just cross that bridge when we came to it.

Another point of contention was the house. They had owned it for three years, and it had a limited amount of equity. Shirley admitted that a large portion of the initial down payment had come from her husband and that it had been financed through his connection with his former bank employer. However, she stated, since the time of his job loss, she had carried the bulk of the financial burden with regard to maintaining the currency of the mortgage account. Shirley was afraid that her husband would insist either on taking the house away from her or on an unreasonable buyout because of his initial contribution to the house purchase. I pointed out that real estate commissions, bank fees, points, code-violation repairs and other sale-related expenses would diminish the proceeds from the sale. Even though the estimation of those costs exceeded the current equity in the home, we decided that we would offer her husband a thousand dollars to get out of the house and deed it over to Shirley as part of the divorce settlement.

The day of Shirley's divorce dawned. She arrived promptly with her sister (her witness) and met with me and my assistant in the hallway by the judge's chambers. I checked in with the judge's staff and was told that although several other divorces were scheduled, the judge would do the uncontested ones such as ours first. I went back down the hallway to work on the "uncontested," "simple" divorce.

Although Shirley's husband had not filed an answer to our divorce complaint and did not have a lawyer, he did have an attitude. He had consulted with one (whom he did not pay to come) and knew all of his "rights." He had gone over the computation form with someone and knew we could not prove his actual income. He offered not a penny more than $150 a month, and Shirley wanted $250 a month. Consequently, we were stuck on the first item of business.

I told Shirley's husband that since he was not legally in court, we could put down whatever amount we wanted without his approval. That comment evoked a little more cooperation and he upped his child support offer to $200 a month. Shirley agreed, and they both signed that part of the form.

Now about the house. No, Shirley's husband was not ready to deal with that part yet. He wanted joint custody of his son! He wanted to be able to go up to school (when his son started) and have some input. That threw Shirley for a loop. Although their son was not yet in school, she still did not want to have to deal with making child exchanges in the middle of the week. Moreover, she did not want to give him up for entire summers at a time in alternating years as was proposed by her husband. And what about Christmas? His upcoming birthday? Easter? The only holidays they could agree on were Mother's Day and Father's Day, respectively. Otherwise, we were stuck again.

At an impasse on the child custody issue, I went back to the house. Upset and distracted about the custody of their son, they played a little ping-pong with the house question. However, after we began with a $1,000 buyout offer and he made a $3,000 counter proposal, they quickly signed off on a $2,000 compromise for his equity in the house. I attached a copy of the real estate description culled from the deed of their house to allow the Journal Entry to be used as the new deed after docketing by the court. That point was settled.

The custody matter still loomed before us. With whom was their son going to spend the majority of his time? Who would sign his report card? Who would sign for his temporary driving permit? (Divorce or no divorce, both would have to sign his financial aid papers, of course, when the time came for him to go to college.)

I was impatient. The divorce negotiation had started at 8:45 A.M. and it was now 10:30. I had an 11:00 A.M. sentencing in the criminal court across the street. I went back to the judge's chambers to report my dilemma. The other uncontested divorces were over. The judge had a hot and heavy contested divorce with both lawyers and both parties going strong in her chambers. They were not about to quit. They were right in the middle of their various debates. Her bailiff would see what she could do about my time problem. I sent my assistant across the street to say that I would be there as soon as possible. The defendant I was representing that day was a "guest of the county" and was waiting for me in a holding cell. I had promised to try to get him out that day.

The judge's bailiff came over to us. She had found a visiting judge who would hear our case, a retired judge who had had a lot of domestic relations experience. I presented him with what we had accomplished so far that day and informed him of our unfinished business, the child custody issue.

All of a sudden Shirley's husband started crying and saying that he did not want any divorce. He wanted his family back. Shirley looked at me, disgusted. She had known he would not be amicable. The judge informed him that since he had not contested it in a timely manner, his protests really were to no avail. Further, the revised domestic relations law had added a ground for divorce entitled "Irreconcilable Differences." The judge informed Shirley's husband that when one party to a marriage was adamant about getting a divorce and the other party was adamant about *not* getting one, that made the case for the "Irreconcilable Differences" ground right there.

With that realization, Shirley's husband continued bewailing the loss of his son. The judge reassured him that he would have reasonable visitation rights. Shirley's husband insisted he wanted more than that. He wanted to be able to instruct and guide his son. To influence his growth and development. To have the benefit of his companionship. To develop a meaningful relationship with him. And anyway, did the judge know about her conviction?

Shirley feared he would bring that up. She and I both groaned at the same time. No! That was not right. The initial child custody information form filled out at the time of filing asked if a party had any civil decisions or convictions related to child or family neglect or abuse or any crimes of violence. Any other conviction was not relevant. The visiting retired judge agreed.

At that point, the judge mentioned that the court had gone to great lengths to develop a visitation schedule that would cover in detail the most minute areas of visitation. With that, I pulled out the five-page court-generated Visitation Schedule. It covered the alternating weekend times that the noncustodial parent could pick up and drop off the child. It covered the alternating holidays that the noncustodial parent could have with the child. It covered the summer periods that the noncustodial parent could have with the child. It pointed out that the noncustodial parent could always have the child on that parent's birthday and on Father's or Mother's Day, whichever was applicable. It indicated that the child was to spend alternating birthdays with the noncustodial parent.

Shirley and her husband signed the Visitation Schedule form. Their divorce [hearing] was over. I left them to do the hard part, to live with it. I went on to my next hearing.

Domestic Relations and Society

Trends in the country in the current law-and-order regime are moving toward strengthening and further institutionalizing the principles of family legal disenfranchisement as regards the Black woman. For instance, in Ohio the General Assembly eliminated recognition of common law marriages alleged to have begun after October 1991. Common law marriages are de facto unions that because of certain circumstances endemic to the relationship are retroactively declared legal and thereby under the jurisdiction of divorce (domestic relations) court by that court.

Shirley's situation described above was ameliorated somewhat by her reliance upon her extended family (also see Martin and Martin, 1978; Stack 1981). That the forms and styles of African American family structure are not "lawful" renders them much more vulnerable to attack by the economic and political forces which sustain the legal system in the first place. For instance, in the *Anderson v. Edwards*[6] case, the Supreme Court undermined the level of welfare support for children in extended family situations. And, while the wealthy can obtain retroactive protection in failed domestic relationships, the poor (disproportionately consisting of ethnic and racial categories such as Hispanic and African American) are left without recourse within the legal system. Of course, the defendants against whom action would be sought are disproportionately "uncollectible," meaning they do not have a source of income from which judgment could be enforced.

One resource that in the past was particularly helpful to Black single-parent families in the area of domestic relations was the Legal Services Corporation. When Reagan entered office, however, he complained that federally funded lawyers bring lawsuits which are in reality attempts to enforce a judicial resolution of political and public policy issues properly left to the electorate. Nevertheless, in terms of bringing legal relief to the deserted family, the Legal Services Corporation fills a crucial gap, because lawyers have a monopoly on entry into the court system. Generally, no one but a lawyer can obtain an order restraining an abusive ex-spouse or former boyfriend[7] or procure an award of child support or regain legal custody of offspring spirited away by a spiteful parent. Prior to the establishment of Legal Services, the poor did not have access to these services.

In fact, it seems difficult to conceive that the Reagan-Bush plan to put greater reliance upon child support enforcement for the reduction of AFDC payments would have much success without the cooperation of Legal Services. For one thing, who would obtain the paternity determinations necessary in many cases and then the child support award judgments? Obtaining such judgments through private resources is a time-consuming and costly procedure that few African Americans, particularly female-headed families, can afford.

The Uniform Reciprocal Enforcement of Child Support Act, the Uniform Child Custody Jurisdiction Act, the Parent Locator Service (see the Family Support Act of 1988 in Chapter 5), all invaluable legal tools to the single-parent family, would be much less effective aids without Legal Aid.

The Family Situation of the Black Woman

The normal functions of the family institution as supportive mechanisms for the Black woman are thwarted by their interaction with the other social institutions that exercise negative influences upon them (Hill-Collins, 1990). By design and by default then, the family institution operates under severe socioeconomic constraints for African Americans. Many Black couples have difficulty in forming social, religious, economic and political bonds that make up the firm foundation capable of resisting normal societal onslaughts on the viability and integrity of their union. The societal supports of employment, education, empowerment and equity that should surround any such union are either grossly restricted or completely lacking. Hence, societal racism, classism and discrimination that have been aggravated in the New World Order have operated on the Black family not just to complicate its survival (cf. Jewel 1988), but to threaten its very existence. In short, these forces devastate the male-female relationship to the point that the parties turn on each other, leading to its termination. Or, if the parties do not separate or divorce, the quality of their relationship is greatly impaired. The premise that the New World Order has exacerbated the debilitating forces is based upon historical reference. Billingsley (1992, 107) maintains that the African American family was "re-created and reconstructed" during slavery. Billingsley further cites sources that corroborate the thesis that during the period of Reconstruction after slavery, husband-wife families predominated among African Americans comprising almost 80 percent of all Black families in some counties (1992, 120). It can be inferred from period descriptions of the aftermath of migrations, wars and technological changes as reported by Billingsley that political and economic upheaval substantially decreases the ability of the African American family to maintain a two-parent [and thereby] upwardly mobile structure (1992, 124–125, 139).

The African American family, defined in administrative and academic terms as a predominantly single-parent entity, is correspondingly assessed on nearly every variable—employment, education, income, health—as being among the least of these. Ironically, the blame for its substantially diminished viability is primarily placed not upon the shoulders of the discriminatory society, but upon those of the Black woman. The Black woman is called emasculating, promiscuous, domineering, excessively fertile and lazy; it is she who fails to rear her children to avoid the lure of drugs, crime, violence and more children in lieu of jobs, education, self-discipline, obedience and abstinence.

The proportion of never-married Black women is almost twice that of never-married White women. Of all Black women in the U.S., 38.7 percent have never been married as opposed to 20.8 percent of all U.S. White women.[8] Similarly, 44.8 percent of all African American men have never been married versus 28.0 percent of all European American men. Combining the categories of the never married, the widowed (11.9 percent) and the divorced (11.0 percent), one comes up with the fact that 61.9 percent of all U.S. Black women are single.[9] Combining the approximately 8.9 percent of all White women in the United States who are divorced, and the 11.2 percent who are widowed with the never married, about 40.9 percent of all White women are single. From another angle, 43.1 percent of all Black men in the United States are married compared with 62.4 percent of their White counterparts. Using simple subtraction, it can be deduced that almost 60 percent of Black men are single as are almost 40 percent of White men, meaning that the Black/White single ratio for men approximates that for women, pointing to about 20 percent more single Black persons than White persons.

Further, these figures have consequences for children, as only 35.9 percent of all African American children live with two parents as compared with 78.5 percent of all European American children. These figures are significant because the poverty rate for U.S. children living in Black female-headed households is 68.2 percent as opposed to 47.2 percent for children in White female-headed households. The poverty rate for children who live in Black married-couple families is 15.1 percent, while for children who live in White married-couple families it is 9.8 percent. That difference is less significant as an indicator of well-being for Black children in view of the fact that there are markedly fewer Black married-couple families.

The crux of the matter lies in the fact that U.S. societal forces currently preclude the attainment of married-couple family status for most African American adults. Such a status requires economic, religious, educational and political support networks that are purposely denied African Americans in the New World Order. Access to educational, employment, entrepreneurial, emotional and other economic resources elude African American women and men in their search for stability and security in their lives. To make a long story short, it costs money to be married.

Black Family Case Study: Divorce Involving a Business

My summary account of Elaine's divorce probably reflects a more participatory than observatory participant-observer case analysis. Elaine was a long-time friend from junior high school. She was gregarious and outgoing then and had remained so. At that time she and I had not been that close because I had been placed in a college-bound track somewhat removed from our more extroverted counterparts. Because of neighborhood proximity and the convergence of our lives during our adult years, however, Elaine and I developed close regular contacts. For the civic activities in which we both participated, if given notice in the morning, Elaine could have a crowd gathered for an evening rally. Networking was her forte.

Our closeness was partially the reason that I enlisted the aid of co-counsel in handling this domestic relations matter.

Elaine had been through three previous divorces and had two sons from two of those marriages. She had maintained good relations with all of her former spouses, who were all willing to come into court and testify on her behalf.

I had never met Elaine's fourth husband. He had come up north to join his mother and several of his ten brothers and sisters from a small town in Georgia. He was seeking a better life from the one he left down south, where he had been incarcerated as a juvenile (although Elaine did not know that at the time she married him). When Elaine met Joe, he was working as a baker in a doughnut shop. He said he made the best doughnuts in the world. He was making six dollars an hour. He had a grown son from a former relationship. He was living alone in the attic of Elaine's aunt's house but was due to move in with another woman shortly. After he met Elaine, however, he changed his mind and became engaged to her.

Elaine's wedding was the most elaborately beautiful one she had had. She wore an exquisite light peach gown covered with fine embroidery and lace. Her bridesmaids were likewise adorned. My husband and I watched in wonder. It was like a fairy tale. Joe was resplendent in his tuxedo and had trimmed his "Jheri Curl." A sumptuous dinner was served in the church basement, and I took an extra plate of soul-food vegetables home.

After the marriage, Joe's son moved in with them. Joe helped to remodel totally the first floor of the two-family house where they lived, which was owned by Elaine's parents. Joe's father, who had owned a popular doughnut shop during the sixties, also helped. As Joe did not have any credit, they used Elaine's to purchase the materials. Elaine helped to get Joe a manufacturing job paying fourteen dollars an hour at the company for which she worked as a secretary.

All was going well, except for one thing. Joe had a *dream*. He wanted to own and operate his own doughnut shop like the one that his father had had years ago. After all, he was the best doughnut maker in the world.

Elaine took him to her credit union. Joe found a lawyer who connected him with a benevolent Italian investor kind enough to set him up with a "Triple-A Net Lease" (the investor would get paid first out of any income). Elaine got several of her friends to come up with a thousand dollars each. (I made a personal loan to her for four thousand which she promptly repaid when the business got on its feet a little more.) Elaine's credit union loaned Joe six thousand. Elaine's parents loaned him three thousand. The investor provided the loan for the refurbishing of the old doughnut shop building and the purchase of the necessary equipment and initial supplies. The lawyer incorporated[10] the endeavor, giving Joe 51 percent of the shares, Elaine 19 percent and the investor the remainder.

During the negotiations and refurbishing of the old building to get the business started, Joe left his manufacturing job to concentrate on starting his business.

Opening day dawned. The doughnut shop was open twenty-four hours a day in the predominantly Black suburb, which had a higher poverty rate than the adjacent metropolitan city. They hired four "girls." (Joe called them that although they were all grown women.) Joe, his father and his uncle made the doughnuts at night. Elaine and a couple of her investor friends served as shift managers. Elaine's sister, fourteen years her junior and a newlywed, left her job as a group home supervisor to serve as a manager. Elaine passed out flyers at every church she knew—and there were a lot. She gave flyers at all the neighborhood centers to individuals whom she had met when she worked at one. She flooded the community stores, nail salons, bars, beauty shops and barber shops with flyers. She gave them to her friends who were school teachers, teacher's aides, nurses, nurse's aides, clerks, day laborers, social workers, drug counselors, computer operators, waitresses, receptionists and child care workers. She went to the professional organizations of the attorneys, accountants, data processors and the pipe fitters union (to which one of her former husbands belonged). She put signs up at the credit unions. She stood outside factory gates. She passed out flyers at the parties given by the Black transit, postal and city workers. She frequented charity and political functions—Black organizations, White organizations, Greek organizations. She gave theater and cabaret parties.

She took out booths at community fairs and picnics. She had us on bus trips visiting everything from cathedrals to casinos. She organized tours to every place from passion plays, to underground railroad slave stops, to wholesale outlets, to museums, to Amish country,[11] to horse races, to amusement parks. She got in touch with businesses whose employees left home without breakfast. The doughnut shop started serving pop and sandwiches. She got in touch with companies whose workers got hungry at lunchtime. She provided the doughnuts for breakfast at a conference one of my organizations had (but also see Chapter 7 on health). The company for which she worked ordered doughnuts regularly for employee meetings and celebrations. The local police doughnut discounts helped to keep away the druggies. She put flyers in my trunk. Business was booming. They got corporate credit cards. Joe went to Georgia twice in six months, to the Bahamas, Las Vegas and Myrtle Beach once each within the year. He got a new truck. He got a bicycle to ride as part of his weight loss program. He got a bunch of new suits.

Elaine kept the books and paid the restaurant bills. They procured the services of a payroll company to make out the checks for the employees. When she left work every day she came to the doughnut shop to help manage until the third shift (Joe's father and uncle) came on at eleven. She also worked every weekend, coming in at seven in the morning on Saturday and Sunday and staying until someone else was available. She had not been able to go to morning services at church for months. She was lucky to get to the evening services. She was not able to attend her Church Courtesy Club meetings either. No more bingo, bowling or Bible study classes. She had missed so many choir rehearsals that she almost felt obliged to resign. Joe's only job was the doughnut shop. Elaine kept him covered under her health insurance at her job. He brought home $387 every week from the doughnut shop. He gave Elaine $300 for the bills and kept $87 for spending money, except for the weeks in which he travelled. He charged the things for which he did not not have the cash. For her work at the shop, Elaine was paid $200 a week.

The managers hired by Elaine began to have conflicts with those hired by Joe. Joe began to complain that too many people had control of the key to his inner office, where the safe deposit box held the money. He changed the locks on the door and the desk so that neither Elaine nor the managers could get into them. He would not let his father or his uncle into that back office either.

One day Joe claimed that the cash register tapes of Elaine's sister were short by $27. He fired her. (It was only during the later divorce proceedings that Elaine learned that the relationship between Joe and her sister had begun to deteriorate after he made a pass at her in his back office.) He also fired the two managers who had been hired by Elaine, claiming that they too had mismanaged his money.

Feeling that Joe had taken advantage of her, Elaine withheld the last $3,000 payment on the $10,000 required to purchase the initial stock offering for their company. Furious, Joe said he could get a lot of women to help him. She told him to get out and go find one. He left, but his son elected to stay with Elaine.[12]

Elaine took the breakup of this marriage rather badly. She went back to her church and consulted with her pastor. Each evening the week after Joe left, a group of her friends met to console her at a dinner club. The band that week was from New York and Elaine went there so often she began to mediate the conflict between the singer and the drummer. Listening to the consolation team ruminate about male-female relations in that atmosphere was for me like flashing back to a scene out of one of Langston Hughes' 1953 stories from *The Best of Simple*.[13]

Without legal counsel, Elaine signed an agreement with Joe that if he would not step foot on the residential premises, she would not come onto the business property. He stopped paying her the $200 a week. He called the credit card companies to cancel her charging privileges. Joe refused to pay for the $1,900 in expenses he had charged or for his father's $600 trip to Arkansas, or for the $3,000 credit union installment on the shares for the business, or for the $3,000 loan from Elaine's parents, or for any of the $10,000 in household furnishings and $20,000 in remodeling or clothing, restaurant and other personal bills he had incurred while "living large" with Elaine.

Elaine had to get a second job as a cashier in the evenings and on weekends to keep up the payments on these bills. Joe had left on September 14, 1993. While out of town at a conference during March of 1994, I received an emergency phone call from Elaine, who had been admitted to the heart ward of the largest hospital in the city. She stayed there over two weeks as they tried to get her stabilized. Once home, it was another two weeks before she could go outside. The father of Elaine's younger son, her third husband, voluntarily increased his child support payments. Although her father had a stroke during this period and her mother had to put off her retirement for a year, her parents decided to forego rent from her until she got back on her feet.

Elaine's old boss had been bought out in January of 1994, and since February she had been the executive secretary for the new head of the company. In the middle of April, one of his vice presidents called to ask her to come in off sick leave for one day and straighten out some of the files, as well as show the temporary the nuances of the computer software packages Elaine had installed. When she did so, she found the place in such a mess that she came in every day after that even though her doctor had not released her yet for work. On the Friday of the last week in April, the personnel director asked her to come into his office at 2 P.M., when he informed her that her employment was ended and her health benefits were terminated effective immediately.

Flabbergasted, Elaine asked, Why? He said she had violated the company's code of corporate conduct. How? She had received periodic pay increases after every personnel review she had had. The personnel director informed her that when making travel arrangements for the company's executives, she had kept the frequent-flyer miles, in direct contravention of company policy. In addition, she had used those companies that gave her the most travel bonus points. Those bonus points belonged to the *company!* What she had done was a conflict of interest, an infraction of the company directive that prohibited an employee from accepting favors from a firm doing business with the company. She pointed out that she had done it under her old boss with his knowledge and that her new boss had not told her anything different. It did not make any difference. A security guard escorted her out the door. The next day, Saturday, at 7 A.M. she was allowed to get her personal belongings out of her office with a guard standing over her.

The company disputed her unemployment claim with the state Bureau of Employment, and the referee upheld the company through both her hearings. She filed a complaint in the state trial court, but after a year, that complaint was still pending.

Elaine was replaced with a White secretary. (Elaine's office at the company had been completely remodeled in February when her new boss came, and she had been given the most up-to-date computer and communications equipment. She said she should have known that they were not doing all of that "just for me.") Elaine filed a discrimination claim with the Equal Employment Opportunity Commission. After a year, that complaint was still pending.[14]

Although I had had Elaine retain another lawyer for the case, Joe was so adamant about not giving her a dime of his business that he kept both of us busy. In addition, although it was almost a year since they had broken up, he still refused to pay any of the bills he had left.

The judge to whom the case was originally assigned repeatedly had tried to get them to settle, to no avail. Joe would not relinquish anything. He would not pay Elaine a penny. It was his business; he had built it up. She did not deserve anything. She got the furniture and other household furnishings as well as the work he and his father had put into helping to remodel her parents' house. At a standstill, with no settlement in sight, the judge originally assigned to the case spun it off to a retired visiting judge.

The trial started June 21, 1994. The fact that Elaine had so many friends served us well during the two-and-one-half weeks we spent in trial at the Old County Court Building that housed domestic relations. Every day Elaine's supporters filled three rows of the courtroom. They wore their Sunday best. I wore one of my seventeen blue lawyer suits; I had enough to worry about. For his part, Joe had cut off his "Jheri Curl" and sported a very short, neatly trimmed haircut; he was a businessman.

The first witness called by Joe was the personnel director from Elaine's old company. He reiterated Elaine's duplicity in taking the bonus points. How could anyone trust a person who would "steal" a company's frequent-flier miles? My co-counsel asked where the company code book was located because Elaine had never seen it. The personnel director said it was in the personnel office, available to all employees, who were specifically advised to review it when they were hired. Co-counsel also asked the personnel director about conflict-of-interest examples. During that line of questioning he elicited from the director the fact that the company had purchased doughnuts from Elaine's shop. My co-counsel then asked the director if he considered that a conflict of interest. The director just looked blank. When prompted and told to answer by the judge, he said he didn't know. When co-counsel asked him if Elaine's dismissal had been *pretextual*, a pretense rather than a valid reason, the director said it had not and stated in so many words that the reason that Elaine was fired was the reason she was fired. Other secretaries around the region in other branches of the company who had done the same thing were remarkably silent; although one especially was supportive when Elaine talked to her on the phone, she would not come to court and testify on Elaine's behalf.

Our witnesses consisted mainly of character references from Elaine's church and, for corroboration purposes, friends who had worked with the couple at the doughnut shop and/or loaned them money for its startup. We had subpoenaed both Joe's mother and his father as well as the uncle and the aunt who had worked at the doughnut shop. His mother was willing to testify on Elaine's behalf, but in the end we decided not to call her. The night before Joe's father was scheduled to appear, we went over to his house and discussed the matter with him. Joe had fired him also in a dispute over management monies and banned him from the premises. Although he was familiar with facts that would have benefitted Elaine's cause of action, he was ambivalent about coming. He did show up the next morning for court, but we did not use him because of that ambivalence. We also decided that Joe's uncle and aunt would do more harm than good even though his uncle had also been fired by Joe. Joe's aunt said, "There are two sides to every story." That statement was ominous enough for us to forego her testimony, as well.

While Joe was on the witness stand my co-counsel brought out the fact that in the year prior to their marriage, Joe had made $13,000. Elaine had made $33,000. (As Elaine had done their taxes, which they had filed separately that year, she had both of their W-2 forms in her files.) In addition, a copy of Joe's credit report containing information about the years immediately preceding their marriage indicated that his credit had left much to be desired.

The investor with whom Elaine and Joe had the Triple-A Net Lease brought in income statements from his accountant showing that the latest figures indicated that the doughnut shop had brought in $293,000 for that year.

Elaine was amazed. She was existing on food stamps and a Medicaid card from the county as well as the on the largess of her parents in foregoing the rent.

The bottom line legally, however, rested upon an accurate appraisal of the net worth of the doughnut shop. Joe claimed a lot of expenses, which had shot up even more after Elaine was precluded from managing the business end of things.

Joe and his lawyer went around and around about providing the necessary paperwork for appraisal. After the trial, the judge kept setting hearing dates for the discussion of the appraisal issue, and either Joe would not show or his lawyer would ask for a continuance.

Elaine could hardly pay for the co-counsel, let alone for a qualified business appraiser. Nevertheless, she rounded up $500 from various sources. Still, the procrastination continued, with Joe saying the business was in the hole and wasn't making any money and he was keeping it together by a shoestring. Therefore, it was worth nothing and Elaine should get nothing.

A year after the trial, Elaine's domestic relations complaint was still pending. The judge would not even give her a divorce until the property division[15] element of the case was resolved. At the time of the trial in the summer of 1994, the judge was 89 years old.

Choices for the Black Woman

Elaine's situation is a classic example of the way other social institutions interface with the institution of marriage to help "make or break" it. Although her marriage was broken, a major reason Elaine was not was due in large part to her extensive social network (see also sociologist Gay C. Kitson's book, *Portrait of Divorce*). Kitson (1992) found that Black people adjust better to divorce. There might be several explanations for her finding. One may be due to the fact that Black people are more accustomed to crisis situations in general. Another may be that as a greater proportion of Blacks as earlier indicated are single anyway, they are less of an anomaly in the context of their group. In addition, although marriage increases economic stability for Blacks (see below), proportionately, there are fewer married Black people, so marriage in and of itself has a less stabilizing influence in the Black community than it does in the White. In Parsonian terms, the tension management function of marriage, then, is not as salient for Blacks as it is for Whites. Finally, relating back to Elaine, her extensive social network not only gave her friendship. It gave her a place to stay. It gave her

her day in court—for whatever that turns out to be worth, she at least could meaningfully exercise her right to call witnesses on her behalf. It gave her (or at least her husband) a business. But whether or not she ever reaps any benefits from that, alliances, partnerships—networking gave her choices.

It is not marriage in and of itself then, that provides such a greater level of equanimity (tension management) and equilibrium in the personal lives of people. Rather it is the legal, social, economic and political advantage that such a status confers and reinforces. Elaine would have had even less of a chance of one day prevailing and obtaining some of the equity out of the doughnut shop had she merely been living with Joe rather than married to him.

By the same token also, the children of persons who are not married are stigmatized as "illegitimates" (*Labine v. Vincent;*[16] *Mathews v. Lucas;*[17] *Lalli v. Lalli*[18]) and classified under the *bastardy* laws of many states.[19] Forty-six percent of all Black children were born to teenagers who were never married. This figure contrasts with the 11 percent of all White children who were born into such a situation.[20] Hence, "illegitimate" Black children are more likely to be born in the more vulnerable situation of having a teenage parent than their White counterparts. The hazards of bringing a child into the world under debilitating social and economic conditions are what lead some women, Black and White, young and older, to seek abortions.

The treatment of the abortion issue has evoked much controversy in the New World Order at all levels of society.[21] The Black community has some ambivalence surrounding abortion (Billingsley 1992, 148, 149). Angela Y. Davis (1983, 204) writes that any such perceived ambivalence can be clarified if advocacy of abortion is distinguished from advocacy of *abortion rights*. Introductory to this discussion is the problem of Black women's having adequate information about the issue (Hill-Collins 1991, 163). Davis maintains that given the social conditions that many Black and Latina women must endure, abortions are used as a last resort from misery rather than motherhood (1983, 204). Davis also decries the fact that the passage of the Hyde Amendment[22] in 1976 precluded poor women from being able to obtain abortions (see below). The availability of safe, legal abortions is also an important health concern of Black women (Aldridge and Rodgers-Rose 1993, 16). The ability to perform abortions seems to be a rare skill among obstetricians, so much so that the Accreditation Council for Graduate Medical Education voted "to require that prospective obstetricians be taught abortion skills, saying it wanted them to receive the fullest possible training from the teaching hospitals where they work as medical residents."[23] That decision was also "supported by the American Board of Obstetrics and Gynecology, which certifies obstetricians, and by the American College of Obstetricians and Gynecologists. The change also had the support of the American Medical Association, one of the council's five parent organizations."[24]

The Hyde Amendment, however, prevents the government from paying for "elective" abortions. The Supreme Court held a few years after Hyde that Medicaid regulations in Title XIX of the Social Security Act did not require states to pay for medically necessary abortions for which federal funds were unavailable, in *Harris v. McRae.*[25] Davis's concern also stemmed from the fact that such denial not only drove many Black and Latina women back into the hands of the "butcher" (1983, 220, 221) but also thrust them into the clutches of mass sterilization programs. Such a situation evades the spirit of the Supreme Court decision, *Skinner v. State of Oklahoma,*[26] in which involuntary sterilization of persons convicted of multiple larceny offenses was held to be unconstitutional. With reference to teenagers, abortion rights of the young as well as the poor have been further complicated by the Supreme Court's decision in *Planned Parenthood of Southeastern Pennsylvania et al. v. Casey.*[27] With reference to poor young women, the abortion issue has been further complicated by New World Order mandates tying levels of welfare support to age at pregnancy, number of children in a family and additional children born while under the auspices of AFDC.[28] For instance, 39 percent of teenagers, 15 to 19 years of age from poor families (those earning below the federal "poverty level of $14,800 for a family of four in 1994") terminated their unplanned pregnancies compared to 54 percent of those from low-income families (income 100 to 199 percent above poverty level) and 70 percent of those from higher income (more than 200 percent of poverty level) families. There is concern by some that reductions in welfare would increase the number of abortions by poor teenagers.[29]

This trend is also reflected somewhat in the abortion rates of women in general. The abortion rate among poor women aged 15 to 44 was 43 percent. In comparison, both low-income and higher-income women aged 15 to 44 terminated their pregnancies at the rate of 51 percent (figures from 1988).[30]

Before addressing the *Casey* decision, in order to get a sense of the pre-New World Order direction to the abortion rights issue, we should examine *Casey's* legal precedents.

The unequivocal right to an abortion in the first trimester of pregnancy was upheld in 1973 in *Roe v. Wade,*[31] which also provided for doctor-approved abortion in the second trimester. *Roe v. Wade* was a landmark decision that invalidated the human reproduction laws of thirty-one states.[32] The Supreme Court decision in *Bellotti v. Baird*[33] was also precedent-setting in that it invalidated the requirement that minors have parental consent before receiving an abortion. Parental *notification* was later upheld in *H.L. v. Matheson.*[34] A husband's permission was held by the Supreme Court not to be required, in *Planned Parenthood of Central Missouri v. Danforth.*[35] Likewise, a twenty-four-hour waiting period before a woman could receive an abortion was scuttled in the *Akron v. Akron Center for Reproductive Health*[36] case. In combination, except for the Hyde Amendment, abortion rights seemed to have been incorporated into the Constitution until the institutionalization of the New World Order.

An abortion rights case which is most representative of New World Order policy is the aforementioned *Planned Parenthood of Southeastern Pennsylvania et al. v. Casey*. In efficient fashion, *Casey* upheld the twenty-four-hour waiting period that had been rejected in *Akron* and shelved *Bellotti* and required parental consent for minors. *Casey*, in a compromise decision, did retain the *Danforth* feature declining the need for a husband's consent. However, Justice O'Connor repudiated the trimester framework in the statement that we "abandon the trimester framework as a rigid prohibition on all pre-viability regulation aimed at the protection of fetal life."[37] The impact of the trimester framework rejection can be measured by the observation of Justice Stevens, concurring and dissenting, as he notes that 90 percent of all abortions are performed during the first trimester,[38] anyway.

Greater restrictions upon abortion theoretically might be slightly mitigated by greater use of the "Morning-After Pill." However, gynecologists "seldom prescribe them because they wait for women to ask. . . . And most women . . . do not know enough about the pills to ask for them."[39] The "pills must be used within 72 hours of intercourse but . . . they prevent 75 percent of the pregnancies that would otherwise occur."[40] The nausea that may last for a day or so would be less than the discomfort of an abortion experienced by a woman unable to care for herself let alone young ones.

Again, the Black woman's predominantly single status is due more to the societal constraints on any Black couple attempting to form a lasting relationship than to the individual Black man (the "Joes" of the world notwithstanding) or Black woman. Access to socially approved accompaniments of respectable adulthood such as a decent income and a technologically up-to-date education greatly enhance one's ability to begin and maintain a relationship. One-on-one interactions between couples cannot be viewed in a vacuum. Such interactions are greatly influenced by their milieu. If that environment does not support responsible adulthood, then necessarily one or both of the parties is seen as "irresponsible." The women in the case studies were more likely to go through with their divorces if their husbands were financially aberrant than if they were emotionally duplicitous (adulterous). Corroboration for this assertion can be found in the fact that the income of two-parent Black families was *more than twice* that of one-parent Black families which are 90 percent female (see Chapter 3).

Given these legal results with reference to the African American family, it is somewhat unreasonable to expect a European American–dominated legal system to render justice for African Americans (cf. Hutchinson 1990; X and Haley 1965; Amaker 1988; Cleaver 1968; Freire 1993). A "trigger-happy social order" is more responsible for legal injustices to Blacks than "trigger-happy cops," according to Eldridge Cleaver (158) in his book, *Soul on Ice* (see also the Rodney King situation[41] as well as Chapter 8).

Along these lines also, Molefi Kete Asante, in his book *Kemet, Afrocentricity and Knowledge* (1990), describes how the fundamental principles of justice derived from the Kemet (Egyptian/African) priests Imhotep and Pepi rather than Anglo-Saxons or Greeks or other Eurocentric models. Asante points out that ideals of proof as a rational way of demonstrating valid and reliable versions of reality were developed by Egyptians. Prior to their co-optation of the Egyptian model of jurisprudence, European Germanic tribes trusted methods such as trial by fire and water to "deduce" the truth. Using the axioms of the African Egyptians, logic was developed as the underpinnings of decision making and problem solving. In this fashion, Anglo-Saxons of England developed a court system which was based ideally upon the persuasion techniques of opposing parties. In an ironic twist of fate, the system that stems from the African development of logical thinking has been distorted to oppress and subjugate the African American.

The legal system as a vehicle of subjugation has been oppressing Blacks since the country was first conceived (the Supreme Court decision in *Dred Scott v. Sanford* in 1857, which decided Congress could not eliminate slavery in a federal, pioneer territory, and *Plessy v. Ferguson* in 1896, which sustained the separate but equal doctrine). Recent legal onslaughts against the integrity of the Black family include the *R.A.V. v. St. Paul*[42] in a 1992 decision that struck down an ordinance prohibiting crimes of hate, such as the burning of a cross in a Black family's front yard.

These legal examples illustrate the point that U.S. political, social and economic forces (Billingsley 1968) have coopted the legal system with respect to African Americans and their families to their detriment, as could be predicted from the theoretical propositions of Parsons and Merton.

The undermining of the Black family in the legal system has been further documented by the writings of some social scientists (e.g., Rainwater [citing Moynihan 1967]; Liebow 1967). Other social scientists have refuted the negative portrayals of the Black family and striven to develop social policy (e.g., Billingsley 1968; Glasgow 1981; Hill 1972; Ladner 1973) that would help negate the work of the power elite in its attempt to destroy African American family life.

Many of the legal issues for social scientists are not so salient as a forum for the antagonistic parties as they are as precedent-setting indicators that affect policies with regard to the standard of living for the Black family. In deciding issues concerning housing, child care, credit, health, employment and other social welfare concerns, the court also decides the fate of the Black family. Unless the resolution of these issues takes into consideration the overall well-being of the African American family in a social frame of reference as well as from the legal perspective (Blackwell 1975), the legal system will continue to wreak havoc upon the Black family.

These issues affect the ostensibly private concerns of the African American male/female relationship (Staples 1981; Rodgers-Rose et al. 1985; Aldridge 1991). Such personal relationships are inevitably influenced by the presence or absence of educational, job, health, housing and even entrepreneurial opportunities. It would be surprising to both the power elite and many Black women to find out that many more Black men would "act right" if such opportunities were available to them on an equitable basis.

This discussion has been greatly informed by James E. Blackwell's presentation (1991) of controversial family issues in the Black community. Divorce, illegitimacy, public welfare, and "the black matriarchy" are identified by Blackwell as such issues. These issues formed the basis of the foregoing analysis of the manner in which the U.S. legal structure affects African American and poor families. That the legal system, as an "operative" of the other social institutions, is clearly obstructionist as pertains to the Black family is rather obvious and has been documented elsewhere.[43] African American women have been pawns in highly regulated and highly monitored systems of control that have subjected them to double jeopardy.[44]

SUMMARY

The foregoing thesis that political and economic forces undercut marital unions among African Americans also has a historical basis. Black single-parent family structures are rooted in slavery (Myrdal 1944; also see Billingsley 1992, above). The same legal and economic injustices that kept slaves from marrying and forming legal unions, keep their descendants from doing the same (Akbar 1984; Hornsby 1991). Through the law, Blacks were robbed of the opportunity to earn a legitimate income and provide an adequate living for their families. Nontraditional activities spawn nontraditional unions. Economic crimes and participation in the black markets of drug, liquor, lottery and gun dealing are not supportive of a "Dick and Jane" lifestyle with a wife and children and a white picket fence to come home to every evening. Many African American men and women see such a lifestyle as an impossible dream.

The unions that the majority of Black men and women have are hence unsanctioned by the prevailing legal system. They hence are subjected to further disenfranchisement and alienation as a family as well as individuals. This alienation serves to increase inequities in income, education and employment (Swinton 1993) because the society comes to see them as too aberrant to participate in gainful economic activities. Such alienation is thereby intentional as is documented by some African and African American scholars (Madhubuti 1990; Fanon 1965; Hare 1984; Asante 1990; Kunjufu 1984). Sociologist Robert Hill (1972) maintains that the Black family survives in spite of rather than because of legal support systems. Although the Black family has developed strengths out of weaknesses, the lack of legal system support is a disadvantage the New World Order has further entrenched, making it more difficult for even the most resolute and resilient to succeed. Even in such a sociolegal context, however, African Americans make the most of the relationships they can sustain in their worlds of poverty and uncertainty. For the legal system to ask more from them, without the support of other social institutions, is not fair—nor is it just.

NOTES

1. Cf. *Ohio Revised Code* Sec. 2151.03.
2. Cf. *Ohio Revised Code* Sec. 2151.03.1.
3. *Ohio Revised Code* Sec. 3113.31 defines Civil Domestic Violence as the occurrence of one or more of the following acts between family or household members who reside together or have resided together: 1. Attempting to cause or recklessly causing bodily injury; 2. Placing another person by the threat of force in fear of imminent serious physical harm; 3. Committing any act with respect to a child that would result in the child being an abused child as defined in R.C. 2151.031.
4. *Ohio Revised Code* Sec. 3105 et seq.
5. Angela D. Chatman, "Housing Cuts: Restructuring HUD Will Shred the Safety Net for the Poor. But the Pain Will Be Shared by All," *Plain Dealer*, March 26, 1995, C1, C4.
6. 115 S.Ct. 1291 (1995).
7. Willa M. Hemmons, "The Need for Domestic Violence Laws With Adequate Legal and Social Support Services," *Journal of Divorce* 4, no. 3 (Spring, 1981): 49–61; V. Micahel McKenzie, *Domestic Violence in America* (Lawrenceville, Virginia: Brunswick Publishing Corporation, 1995).
8. U.S. Dept. of Commerce, Bureau of the Census, "Marital Status of African Americans 15 Years and Older, by Sex: 1991, *The Black Population in the United States: March 1991*, Current Population Reports (Washington, D.C.: GPO, 1991, Series P-20–464, Table C): 5.
9. Ibid., 5.
10. *Ohio Revised Code* Sec. 1701 et seq.
11. Keith Schneider, "Fleeing America's Relentless Pace, Some Adopt an Amish Life," *New York Times*, March 22, 1995, A8.
12. Also see, Susan Chira, "Struggling to Find Stability When Divorce Is a Pattern: Fractured Families Dealing With Multiple Divorce," *New York Times*, March 19, 1995, A1, A17, for news report with reference to minor children in divorce situations.
13. Langston Hughes, *The Best of Simple*, Ill. Bernard Nast (New York: Hill and Wang, originally appeared in *Simple Stakes a Claim*, 1953, thirty-seventh printing under special arrangement with Holt, Rinehart and Winston, Inc., 1993).
14. See (in Chapter 3 also) Peter T. Kilborn, "A Family Spirals Downward in Waiting for Agency to Act," *New York Times*, February 11, 1995, A1, A7.

15. *Ohio Revised Code* Sec. 3105.18; *Cherry v. Cherry*, 66 Ohio St. 2d 348 (1981); and, *Black v. Black*, Case No. 43005 (1981), an Eighth Appellate District of Ohio Court decision in which it was held that marital assets include property accumulated as a result of parties' joint efforts and do not include property separately acquired by gift or inheritance during marriage.

16. 401 U.S. 532, 91 S.Ct. 1017, 28 L.Ed.2d 288 (1971).

17. 427 U.S. 495, 96 S.Ct. 2755, 49 L.Ed. 2d. (1976).

18. 439 U.S. 259, 99 S.Ct. 518, 58 L.Ed. 2d 503 (1978).

19. Walter Wadlington, Charles H. Whitebread, Samuel M. Davis, *Cases and Materials on Children in the Legal System* (Mineola, New York: Foundation Press): 117, citing 5 Am.Dig. System 1966–1976 (Eighth Decennial Digest) 939–40 (West 1978) use of the 106 Key Numbers under the heading "Bastards."

20. U. S. Dept. of Commerce, Bureau of the Census, "Number of Children Ever Born to Teenaged Women by Race and Marital Status: 1990," *Statistical Abstract of the United States: 1992* (Wash., D.C.: Government Printing Office): Table 4, 71.

21. Ann McFeatters, "Clinton Tells Pope He's Wrong on Abortion," *Plain Dealer*, June 3, 1994, 1–A; 12–A.

22. P.L. 94–439, 90 Stat. 1434 (1976).

23. James Barron, "Group Requiring Abortion Study: Requirement Would Apply to All New Obstetricians," *New York Times*, February 15, 1995) A1, A10.

24. Ibid.

25. 448 U.S. 297 (1980).

26. 316 U.S. 535 (1942).

27. 112 S.Ct. 2791 (1992).

28. Robert Pear, "Catholic Bishops Challenge Pieces of Welfare Bill: Fear a Rise in Abortions; While Unhappy With Current System, They See a Moral Test in House Debate," *New York Times*, March 19, 1995, A1, A13; Tamar Lewin, "The Nation: Abortion Foes Worry About Welfare Cutoffs," *New York Times*, March 19, 1995, Sec. 4, 4.

29. Lewin, "Abortion Foes Worry About Welare Cutoffs."

30. Ibid.

31. 410 U.S. 113 (1973).

32. Donald Brieland and John Allen Lemmon, *Social Work and the Law* (St. Paul, Minnesota: West Publishing Company, 1985), 259.

33. 428 U.S. 152 (1976).

34. 450 U.S. 398 (1981).

35. 428 U.S. 52 (1976).

36. 462 U.S. 416 (1983).

37. *Planned Parenthood v. Casey*, 112 S. Ct. at 2818.

38. Ibid. at 2843.

39. Gina Kolata, "Scant Use of Morning-After Pill Is Analyzed: Birth Control That Few Women Request or Understand," *New York Times*, March 29, 1995, A13.

40. Ibid.

41. "Jury Acquits Los Angeles Policemen in Taped Beating," *New York Times*, April 30, 1992, A1, A8.

42. U.S. Supreme Court Case No. 90–7675 (1992).

43. Rose Brewer, "Black Women in Poverty: Some Comments on Female-Headed Families," *Signs*, 13, no. 2 (1988): 331–39.

44. Frances Beale, "Double Jeopardy: To Be Black and Female," *The Black Woman: An Anthology*, ed. Toni Cade Bambara (New York: Signet, 1970), 90–100.

CHAPTER 7

Black Women in the World Order of Health

HEALTH CARE AS A SOCIAL INSTITUTION

A discussion of the African American woman's health is an endeavor that is almost as appropriately placed in an economic, education, social welfare, family or indeed criminal forum as by itself. (When Parsons was writing in 1951, the health care industry was not suffering from the type of megalomania it is today.) Economic issues in particular, permeate any analysis of the U.S. health institution and its reform.[1] Further, although economics is the driving force that largely formulates health policy in the United States, the political institution is the vehicle through which such policy is effectuated.[2] Politics often leaves health priorities at the bottom of the governing agenda[3] or reflecting the agenda of the more powerful. Politics may drive[4] health care policy but, using superior resources, disguise the true origin of the purported movement. The problem of adequate health care provision for everyone is intensified because the private sector of the health care industry is rapidly instituting its own health care initiatives[5] which are, in the absence of governmental action responsive to the needs of the public, unilaterally altering health care in the United States.[6] Further, these changes will be firmly in place before any governmental health reform can be instituted; indeed they will probably influence governmental reforms before governmental reforms influence them.[7]

This prediction is exemplified by hospital staff layoffs and bed reductions undertaken by hospital administrations in response to perceived mandates to become competitive as well as a wish "to make the agency's hospitals more attractive to managed-care companies."[8] Even with all the cost-cutting measures, however, the profits of the profit-motivated hospitals are languishing,[9] potentially jeopardizing the quality, nature, degree and availability of patient care. Hospitals are presently forced to "grant price concessions to the insurance companies, employer health plans and health maintenance organizations." They are faced with federal and state payments that "are already too low to cover Medicare and Medicaid costs" for the poor urban patients, who usually rely on the latter.[10] With such pressures on revenues, hospitals are "discharging patients sooner,[11] performing more surgery without keeping patients overnight, closing underused facilities, and eliminating executive and staff jobs."[12] What this means for the Black woman in the New World Order is that she is much more likely under such auspices to be diagnosed as untreatable, to be given limited treatment options and even to be denied hospital admission entirely. Such possibilities may make doctors and clinics loathe to refer to a hospital the Black woman who is poor, lacks adequate health insurance or is subject to the restrictive payment schedules of Medicare[13] and Medicaid.

In such a compromised health position, Black women, along with other poor and minorities, are more likely to be deprived of options such as radiation or chemotherapy in cancer, dialysis in kidney failure, and by-pass or balloon surgery and pacemakers[14] in heart disease. Also denied may be advanced treatments awaiting Food and Drug Administration (FDA) approval, such as protease inhibitors (Merck & Company's L524 or Abbott's ABT-538)[15] or 3TC (Glaxo Holdings, Inc.,'s) along with AZT[16] in AIDS[17]; the drug hydroxyurea (Bristol-Myers Squibb's, currently $100 per month) for Sickle Cell Anemia[18]; and the results of dealings Dr. Douglas Ishii has with the replacement of the hormone I.G.F.- 2.[19] Given the Black woman's current rates of the disease, the successful "PCI" protein reduction techniques and insulin[20] for diabetes would be especially helpful in regard to the health of the Black woman.

The position of the Black woman in the New World Order almost dictates where she will stand medically in terms of the competition for respirators, special feeding procedures and other life support mechanisms. Her problem would likely be just the opposite of a Karen Quinlan[21] or a Nancy Cruzan,[22] who were on such mechanisms for prolonged periods of time. More and more, death involves a human decision not to affirmatively intervene rather than a result of totally natural processes. Health care system issues now involve who or what (e.g., insurance companies) is going to make the decision to treat or not to treat; that is the question that will increasingly affect the ill in the near future, as it does to a substantial extent today.[23] In the cost-benefit analysis[24] (bottom line) of nearly every area of New World Order life, whose benefit will be considered paramount, that of the patient or that of the profiteer?

For instance, increasingly doctors are reimbursed on a "fee per service" basis rather than a "fee per person" one. In a fee per service arrangement, doctors are paid on the basis of how much work they do. Each separate medical procedure or action is a billable unit. With a fee per person agreement, "[t]he same monthly fee is paid for each patient. The doctor's total fee remains the same, regardless of how much work [she or] he does."[25]

Under a fee per person policy, the fewer services provided, the more profit is made. Such a method, while in line with typical New World Order perspectives, will eventually have a negative effect on everyone, not just the Black woman. But, then, if the point is just to make profits then such an effect would not be controlling.

The United States is the only Western industrialized country without a universal health care system, nor has any pending executive or legislative proposal even sought to approximate such a goal.[26] In addition, as states become unable to make up the difference left by the federal government, more and more people are becoming uninsured.[27]

Any approach to revising health care delivery will undoubtedly incorporate individual wealth-related connections to health care quality. For example, the Supreme Court in 1975, ruling on the education case *San Antonio Independent School District v. Rodriguez*,[28] held that it is not unconstitutional to finance public education primarily by property taxes. They upheld this financing structure even though the result was unequal economic support among the varying school districts of Texas. The districts with the poorest property-tax basis received the least funds.

One of the relatively rare African American physicians who happened to be a client of the author is also a male cardiologist (board certified and licensed in two states as well as the Virgin Islands). Interviewed on the issue of health care, he stated that one concern about an executive plan for health care reform[29] was that it segmented out different categories for treatment by specialized medical units. For example, Medicare patients (the elderly) would have certain health providers, Medicaid patients (the poor) would have theirs, those in the military would have others and patients with jobs would have still others, who would be reimbursed at various levels by their employers. The built-in economic distinctions that could easily be integrated into such a program are rather easy to see. In fact, the physician saw it as very unlikely that a millionaire and a pauper would ever compete for care in the same waiting room.

His pessimism was shared by a journalist who compares Canada's universal health plan with the U.S. medical system, which he describes as being "profit-oriented, inequitable and the most expensive in the industrialized world."[30] The physician's cynicism was also augmented by his observation that the current chief executive working on health reform had been beset by personal attacks on himself,[31] which substantially diverted his attention from health issues, no matter how pressing for the people in the United States. In fact, just about any serious proponent of a plan advocating anything even remotely approximating universal health care faces political scrutiny.[32] The doctor's take on health care reform was that some kind of diluted facsimile of a plan would sooner or later be passed.

The health care needs of Black females are even more exigent than those of others. Whites go to the doctor for preventive care, while Blacks wait until there is an obvious problem. By the time many Blacks enter the doctor's office, they are in such advanced (often untreatable) stages of cancer, heart disease or kidney failure that all that can be done for them is the "morphine drip." Asked what could be done about the high probability that meaningful preventive health care measures would not be forthcoming for Blacks, the doctor replied, "We're all going to die, some sooner than others." With new governmental mandates with titles such as "Advanced Medical Directives,"[33] by which medical personnel are allowed not to treat or even to feed patients in certain conditions deemed inevitably fatal, sooner will be even sooner for more vulnerable populations such as Black women. It is one thing to die of a primary or secondary disease, it is another thing to be starved to death. Persons who are less well educated as to their rights may be more likely to sign a *premature* DNR (Do Not Resuscitate) order, designed to lower the medical costs of maintaining "sooner or later" terminal cases (see preceding hospital cost-containment discussion).

The doctor further indicated that insurance companies do not encourage *preventive* care. Elaborating, he stated that, for instance, if a patient's office visit were for a routine medical examination, most insurance companies would not pay for it. A routine physical including tests for such things as cholesterol levels, blood work, a mammogram, checking for blood in stool, stress tests and other screenings might run between $1,000 and $1,200, a prohibitive cost for many Black people, to say the least. He noted that most people should get physicals at least once every two years before the age of forty. After forty-five, the average person should get a complete physical once a year. For Black women, though, the National Medical Association (the Black corollary of the American Medical Association) indicates that another consideration influences how often they should get a physical checkup. Breast cancer is the number one cancer killer of Black women, and the onset of breast cancer is earlier for Black women on average than for White women.

Further, breast cancer kills Black women more frequently than it does White women. Therefore, it is recommended that Black women have a "baseline mammogram" at age thirty-five, mammograms every year or every other year after that and annual mammograms beginning at age forty.[34] Local health departments for cities and counties may be contacted for information on where mammograms may be obtained, perhaps free. They may be available at community clinics and neighborhood centers. (Research is evolving which will even make it possible to determine one's *predisposition* to develop cancer—although the ethical considerations of obtaining that knowledge are also being explored.[35] At any rate, at a cost of "$800 for the first family member and $250 for each additional member,"[36] the taking of cancer prediction tests will not be available to most Black women—poor or middle income. Another prohibiting consideration is the fact that government-financed health care (e.g., Medicare or Medicaid) does not pay for *experimental* procedures. Generally, also, private insurers follow the government's lead in determining what is experimental and what are standard medically approved practices.

Disallowance by private insurance carriers may be avoided if a specific problem rather than a routine medical examination were the asserted reason for the visit. "I have a pain here; would you check it out for me?" Even if nothing were found to be wrong, the insurance company would be more prone to pay.

In addition, certain insurance companies have ways of holding down their payouts.[37] For example, if most doctors charge, say, $1,500 for a certain procedure, some insurance companies or health groups might say to a group of doctors, "We will pay $1,300 for the procedure. We have a huge number of insureds and. . . ." An expensive operation that used to be a money maker for most hospitals "now is a drain on revenues."[38]

Thus, the doctor's insurance allegations are somewhat corroborated by a media account which related that in the past "health plans have rewarded hospitals and doctors for keeping the patient in the hospital longer or performing more tests and surgical procedures, by paying them for each service performed."[39] However, as very probably a sign of future insurer, health maintenance organization and managed-care organization policy, "a growing number of insurers now pay a flat fee for treatment of a particular ailment, no matter how many tests are done."[40] Going even further, some health maintenance organizations pay a hospital "a set monthly amount for each health plan member, whether or not the person requires hospital care."[41] It is not hard to imagine how an alleged hospital "obsession with efficiency"[42] might evolve pursuant to these priority pressures. In light of such medical restructuring, Dr. Arnold S. Relman, editor emeritus of the *New England Journal of Medicine*, opines, "in this process businessmen and their agents will begin to exercise unprecedented control over the allocation of medical resources."[43]

Such cost containment strategies do not bode well for the Black woman. The bulk rate may or may not address her particular health care needs. Her life expectancy is one indication of her diminished health care level. While the average life expectancy of the White woman is 79.7 years, the Black woman lives on average to be 74.3 years of age.[44] The Black man on average lives to be 65.6 years of age, while the average life expectancy of the White male American is 73.0 years. Based on race, the Black woman is being cheated out of approximately 5.4 years of life and the Black man, 8.6 years.

Another health indicator is the infant mortality rate (number of deaths per thousand live births for infants through the first year of life). Female African American infants die at a rate of 17.2 per 1000. The rate for Black males is worse at 20.0 per 1000. White male infants die at a rate of 9 per 1000, and White female infants at 7.1 per 1000.[45] Further, there is evidence that although the infant mortality rate overall is decreasing, the mortality rate for White infants has been dropping faster than the mortality rate for Black infants.[46] Factors such as housing, income, stress and "cuts in federal public health programs that provided pre-natal visits for people in the black community"[47] were suggested as possible contributors to the racial difference in the infant mortality rate.

Such health-related statistics are made salient for health care reform issues when it is recalled that the Black woman has fewer resources than other racial and gender groupings in the United States. There is evidence, however, that economics is not the only problem. One study reported in the mass media indicated that the "effects of poverty linger for generations" even after Black women achieve middle-class status.[48] In that study, the researchers inferred that factors such as psychosocial stress, prenatal care and nutrition helped to cause the statistic that Black women had low-birth-weight babies at twice the rate of their White income-level counterparts, of whatever socioeconomic status.[49] Hence, efforts to address health care reform among Black women in the New World Order must be comprehensive to be meaningful. Paradoxically then, health care reform must be responsive to as well as irrespective of socioeconomic status.

Health Care Case Study: Author's Personal Preventives

Getting down six to eight glasses of water a day was perhaps the most challenging personal health reform to my lifestyle. Almost equally challenging was the incorporation into my daily regime of exercise, part of which was accomplished before a shower with the practice of techniques recalled from a Tae Kwon Do (Korean martial arts) class. Although there was one other Black woman in the class, and a couple of Black men, there were many more White men and women. There are many more White women in fact at the swimming pool during lunch hours, on the tennis courts, in aerobics class, hiking, walking around the block and playing racquetball. (Jogging was too hard on my knees.[50]) Perhaps now that there are many more hairstyle alternatives, Black women will be more prone to engage in swimming. Being able to afford regular attendance at a health spa is something that is definitely related to economic status.

Black women are more likely to be observed in line dance courses and at bowling than at health spas. Some middle-class Black women even have golfing parties. A couple of Black teacher retirees I know go to a golf course once a week during the summertime. A retired dietician told me that she regularly visited a predominantly White suburban golf course in a district which had been sued for racial discrimination in housing.[51] She said that when she first started going, driving her car in her golfing attire, she would be stopped on the way to the golf course "just about every time" she went. After several such episodes, she drove there in regular clothes and put on her golfing outfit once she got to the golf course.

Once they graduate from high school, Black women generally never again pick up a basketball or run track. Black women do participate in softball and volleyball games at Church picnics and family reunions, but other than that they generally are too busy trying to feed their families. And again, the fact must be recognized that some Black women have succumbed to the indomitable forces of society and are already too debilitated by diabetes, high blood pressure, heart disease, AIDS, chemical dependency and stress disorders—all health problems that afflict Black women at higher rates than White women—to be still active. The Black female experience with regard to AIDS helps to illustrate how vulnerable is Black women's health. For instance, Black women are contracting HIV, "the virus that causes AIDS, faster than any other single group of Americans."[52] In fact, "Black women are nearly 15 times more likely than white women to have AIDS, while black men are five times more likely than white men to have the disease, the Centers for Disease Control and Prevention said."[53] Further, according to the Centers for Disease Control and Prevention, of 106,949 AIDS cases reported in the United States in 1993, 55 percent (58,538) were among racial and ethnic minorities, of which 38,544 were Black. The report stated that "There were 73 AIDS cases among every 100,000 black women, while the rate for white women was 5 per 100,000."[54] The study also reported that "Forty-seven percent of AIDS cases among minority women were caused by intravenous drug use, while 37 percent were due to transmission of H.I.V., the virus that causes AIDS, through heterosexual intercourse."[55] More education and community awareness must take place regarding this devastating health concern, not to speak of social action and mobilization on the political front.

Getting back to my own set of personal lifestyle changes, I next nurtured the development of the definitely acquired taste for (assuming there is no boycott) lettuce. Lettuce, in different varieties, is the foundation for many different types of salads (spinach is my second most popular).[56] Next, the substantial reduction of white flour, sugar, salt and dairy products[57] in my diet limited me to such foodstuffs only at parties, social occasions and weekend celebrations (lapses). Trips to fast-food restaurants[58] involved selecting from their salad and juice selections, which were excellent at-home choices, also. There are indications that soy protein is a "potent weapon in lowering cholesterol" so perhaps there might be more efforts to develop tasty "soy burgers" in the future.[59]

After fast food lapses, however, if I were out of any of the herbs described below, I would visit my favorite health food store and carefully reading the labels (made more extensive, thanks to the FDA[60]) I would obtain some of the following items. For instance, I purchased aloe vera for its cleansing properties.[61] For energy, I combine the herbs cayenne and ginseng.[62] Oddly enough, for my eyes I get eyebright,[63] and to strengthen my hair as well and my fingernails, horsetail or sage.[64] For my bouts with acne, I bring out the aloe vera again, along with red clover.[65] And, to assist in fighting off obesity (besides sticking to fruits and vegetables[66]—or trying to), kelp[67] and chickweed[68] come in handy. To offset the stress variables described below and, indeed, throughout this book, a couple of nursing students taking one of my courses suggested vitamin B-12; it seems helpful. During the cold season, in addition to taking my multiple vitamin, including vitamin C and iron, I load up on golden seal[69] and fenugreek.[70] I lost too many friends taking my garlic[71]/cayenne combination, for imminent flu problems. Of course, such supplemental herbal foods are expensive and would be more cost effective if grown in one's garden. It would probably be desirable to try to revitalize the earthy skills that were had by the African ancestors. Some plants grow very well in one's window. I have had enough criminal clients who quickly acquired the art of growing marijuana plants on their verandas, porches and window sills even in the projects to know that Black women can learn how to cultivate vegetation if they are sufficiently motivated to do so. The incentive of passing on later as opposed to sooner is a pretty great motivating factor.

The Black Woman and the Medical-Industrial Complex

With reference to comprehensive rather than individual health care efforts, most health reform plans are being proposed in the "survival of the fittest" mode. Further, they are beginning to put more emphasis on "prevention."[72] One community service bill-board located in the heart of an inner city proclaimed that health is threatened by certain "preventable factors": obesity, smoking[73], stress, lack of exercise, substance abuse and poor diet. The assertion that these factors are within the control of the individual is ominous for the Black woman. As noted above, it takes generations to effectuate certain lifestyle and cultural behaviors.[74] In addition, unremitting societal pressures are not totally, or sometimes even partially, within the discretion of the recipient (see other chapters). Such assertions also reject the idea that substance abuse is itself a disease. Folk wisdom acknowledges that most programs to lose weight are unsuccessful, even when attempted by highly educated, highly motivated persons who lead relatively stress-free lives. The individual responsibility approach also minimizes the role of the physical environment and one's health—particularly those persons that reside in the reputedly more vulnerable African American communities (cf. Bullard, 1994). Further, as the New World Order gains momentum, regulations regarding environmental health and protection issues will probably diminish in effectiveness and number.[75]

From the way the health reform values are developing, then, it appears that the Black woman will be punished if she continues to succumb to a certain extent to her heritage of discriminatory treatment operating in the context of her second-class socioeconomic and physical environment. Further, as is a major contention of this book, those realities are being exacerbated by the plannings and workings of the New World Order—particularly as they affect the Black Woman, her family and her community.

The maxim, "man [sic] does not live by bread alone" is important. Black women have always known implicitly or explicitly that stress is a key factor in hindering their health (Aldridge and Rodgers-Rose 1993). Also, news articles sport titles such as "Faith and Social Activities Help to Heal, a Study Finds."[76] In that particular study it was shown that surgery patients who said that they found

No comfort in religious beliefs had a death rate almost three times higher than those who said they found some strength in their faith, other measures of religiosity were not nearly so strongly related to survival.

There was no such effect on the death rate from frequency of participation in religious services, . . . or from a feeling of being deeply religious.[77]

In other words, the benefits of a "calm" mind were life saving. Unfortunately, as has been pointed out before, in light of the increasing life challenges, exacerbated by the intense and rapid growth of the New World Order, the Black woman is hard pressed to find stability in an unstable world, reasonableness in an unreasonable world, kindness in an unkind world and support in an unsupportive world. Such a situation, to say the least, can be stressful. As history and Sojourner Truth, Phyllis Wheatley, Harriet Tubman, Ida B. Wells, Mary McLeod Bethune, Madame C. J. Walker and Maya Angelou, among thousands of others, have attested, without faith in some strong sustaining force the Black woman is that much more vulnerable to the capriciousness of the New World Order.

In terms of the political front, a key to any set of health care preventives is education. Health care preventive concerns were among the priorities developed at a health care forum convened by Congressman Louis B. Stokes (D-Ohio), a member of the Congressional Black Caucus. (Although health care is almost as much an economic issue as it is a medical one, its resolution for the African American woman is inherently political (see the book by Delores P. Aldridge and La Francis Rodgers-Rose, *River of Tears: The Politics of Black Women's Health*, 1993).

Another prevailing theme at the congressional forum was need for the elimination of disparities in health care access and treatment, a theme that has been shown to be a very real concern.[78] For instance, one study has shown that only 47 percent of very sick Black and poor Medicare patients were put into intensive care units as opposed to 70 percent of other, similarly ill Medicare patients.[79] The researchers looked at patients treated at 297 hospitals in 30 cities and towns. The study "suggests that the quality of care varies tremendously with a patient's race, and not, as other studies have suggested, based on whether a person has health insurance."[80] Another consideration with reference to the fewer preventive visits to the doctor made by African Americans relates to distrust by Blacks of the medical profession. For instance, one Black woman pointed out that doctors were engaged in the "practice" of medicine, and she felt that term to be particularly salient with respect to Black people. In addition to issues of neglect and fiscal concerns, the historically relative "expendability" of poor Black people has reportedly also resulted at times in their "abuse and exploitation" by the medical industry in terms of experimentation.[81] Without either racial advantage or insurance one is at a decided loss in terms of health care in the United States. Such a situation is made more ominous for the Black woman by the fact that, according to the Washington-based nonprofit Employee Benefits Research Institute, the "number of working-age people without insurance increased by 6.5 million in four years to 40.9 million in 1993."[82] Even worse, for the Black woman, such statistics are exacerbated by the fact that of that estimated 40.9 million, 25 percent are African American. This means that the Black woman is in double jeopardy if both her race and either her lack of insurance or her possession of insurance such as Medicaid, which possibly mitigates against quality of care, are suspect. Hence, if even the quality of care of employed persons is increasingly being undermined, hers is even more probably seriously in danger of being compromised.

Such concerns were addressed by the Stokes Health Care Forum held in Washington, D.C., on March 11, 1994, and aired on public television. The following are some of the ideas presented at that hearing, which was convened and chaired by Louis B. Stokes. At this congressional forum the legal viewpoint was provided by Maya Wylie, assistant counsel with the NAACP Legal Defense Fund. At the forum, Ms. Wylie represented the views of both the Congressional Black Caucus Foundation Health Task Force and that of the Defense Fund, which she indicated were one and the same. Attorney Wylie stated that both organizations were concerned that consumer issues include antidiscrimination issues, civil rights issues and strong consumer protections that include an enforcement system that allows consumers to proceed through some process if they are having trouble getting the services they are supposed to get. An informational network embodying these issues should be developed in order to monitor these problems.

The president of the Congressional Black Caucus, former Congressman Kweisi Mfume, presented an overall list of consumer health concerns that he declared should go into any Congressional health care reform legislation, including:

1. A quality control mechanism
2. A basic package of benefits for high risk groups
3. An increase in the number of African American providers to improve and educate the community for prevention
4. An increase in federal authority and enforcement

5. The strengthening and expansion of the community health care infrastructure
6. Universal coverage as well as universal access (different concepts)
7. Civil rights standards and affirmative action provisions
8. A way to expand prohibitions against redlining

In addition to these concerns, at the forum's end, Dr. Gloria Maxwell, a physician helping to moderate the session along with the facilitator from the National Urban League, Robert McAlpine, recorded priorities suggested by the participants. These included:

1. Universality of access and coverage, along the lines of the public health care model (meaning that health care is regulated by a governmental entity rather than a private body)
2. Financing, including governmental subsidies for all affordability, employer mandate, co-payments, government subsidies for the low income, tax deductibility, no Medicaid/Medicare cuts
3. Federally mandated civil rights and affirmative action standards, including race-based data collection and not just data collection on persons considered high-risk and expensive to cover; Note: Comment was made that the Office of Civil Rights should have an assistant secretary at Cabinet level as is the case at Health and Human Services.
4. Quality assessment with enforcement mechanism
5. Mandated standards for health certification, more than portability; provider competition; private right of action

It was agreed that embodied in all of the provisions for national health care legislation should be a "Defined Comprehensive Health Care Package." The Black health care practitioners and representatives from Black organizations at the Forum wanted to be sure that such a package would adequately address such concerns as prenatal care, reproduction education, wellness promotion, prevention, prescription drugs, mental health, substance abuse, durable medical equipment, outreach and technical assistance, appropriate health education for adults and children, well child programs, homecare, respite care, rehabilitative services, dental services and pharmaceuticals prescribed by health professionals.

It was also a consensus of the forum participants that any health care legislation should include consumer education on how to access the system and what services are provided and by whom, where and when.

Reflecting the current state of affairs, however, Dr. Ethel Hoytt, a doctor from the National Medical Association, reported that many women physicians she knew could not get health care because of preexisting conditions.

At the Ninth Annual Lawyers' CLE Seminar (see Chapter 2) held in 1993 a proposal for legislation preventing discrimination in health care was presented. The presentation was made by law professor Vernellia Randal of the University of Dayton School of Law. Her proposed act included the following purposes:

1.   To provide a clear and comprehensive national mandate for provision of health care that is nondiscriminatory in service delivery, in accessibility, or in treatment modalities.
2.   To provide clear, strong, consistent, enforceable standards addressing discrimination in the health care industry.
3.   To ensure that the federal government plays a central role in enforcing the standards established in this act.
4.   To invoke the sweep of congressional authority, including the power to enforce the Fourteenth Amendment and to regulate commerce, in order to address the major areas of health care discrimination.

SUMMARY

Hence, the knowledge and insights for health care reform exist. To effectuate the health care concerns identified by legal, organizational and health care professionals will require focus, discipline, direction and mobilization by the parties who desire change.

However, the current health care institution is serving an important purpose for certain powerful interest groups. That makes health care reform, like welfare and criminal justice reform, intensely political as well as fundamentally economic. The effort to effectuate reform in any of these areas is an uphill one—in fact, the analogy should be to climbing Mt. Everest. Given the political methodology in making legal changes, there are political casualties (also see Chapter 8, addressing the purpose and process of incrimination).[83]

The health care institution is maintaining those interest groups in the society, allowing them to wield influence and authority in other sectors of the social structure, and vice versa. Therefore, the universal system typified by Canada's, in which everyone has access to health care irrespective of position, employment, wealth and pre-existing conditions, probably is not a likely result in the United States. Health care for the Black woman in the New World Order will probably still be a matter of "catch as catch can," in other words, a matter of her physical, economic, social and educational position.

NOTES

1. Mike McNamee, "So Far, the Health-Care Numbers Are Crunching Clinton," *Business Week*, December 20, 1993, 53.

2. Douglas Jehl, "Surgeon General Forced to Resign by White House: G.O.P. Applauds the Move; Clinton Had Warned Dr. Elders to Curb Tendency to Make Controversial Remarks," *New York Times*, December 10, 1994, A1, A9.

3. R. W. Apple Jr., "Crime Bill Clears Hurdle, But Senate Is Going Home Without Acting on Health: Clinton's Smiles on the Crime Bill Mask the Pain over Health Care," *New York Times*, August 26, 1994, A1, A10; Adam Clymer, "Clinton Is Urged to Abandon Fight over Health Bill: A G.O.P. Threat on Trade; Longtime Democratic Backer of Medical Care Overhaul Seeks a Tactical Retreat," *New York Times*, September 21, 1994, A1, A16.

4. Elizabeth Kolbert, "When a Grass-Roots Drive Actually Isn't," *New York Times*, March 26, 1995, A1, A12.

5. Michael Quint, "Merger to Create Largest Company for Health Plans: Industry Consolidating; United Healthcare to Acquire Metrahealth in the Trend to More Managed Care," *New York Times*, June 27, 1995, A1, C4.

6. Erik Eckholm, "While Congress Remains Silent, Health Care Transforms Itself: Healing Process, A Special Report," *New York Times*, December 18, 1994, A1, A22.

7. E.g., Erik Eckholm, "H.M.O.'s Are Changing the Face of Medicare: H.M.O.'s Woo the Elderly, and Win Over Many," *New York Times*, January 11, 1995, A1, A8.

8. Melinda Henneberger, "New York's Hospitals Chief Sets Layoffs of 3,000 Workers and Reductions in Beds," *New York Times*, September 21, 1994, A20.

9. Milt Freudenheim, "Profit Levels Stagnating at Hospitals," *New York Times*, February 6, 1995, C1, C4.

10. Ibid.

11. Cf., Associated Press, "Cost Cuts Shrink Hospital Stays for Childbirth: A Medical Group Is Concerned That New Mothers May Be Shortchanged," *New York Times*, May 6, 1995, A9. For example, the article notes that the "average length of stay for hospital deliveries dropped to 2.6 days in 1992 from 4.1 days in 1970, and the decline has not stopped, the Centers for Disease Control and Prevention said."

12. Freudenheim, "Profit Levels Stagnating at Hospitals."

13. Robin Toner and Robert Pear, "Medicare, Turning 30, Won't Be What It Was," *New York Times*, July 23, 1995, A1, A12.

14. Lawrence K. Altman, "Bias in Choice of Who Gets a Top Pacemaker," *New York Times*, February 15, 1995, A16.

15. Gina Kolata, "Researchers Report Finding New Early Battlers of H.I.V.: Drugs' Short-Term Results Are Effective," *New York Times*, January 29, 1995, A12.

16. *Plain Dealer*, February 2, 1995, 4-A.

17. Gina Kolata, "Top Official Says AIDS Fight Is Inefficient: Scarce Resources Are Poured into Testing Drugs That Have Minimal Promise," *New York Times*, February 3, 1995, A9.

18. Warren E. Leary, "Sickle Cell Trial Called Success Halted Early," *New York Times*, January 31, 1995, B5, B8.

19. Sandra Blakeslee, "Deficient Hormone May Be Culprit in Painful Diabetes Complication," *New York Times*, January 24, 1995, B8.

20. Sandra Blakeslee, "Overproduction of a Protein Is Linked to Adults' Diabetes," *New York Times*, February 2, 1995, A12.

21. *In re Quinlan* , 70 N.J. 10, 355 A. 2d 647 (1976) cert denied *sub nom.*

22. *Nancy Beth Cruzan v. Director, Missouri Department of Health*, 58 L.W. 4916 (1990).

23. Gina Kolata, "Withholding Care from Patients: Boston Case Asks, Who Decides?" *New York Times*, April 3, 1995, A1, C10.

24. E.g., Milt Freudenheim, "Health Costs Paid by Employers Drop for First Time in a Decade: Growth of Expense-Cutting Medical Plans Cited," *New York Times*, February 14, 1995, A1, C7.

25. Michael Quint, "Health Plans Force Changes in the Way Doctors Are Paid," *New York Times*, February 9, 1995, A1, C5.

26. Associated Press, "Congress to Start Work on Health Reform," *Plain Dealer*, February 28, 1994, 9–A.

27. Milt Freudenheim, "States Shelving Ambitious Plans on Health Care: More People Uninsured; Severe Budget Deficits Force Legislatures to Back Down on Universal Coverage," *New York Times*, July 2, 1995, A1, A14.

28. 411 U.S. 1 (1975).

29. E.g., "Clinton's Health Plan Hits the Ground Limping," *Business Week*, February 21, 1994, 36.

30. Keith Epstein, "Ills and Bills: Would Canada's System Work in U.S.?" *Plain Dealer*, 1994, 1–C, 4–C.

31. See again, Lee Walczak, "How Clinton Can Keep His Head Above White-water," *Business Week*, March 21, 1994, 41; Stephen Labaton, "$830,000 Debt for Clinton Legal Fund: Half-Million Raised But Far More Owed," *New York Times*, February 4, 1995, 7; and, Susan B. Garland and Gail DeGeorge, "Can Hillary Put the Pieces Back Together?: The Sharks are Circling; So She's Hitting the Road to Spruce up Her Image," *Business Week*, March 21, 1994, 40.

32. Associated Press, "G.O.P. Senator Investigates Finances of Retirees' Group [AARP—The American Association of Retired Persons]," *New York Times*, April 9, 1995, A13.

33. E.g., Cleveland VA Medical Center, "Advance Directives: Recognizing the Right of Patients to Participate in Health Care Decisions," Brecksville, Wade Park, Canton, Youngstown, Department of Veterans Affairs Medical Center, 10701 East Boulevard, Cleveland, Ohio 44106, July 1, 1992. Quoting Carl J. Berber, M.D.: "An Advance Directive is a statement you make of your medical treatment choices and/or a designation of someone to make choices for you in the event you lose your decisionmaking capacity. VA has three forms available on which you can state your Advance directives: (1) a Living Will Form, (2) a form to designate a Durable Power of Attorney for Healthcare, and (3) a Treatment Preferences form."

34. Laura B. Randolph, "Why Breast Cancer Kills More Black Women: Alarming Statistics Spark National Search for Answers," *Ebony*, March, 1995, 122, 126, 127, 128.

35. Gina Kolata, "Tests to Assess Risks for Cancer Raising Questions: Wide Marketing Debated; Scientists Divided Over Ethics of Telling People They Have a Gene for the Disease," *New York Times*, March 27, 1995, A1, A8.

36. Ibid.

37. Also see Erik Eckholm, "While Congress Remains Silent": "Tens of millions more people are in looser forms of managed care like 'preferred provider' networks that require use of doctors who have agreed to work for a discount, but that do not oversee daily medical decisions as closely as the H.M.O.'s do. Insurers, hospitals, doctor groups and new kinds of hybrid health care companies are buying each other out, engaging in cut-throat price wars as they seek to position

themselves for the coming competition. No one is chasing after the uninsured, whose plight may actually be worsening as financially strapped hospitals cut back on charity care." (A22).

38. Erik Eckholm, "A Hospital Copes With the New Order," *New York Times*, January 29, 1995, Sec. 3, (Business), 1–7.

39. Milt Freudenheim, "Hospitals' New Creed: Less Is Best: No Areas Immune From Cost-Cutting," *New York Times*, November 29, 1994, C1, C15.

40. Ibid., C15.

41. Ibid.

42. Ibid.

43. Eckholm, "While Congress Remains Silent."

44. U.S. Department of Health and Human Services, National Center for Health Statistics, "Annual Summary of Births, Marriages, Divorces, and Deaths: United States, 1991," *Monthly Vital Statistics Report*, 40, no. 13 (Washington, D.C.: GPO, September 30, 1992): Table 7, p. 16.

45. National Center for Health Statistics, "Annual Summary of Births, Marriages, Divorces, and Deaths: United States, 1991," *Monthly Vital Statistics Report* (Washington, D.C.): 40, no. 13, September 30, 1992): Table 11, p. 22.

46. A J. Hostetler, "Mortality Rate Gap May Rise by 2000: Black Babies May Soon Be Three Times More Likely to Die Than White Babies," *Tallahassee Democrat*, April 30, 1994, 4–A.

47. Ibid.

48. Brenda C. Coleman, "Poverty's Effects Linger for Black Babies," *Plain Dealer*, June 5, 1990, 1–A, 8–A.

49. Ibid.

50. But see, Jane E. Brody, "Study Says Exercise Must Be Strenuous to Add to Lifespan," *New York Times*, April 19, 1995, A1, B7 that notes "To achieve the level of exercise associated with longevity, a person would have to do the equivalent of jogging or walking briskly for about 15 miles a week."

51. *U.S. v. City of Parma*, 494 F. Supp. 1049, 1049 (N.D. Ohio 1973), aff'd, 661 F.2d 562, rehrg den'd 669 F.2d 1100, cert. denied 102 S.Ct. 1972.

52. Muriel L. Whetstone, "New AIDS Scare for Heterosexuals: The Increasing Threat to Black Women," *Ebony*, April 1994, 118–120.

53. *New York Times*, "Blacks Far More Likely Than Whites to Have AIDS, Agency Says," September 9, 1994, A8.

54. Ibid.

55. Ibid.

56. Helen Robinson (Queen Afua), *Heal Thyself: For Health and Longevity* (Brooklyn, New York: A & B Books, 1992): 42.

57. Llaila O. Afrika, *African Holistic Health* (Brooklyn, New York: A & B Book Publishers, 1993): 41, 109, 118–119.

58. Marian Burros, "For the Takeout Bunch, Bad News on Sandwiches," *New York Times*, March 22, 1995, B8.

59. Natalie Angier, "Health Benefits From Soy Protein; Study Finds Potent Weapon in Lowering Cholesterol," *New York Times*, August 3, 1995, A1, A9.

60. Justin Dorgeloh, M.D., Retired Associate Clinical Professor of Pathology, University of California Medical School (Letter to the Editor dated February 12, 1995), "We Still Need a Strong Food and Drug Agency," *New York Times*, February

15, 1995, A14 including statement that "From 1957 to 1961 it [thalidomide] was taken by pregnant women for morning sickness, but it had an unexpected side effect that resulted in 8,000 cases of babies born with malformed arms and legs. Virtually all of those tragic cases occurred outside the United States. Dr. Frances Kelsey of the Food and Drug Administration had virtually singlehandedly prevented marketing of the drug here despite pressure from irate American pharmaceutical companies."

Also see, Philip J. Hilts, "F.D.A. Becomes Target of Empowered Groups," *New York Times*, February 12, 1995, p. A 12. This article notes that "Among the Republicans in Congress and their allies in conservative advocacy groups, the Food and Drug Administration has become the first and biggest target in the push for deregulation. The attacks on the drug agency are coming at a time it has begun to speed up the approval of drugs by working with the pharmaceutical industry under a new plan, the User Fee Program."

61. Afrika, *African Holistic Health*, 67; and Penney C. Royal, *Herbally Yours* (Provo, Utah: Sound Nutrition, 1982): 14.

62. Royal, *Herbally Yours*, 72.

63. Afrika, *African Holistic Health*," 63; Royal, *Herbally Yours*, 25.

64. *African Holistic Health*, 65; *Herbally Yours*, 30.

65. *African Holistic Health*, 69; *Herbally Yours*, 39.

66. Jane E. Brody, "Health Factor in Vegetables Still Elusive," *New York Times*, February 21, 1995, B5, B9 in which it is stated: "recent evidence from both laboratory and human studies strongly suggests that carotenoids may be most powerful as a team, working perhaps in combination with a large group of substances in plants called phytochemicals—among them, indoles and flavonoids—that appear to have value as disease preventives [e.g., heart attacks, strokes and cancer]" (B5).

67. Royal, *Herbally Yours*, 32.

68. Ibid., 21.

69. Afrika, *African Holistic Health* , 62; Royal, *Herbally Yours*, 28.

70. Ibid., *Herbally Yours*, 26.

71. Ibid., 27.

72. Associated Press, "Congress to Start Work," 9–A.

73. See also, Philip J. Hilts, "Black Teen-Agers Are Turning Away From Smoking, but Whites Puff On—The Shift Reflects Social Pressure, Scientists Say," *New York Times*, April 19, 1995, B7.

74. Coleman, "Poverty's Effects Linger for Black Babies," *Plain Dealer*, June 5, 1990, 1–A, 8–A.

75. E.g., John H. Cushman Jr., "G.O.P's Plan for Environment Is Facing Big Test in Congress: Votes Planned on Curbing Regulatory Powers," *New York Times*, July 17, 1995, A1, A9; also see, John H. Cushman Jr., "Democrats Force the G.O.P. to Pull Anti-Regulation Bill," *New York Times*, July 19, 1995, A1, C18.

76. Daniel Goleman, "Faith and Social Activities Help to Heal, a Study Finds," *New York Times*, February 4, 1995, A9.

77. Ibid.

78. *Plain Dealer* (from *New York Times*), "Medicare Treatment Biased: Study Says Blacks Get Less Care," April 21, 1994, 6–A.

79. Ibid.

80. Ibid.

81. Harriet A. Washington, "Blacks Have a Long History of Abuse and Exploitation in Experiments," *Plain Dealer*, March 19, 1995, 1–C, 4–C.

82. Freudenheim, "Health Costs Paid by Employers Drop."

83. David Johnston, "Feds Accuse Rostenkowski of Plundering Government," *Plain Dealer*, June 1, 1994, 1–A, 6–A;"Rostenkowski's Fall to Have Large Impact," *Plain Dealer* (New York Times), June 1, 1994, 6–A; Tom Diemer, "Clinton's Team Is Still Confident," *Plain Dealer*, June 1, 1994, 6–A.

CHAPTER 8

Black Women as Ordered by the Criminal Justice World

CRIMINAL JUSTICE AS A SOCIAL INSTITUTION

Crime has been developed to supplant the more positive attributes of a community once it becomes defined as the inner city. The functionality of crime for the Western world was first set forth by Cesare Beccaria in his 1764 treatise, *On Crimes and Punishments*.[1] Beccarria states that "Laws are the conditions under which independent and isolated men united to form a society."[2] When "men" have united to form a certain society's structures, relationships and values, the implementation of the law is done by organizations known as the courts. The courts thus function to preserve the aforementioned societal structures, relationships and values. Further, because legislators make the laws and because those legislators generally come from the powerful echelons of the society, the laws those legislators make, unless certain unusual political events operate, basically preserve the structures, relationships and values of the powerful in the society. In the nineteenth century, Emile Durkheim was one of the first sociologists to outline the functionality of crime. In his 1893 doctoral thesis,[3] Durkheim maintained that the law is necessary to reinforce uniform group values and regulate interactions of various parts of a diverse society. Hence, Durkheim went on to postulate that crime is a normal force of social control and its purpose is to restrict segments of the society that for some reason are seen as "deviant."[4] Durkheim's view is translated here to mean that criminality for the Black female is more a function of power relations in the society and a proclivity by virtue of her race and gender to be typecast as "deviant" than any actual villainous conduct on her part. Other rationales forwarded by theoretical constructs in criminology such as differential association, role strain, social reactivity, and even conflict theory serve to illustrate different components of functionalism. The set of propositions that best explains the criminality of the Black female defendants in this population is seen to be that of the Functionalist Theory. The function of crime in maintaining the inferior position of Blacks in the United States and elsewhere has become even more important as the vestiges of the U.S. civil rights movement and the global human rights movement have outlawed the more overt manifestations of racism and discrimination. Though it might be illegal to discriminate on the basis of race in an employment, education or entrepreneurial opportunity situation, it certainly is politic to discriminate on the apparent basis of one's past criminal record.

One blatant example of the convenience of criminal labelling for ruling society is an incident that occurred the first day the Brady Bill (gun control) went into effect. A Black male lay preacher went into a pawn shop located in a small Georgia town as he had many times before, and was discovered to have a twenty-three-year-old felony assault conviction. Reporting the event, the CNN TV announcer proclaimed that local and federal (ATF) law enforcement authorities were elated that the Brady Bill was doing what it was "supposed" to do. The portly middle-aged minister and his wife, standing outside their Georgia home, were flabbergasted. They did not know what had hit them. It was covert racism as executed in the New World Order, operationalized by legislative edict using the organizational structure and modern computerized technology of the criminal justice system. Although this particular maxim is less likely to affect Black women than Black men, because the former are convicted more often of nonviolent, economic crimes, the mission, message and meaning are the same—to disenfranchise, discredit and render dysfunctional Black people. Since the Black woman's transgressions are generally more passive, the state must be more proactive in generating her criminality. It does so by taking the manifestations of Eisenhower's military-industrial complex such as monopoly, exclusion of the masses from resources, corporate tax favoritism, restrictive personnel promotion and subtle support for questionable business practices regarding environmental issues, product quality and profit dissemination and putting the blame of their negative consequences such as welfare and drugs on the Black woman.

In other words, the Black woman functions in U.S. society as a scapegoat to divert attention from the fundamental, universal societal problems that affect nearly all but the power elite. This purpose is perhaps most obvious in the design, operation and results of the criminal justice system, although this criminal function served by the Black woman for overall New World Order posturing is just as real and just as devastating for her when played out in the social institutions of politics, economics, education and the family.

Criminalization of the Black Female: Observations of a Justice System Participant

This chapter presents an analysis of the societal situation of Black females in the context of the criminal justice system. According to the *National Law*

Journal, although women make up less than 6 percent of prisoners nationwide, "new sentencing laws have affected women most detrimentally."[5] While the U.S. male prison population increased by 112 percent, the female population increased by 202 percent since 1985. Further, 59 percent of the state female prison population were sentenced for nonviolent offenses: 41.2 percent for property offenses, 12 percent for drug offenses. Of those women who were sellers, most were used as "mules," carriers of drugs for their male companions."[6] (In general, Black people get arrested at four times the rate of Whites even though the two groups use drugs at almost the same rates; 53 percent of all incarcerated people are sentenced to prison for possession of "one gram or less of an illegal substance."[7]) While Black men go to prison at seven times the rate for White men, a Black woman is eight times more likely to go to prison than a White woman.[8] Thus, 54 percent of the 90,000 women in prison are women of color. Also, Black women are twice as likely to be convicted of killing their husbands while in an abusive relationship than are White women; on the average, Black women receive a longer jail term as well as higher fines than do White women in the U.S. court system.[9] In addition, 63 percent of women generally who are in prison for violent crimes are there for attacking relatives, intimates or acquaintances. Often their attacks were made to defend themselves and/or their children from abuse.[10]

The basic premise here is that the criminal justice system reflects the purposes of the society and in doing so maintains and reinforces the relative status configurations of the overall social structure. It is written from the viewpoint of the author, a sociologist-lawyer, who represented approximately one hundred women of African descent accused of criminal activity in a midwestern trial court system. The two case studies below are presented to give a flavor of the situational factors behind black female "criminality." The ethnographic inquiry as to the sociological implications was done concurrently with the legal representation with the objective of identifying the interrelationships between the legal consequences and the social conditions. For instance, the poverty and related powerlessness of the women described in the case studies form a backdrop to the evolution and nature of their criminality. One woman's incrimination was caused by her "defiance" of an authority that to her was both threatening and ambiguous. The other's incrimination was caused by her surrender to the forces of the drug world. These forces have been superimposed upon the Black community as diversionary tactics camouflaging the flight of jobs, opportunities and the minimal amenities of a decent standard of living, (e.g., grass, trees, parks, tennis courts, swimming pools, recreation centers, libraries, supermarkets, department stores, neighborhood pharmacies and doctor and dentist offices).

Background of Study

This examination began (and ended) with the premise that in some instances one's social circumstances are more determinative of one's chance for being labelled (typecast) as deviant than one's personal predilections. That premise was felt to be particularly relevant to the Black female in the case load studied and in general, given the widespread social status of the Black woman.

Observations were made of the one hundred indigent Black women who were assigned to the writer in a rotational attorney assignment system over an eighteen-year period of law practice. These women were convicted primarily of welfare fraud, theft and drug offenses. The vast majority of them were single parents who had ephemeral but yet intense ties to an extended family system (e.g., mother, grandmother, siblings, aunts and cousins).[11] Their age ranged from 22 to 30. Three quarters of them had never before been charged with a felony offense. The age of these women was higher than the age at which Black males first get in major trouble with the law. Likewise, these women had a higher average school completion grade than Black males. The average Black male in this felony court system had not completed the eleventh grade. These women, on average, while not having a high school diploma, had completed the twelfth grade, and many of them had GEDs. This, however, was more true of those accused of welfare fraud and the theft offenses than those accused of drug offenses. One of the underlying themes of this article is that there is not much difference demographically in terms of education, number of children, family background and occupational skill levels between those who have been convicted of welfare fraud and other poor Black women, including others who are or have been on welfare (see also McClain 1988). The study was done during a time when prosecutions were escalating in the county. For instance, according to county court records felony arraignments "nearly doubled in five years, climbing from 8,922 in 1987 to 16,953 in 1992"[12] (the county population approximates one million). The rate for the female defendants, two thirds of whom were Black, increased likewise.

Conclusions from the case histories are presented here in a cumulative manner, with more concern with broad demographic issues and universal theoretical applications than individual idiosyncracies. The Black female defendants are demonstrative of people who are swept up in social and legal situations that have many dimensions that are essentially beyond their control. Of course, further research in this pioneer area is needed. However, as described below, debilitating demographic factors, represented by this population of client-defendants, seem to describe, to explain and, in large part, to predict the legal predicament with criminal consequences in which they found themselves.

In a study in which the investigator performs a dual role, there is an obvious opportunity for undue bias. Here, one role was as a defense attorney (advocate) assigned to represent indigent persons accused of criminal activity. The other was as a sociologist (scientist) studying the relationship between the demographic aspects of the Black females' social condition and the legal aspects of their situation in the eyes of the law. Nevertheless, this longitudinal examination provides evidence of the importance of certain variables in anticipating criminal behavior in certain categories of individuals. These are poor Black females unaffiliated, for the most part, with strong legitimate organizations such as churches, lodges, community centers, civic leagues, trade associations (practical nurses, cosmetologists, entertainment artists and the like), schools, sororities or street/ward clubs (Hill-Collins, 1991). In short, lack of established "legal" group affiliation coupled with poverty was a prevailing factor in the characterization of the Black female defendants who involuntarily, by virtue of being incriminated, participated in this study.

Although the study was dependent upon women randomly assigned to the investigator as part of a routine attorney assignment process, it was effected in the tradition of Elliot Liebow (1967) as described in his book, *Tally's Corner*. Liebow examined the relationships of neighborhood men with each other and with the greater community. In doing so, he was able to come to conclusions about their overall societal condition that would have been less meaningful without the microanalysis at the individual level. Likewise, the women studied in this investigation interacted with the investigator on a personal basis such that the latter was able to gain considerable insights into their social condition while in no way compromising their defense, inasmuch as the data collected was crucial to the preparation of an adequate defense. Moreover, the material gathered was probably much more comprehensive than that given to a traditional social service agency and is just as protected from an individual perspective because of the privacy constraints mandated by attorney-client privilege. Further, the trust level inspired by the nature of such an interviewer-client relationship assists in increasing the validity of the data.

The material was collected while the subjects were in somewhat of a natural habitat. The dynamics of attorney-client interaction were based upon such high stakes that truth was at a premium and most defendants were aware that there was little to be gained by mendacity. How this scenario played out is demonstrated by the fact that the safest place to leave one's purse is on the defendant's table in the courtroom, even among previously convicted theft offenders. This would undoubtedly not have been possible at Tally's Corner. Hence, the women shared far more than was necessary to prepare a defense, in terms of not just their economic and educational states but their emotional and attitudinal ones as well.

Nevertheless, from a methodological perspective, though making the type of leaps of faith inherent in a Tally's Corner type of inquiry carries with it a rather large probability of also making an ecological fallacy, the wealth of valid information obtainable justifies the risk. Other investigators have utilized similar methodological approaches in attempting to get a handle on a portion of reality in their subject area. An example of this is the ethnographic research of George W. Noblit (1987) who, as part of the social scene of the classroom, employed qualitative methodological techniques. Sociologist Wilbur H. Watson (1989) used the ethnographic study technique, also. Watson went back to his home community described in his book, *The Village*. There he obtained oral histories from the "old timers" in order to get a firsthand account of Black empowerment in the village during the early years of the twentieth century.

In the examination here, a concerted effort was made to separate out the legal advocacy from the scientific inquiry, such that the relevant social factors were ascertained and recorded while the investigator was mounting a criminal defense. Fortunately, as these dual endeavors were entirely congruent and supportive of one another, neither effort suffered in the process. (As a defense attorney, the writer obtained acquittals in six of the last eight criminal jury trials. Of course, 95 percent of the criminal cases before the court system in this study "plead out," and that figure is also reflective of the specific criminal cases undertaken by the researcher-participant. Trials generally are undertaken only after an assessment has been made that there is a fairly good chance of winning them.) However, the ability of any criminal defense attorney representing Black defendants to win jury trials will probably become more problematic in the future inasmuch as the Supreme Court is allowing prosecutors to dismiss potential Black jurors on the basis of the slightest, most implausible pretense (*Purkett v. Elem*[13] allowed the dismissal of two Black males on the basis of their having mustaches and sideburns—one also had a goatee).

Criminal Case Study: A Black Woman and an Offense of Violence

Gail, a thirty-one-year-old Black female, worked part time as a janitress in the public housing complex in which she lived. Currently separated from her second husband, she had no children. Her mother had died when she and her brother were "kids," and she had been raised by her father with the assistance of one of her aunts. She had graduated from a suburban high school that, at the time of her attendance there, had a 50 percent Black enrollment. When I was assigned to defend her, Gail was living in a one-bedroom apartment in an inner-city project where she had lived for ten years. She was totally independent of anyone else and received no public assistance. She told me she had been living on her own since she was eighteen years old. I wondered at this, as she was a highly nervous type, although the circumstances may have affected her demeanor. Her appearance belied her anxiety level. On one of the coldest days of the year, when

I first met Gail, she had come down to court by bus, wearing three jackets. The top jacket was of the motorcycle variety with more metal on it than a five-star general's. In addition, her hair was all down her back, wet and dripping with various hair-care products. There are times when lawyers wish, rightly or wrongly, that they could change something about their clients' appearance or behavior to appeal to what they expect will be a middle-class, suburban, predominantly White jury (See Evelyn Williams' book, *Inadmissible Evidence*, 1993, in which she describes her defense of her niece, Assata Shakur, "slave name" JoAnne Chesimard[14] during the 1970s). Typically, lawyers will emphasize whatever qualities in their clients that they think will be most endearing to a jury.[15]

In this case, I thought Gail should think about the exotic duplicate set of eyebrows that she meticulously drew with eyebrow pencil every morning over her own, more or less.

By the same token, there are times when many clients reject their lawyers' middle-class notions of propriety and insist upon retaining their own identity—win, lose or draw. In this instance, Gail responded by smiling and telling me that she had thought about it. She continued to wear two sets of eyebrows. (Also see the book by Assata Shakur, *Assata: An Autobiography*, 1987, telling her side of the story, in which she too decided to retain her identity—win, lose or draw).[16]

Prior to this case, Gail had never been charged with any offense. Although poor, she had lived a law-abiding life and had even been able to afford a twelve-year-old car. The car and living alone in a high-crime area are where the story of her "criminality" begins.

Gail left work about 5 P.M. on the evening of Friday, October 29, 1993. After doing her banking and paying her bills, she stopped by to visit her uncle in the hospital at approximately 6 P.M. She then returned home and watched TV. She drank a beer between about 7:30 and 8:00 that evening after which she fell asleep on the couch. (Gail said she never drank any hard liquor and began drinking beer only after her "nerves got so bad"; indeed, her fingernails were bitten down to the nub.)

Upon awakening, discovering that there was nothing in the refrigerator to eat, she went out about 10 P.M. to find an open restaurant. In the back of her mind, Gail knew there was a McDonald's Restaurant a couple of blocks south of her apartment. Driving toward the restaurant, she saw a plain car behind her flashing its headlights. Anxious, being alone at night, she continued cautiously towards her "burger" destination. The car pulled up beside her. The two men inside, one White and one Black, were dressed in leather jackets and looked liked "cooties" [hoodlums]. She became more apprehensive. At that point, all she wanted to do was get to a crowded area and yell for help. The men were shouting at her by this time. Finally, she made it to the McDonald's parking lot. The car pulled in behind her. She got out to make a run for the door and get help. One of the men, looking just like an everyday person in jeans and sneakers, came up to her. The White guy was tall and big. The Black guy was medium in height with "a little gut." They wore working clothes and looked like the type of thugs "that might get in a whole bunch of trouble." Gail said, "The guy confused the mess out of me." He mentioned something about her headlights were off, which for Gail was meaningless; she saw no connection between her headlights being off and a couple of thuggish-looking hoodlums following her.

As Gail tried to get to safety, one of the guys grabbed her, put her in the back of their car, and handcuffed her. Terrified, Gail was left in the back of their car. Gail's wrists were very flexible because they had been broken several years before. She was so scared that she wriggled out of the handcuffs, got out of the car and hid in the bushes. The men had not told her they were plainclothes policemen. Finding her crouched in fear under some McDonald's shrubbery, they dragged Gail, kicking and screaming, back to the car.

When Gail told the desk team back at the police station (the staff sergeant, the matron, the booking clerk, etc.) her story, they all laughed and assured Gail that the arresting officers probably would not pursue a criminal charge against her. However, the two members of the SWAT team who had arrested Gail held firm. They prosecuted Gail for a violent felony. Gail was charged with the felony crime defined as "escape" in violation of Ohio Revised Code 2921.34 (along with failure to use headlights after dusk, a misdemeanor to which she pled in Municipal Court). Escape is an "offense of violence" pursuant to Ohio Revised Code 2901.01(I)(1). On December 22, 1993, the grand jury found that Gail, knowing she was under detention or being reckless in that regard, did break or attempt to break such detention. Thus, Gail was under indictment for her first felony offense. She was assigned to me for legal representation after her arraignment on this charge on January 10, 1994.

At our interview, Gail said she was scared and "didn't really believe they was police." She said, "Miss Willa (her appellation for me), I didn't know what they was up to—I still think they was up to something." "I know they was going to take me somewhere and do something they had no business." She also stated, "They didn't read no rights—they didn't tell me what I was under arrest for." When she got to jail, she told them that she was going to sue. (I imagine that must have scared them, coming from an indigent Black woman.)

During the pre-trial of her case, I presented Gail with her options. She could go to trial and risk prison if she lost, or she could plead guilty and stand a better chance, upon a showing of "repentance and contriteness," of receiving probation. Gail said she did not "even think you could get charged with escape—unless you bust out of prison." She was also distraught with the conduct of the police, commenting, "They can do what they want to do." Even thinking about "going in that place" (prison) made her, she stated, "go crazy." She went on to say that the police "told me I should know what a vice car look like." "I didn't know what a vice car looked like." During the discovery process, the assistant prosecutor provided the police report, in which the arresting officers claimed that their unmarked police car was "well-known" to members of the community in which they operated. (One wonders what was the point of the car being unmarked and their function as undercover officers.)

Gail was further distressed because, "When I got my car out, the gears were messed up. People say they should be liable for that. They [the police] do what they want to do." Since the episode, Gail has been on foot, which is why she had to take the bus to her court appearances.

Gail insists that while waiting for a bus she saw the same two police officers, in plainclothes, and that they waved as they passed by. Gail lamented that before she knew who they were, she waved back. The Black officer had on the same little "cootie" cap he was wearing the night he arrested her. They laughed as they drove past.

(Their actions almost make one rethink Eldridge Cleaver's pre-conversion remark that a trigger-happy social order is the problem with the justice system, rather than trigger-happy cops[17]; also see Chapter 6). But, then, it must be recognized that individuals generally act within the confines of their social system and their behavior, for the most part, is only that which a given society will tolerate.)

We started plea bargain negotiations on this set of facts. Both the assistant county prosecutor assigned to the case and I agreed that Gail would be eligible for a new program known as Diversion. It was modeled after one begun down in Miami by Attorney General Janet Reno before she became the chief prosecutor for the United States. Our county prosecutor and one of her supervisors had gone down to Florida for a seminar to learn more about Diversion as an alternative to criminal prosecution. Upon successful completion of this Diversion program, Gail's felony record of her "escape" charge would be expunged, and her record would not show a conviction. A first felony offender not in the Diversion program cannot have his or her record expunged until the case has been closed (final discharge, probation over, fines paid, etc.) for three years.[18] A first offender convicted of a misdemeanor has to wait one year after the case is closed before having his or her record sealed (expunged).[19] An expungement is analogous to an annulment in marriage in that the offense, felony or misdemeanor, is treated as if it never happened. A person whose record is expunged can respond to questions about convictions asked by private and state entities in the negative: The answer to, "Have you ever been convicted of a felony [misdemeanor] offense?" would be "No." (Unfortunately, the federal government does not recognize state expungements. In the federal government's expungement program, the only eligible first offenders are persons whose offense was committed before the age of twenty-six.) The criteria of eligibility for the state Diversion program discussed here included (1) No prior felony convictions; (2) The consent of the arresting agency and victim; (3) The pending charges must be non-violent or unrelated to drugs; (4) Supervision by the Probation Department's Court Supervised Release Program/Diversion Unit, in non–public assistance fraud cases; (5) The applicant must admit his guilt, in regard to the pending charges, in a written statement; (6) The applicant must waive his right to a speedy trial, and any statutory limitations of action; (7) The applicant must give consent to the Diversion Unit to perform periodic record checks, along with several other procedural requirements.

In addition, persons on Diversion generally were placed under supervision by the Probation Department for a period of six to eighteen months, with the average supervisory period being about a year. During this supervision, such "Divertees" were generally subject to all the rules of probation including needing permission to travel or to marry, regular reporting, restriction of "undesirable" associations, reduction of civil rights such as freedom from unreasonable search and seizure (Fourth Amendment), the privilege against self-incrimination (Fifth Amendment) and the right of confrontation of accusers (Sixth Amendment), and periodic urinalysis. However, the prospect of leaving the criminal justice system with no felony-criminal record made such restrictions worthwhile for most defendants.

Thus, on Gail's behalf, I made a motion for her to be accepted into the Diversion program. As she still did not have any transportation, I met Gail down at the court in order to have her read and, at the appropriate places, fill out the nineteen-page Diversion application form. Gail was eligible to get a lucky break.

Gail had no prior felony offenses. The Municipal Police Department had no objection to her being on the program. The charge of escape did not involve drugs and was certainly nonviolent. Every other Wednesday she reported to the probation officer assigned her in the Court Supervised Release Program and "dropped a urine." On the alternative Wednesdays that she did not report in person, she phoned into the office and spoke to her "P.O." by phone. She willingly waived her rights to speedy trial and any other statutory limitations. Upon receipt of her paperwork, however, a problem for the Probation Department with Gail's eligibility appeared on the part of her application calling for her admission of guilt. That part ("Client Statement") requires that:

You are to provide a complete, accurate, and truthful statement concerning your present criminal charge(s). Please state clearly the *date, time, location, and reason* for your arrest, or the reason for the current charges. You may include the name(s) of any other person(s) involved in the offense, and their role(s). You must state whether you believe you are guilty or innocent of the charge(s).

This is the part Gail failed. Her statement reflected the fact situation described earlier, and the probation officer said that did not reflect a criminal offense. When I reported this information to Gail, she said anything else would be a lie, and she could not do that.

I reiterated that she had the option then of going to trial. Gail started crying and emphatically informed me that "This is my life." She fretted that she would lose her apartment. Gail wondered what would happen to her furniture if she went to jail. She was almost finished paying for it. Her father had died two years prior to this incident, and she would have no place to store her belongings. She had no one else she could depend on to take care of her business. She had made too many sacrifices and worked too hard to see everything she had "go up in smoke just like that." What would happen to her dog? (I was glad she did not have any children.) Gail was not enthusiastic about the free receipt of "three hots and a cot" that some other female defendants try to use as rationalization that prison would be bearable.

Gail did not have much faith in what, according to her, "a bunch of White people" would find. Although she maintained that all she did anyway was go to work and come home and go to work again, Gail promised that if she ever got out of this she would keep "such a low profile, they wouldn't even know I exist on earth."

Since she was so terrified of going to trial, Gail would have to enter a guilty plea to the criminal offense—or at least be found guilty by a judge after a reading of the facts of the situation by the prosecutor. (See also *North Carolina v. Alford*,[20] a Supreme Court case in which it is permitted to plead guilty without admitting guilt. Although I have seen some judges in Ohio unwilling to accept such a plea, many others are willing to do so.) Gail's judge required that the assistant prosecutor provide a "factual basis" for her plea. To comply with that requirement, the prosecutor read the police report.

Earlier, however, the assistant prosecutor and I had searched through the code [criminal statute] book to find a misdemeanor that would "fit the crime" appropriately. His supervisor had approved a misdemeanor for Gail so that she would be allowed to plead guilty to a lesser offense than the "felony escape" with which she had been originally charged. After reviewing several misdemeanors, we found one that looked promising, titled, "Failure to comply with order or signal of police officer," as set forth in Ohio Revised Code Section 2921.33.1(A): No person shall fail to comply with any lawful order or direction of any police officer invested with authority to direct, control, or regulate traffic." The two officers sat in the courtroom watching as Gail pled to this misdemeanor, was fined twenty-five dollars plus court costs and sent on her way, back into her world to continue to negotiate life the best she could. Gail was given sixty days to pay the money to the court clerk. Case closed.

Gail said, "The killing part about it—I never did get the burger."

THE NEW WORLD ORDER AND THE ROLE OF CRIMINAL JUSTICE

Criminal codes are purportedly the legal embodiment of society's folkways (in misdemeanors) and mores (in felonies). They are governmental enactments, and the government is imbued with the power to enforce them. That power is awesome, and in the hands of the unscrupulous it is easily abused.

The government is responsive to those who govern and to those who influence those who govern. Those who lack such influence (e.g., Black women) are much more likely to be subject to laws and legislation that define their behavior more directly than the behavior of the more influential. This is the problem with theoretical constructs that attempt to predict and explain crime. Criminal codes vary from country to country, state to state and city to city. What may be criminal in one state may not be in another. By the same token, what may be criminal in one city or county may not be in another. Thus, the law-abiding citizen of one county may drive to obtain liquor in another, then come back as a criminal. The problem for African Americans is that because of differential living circumstances and treatment what may be criminal for them may not be for European Americans. The true issue in the criminality question is, "What evokes the wrath or loathing of the members of a community so much so that those mores or folkways are codified into criminal officialdom?" Further, what is there about African Americans in general, and African American women in particular, that the wrath or loathing of the community is disproportionately meted out upon them in the form of incrimination? Or, more accurately, what is there about U.S. society that this result obtains? Of course, a primary thesis of this book is that the answer to this latter question is found in the programs, policies and practices endemic to the New World Order. Those New World Order policies have refurbished and refined the strategies and the methodologies that institutionalize and reify the American caste system.

In essence, everyone knows that the general members of a community are not the real arbiters of the law. Laws, criminal or otherwise, are created by either the ruling elite (Mills 1959) or the politically mobilized, such as organizations from the Women's Temperance Union to the highly organized MADD (Mothers against Drunk Driving).[21] "Society" just does not decide that some behavior is repulsive to it and needs sanctioning; rather, some influential party or group in the society makes that decision and acts upon it. That is the most euphemistic interpretation of lawmaking.

What has happened in practice and has been elevated to the stature of policy is that the politically powerful have directed their sanctioning authority toward those with a certain status rather than a certain behavior. There has to be method behind the madness of incriminating the relatively powerless, penniless and problem-filled African American women who have succumbed to the desperation of their life situation (Piven and

Cloward 1971, 1980). The criminal label has become so easily applied that the prostitutes, debtor's prisonettes and substance abusers of the Middle Ages now comprise the bulk of the female criminal population. Between the welfare system and the criminal justice system, it is hard to determine which is the more effective and efficient social control mechanism. Both are formidable, omnipresent/potent forces in the lives of low-income Black women. It has been the author's experience that many defendants would rather plead guilty than lose the welfare benefits needed to feed, clothe and house their children. Both the welfare system and the criminal justice system provide more support and benefits to the middle classes than to the working and grassroots echelons. Both help to "document, divide and database" the society's marginals. Increasingly they work hand in hand to form a screening network that creates unsurpassable barriers between the haves and the have-nots in the New World Order.

As mentioned above, the conclusions here are based upon information gathered from Black women studied over eighteen years of legal practice and represented in the same midwestern court system. Although that system through the years consisted at any given time of thirty-four different judges, dozens of different prosecutors and a multitude of other court and law enforcement personnel, there is a consistency of situational factors that transcends personnel. In other words, the most pertinent factors relating to the incrimination of the Black female in the U.S. justice system are systemic, which means that the issues are basically the same as one goes from case to case. Therefore, the solutions to the problematic issues should be seen more as societally required than as individual necessities.

Criminal Case Study: A Black Woman Drug Offender

The process resulting in Moonie's criminalization was different from Gail's, but Moonie's criminal outcome was similar insofar as it was a consequence directly and/or indirectly of powerlessness within the society.

On or about February 15, 1994, at approximately 1:25 A.M., according to an assistant county prosecutor, a Black and White [police car] was checking an area known for its high crime and drug activity. Two females were observed by the officers standing on a corner flagging down automobiles. They stopped the females, patted them down and located a long hard object, in the right coat pocket of one of the females. The officer asked the subject female to remove the object, which turned out to be a glass pipe with suspected residue. As the amount of residue was too small to measure, the lab report merely listed it as residue (as far as a drug possession charge is concerned however, residue results in the same offense as does any amount up to ten grams or twenty-four rocks of crack cocaine).

Thus Moonie was charged with her third drug-abuse offense within one year in violation of Ohio Revised Code Section 2529.11. Because she had two previous drug offenses on her record, she was charged with a felony of the third degree, an F-3, rather than a felony of the fourth degree, an F-4. A felony of the third degree of this nature (nonaggravated) is punishable by a term of imprisonment of one to one and a half up to two years. In addition, Moonie had been sentenced to a period of probation of two years as punishment for her two previous drug possession (two rocks of crack cocaine and pipe residue) charges.

Moonie, in the course of her conflicts with the law, had met me before, and when she was in the arraignment room she asked for me. The arraignment room judge did not have to honor her request, operating on the theory of "beggars can't be choosers." Also, all the Constitution requires is "adequate assistance of counsel," not a certain attorney.[22] However, I had just won a jury trial before that judge in which I had defended a police officer accused of felonious assault with a deadly weapon. I think the judge was glad the officer won because the officer had two Purple Hearts from Vietnam and the judge had also served in Vietnam. (It turned out that they both had been involved in the Tet offensive.) At any rate, the judge assigned Moonie to me.

In the county jail, a relatively new modern structure, built in response to a 1971 federal lawsuit, Moonie had written a letter asking for psychological help as well as one to the judge assigned to conduct any trial she might have or to take her plea, whichever was the case. She told me that she had talked to the corrections officers, and they had shown her the error of her ways. She said that if she were to be granted another chance at probation she would go to the project [drug rehabilitation] that she had been ordered to go to previously by the trial judge; she told me that she had not trusted the people from that project before.

I asked her how she had gotten into this predicament, and she said that she had to face it, she was a "hard-core drug user." I asked her what she was doing when she was flagging down cars on the corner. Moonie was insulted at the tone of my question, which she interpreted as implying she was a prostitute. She told me indignantly that she was a "hustler." She did not sell her body for drugs! I then asked, "Well, what is a hustler?" She said that is just what people called her. In other words, she dealt in drugs, not her body, to support her habit. I felt I had made an honest mistake because the project to which she was applying had been started especially for prostitutes.

A few days later I had an opportunity to question another female defendant who was an admitted crack-cocaine abuser. This young woman was a year older than Moonie and the mother of two "estranged" children. The oldest daughter of this defendant was in the custody of the toddler's father, who lived with his mother, father and two sisters. Two "fathers," one with his mom, had shown up at the hospital for the youngest baby, a newborn. As this defendant had left the hospital without either taking the baby with her (she had a pressing date with the county's correction center) or identifying the father, the hospital social worker had placed the baby in the custody of a (maternal) family member.[23] Except for an initial rough start, for which the baby was placed in intensive care, after two weeks the baby was pronounced healthy, even though the mother had received absolutely no prenatal care. The mother did claim during one of her court hearings that she had refrained from smoking crack cocaine during the last two months of her pregnancy. That assertion rather strains credibility inasmuch as three days prior to the infant's birth, the mother was arrested by police after jumping out of a crack house window during a drug raid. This defendant was let go immediately after booking, despite being in an advanced state of pregnancy, because she was not apprehended by the police officers who usually picked her up; she was in a different territory. She had given those "stranger" police officers a cousin's name and birthdate; the cousin was a premed student then attending college in another state. She later had me clear up that misrepresentation because, once she got back to the women's reformatory, she decided she wanted to stay there longer. She called me (collect, of course) at 6:23 A.M. one day to tell me what she had done and had me go down that day to criminal records so that the misstatement could be identified. This done, she could be brought back to court for further sentencing to the women's reformatory under the state's drug-recidivist statutes[24] on the additional drug-abuse and drug-trafficking charges (involving eleven rocks of crack cocaine).

For this woman's infant, after such harrowing in utero experiences as well as a touch-and-go first couple of weeks, to be pronounced healthy upon discharge from the hospital represents a primary reason that I prefer to term such infants "drug challenged" rather than "crack babies." The latter phrase puts an additional stigma upon the children that is not warranted. Furthermore, at least one health professional has editorialized that given "a consistent, loving, supportive relationship with their primary caretaker"[25] in a nurturing situation where a secure, trusting bond is formed, children whose mothers used cocaine while pregnant with them can nevertheless thrive. Of course, such a nurturing scenario cannot be complete without being expanded to include the greater societal institutions of education and health as well as those of the family and the economy in general. The welcoming committee for such children has to be rather broad, to say the least, in order for a significant portion of the next generation not to be permanently scarred. At any rate, I put a hypothetical question outlining Moonie's "badge of honor" (being a nonprostituting hustler) to the other female drug-abuse defendant during a telephone jail interview (she had called me collect again as per usual). This other Black female defendant told me very bluntly that whoever the girl was who claimed she was flagging down cars but not selling her body for drugs was lying.

In addition with regard to Moonie's case, in their report the police had stated that the Black female suspect from whom the glass (crack) pipe had been confiscated was a known prostitute in the area. In fact, Moonie had told me herself the first time I interviewed her face-to-face at the county jail that she was just walking down the street and this girl had joined her. She said she had "told the girl to get away from me" because the police in the area knew her and would stop her on "GP" [general principle] if they saw her with somebody.

In short, because of a credibility problem with regard to the defendant in this case, Moonie, we cannot conclusively determine what Moonie meant when she stated that they called her a "hustler." Gathering more information about Moonie's background, I realized that she was just about a week younger than my own twenty-one-year-old daughter, who was graduating from college in the spring. I told Moonie that, and she informed me that she too wanted to go to college, when she got her life together (a common response among my female drug-offender clients).

Moonie's children were with their respective fathers, each of whom obtained custody after Moonie had lost it. (The daughter of one imprisoned father was with his parents.) Moonie maintained she had been on her own since she was thirteen years of age. Her oldest sister had her own father, to whom her mother had not been married. John David Williams (Moonie was specific about the *each* of the names of *each* of her stepfathers) was the name of her next sister and oldest brother's father. After him, her mother had been married to the father of her next brother and next sister, Walter Lawrence. That stepfather died before Moonie was born. Her mother had kept his name throughout all her other liaisons. Moonie informed me that that set of children were the Lawrences.

Finally, Moonie, born when her mother was forty-one years of age, had her own father. Moonie said that when her mother was forty-eight she got pregnant again. According to Moonie, "She was out doing something she had no business." Moonie said that she told her mother that if she had that baby she would do something to her [the mother]. *She* was the baby of her family! Her mother had an abortion.

Moonie claimed that her mother "made a difference" between the children to whose fathers she had been married and the others. She treated those children better than Moonie. She always told Moonie that she never should have had her. Moonie said that her oldest brother, ten years her senior, had been like a mother and a father to her. He had told her about her period. Moonie said that her mother was not around at the time. Moonie said that "he raised me."

When asked why she had tried drugs in the first place, she said that she had kept getting into it with her mother so she left when she was thirteen years of age. I asked her, "You ran away?" Moonie replied, "No, I didn't run away. I just went over to live with one of my sisters." (The other female drug defendant had also 'left' home as a sort of self-emancipated teenaged minor and returned sporadically only to leave again after some sort of confrontation with her mother and/or stepfather. They both blamed their mothers for a lot of their problems, implicitly and explicitly, in talking with social workers, counselors and lawyers.)

At Moonie's sister's, she met a boy a little older than she. She moved in with him. They lived together at an inner-city motel. He took care of her, Moonie said. He sold drugs and she went to school. When he went to jail (a juvenile facility), she went back home to live with her mother. Things with her mother went downhill, and she was taken away from her mother and placed in a children's home when she was fifteen. She was released from the children's home to her brother's girlfriend. She left there she said because the girl kept taking her checks. She was pregnant with her first child by the boy with whom she had lived at the motel when she went back home to live with her mother. She managed to complete the eleventh grade. As part of her aforementioned education plans, Moonie told me, she wanted to get her GED (General Education Degree).

Her mother had had a heart attack, and Moonie had moved in with her to help. They moved to a high-rise. Her mother, she said, took her checks (from welfare for the baby) and did what she wanted to with them. At the high-rise she met the man who would become her second baby's father. She moved in with him. He would do anything for her. Unfortunately, he would on occasion "go upside her head for no reason at all," and he continued to get high constantly. She left.

On probation for her first drug offenses, Moonie claimed that she had been doing fine. She said she never gave him (her probation officer) a dirty urine. I asked her how she had managed that, as she had already informed me that she was a hard-core drug user. She looked at me and smiled. I asked, was it a matter of timing because cocaine, unlike heroin which is an opiate, supposedly disappears from detection in the urine after three days. She said something like that. She then went on to tell me it was timing along with the use of golden seal, which she claimed is a blood purifier that cleanses the system (I had heard that bit of folk wisdom from some other defendants, too, but they nevertheless seemed to always get caught if they did actually use drugs on probation. The drugs would still be detected by urinalysis and the defendant would consequently be charged with a probation infraction).

Moonie's initial probation violation, however, was prompted by something she maintained was out of her control. She said her oldest sister, a cosmetologist in Decatur, Alabama, had gotten chemicals into her eye. Moonie said she was in need of a family member to assist her during her medical emergency. The family scrambled around, and Moonie stated that she was the only one able to go, financially. I asked her how it was that she had been able to afford the trip, and she replied that she had a "sugar daddy," an older man in his forties. He told her that if she wanted to go, he would pay her bus money. This he did, and he sent her money to come home. (I did not ask her why she had not requested plane fare instead, because she probably had paid dearly for that ticket.)

She had gone to her probation officer and asked if she could make this trip to Alabama. He said, "Not now," but Moonie left anyway. Hence, the violation.

Because of this experience, Moonie maintained that she took the stance that she did during plea negotiations. The prosecutor had offered to drop the two "furthermore" clauses, putting this new charge down to a felony of the fourth degree, F-4. This exposed Moonie to a term of incarceration of six months, a year, up to a year and a half. The judge intimated that in exchange for a plea, he would consider terminating the probation and shipping Moonie on the new charge only. During the plea hearing, when the judge asked Moonie if she understood all of her rights as he had read them, she said she didn't understand about the revocation of the driver's license requirement since she had never learned how to drive anyway. The judge informed Moonie that since September of 1993, anyone convicted of a drug offense would have his or her driver's license revoked for anywhere from six months up to five years (the legislature had added this disincentive, of course, but the punishment was lost on persons who never had such basic societal privileges "anyway").

Further, there was a mandatory fine of $1,500 for the level of drug abuse to which she was pleading. (Defendants convicted of more serious drug offenses are supposed to receive higher levels of mandatory fines, accordingly.) The problem with this scenario as orchestrated by the state's legislative body is that most of the drug offenders who plead are generally eligible for the indigency waiver, and the others are not really concerned about fines ranging from $1,500 to $4,000 or $5,000. I observed one drug offender (I had the codefendant) willingly sign a confiscation agreement to $11,000 in cash but refuse to plead guilty until his portable computerized answering-machine phone was returned; it had a lot of phone numbers recorded in it. The two major felony prosecutors for the county agreed to give it back to him, but I noticed that within seven or eight months his convenience store in the inner city had been closed down and he was serving time in one of the state penitentiaries. My client, who was a second defendant on this man's case, had to give up a 1988 Lincoln Towncar. Actually, a small bank from a place two counties over owned most of the car and entered a writ of replevin to have the car returned to them from the police impound lot. My client, a fifty-four-year-old Black male, first offender, had just purchased the Lincoln used from that bank and after three car payments still owed $16,000 on the five-year-old car; it had a list price of about $6,000.

Moonie had said to me, "Miss Hemmons, I can't do paper [probation]—if anything happens to my sister, I'm gone." The judge accepted Moonie's guilty plea, approved the indigency waiver whereby jobless Moonie was relieved of paying the mandatory $1,500 fine, and Moonie was shipped (sent to the Women's Reformatory) for six months.

NEW WORLD ORDER CRIMINAL/DRUG CASE IMPLICATIONS

By the age of twenty-one, Moonie had had two children, both daughters. Her daughter Nora, named after her mother, was four years old, and her second daughter, Nina, was two at the time. I noticed that both Moonie and the other previously mentioned female drug defendant had configured some type of pattern in naming their respective daughters. This common bond that the defendants tried to establish between their children was attempted even though the offenders could not follow through by providing any other continuity in their daughters' lives; both sets of half-sisters were being raised by different families with little or no contact between them. Both clients informed me that they intended to get their children back when they "got themselves together"; however, neither could provide any concrete plans for the achievement of that eventuality. "Well, I need a place to stay." "I didn't want anything to happen to her." "It's hard to get people [from the drug world] to stay away from me." "I don't have any money."

According to the Bureau of Justice Statistics (1991) the children of Black female inmates who are in state prisons are less likely to live in a foster care or institutional setting than those of White female prisoners. (See Table 8.1.)

Table 8.1
Living Arrangements for the Children of Female State Inmates by Race*

Where Child(ren) Under 18 Live(s) Now	*All*	*White*	*Black*	*Hispanic*
Father/Mother	25.4%	35.2%	18.7%	24.4%
Grandparents	50.6	40.6	56.7	54.9
Other relatives	20.3	14.7	23.7	22.8
Friends	4.1	5.7	2.7	4.2
Foster home	8.6	12.6	5.8	6.5
Agency or institution	2.1	2.1	1.8	2.1
Alone	2.0	1.9	2.3	1.5

*Percents add to more than 100% because inmates with more than one child may have provided multiple responses.

Hence, the work of researchers such as Carol Stack (1981) and Elmer and Joanne Martin (1978) could be interpreted to have anticipated this result. That result is the somewhat greater use of the extended family by Blacks when compared to Whites in regard to placement of the children of female incarcerated offenders.

It is interesting to note that the "trying to get my life together" statement was a theme repeated in the lives of other Black women trapped in the inner-city world of drugs.[26] Indeed, it appears that though the criminal justice system pursues prosecution of Black women caught up in the street drug scene with a tenacity and relentlessness that would put Singapore[27] to shame, it does not do the same job of protecting them from crime. One victim advocate and liaison with the state attorney general's office said, "The criminal justice system provides fewer resources to the investigation of crimes against poor black women."[28] Further, given the presence of drugs even there, being incarcerated in prison in the United States does not seem to protect one against one's drug addiction.[29]

Another common bond between the two subjects being considered here was that the education of both ladies consisted of having completed the eleventh grade. A high school diploma eluded both of them, as did formal training for any but the lowest of minimum-wage jobs. However, both were extremely bright in terms of "catching on quickly," even in the context of the definitively constraining influence of incarceration.

It might also be pointed out here that neither defendant was on "welfare" at the time of their prosecution and subsequent conviction. Neither of them, as drug-addicted mothers, had the stability, perseverance, tenacity, commitment, skill, ability or attention span needed to keep together an independent household that included their children for any appreciable length of time. In other words, they lacked the capacity of even some teenage mothers to form a family unit long enough to collect welfare. As far as becoming "welfare mothers," they could not get it together for two days, let alone two months or two years.[30] The title of welfare mother would have been a step up for either of them.

The New World Order seems to have forgotten that being a mother is hard work. Hence, the role of mother and caretaker has been devalued, debased and discredited as one that lacks dignity and worth. This is particularly true when the male partner in a two-party parental relationship is subject to such high unemployment rates that his ability to live up to "traditional" values requiring something like a traditional breadwinner role has been severely compromised. If drugs for both parties are part of a recourse of escapism from such a political and economic disenfranchisement, then the loss of welfare has meaning only for those still somewhat in touch with majoritarian society. For many the loss may mean that the last thin shred of legitimate contact with the establishment is cut. As control is such an essential factor in New World Order monitoring, maintaining and managing of the designated outgroups, delegitimized contact would probably be intensified in the form of increased interaction with the criminal justice system. The precepts of the New World Order require that such control be manifested even more efficiently, with less hindrance by "technicalities" and individual-rights restrictions than in the past.[31]

For some reason, the fact that these two female drug defendants avoided welfare in this manner, as opposed to other young mothers who did not, does not seem to be a preferable alternative in seeking the elimination of the welfare state. The fact that the society no longer seems to need the reserve labor pool that the welfare state maintained is no reason to send even more Blacks and women into the underground economy and lifestyle. However, more Moonies might be a logical consequence of such welfare-state reductionism as the New World Order seeks to cultivate a nation of competitive hustlers of one type or another, on one level or another—corporate, criminal or community.

Neither of the two female drug offenders in the case study was on welfare; they supported themselves through means derived from the drug world, a world in which their status was also at or near the bottom. (Both had been convicted of offenses involving "crack cocaine," as opposed to the powdered variety. There are allegations that penalties are stricter for the former and that, since crack is the drug of "choice" of poor Blacks and Hispanics, such penalties are tantamount to discrimination.[32])

Another issue which is inextricably tied up with drugs is that of the use of the "informant." Both the drug defendants noted in the case study above had been charged with two different drug offenses, occurring at different points in time. They, along with several others of my clients, had complained that their respective arresting officers had participated in a practice of breaking up the "rocks" of crack into smaller pieces so that they could be charged with more stringent offenses or would not be able to get as favorable a plea bargain. If one were caught with less than three "rocks," the prosecutor, weighing other factors, would allow one to plead to a misdemeanor as opposed to a felony.

Further, if one can believe an informant, some credence might be given the allegation of "rock breaking" by some law enforcement personnel for the purpose of receiving credit for a "bigger bust." The informer revealed the nefarious details of a sting operation involving entrapped postal employees in which I had defended one of the Black male defendants. During his defense, I had requested the name of the confidential informant (listed on the police report during my discovery of the state's case only as CI) on Sixth Amendment grounds involving the right of confrontation and cross-examination.[33] The prosecutors had denied my request, asserting the twin rationales of informant safety and security. That case was in 1991. Subsequently, the state Supreme Court held that such a right existed, in *State v. Brown.*[34]

In his disclosure in the above-cited postal employee case, the informant claimed that one postal inspector had indeed crushed rocks in order to secure a conviction for drug trafficking[35] rather than for the less serious drug possession.[36] As 24 "rocks" was the cutoff point (for a determination of bulk amount, 25 or more were needed), the inspector allegedly split the drug units until they numbered 27.[37]

Another case also illustrates the ubiquity of confidential informant programs in the country's evolutionary development towards a more *definitive* New World Order. Despite such rulings as in the *Brown* case, the use of confidential informants (CIs) is becoming almost the preferred strategy of investigation among state and federal law enforcement authorities.

In addition, the use of "surveillance authority" for drug arrests as was done with the postal employee is more the norm for federal agents than the way they have been employed against some more overtly dangerous threats against society. For instance, one report indicates, "Data Show Federal Agents Seldom Employ Surveillance Authority Against Terrorists."[38] Hence, federal law enforcement surveillance authority was able to apprehend a Quibilah Bahiyah Shabazz[39] and totally miss a Timothy J. McVeigh.[40]

The illustrative case is the prosecution of Malcolm X's daughter, Quibilah Bahiyah Shabazz,[41] "on charges of conspiring to kill Louis Farrakhan" and the use of her "friend," CI Michael Fitzpatrick aka Michael Summers, against her.[42] Indeed, in this governmental climate of the New World Order apparently some persons become professional "set-up artists," as Mr. Fitzpatrick was characterized by a Steven Dennel, "a former member of the J.D.L. [Jewish Defense League] who attended high school at the United Nations International School in New York with Ms. Shabazz and Mr. Fitzpatrick."[43] For instance, Mr. Fitzpatrick, whose mother was Jewish, was also used as a CI against the J.D.L., prompting a defendant in that case, Chaim Ben Pessach, to state that being a CI was a "high point" for Mr. Fitzpatrick.[44] Although the federal investigating authority, the F.B.I. indicated that Mr. Fitzpatrick was scheduled to testify at any trial of the case against Ms. Shabazz, Mr. Fitzpatrick's lawyer for a drug case in Minneapolis, attorney Dennis Palm, "said he did not know how his client could be reached" at the time of Ms. Shabazz's indictment.[45] In fact, Mr. Fitzpatrick first went to Minneapolis as a government informer under the auspices of an arrangement, inevitably to be institutionalized under a New World Order system of the widespread use of spies, entitled the "witness protection program."[46] Another dimension of such prolific use of informants was brought out by Director Roscoe Brown, Jr., of the Center for Urban Education Policy at the City University of New York. Director Brown is a longtime friend of Dr. Betty Shabazz, widow of Malcolm X and mother of his six daughters, including Quibilah Bahiyah Shabazz.

Expressing that other dimension of informant use with regard to Mr. Fitzpatrick, Roscoe Brown explained, "This guy is an informer. Anything they say has to be suspect."[47] This aspect has particular salience given the situation of many informants of being under criminal investigation themselves and therefore in inherently compromised positions. The payment of such informers[48] is another authoritarian feature growing under the auspices of the New World Order, and hence the suspect nature of their credibility.[49] That is the nature of the beast—a feature reminiscent of the tactics of the Star Chamber or Nazi Germany, which in Ms. Shabazz's case subjected her to a possible "90 years in prison and $2.25 million in fines."[50] This particular feature, however, was thought to be more a part of a totalitarian form of government than of the democratic adversarial criminal justice system so strongly touted as protective of individual rights in the United States. The relentless finger of the New World Order orders, however, and having done so moves on to order, again. If a 34-year-old does not know whom to trust, how does a 14-year-old, a 24-year-old, or a 54-year-old?

Theoretical Implications

From the foregoing, it is obvious that a fundamental premise underlying this analysis is that there is a correlation between economic deprivation and being accused of a crime. Of course, the data presented here is understandably biased, as the investigator would not have been assigned to the Black female defendant had she not been poor. Still, there is evidence that most criminal defendants are poor, as approximately 60 percent of all those in prison had incomes of less than $10,000 when arrested.[51] The contention here is that, almost by definition, being poor and being criminal are two sides of the same coin, a connection that has plagued social science almost since its beginning. For instance, Herbert Spencer (1971), perhaps coming out of the tradition of debtor's prison, infused the embryonic sociology with the Social Darwinist philosophy that the poor somehow are unworthy. By 1968, Andrew Billingsley observed that low-income Black families being victimized by discrimination, poverty and the lack of opportunity were thereby unstable, dependent and *deviant*. Picking up on the theme of victimization of the poor in 1972, William Ryan discussed the idea of how societally generated ills were transposed onto the poor, with the latter being then transformed into the perpetrators of their own social problems.

It was Daniel Patrick Moynihan, however, who developed the application of these ideas of the poor as perpetrators of their own fate into an art form in describing Black women. It was his 1965 Moynihan Report (Rainwater 1967) that turned the ill-fated welfare-dependent mother into the notorious "matriarch." That label helped to justify the heavy-handed social policies that followed (Hill 1972). Emasculating, intimidating and a contradiction in femininity, the Black female deserved whatever punishments life handed out to her. This was the background that led to a federal and state welfare-fraud enforcement code (e.g., *Ohio Revised Code* Sec. 2913.02) that equated its transgressors with the most despicable of society's villains. In later years, it was her failure as a maternal figure that was blamed in large part for the need to enact drug abuse laws focused more on punishment than treatment. If she had not been so domineering, controlling and possessive—or, conversely, so apathetic, promiscuous and licentious—then her children, it was argued, perhaps would not have had such a desperate need to turn to drugs. Little heed is paid in such arguments to the role of such social factors as lack of opportunity, poverty, illiteracy and unemployment, in fostering drug-related criminal activity (see Supreme Court case, *Minnesota v. Dickerson*[52]).

Unfortunately for minorities and women, generally, social science theory is overlooked by judges, decision makers and planners in the criminal justice system. For instance, during this observation, ideas forwarded by social theorists that could add great insights into the cause and effect of "criminal behavior" (Du Bois 1903; Thomas 1931; Merton 1954; Durkheim [Lukes and Scull] 1983; Cloward and Ohlin 1960; Glaser 1972; Cressey 1969; and Goffman 1963) would never have been taken into consideration during judicial guilt or sentencing deliberations. Neither is theory a serious contributor during legislative contemplations, which are really the start of the criminalization process. Theoretical innovations have had an easier time being adopted by the corollary applied fields of the hard sciences, which is probably why technology is so much further ahead of the development of human rehabilitative and interventive strategies. This brings us back to the unrelenting fact that incrimination is basically a political process, determined and orchestrated by the politically powerful or their agents.

In truth then, it is the Black female's very lack of empowerment, fate control and assertiveness (Bynum 1991; Rose 1980) that keeps her disproportionately defined as criminal when compared to her White sisters and brothers. She also has a higher gender-specific crime rate than her Black brethren compared to his White counterpart. Hence, causal explanations of female crime based in the women's movement have to be rethought (Adler 1975), particularly as such explanations might relate to the Black female. One former female inmate, now an author, claims that the increased incrimination of women is "the dark side of the women's movement. With equal rights comes equal responsibility."[53] That statement is true, except that women have yet to receive equal rights.

Another female who is a former offender feels that her entrée to the drug world was her environment. In order to overcome that factor, she states that she had to leave behind all her former companions and hangouts. She also had to overcome feelings of anger and hopelessness. But, more than just mobilizing her personal strengths, she had to deal with the society's refusal to forgive and forget, when she was fired from a job after an employer learned of her felony record.[54] Felony convictions are a readily acceptable way in which U.S. society further rationalizes the refusal to admit many African American men,[55] as well as women, to the mainstream. Thus, when one falls prey to the devastating blows of poverty, discrimination or deprivation by resorting to drugs, society adds insult to injury and further undermines one's access. The computer age has made this consequence of criminality particularly effective, as it fills in the gaps of one's credit reports, employment history, family background and general standing in the community. Hence, there is another reason that, for instance, although women are just about 6.0 percent of all inmates, the number of female prisoners increased 24.4 percent, as opposed to 12.5 percent for men, just in 1989.[56] According to a news report regarding female inmates, "at least 80% were convicted of crimes while on drugs or to get drug money."[57]

Demonstrating their lack of empowerment, the women in the drug world observed in this study were essentially in a "gopher" capacity. They were "waterboys" to be used and reused as needed. One of the author's twenty-year-old Black male clients was asked by an interviewer (male) why he was carrying counterfeit dope. The young defendant replied that he and a buddy had planned to use it to give to "this girl" after having sex with her; he, of course, had been arrested before this intention was effectuated. (It is also interesting, albeit sad, to note that even though given such grocery-store (with baking soda as about the only ingredient) concoctions, some addicts reportedly still get high.)

Indeed, there is further evidence that Black women drug defendants are used not only by fellow male drug compatriots,[58] but also by law enforcement personnel. The latter use them as informants, scapegoats and bargaining tools as well as for their own drug habits and prurient interests. In fact, one prison observer writes that "Regardless of their offense, most were sexually or physically abused by men." For example, a thirty-seven-year-old female defendant being represented by the author arrived for her morning court hearing in a terrible state. She had lost twenty pounds since the previous month's hearing; she had been beaten up; her mascara was running down her face with her tears; her hair piece was in disarray; and although we were supposed to "plead" that morning, she begged for a three day continuance for some reason (co-counsel on the case offered to bet a quarter that if her request was due to a possible dirty urine, it would still be dirty after the grace period—that bet was not taken). When asked why that was the case as during the winter she had completed a thirty-day, in-patient drug treatment program at the V.A. (she was a veteran), she replied, "'Gregory' was my program." Thus, many female offenders have gotten into crime because of a husband or boyfriend; and it was also observed by the aforementioned prison writer that "Less than 10% committed violent crimes—most stem from domestic disputes."[59]

The Supreme Court outlawed punishment based purely on a person's status in the *California v. Robinson* case in 1962 (state prohibited from creating the offense of being a drug addict). Nevertheless, the law as it has evolved can be used arbitrarily to target certain individuals as criminal. Criminology theory has been inadequate in its explanation of criminal behavior. It is because *the law in and of itself can create criminals*, especially with *strict liability* crimes, in which there is no *mens rea* or criminal intent. The majority of the defendants observed in this study were charged with crimes that fit that category, where intent is minimized as a criminal element.

Most of the Black females assigned to this writer were charged with welfare fraud or drug possession. Welfare fraud as a crime is strictly a matter of statutory construction in which only the act is required for conviction of an accused offender (*U.S. v. Marvin*, cert denied, 1983). Similarly, knowing possession is defined as act sufficient in and of itself to incriminate one. In the case *Jenkins v. State* (1957), the Court of Appeals of Maryland in discussing the appropriateness of the offense of marijuana possession stated that

The statute was properly enacted under the general police powers of this State; it is a mandate of the legislature designed to promote the public health, the public morals, the public safety and the general welfare of the State. It requires no elaborate discussion nor lengthy argument to demonstrate that if our citizenry, young and old, become addicted to the use of narcotic drugs, the public health, morals, safety and welfare will be directly and seriously affected. (137 A. 2d 113)

The reason that legislatures and the courts chose punishment as a solution to drug addiction (e.g., *Ohio Revised Code* Sec. 2925.11) can be found in the theoretical propositions set forth by "conflict" criminologists (Vold 1958; Dahrendorf 1959; Skolnick 1966; Scheingold 1984; Chambliss and Seidman 1971; and Quinney 1977). These theorists acknowledge the changing nature of social control in the form of changing governmental and societal edicts as power fluctuates from one group to another or as the interests of and challenges to those in power change. For the women in this study, these theorists probably posit the most viable explanations of how and why they came before the criminal courts. With regard to welfare fraud, if one stays on welfare long enough, with its myriad of rules and regulations (Glueck 1952), one is highly likely to break one of them, get caught and turn into a criminal. This book contends that the state makes laws that differentially define certain categories of persons as criminal rather than that the "criminal" becomes so by selecting certain nefarious friends and associates (Sutherland and Cressey 1974). For the most part the criminal behavior of these women accused primarily of strict liability crimes was invented by the government rather than the individual.

The law is much more magnanimous towards those who poison the water and air, overprice goods and services, sell defective merchandise, defraud stockholders, engage in insider trading, misuse others' life savings, abuse public office, mutilate workers through hazardous work sites and abandon dangerous equipment in public places than to such individual women. The persons and entities who engage in these criminal behaviors are more likely to be politically influential and therefore more likely to be immune to the general application of the criminal law. While the Milkens and Boeskys of the world get a lot of press, as a class they are not generally prosecuted. Oliver North's situation was an aberration that was ultimately "corrected" by the Supreme Court. Along these lines, in the English common law, white-collar crime did not even exist (Sutherland 1961), and it was primarily the poor who were whipped and hanged. As modern society enters the twenty-first century it is still primarily the poor who are subject to punishment (Quinney 1975).

The primary presumption of this inquiry is that the Black woman is most vulnerable to incrimination because she is the one who is most vulnerable to poverty and economic deprivation, which derive mainly from her lack of access to power. Further, what is illustrated in this examination is that this vulnerability exacerbates her criminality and increases her inability to escape from her impoverished social condition (Davis 1983). Lacking control over her destiny (Phillips and Votey 1974), she falls victim to the criminal justice system and in so doing becomes an even less vital contributing member of society. This "subproletarian status" (Marable 1983; 58, 59) sentences her permanently to the inner-city ghetto. Once she is pronounced a felon, her prospects for reentry (more appropriately, meaningful entry) are essentially nil.

A particular injury is done by the application of the basic tenet of criminal justice personnel that "the first step in rehabilitation is admission of guilt." As outlined in social reactive theories of crime (Cooley 1902; Yochelson and Samenow 1976), the already tattered self-image of the Black women observed here was further damaged as they had to publicly declare their deviance and add another humiliating identifier to their growing list of negatives. After pleading guilty, they return home even less able to mobilize enough credibility to allow them to make a decent living.

Demographic Implications

It was stated earlier that the Black females in this investigation were poor. Actually, that is a gross understatement. They fit the category treated by Douglas Glasgow (1981) in his depiction of the *underclass*. In fact, these women were not so much poverty stricken as unempowered. Several of them were too little in touch to get themselves back onto General Assistance when their eligibility status returned. The state had initiated a six-month-on/six-month-off program to save money during a period of budget cuts in 1992. At least three of my clients could not mobilize themselves enough to go back down to the welfare office to get reinstated. One problem was that they had lost custody and/or control of their children. One thirty-seven-year-old drug addicted grandmother's son was in the care of her twenty-one-year-old daughter, whose name the older woman had given at the time of her arrest. This act made them both criminal, although I tried to exonerate the daughter at the time of her mother's sentencing, when her mother confessed her transgression on the record before the judge. Although the mother's exonerating statement is buried somewhere in a stenographer's notes, the criminal court computer network still lists the daughter's name among its felonious inhabitants.

The women in this study were not inherently degenerate. The sold their food stamps for Christmas toys. They hopelessly turned to drugs for solace. They relied upon unreliable boyfriends and husbands. But their real problem can be related to nationwide statistics that give greater insights into the reason that the state, the epitome of power and control, came ultimately to define them as criminal. Again, this problem derives from their predetermined position in the New World Order which seems to relegate them to a subordinate status regardless of the legality or illegality of any particular organizational entity. As slightly over forty percent of all Black households live within the central cities of large metropolitan areas, compared with sixteen percent of all White households, Black families are that much more prone to be affected by the social ills that plague the central city. All but a couple of the Black women in this client population came from the central city. Fifty-one percent of all Black children reside only with their mothers, as compared to sixteen percent of all White children nationally (Bureau of the Census, *Current Population Survey*, March 1990). Again, the women who were sent to the writer were predominantly single mothers who, including even most of the drug offenders, had primary responsibility for their children.

Whether or not they were the primary caretakers, they generally defined themselves as individuals, not so much as mothers or girlfriends or homemakers or the like. Certainly, even after the sentencing process, they did not define themselves as criminal. In fact, one of the White female defendants was amazed that after sentencing she had to perform the actions required for her urinalysis test in full view of an observer. This was the first time the procedure was brought to the writer's attention, which meant that the dozens of other women who had been subjected to it, most of whom were Black, had not shared that information. It is unclear whether this was because of some culture-specific norm not to disclose such private affairs or because the humiliation was so great and verbalizing it would have further reinforced the dehumanizing reality. Of course, the failure of a drug test must be viewed in context. If the stakes are too high, a drug-test failure can be put in a noncriminal context.[60] In short, if the "human resource potential" is high enough, as with certain sports, habits such as drug use can be monitored and "any potential problem could be headed off right from the start" if the user "is careful" and "we watch over him."[61] If such an approach could be sufficiently magnified to include vulnerable Black women, the devastation of drug abuse could be purged from the community. Such an approach would mean that the Black women involved were considered to be valuable human resources, whose loss to the community, the country and the cosmos would be intolerable.

Most of the public probably does not realize that being convicted of food-stamp abuse, possession of a "crack" pipe (e.g., small glass tube), check overdraft (forgery and uttering), riding with someone else in a stolen car (receiving stolen property), visiting a friend's house when it is raided and cocaine residue is found on the premises, shopping with friends who use stolen credit cards or working over the limit while on welfare means that one has to urinate in front of an observer. Nor does the public probably care. The public would care if it knew the people affected by these determinations, but, for the most part, the people so affected are of a different race, a different class, a different subculture. They are people too disenfranchised already to have ready recourse to a policy maker who would or could be responsive. They are people without a voice not only in their own country, but in their own community. They are Black, and in these cases they were female. The public does not realize that the more it allows such intrusions, the more freedoms it loses as well. Urinalysis did not become the detective device of choice in the sixties and fifties when marijuana and heroin were rampant. If the middle classes were affected, hair sampling would probably quickly gain favor among drug detectors—if drug testing were retained as such a universal feature of life at all. Now, though, we are losing the middle class. Now, urinalysis is widely accepted as the protocol even for obtaining middle class jobs. Now, however, the bulk of the burden for taking drug tests in this manner falls upon the poor and minorities.

To illustrate this point, figures from Chapter 3 must be recalled. The Black female headed a family with a median income of $12,537 in 1990. In contrast, the median income of a household headed by a White female was $20,867 for that year. Black male-headed households did considerably better, with a median income of $24,048, and White males did best, having a median family income of $32,869. The implications of the family income situation facing many Black women are clear when it is pointed out that in 1991 a family of four was deemed to be poor if it existed upon a cash income of less than $13,924 (*New York Times*, September 4, 1992, A1, A12). Hence, being Black and female is almost tantamount to being poor, and being a poor Black female makes one a considerably more probable subject of the criminal justice system by virtue of not only one's poverty, but also one's unempowerment.

Demographic figures show that Black females comprise only about six percent of the population. However Black female headed-families make up approximately forty percent of those who are on welfare (Aid to Families with Dependent Children). The social significance of this statistic relates back to the fact that just receiving AFDC gives one a high probability of eventually facing criminal charges because of the impossibly inconsistent regulations. As far as the women in this investigation were concerned, the state polity defined what is criminal in terms of who is the most dispensable and the most despicable. Forty-six percent of all women in state prisons in 1991 were Black (Bureau of Justice Statistics, 1991). Further, nearly one-third of all female inmates were incarcerated pursuant to a drug offense in 1991 as compared to one out of eight in 1986. Harsh, criminally oriented penalties were devised for infractions expected to be made by low-status persons, White or Black, who were economically dependent upon welfare or emotionally dependent upon drugs. Reflecting the shift in criminalization practices from property offenses such as welfare fraud to drug offenses, the Bureau of Justice Statistics also reports that "[t]he percentage of women in prison for property offenses declined from 41 percent in 1986 to 29 percent in 1991. Either way, higher-status persons, of course, would not be on welfare, and they would be able to afford anxiety-relievers and mood-elevators prescribed by law-abiding, licensed physicians. These respectable citizens could remain beyond reproach. Criminalization, of course, takes respectability further away from the reach of low income (and, increasingly, middle-income) Black women. Also, the change anticipates the criminalization impact of the diminution of the welfare state and the corresponding expansion of the criminal justice system as the replacement control mechanisms of the poor and minorities (Piven and Cloward 1971; also see again Chapter 5).

The criminal situation of the African American female cannot be fully understood without looking at some demographic figures with regard to the views of "respectable" citizens. Data relating to the beliefs of such citizens are as important as those relating to the people defined as the country's crooks. The former are at least ostensibly responsible for the making of the laws that render certain portions of the population criminal. Data concerning the values, attitudes and beliefs of such law-abiding folk provide information as to the values, attitudes and beliefs behind the criminal law. As indicated earlier, the criminal law is the formalization of an empowered group's folkways and mores. Although the average Jane or John Doe usually does not have direct input into the formulation of the law, their views generally result from the same mass communications that have informed the votes of their legislators. Indeed, such images are sometimes used to camouflage actions by majority-group members. The fear of the sinister Black criminal is such a reality that an assertion of Black culpability can deter law-enforcement officials from vital investigative evidence for days (cf. the case of Susan V. Smith, confessed drowner of her two sons aged 3 years and 14 months, who for nine days claimed that they had been kidnapped by a Black carjacker[62]).

Some interesting numbers describing the views of citizens were obtained from a seventy-five-question telephone poll done for the *National Law*

Journal (NLJ) by Penn and Schoen Associates in March of 1994 (the margin of error was 3.5%). First, 82 percent of the White citizens questioned and 95 percent of the Black ones saw "racism in the American criminal justice system." The poll's findings showed that 68 percent of Blacks as compared with 49 percent of Whites found the "black rage"[63] defense a compelling one. Recalling that females who are incarcerated for violent offenses generally have been convicted of domestic violence, 41 percent of all those polled said the "battered woman syndrome" was a very compelling defense and an additional 40 percent said it was a somewhat compelling defense. This could be interpreted to mean that, if one separated out from criminality the women convicted of economic crimes and anomic (Merton 1954) crimes such as drugs and prostitution, then what is left are the "violent" crimes. If the *NLJ* poll on the issue of the "battered woman syndrome" can be believed, most women would be knocked out of the criminal category and left to the societal devices of economic and human service intervention. Of course, these policy questions would require the intervention of the political institution, an intervention that will probably not take place until African American women are empowered sufficiently to hold the keys to meaningful political decision-making (see Chapter 2).

According to the *NLJ* poll also, 78 percent to 85 percent of the total sample of U.S. citizens were unwilling to sacrifice basic civil liberties in the name of the enhancement of their personal safety.[64] Police wiretaps without prior court approval were anathema to 85 percent of those questioned, and 82 percent did not believe that police should be permitted to search people randomly, without probable cause.[65] These findings, along with the finding that 78 percent approved of the oft-maligned *Miranda* warnings, surprised the president of the American Civil Liberties Union, Nadine Strossen, who also stated that she was "heartened" by the report.[66]

In terms of the causes of crime, the citizenry was not so surprising. The poll compared their responses in 1989 with those in 1994. In 1989, 66 percent felt that most crime was caused by drugs. In 1994, five years after the introduction of crack cocaine into major cities such as Detroit, Los Angeles, New York, Washington, D.C. and Atlanta, 28 percent of those polled felt that drugs were "the greatest cause of crime today." Causes such as the "breakdown of the family" (5 percent in 1989 versus 15 percent in 1994) and "moral breakdown" (1 percent in 1989 versus 11 percent in 1994) had grown significantly more important in the public mind. Such increases in these crime rationales means that the public became more likely to blame crime on forces ostensibly within the control of the accused rather than upon external factors such as drugs. Blaming the victim thus seemed to be the trend, except for the increase in crime attribution to unemployment. In 1989, 5 percent of those polled believed unemployment or the economy was a factor in crime causation. By 1994, this figure had increased to 10 percent. That increase leaves some room for hope that the national community does not pin all the onus of crime upon intrinsic moral degeneracy. Some room is left for societal conditions even by the rather easily influenced public.

With reference to what the report termed "Reasons That Excuse Crime," long-term institutional racism received mixed reviews. Among those questioned, 24 percent felt that it was not at all a reason and 22 percent felt that it was not a very salient reason. Sixteen percent felt that it was a very good reason to snap, and 33 percent felt that it was somewhat of a reason to excuse law-breaking.[67]

Another comparison between pre- and post–New World Order years found that although half of all Americans in 1989 felt that crime would not be curbed until social conditions were improved for the poor, 60 percent felt that way in 1994. That is possibly another heartening statistic, if its message can be implemented in a meaningful way following such reforms as treatment, therapy and employment rather than incrimination for such situational offenders. The likelihood of this possibility is lessened however, when one considers another 1989/1994 comparison that is not quite so charitable.

In 1989, 52 percent of the polled subjects indicated that they were in favor of the death penalty for those under twenty years of age. In 1994, that percentage had increased to 75 percent. The support for the teenage death penalty paralleled that for adults. The percentage upholding the death penalty was 73 percent in 1989 and 77 percent in 1994, which given the margin of error meant that it was pretty much the same for both years. Senator Joseph Biden is quoted in the article as stating that anger directed at "law-breakers" has reached such a fever pitch that barbed-wiring the ankles of jaywalkers would probably pass.[68] Also less than heartening was the news from the report that almost "one out of five" (18 percent of persons) believed that some wrongful convictions are "inevitable and acceptable."[69]

The next "logical" step in the U.S. system of justice to "respectable" citizens will probably be the readoption of corporal punishment. The implementation of a caning law would probably attract more firsthand observers than are allowed at the execution of a death penalty. Given the public attitude espousing tough law and order, schools would probably be encouraged to bring schoolchildren—particularly those from the central city—to the event in order to teach them a valuable lesson. As public schools were one of the last forums in which corporal punishment had been approved by the Supreme Court (*Ingraham v. Wright*[70]), it would be consistent with their charge. In light of how Black men and women are disproportionately criminalized, it does not take much imagination to figure out who would most likely be featured in the sports/entertainment arena experiencing the pain and humiliation of corporal punishment.

Social Processes and the Criminal Law

Now that the rationale behind criminalization has been explored, the societal process of criminalization should be considered. Looking at the process of criminalizing the Black woman necessarily involves considering such questions as, "Why are certain actions made criminal?" "Why are certain persons more likely to acquire criminal labels than others?" "Why do certain crimes have harsher punishments than others even though they do not inflict as much physical or economic damage on societal members as those others?" "Why do certain socioeconomic classes have higher incidences of criminality than others?" "Why do certain neighborhoods have higher incidences of criminality than others?" Complete answers to these questions cannot be found by looking at the individuals who fall prey to the criminal justice system in and of themselves. Criminal justice is fundamentally a policy call. Who is criminal and when, where and how criminality begins are decisions that a society consciously makes in terms of its other needs and priorities.

Looking at economic measures to help explain Black female criminalization, one is reminded that the poverty rate of Black females remains more than three times that of Whites (see again Chapter 3). The unemployment rate of Black females is twice that of White males and females (Chapter 3), and they are much less likely than any other group to own a home—or anything else, for that matter.

By the same token, the Black female is much less likely to have her own advocacy group. While there are group advocates for energy conservation, the environment, taxpayers, the elderly, children, minorities, women and the mourning dove, there are no Washington lobbyists who specifically address the concerns of low-income Black women. Their "special" interests are always entangled with those of other, more resonant groups. Thus, while the pro-choice, pro-life, pro-environment, ban-the-bomb, save-the-whales, gay rights, gray panthers and American Way groups proliferate, the needs of the low-income Black female cohort go unheeded. Laws designed specifically for the further social oppression of her class of persons continue to multiply, to the applause of "legitimate" society. With the exception of the women accused of welfare fraud, the women studied, besides being poor, were largely unaffiliated with any legitimate organization. Welfare offenders were somewhat more likely to have some type of religious affiliation even if they were not active members. The drug offenders were not as anomic as Merton's propositions (1954) might have predicted. Except for the few (four or five) who had gone off the deep end, the women who had been caught in drug violative situations were functional (or dysfunctional depending upon the perspective) in their respective Black neighborhood settings.

The women who were more or less totally strung out were deeply embedded in a revolving-door drug culture and, for the time being, unreachable in terms of a return to "normal" family living. Families and children had lost meaning for them. They were irresponsible as related to the legitimate Black community, although there are indications that their role in the drug community was much more systematized and dependable. When one's life depends upon one's accountability, one may be somewhat more reliable. However, the writer has encountered females who were on the run, having saturated their luck in certain segments of the city. For instance, representation did include early morning calls from hospital emergency rooms where defendants had sought refuge from pistol whippings and bodily assaults.

How deeply a woman became submerged in the drug culture seemed to be a function of age of first drug usage, family relationships, education, occupational skill level and work situation. The clients most at risk were the ones who came into the drug culture with the least of the former as backup resources. In other words, the earlier the onset of drug use in a female's life, the fewer resources she had to fight continued addiction. The earlier her drug usage began, the less likely it was that she had an opportunity to complete high school. The clients with early onset of drug usage were also more likely to abandon their babies in hospitals or foster homes or leave them to makeshift arrangements with grandparents, great-grandparents, aunts, sisters and cousins. Interestingly, although probably part of the drug culture themselves, several fathers came forward to claim their offspring and help raise them in the context of their parental family structures.

The stamp of criminality upon her does little to ameliorate the Black female drug offender's dead-end situation. Having to urinate weekly before an observer, to reveal her intimates, to explain her lack of attachments to economically productive means or to shuffle within the confines of a cell or pseudo-dormitory room does not reinforce the Black female drug offender's humanity or viability. The more the criminal justice system treats such persons in a brutal, punitive, churlish way the more brutal, punitive and churlish they become. In fact, this result may be analogized to the entire society: A law-and-order society devotes itself to turning out law-and-order people. The law-and-order theme continues to be the safest bet for the continuation in office of the country's politicians, as the public endorses such simplistic solutions to Establishment-generated societal problems. Eventually people find themselves urinating for jobs, stabbing each other in the back (figuratively speaking), begging for crumbs, fearing the future and going to prison for debts. Infractions of societal mores and folkways become more and more arbitrary and subject to the discretion of whoever is in charge rather than to impartial, independent rules and regulations. Assisted by greater and greater technological expertise, one's (White, Black, Brown or Yellow—male or female) thoughts and lifestyle become likely targets for intrusion and "intervention" by one's enemies or just by those from whom one is different.

The more likely the female drug client was to be visibly on the streets and in crack houses, the more likely she was to become identified by police patrols, which are better trained in the ascertainment of underclass and working-class criminal violations than those of the upper classes. The police are also much less likely to identify suburban and employed drug abusers. The criminal and constitutional law seem also to differentiate between the crack abuser, usually of the underclass, and the powder cocaine user who, because of the higher costs, is generally of the middle to upper classes. In a publication (*Focus*) of the Joint Center for Political and Economic Studies, Nkechi Taifa, Legislative Counsel for the American Civil Liberties Union, writes that drug laws are "100 Times Harder on Blacks." This proclamation refers to the "Disparate Mandatory Minimum Sentences for Crack Cocaine." In making this assertion, Ms. Taifa cites Congressional discrepancies in penalties for the sale and/or possession of crack cocaine as opposed to the more lenient sentences provided for powder cocaine offenses. Ms. Taifa thus notes that "[o]ne effect of this legislation is to punish small-scale crack cocaine users and dealers more severely than their wholesale suppliers."[71] And, although 64.4 percent of "documented crack users are white," according to a study done by the U.S. Sentencing Commission in 1992, "91.3 percent of those sentenced for federal crack offenses were African American, while only 3 percent were white."[72] Hence, again, low-income persons, Whites and Blacks, males and females who can only afford cocaine in its "crack" form have a higher probability of incrimination if they become addicted to cocaine.

A criminal approach to drug addiction serves the multiple purpose of (1) permanently eliminating incriminated drug addicts from the job market by virtue of their conviction; (2) exacerbating the alienation of drug addicts from mainstream society; (3) increasing the individual isolation and probably the drug habits of addicts; (4) perpetuating the vicious cycle of arrest and incrimination of addicted persons by the justice system; (5) aggravating the destruction of family bonds between the addict and his or her parents, spouses, siblings and children; and (6) overcrowding the nation's jails and prisons with drug offenders who account for between sixty and seventy percent of all inmates, male or female, Black or White. Nevertheless, the "War on Drugs" (Lusane 1991) presses on, inordinately targeting members of the Black community.

Several of the Black female clients in this study were casualties of the police department's SWAT-team raids. They were arrested while sitting in living rooms, dining rooms and kitchens when the SWAT team invaded. The most scientific guess at criminality was determined by what inhabitant or guest was where, vis-à-vis the drug remnant or residue find. A defendant was awarded a reduced misdemeanor charge if she had not been too close to any contraband. The criminal maxim applied at such scenes appeared to be "Birds of a feather flock together." When informed of their alternatives and facing daunting periods of incarceration upon the prospect of loss at a trial, some potentially innocent clients opted for the opportunity to plead to the reduced charge. One client even remarked that, "I'm not going to run for president," perhaps a more telling statement than she knew, in recognizing her deficient status in the United States.

The future for the containment of such abuses looks very grim. Since the Supreme Court's vindication of Dollree Mapp's warrantless break-in and search of her property and the arrest of person by police in Cleveland, Ohio, in the landmark 1961 case of *Mapp v. Ohio*,[73] the exclusionary rule has suffered several major setbacks. In the 1968 *Terry v. Ohio*[74] case, the Supreme Court officially began its retreat by ruling that police had the right to a lesser intrusion of the person through a "stop and frisk" even if they had a "reasonable suspicion" rather than the full "probable cause" that a crime was being committed. Continuing the New World Order march backward, the Court, in the 1984 *United States v. Leon*[75] case, approved an exception to the Fourth Amendment protection against unreasonable search and seizure that allows police to use evidence that although illegally obtained was obtained in "good faith" or, continuing the *Leon* precedent, by mistake, such as computer error, as in the 1995 case of *Arizona v. Evans*.[76]

Further, once the police enter one's home, on the slightest of pretexts, they can just about make an entire "protective sweep" of the house (*Maryland v. Buie*[77]). And, although the Court upheld the prohibition against warrantless searches of houses in *Payton v. New York*,[78] a 1980 case, it still allowed in a 1990 case entitled *New York v. Harris*[79] the use of evidence procured pursuant to a warrantless home entry. When one considers this direction of the Supreme Court towards decreased individual liberties along with such public demands for law and order as represented in the previously described "Contract with America" (see Chapter 5), it is easy to predict the Black woman's future in the New World Order's system of justice. While the Black male's nemesis may strike while he is standing around on the corner (*California v. Hodari D.*[80]), walking down the street (*Minnesota v. Dickerson*[81]), riding around in his automobile (*United States v. Robinson*[82]) or someone else's (*Rakas v. Illinois*[83]) or riding on the bus (*Florida v. Bostick*[84]), the Black woman is not safe from the long arm of the law inside her own home.

The Black woman's home, then, often defined by the police and confirmed by the courts as in a "high-crime" area, far from being a castle is her place of confinement, in which she waits until the telling knock or battering ram on the door as in the days of Nazi Germany when, for certain doomed people, it was just a matter of time. (When the author ran into a former student who had become a municipal police officer at the Justice Center[85] one day during the summer of 1994, he told her that they were averaging fourteen house raids a day; he was looking rather exhausted at the time.) Thus, there is a higher probability than with the rest of the U.S. population that if the welfare system does not criminalize the poor Black woman, the police state will.

SUMMARY

What is concluded from this study of the criminal justice system from the point of view of a participant-observer is that the societal situation of the Black female clients was a primary factor in their criminalization. Remedies, then, for Black female crime should address detrimental social conditions that hinder access to an enhanced quality of life that would, almost by definition, deter participation in deviant criminal activity.

Although it might be presumed from the case studies that Black females in the criminal justice system are all poor, that is not necessarily the case. As resources in the society became more scarce and the society's rulers, blaming the lowered quality of life on the out-groups, led the society into seeking more law and order, more persons from the middle classes fell into circumstances that facilitated their criminalization. The influx of drugs as a medium of control into the Black community resulted in more and more Black middle-class females falling for the lure of drugs, particularly as it became harder and harder to survive during and after the Reagan-Bush regime in America. The entrée of Black females who originated in the middle class, while not heralding major changes in the criminal justice system, has been signaled by some slight differences in its operation. For instance, with the arrival of the middle class into the jails, the author has more extensive contact with corrections personnel regarding such items as contact lens solution, specialized "prescribed" diets, book club arrangements, "therapeutic" cosmetics, grooming devices, dental treatment follow-ups, medical transport visits, tennis shoe delivery and commissary replenishment. The parents, grandparents and family of previously middle-class inmates are also much more demanding as the societal climate has degenerated much faster into the "leaner and meaner" mode than their level of expectations. Many of them are still operating on a rather naive presumption of a "kinder, gentler" society, which means that an attorney has to spend some time in reorienting and resocializing the defendant and his or her parents or people as to the full implications of criminal prosecution within the context of the New World Order. The neo-conservatism era preceding and incorporated into the New World Order society laid the foundations for the drug-ravaged Black community in the same manner as the Antebellum South produced and maintained slavery. The New World Order society is reaping the consequences of that infestation and anomie (Merton 1954).

Overall, the disproportionate criminalization of the Black female, which continues relatively over and above even that of her Black male counterpart as well as her White female one, will continue as long as she remains politically incorrect and impotent. Anomie (normlessness) and alienation from the "greater" society (Durkheim [Taylor 1982]; Merton 1954) will continue to characterize most Black female offenders with reference to their relationship with that society. For more than for any other category of persons, demographics is a poignant predictor of criminality for the Black female. Her chances of incrimination are significantly increased by her preponderance on the welfare rolls, her prevalence in the inner city, her persistence on the unemployment lists, her presence in the school dropout records and her drug of opportunity and choice (crack versus cocaine) albeit a default financial choice. Her empowerment, irrespective of class background, would mean her legitimation. As her economic and educational opportunities have dwindled, her opportunities for criminal engagement have increased because of her lack of economic and educational access.

Further, when those with societal authority know that, unless strong interventive measures are taken, the social welfare and school systems are failing their constituencies, to ignore such information is more than benign neglect, it is intentional malfeasance and as criminal as the conduct it generates and defines. In a speech given to a university audience, commentator Roger Wilkins maintained that as long as "the polls" such as those administered by pollster Stanley Greenberg indicated that "America" is saying, "Do not do anything about Black people, we are sick of it," the needed intervention of jobs and education would not be forthcoming.[86] Professor Wilkins also indicated that such omissions would continue as long as the Black community remained unorganized.

The results of this study suggest that there is a need to develop further research questions designed to explore several possible relationships. The first is the degree of any relationship between the number and extent of a Black female's involvement in legitimate organizations and her criminal involvement; second is the impact of family relationships upon participation in different types of crime by Black females; third is whether or not there is any relationship between the degree and level of political participation by Black females in a jurisdiction and the rate of their incrimination in that area; fourth is whether there is a relationship between Black female unemployment and their criminality, and, fifth is whether there is any significant relationship between Black female education and criminal involvement.

Although the first question may initially seem to be derived from Merton's anomie theory as suggested above in that it implies that greater involvement in established society means fewer criminally oriented contacts, that is not its purpose. Many of the women discussed here, consisting of the author's female law caseload, were highly physically active when not incarcerated. In addition, they were emotionally engaged with others in their surrounding communities. They participated extensively in their worlds. The problem for criminologists is that these women's worlds are so delegitimized and alienated from established society that the women seem anomic. Their norms are the norms of what police have labeled high-crime areas, areas in which the police can run particularly rampant.[87] Still, Black women with otherwise legitimate ties to society are disproportionately criminalized. In essence, Black women are determined to be criminals *in spite of* any active participation in legitimate sectors of society. This should not be surprising inasmuch, for instance, as during the civil rights movement, Black women protestors were criminalized *because* of their desire to participate in legitimate sectors of society (cf. Davis 1983). Similarly, with the encroachment of the New World Order, Black women are again either being delegitimized because they sought legitimate sector participation or because they sought escape from rejection by those legitimate sectors.

The fact is that *all* people in the United States have become "A Nation of Suspects"[88] under the ruse of having to declare martial law on behalf of fighting drugs and crime. Still, even though illicit drugs may be just as prevalent in predominantly White, middle- and upper-class suburban communities, the penalties are not so harsh and severe. The police are not so harsh and severe. The quality of life (as well as of the illicit drugs themselves, one might posit) is not so harsh and severe. Forced to live in their much more harsh and severe environment, with such harsh and severe consequences coming from such harsh and severe people, it is remarkable how much humanity Black women, in this study and otherwise, have been able to retain.

As set forth in the body of this discussion, from this perspective, greater participation means greater empowerment.[89] Greater empowerment is hypothesized to lead to fewer social control mechanisms operating upon Black women; they then come to be criminalized at a lesser rate by the governmental entities. The other questions, in this view, are also related to empowerment: increased familial support is indicative of greater personal stability; increased employment signifies greater economic independence; increased education symbolizes greater self- and community awareness; and, of course, increased political participation in the mainstream societal milieu is reflective of greater societal authority (legitimized power).

A major proposition of this chapter, then, is that an increase in all these variables would result in a decrease in Black female criminalization. The major question that this chapter leaves, though, is how to effectuate the organization, the discipline and the determination such that these respective increases and decreases are obtained. Obviously, the dynamics of the political and economic institutions, to say the least, have to be addressed. Advocacy for Black female offenders has to begin not with making changes in them, but in making changes in the social system that makes their criminality predictable. Advocacy for the Black female would also be found in developing responses to the symptoms of society's sickness, such as drug activity, that would demonstrate positive impact rather than merely increased criminalization of the Black populace. (For instance, a needle-exchange program in New York that has been shown to curb the H.I.V. infection rate among addicts represents a more constructive experiment[90] than the inconclusive workfare[91] mentioned in Chapter 5.)

Political and economic empowerment would necessarily do away with many criminal offenses simply by doing away with many social conditions that create criminal offenses. Some behaviors would be eliminated from the criminal definition. Some behaviors would be eliminated because hope would be born. Some behaviors would be eliminated because there would be no need to react to the conditions that fostered them.

Not to strive toward and achieve this type empowerment and the corresponding elimination of crime would be tantamount to joining the sisters of the drug world in asserting "I have to get myself together," first—and just as immediately probable.

NOTES

1. Cesare Beccaria, "The Origin of Punishments, and the Right to Punish," in *On Crimes and Punishments* (Indianapolis & New York: The Library of Liberal Arts, Bobbs-Merrill Company, 1963), 10–13.

2. Ibid., 11.

3. Emile Durkheim, *De la division du travail social* (The Division of Labor in Society), trans. George Simpson (New York: The Free Press, 1965).

4. Emile Durkheim, *The Rules of the Sociological Method*, trans. Sarah A. Soloway and John H. Mueller, ed. George E. G. Catlin (New York: The Free Press, 1965).

5. *The National Law Journal*, August 8, 1994, 1.

6. Ibid.

7. Ibid.

8. According to the groups Aid to Incarcerated Mothers, 957 Highland Avenue, Atlanta, Ga. 30306, and CLAWS, Wilder Box 16, Oberlin, Ohio 44074, as of November 14, 1994.

9. Ibid.

10. Ibid.

11. See also Carol D. Stack, *All Our Kin: Strategies for Survival in a Black Community* (New York: Harper and Row, 1981).

12. V. David Sartin, "Jail II Soon to Overflow Capacity," *Plain Dealer*, March 8, 1994, 1–B, 3–B.

13. 115 S.Ct.1769 (1995).

14. Evelyn Williams, *Inadmissible Evidence: The Story of the African-American Trial Lawyer Who Defended the Black Liberation Army* (Brooklyn, New York: Lawrence Hill Books, 1993).

15. David Margolick, "Defense for Simpson Attacking Prosecutors' 'Rush to Judgment': State's Case Is Called Character Assassination," *New York Times*, January 26, 1995, A1, A13.

16. Assata Shakur, *Assata: An Autobiography* (London: Zed Books Ltd., 1987).

17. Eldridge Cleaver, "Domestic Law and International Law" in *Soul on Ice* (New York, N.Y.: Dell Publishing Co., 1968), 158.

18. *Ohio Revised Code* Sec. 2953.32, "Sealing of Record of Conviction or Bail Forfeiture."

19. Ibid.

20. 400 U.S. 25, 91 S. Ct. 160, L.Ed.2d 162 (1970).

21. B. Drummon Ayers Jr., "Sobering Effect on Motorists: Tough Laws, New Attitudes Drive DUI Death Rate Down," *Plain Dealer*, May 22, 1994, 1–A, 18–A.

22. *Gideon v. Wainwright*, 372 U.S. 335, 83 S.Ct. 792 (1963).

23. Naomi Karp, "Kinship Care: Legal Problems of Grandparents and Other Relative Care Givers," *NBA: National Bar Association Magazine* (January/February 1994), 10, 11, 16; also see, Linda Greenhouse, "High Court Upholds Definition of 'Family' That Cuts Some Welfare Payments," *New York Times*, March 23, 1995, A11, reporting on the case of *Anderson v. Edwards*, U.S. Supreme Court Case No. 93–1883, written by Justice Clarence Thomas.

24. E.g., *Ohio Revised Code* Sec. 2925.03 and Sec. 2925.11.

25. Diana R. Wasserman, Letter to the Editor (Shaker Heights), "Help or More Pain for Children Who Have Suffered?" *Plain Dealer*, April 24, 1994, 5–C.

26. Mark Gillispie, "17 Slayings, 6 Years—and No Answers: Women's Bodies Found on East Side," *Plain Dealer*, April 24, 1994, 1–A, 22–A.

27. "Singapore Hints Flogging Likely," *Plain Dealer* (Cox News Service) April 24, 1994, 17–A; *Plain Dealer* (*Los Angeles Times*), "Ohio Teen-Ager Lashed with Cane in Singapore," May 6, 1994, 4–A; Associated Press, "Maid Hanged in Singapore," *Plain Dealer*, March 17, 1995, A12.

28. Gillispie, "17 Slayings, 6 Years—and No Answers: Women's Bodies Found on East Side."

29. Matthew Purdy, "Bars Don't Stop Flow of Drugs Into the Prisons," *New York Times*, July 2, 1995, A1, A12, A13.

30. "State of the Union—The President's Address:'We Heard America Shouting,' " *New York Times*, January 26, 1995, A10–A12.

31. Cf. Katharine Q. Seelye, "House Approves Easing of Rules on U.S. Searches: Conservatives Triumph; Bills Allow Evidence Collected Without Warrant and Limit Appeals on Death Row," *New York Times*, February 9, 1995, A1, A10.

32. Mark Tatge, "Drug-User Discrimination Criticized: Penalties Stricter for Crack Cocaine Than for Powdered," *Plain Dealer*, May 30, 1993, 16–A.

33. But see, Ulysses Torassa, "Postal Inspection Chief Ripped Over Botched Drug Probes," *Plain Dealer*, May 13, 1994, 13–A; and, Mark Rollenhagen, "Drug Sting Informant Gets Prison Term,"*Plain Dealer*, May 13, 1994, 4–B.

34. 64 Ohio St. 3d 649 (1992).

35. *Ohio Revised Code* Sec. 2925.03.

36. *Ohio Revised Code* Sec. 2925.11.

37. Ulysses Torassa, "4 Convicts Innocent, Postal Informant Says," *Plain Dealer*, April 21, 1994, 1–A, 8–A; also see Don Terry, "Philadelphia Shaken by Criminal Police Officers," *New York Times*, August 28, 1995, A1, A8 relating the story of a 54-year-old Black grandmother, Betty Patterson, who "[S]pent three years in jail after some Philadelphia police officers framed her in a drug case."

38. Stephen LaBaton, "Data Show Federal Agents Seldom Employ Surveillance Authority Against Terrorists," *New York Times*, May 1, 1995, A8 in which it is reported that "Government records describing 10 years of court applications filed by Federal and state agents show that they have rarely exercised their existing authority to monitor groups and individuals electronically who are suspected of plotting terrorist acts. Instead, the agents have used virtually all of their electronic surveillance resources for narcotics, gambling and racketeering investigations."

39. Ronald Sullivan, "Widow of Malcolm X and Farrakhan to Meet," *New York Times*, April 28, 1995, A16; Don Terry, "Shabazz Reaches a Settlement in Farrakhan Murder Plot Case: 2 Years Probation in Surprise Deal Before Trial," *New York Times*, May 2, 1995, A1, A8.

40. John Kifner, "A Town Where Gun-Toting Individualists Can Blend Right In," *New York Times*, May 1, 1995, A8.

41. Don Terry, "Daughter of Malcolm X Charged With Trying to Kill Farrakhan," *New York Times*, January 13, 1995, A1, A10.

42. Don Terry, "Nation of Islam Says It Doubts Account of Assassination Plan: Questions Case Against Malcolm X's Daughter," *New York Times*, January 14, 1995, A1, A8.

43. Ibid.

44. Ibid.

45. Ibid.

46. Felicia R. Lee, "Anger, Disbelief and Sorrow After an Indictment," *New York Times*, January 15, 1995, A8.

47. Ibid.

48. Don Terry, "Informer Tells of U.S. Payments for His Help in Farrakhan Case," *New York Times*, March 24, 1995, A1, A12.

49. Isabel Wilkerson, "Portrait of Man Who Told of Plot Against Farrakhan," *New York Times*, January 16, 1995, A1, A9.

50. Ibid.

51. Terry, *New York Times*, September 13, 1992, A1, A15.

52. No. 91–2019 (1992–93 term).

53. Andrea Stone (after a visit at the Ohio Reformatory for Women in Marysville), "Surge in Female Inmates Taxes State Penal Systems," *USA Today*, August 29, 1990, quoting former inmate, now author, Patricia McConnel.

54. Rebecca Freligh, "Life Turnaround a Tale of True Grit: Woman Wills Herself Upward-Bound," *Plain Dealer*, May 24, 1994, 1–E, 6–E.

55. Nathan McCall, *Makes Me Wanna Holler: A Young Black Man in America* (New York: Random House, 1994).

56. Stone, "Surge in Female Inmates."

57. Ibid.

58. McCall, *Makes Me Wanna Holler*, 331.

59. Stone, "Surge in Female Inmates."

60. Cf., Mike Freeman, "Sapp Fails Drug Test at N.F.L. Combine," *New York Times*, March 14, 1995, B13.

61. Ibid.

62. "Lawyer Says Mother Will Face Death Penalty in Drowning of Sons," *New York Times*, January 16, 1995, A7.

63. But see, Jan Hoffman, "A Lawyer, A Trial, An Ordeal," *New York Times*, February 14, 1995, A12.

64. Rorie Sherman, "Crime's Toll on the U.S.: Fear, Despair and Guns—NLJ Poll Finds Self-Defense Replacing Reliance on Law Enforcement," *National Law Journal*, April 18, 1994, A1, A19.

65. Ibid., A19.

66. Ibid.

67. Ibid.

68. Ibid.

69. Doreen Weisenhaus, Editor-in-Chief, "Crime's Deep Roots," *National Law Journal*, April 18, 1994, 16.

70. 430 U.S. 651, 97 S.Ct. 1501 (1977).

71. Nkechi Taifa, "Drug Laws 100 Times Harder on Blacks: Disparate Mandatory Minimum Sentences for Crack Cocaine Are Keeping Thousands in Prison, But Equitable Measures Have Been Proposed," *Focus: The monthly mazazine of the Joint Center for Political and Economic Studies* 23, no. 4 (April 1995): 5–6.

72. Ibid

73. 367 U.S. 643, 81 S.Ct.1684, 6 L.Ed.2d 1081 (1961).

74. 392 U.S. 1, 88 S.Ct. 1868, 20 L.Ed.2d 889 (1968).

75. 468 U.S. 897, 104 S. Ct. 3405, 82 L.Ed.2d 677 (1984).

76. U.S. Supreme Court Case No. 93–1660 (1995). No "Orwellian mischief" was found in this case, as reported also in an article by Linda Greenhouse, "Justices Validate Seizure Based on Error on Warrant," *New York Times*, March 2, 1995, A11.

77. 494 U.S. 325, 110 S.Ct.1093, 108 L.Ed.2d 276 (1990).

78. 445 U.S. 573, 100 S.Ct. 1371, 63 L.Ed.2d 639 (1980).

79. 495 U.S. 14, 110 S.Ct. 1640, 109 L.Ed.2d 13 (1990).

80. 499 U.S. 621, 111 S.Ct. 1547, 113 L.Ed.2d 690 (1991).

81. 113 S.Ct. 2130, 124 L.Ed.2d 334 (1993).

82. 414 U.S. 278, 94 S.Ct. 467, 38 L.Ed.2d 427 (1973).

83. 439 U.S. 128, 99 S.Ct. 421, 58 L.Ed. 387 (1978).

84. 501 U.S. 429, 111 S.Ct. 2382, 115 L.Ed.2d 389 (1991).

85. The Justice Center referred to here is in the city of Cleveland, Ohio, Cuyahoga County, and houses county and city courtrooms, county and city prosecutor offices, the county and city jails, county and city clerk of courts offices, county and city probation offices, the city's main police station and a drug treatment agency.

86. Roger Wilkins, the Clarence J. Robinson Professor of History and American Culture at George Mason University, "Goals of Our People" (Keynote address for Black Aspirations Week celebration, Cleveland State University, Cleveland, Ohio, April 25, 1994).

87. Musawwir Spiegel, Letter to the Editor, "Car Searches Perpetuate the Drug-War Myth," *New York Times*, March 5, 1995, A14.

88. David A. Harris, Professor of Law, College of Law, University of Toledo, Letter to the Editor, "A Nation of Suspects," *New York Times*, March 10, 1995, A14.

89. The National Association for the Advancement of Colored People and the Criminal Justice Institute at Harvard Law School (Prepared by Charles J. Ogletree, Jr., Mary Prosser, Abbe Smith and William Talley, Jr.), *Beyond the Rodney King Story: An Investigation of Police Conduct in Minority Communities* (Boston: Northeastern University Press, 1995).

90. Felicia R. Lee, "Data Show Needle Exchange Curbs H.I.V. Among Addicts," *New York Times*, November 26, 1994, A1, A9.

91. Celia W. Dugger with Raymond Hernandez, "Often-Cited Workfare Effort Provides Cautionary Lessons: Limiting Welfare," *New York Times*, November 25, 1994, A1, A12.

CHAPTER 9

Conclusion

RE-ORDERING THE NEW WORLD ORDER

From a social scientific viewpoint, this book presents more theoretical and research questions than answers. It is to be hoped that this synopsis will prompt some action, in addition to continued scholarly investigation of the societal dynamics of societal institutions, that will be directed toward more equitable results for the African American woman.

Such social action is necessary because the Black woman's position in the New World Order, as set forth in this book, is not auspicious. The forces of political and economic re-ordering march forth in a manner which bodes ill for persons of racial, ethnic or gender minority affiliation, a description that epitomizes the status of the African American female. The manner in which these forces are marching appears to be a reactionary retrenchment of White Anglo-Saxon Protestant superiority. The Cold War represented a doctrinal battle between ideologies. It was a conflict based on different belief systems, values and philosophical tenets basically surrounding the economic distribution of goods and services. Its inception could be derived from the writings and teachings of individuals ranging from scholars to statesmen, diplomats to dictators. With the end of the Cold War, around the world, from the former Yugoslavia to the former Soviet Union to the present Rwanda to the present Haiti and, it is contended here, to the present United States, ideological warfare has been replaced with primeval ethnic rivalries and upheavals. In order to further entrench the respective statuses of the various ethnic groups in the United States, the call went out for a meaner, leaner society. That call was answered by a diabolical rejoinder purporting the formation of a "kinder, gentler" society. In this societal environment, crime has become a code word for impending threats from downtrodden racial groups, particularly Blacks. Welfare has become a watchword for the need to scapegoat whoever or whatever is the cause of rising taxes, lowered incomes and a lost way and quality of life. Competition has become the New World Order's most unifying ideological link—albeit a weak one—manipulated with the "fittest" having been pre-selected in many instances. Affirmative action only diversifies the players. New World Order competition dictates the winners. With increased competition as the driving force now behind almost every social institution from health care to education to mass communications to even government—as it becomes "privatized" or vaporized—the New World Order is correspondingly more mean and lean. Was not that the goal? Yes, but was the Black woman the target as well? In this environment, even the lives of most "WASPs" are rendered more insecure, unsafe, unfulfilling and treacherous. And as their lives become even more unsatisfying, not realizing the true source of their frustration, many working and middle-class European Americans call for more of the same meanness and leanness. So much for the kinder, gentler society.

Generally, responsibility for society's failures falls upon those who qualify as the least of these. Because of past institutional racism and discrimination, African Americans emerged in the new, more vicious, less humane (meaner and leaner) societal order as uniquely fit to fulfill the role of scapegoat, to be blamed for other, insidious and relentless world forces set in force by the global multinationals untempered by any viable countervailing ideology—other than that of raw, unmitigated competition. Regardless of merit, Third World countries had used the threat of their vulnerability to predatory communistic forces to extract some advantages from the global corporations, as represented by their respective governments. With the loss of that threat, ethnicity-driven territorial motivations took over. Like the provincialism that preceded the fall of other world civilizations, conflicts degenerated from differences between issues to differences between ethnicities, ever more thinly disguised. The advancement of "me and mine" became the foundation for the new order. The loss of philosophical differences stripped away the thin guise of former global, national and local partnerships that had ostensibly, at least, transcended ethnicity.

In this climate, the New World Order, leaders and followers alike, have fostered such a hateful, mean-spirited rage that the new order has resulted in a new type of disorder,[1] a disorder which lays the foundation for the type of deadly, demented disaster[2] within the borders of the U.S. that two World Wars, a Conflict and an Asian police action had avoided. The loss of humanity in the New World Order has fomented the kind of rage causing treacherous tragedy which U.S. Americans used to attribute to out-of-control autocratic authoritarians in such countries as those of the Middle East, the former Communist bloc and any Third World nations as yet "undeveloped."[3] Imagine our surprise to discover that the enemy is us—the enemy within. For instance, according to commentator Bev Smith, speaking at a university, a house-to-house search was initiated after the bombing of the

Federal Building in Oklahoma City for "Middle-Eastern" looking men. However, Ms. Smith continued, when the suspects in that crime were later described differently, she knew of no such indiscriminate search for "White males with crew cuts and tattoos on their arm." Ms. Smith also summarized that situation with the declaration that, "Hate bombed a building."[4] Further, Ms. Smith, a Black woman, noted in that talk that when the bomb hits Americans it hits her, too. In addition, the Internet has leveled the globe [for at least those who have access to an adequately equipped computer] to one world community of which we are all citizens.

Unadulterated, unbridled White male reactionary fury[5] against this shadow of competition and exploitation run amok has as its logical consequence, the illogical; as its rational result, the irrational; as its predictable end, the unpredictable; as its imaginable finish, the unimaginable; and, as its articuable conclusion, the unspeakable.[6] Actions such as domestic terrorism indicate that when a society declares open season on groups A, C and E but not necessarily on groups B, D and F—unless they get in the way, then sometimes groups B, D and F will get in the way while the exterminators are trying to get to groups A, C and E. But tougher and tougher laws breed tougher and tougher people.[7] Totalitarian states are typified by totalitarian people—and vice versa. More intensive law and order begets more intensive lawlessness and disorder. Ultimately, more extreme measures are taken to defy a police state than a humane one. Justice denied is also injustice which when manifested by the state becomes a role model for the people. The state should espouse standards which seek a higher level of humanity than may be currently found in the masses who have only been selectively informed pursuant to New World Order agendas, anyway.

Who is to say who is the "mastermind"[8]—"spiritual," "substantial" or otherwise—of an explosive New World Order society in an insidious atmosphere in which politicians and national "leaders" desperately try to outdo each other in espousing policies which encourage greater and greater xenophobic myopia and paranoia? In keeping America the preserve of selected groups, the New World Order preservationists have gone off the deep end. H.T. Smith, President of the National Bar Association, noted that in 1995, the 104th Congress, ruled by the "angry white male," not only worked assiduously to eradicate civil rights, but did so in terms that were essentially and unequivocally "race-based."[9] In seeking his vindication from encroaching interlopers, the Anglo male's looking-glass reflection now mirrors destruction and devastation.[10] There are horrible consequences when the facts are misrepresented that a Black teenage mother on welfare or a Black firefighter promoted to sergeant transcending seniority systems that too were grounded in past exclusionism rather than global competition, fast changing technological advancements, computerized telecommunications infrastructures as well as Social Darwinistictype fiscal policies are the cause of rendering human beings more and more superfluous.

To overcome the smallness, the divisiveness and the viciousness of New World Order mandates, society's "rank and file" must outgrow the harbingers of its scapegoating. The end of the Cold War has accentuated the problem, however. Americans in the U.S. have always hated. We have always had a focus group to hate.[11] We hated the Russians. We hated the Germans. We hated the Japanese. We hated the Vietnamese. Then, we hated the Vietnamese War. (Try as *we* might, Ghadafy, Castro or Hussein do not give us the concentration and hate-fulfilling satisfaction as past foreign "threats" have.) Deprived of outsiders to hate, we have turned inward. Now, even more fervently, we hate each other.[12] We have to be taught to hate. So, the people of the U.S. must be re-socialized to look beyond race, gender and ethnicity in order to see another human being.

The employee layoffs which epitomize the New World Order agenda are influenced by the race and gender of the target pool of persons. The ones who are left to a great degree are those who most reflect the ethnicity and gender of the selectors.[13]

The intergroup dynamics described in this book might also be partially explained in Mertonian terms—specifically, that of "relative deprivation." Delivering a presentation entitled "Beyond Polarization: A New Paradigm," at the 90th Annual American Sociological Association meeting, Betty Friedan[14] noted that White male middle-managers were resentful of women and minorities due to the increased vulnerability of their jobs.[15] During the period between 1990 and 1995, White male middle-managers experienced a significant income loss, according to Ms. Friedan. While, relatively speaking, they were better off economically than women or minorities, they blamed those groups for their current insecurity. Ms. Friedan explained that such blame was misplaced inasmuch as the real problems stemmed from deregulation, decentralization and downsizing due to narrow measures of the bottom line, profit[16] and a "culture of greed." In elaboration, she pointed out that in the last twenty years more Americans fell out of prosperity. Forty percent of Americans earn less than $25,000 a year. Those making between $25,000 and $75,000 have shown a decline in income and the only people in the United States who have had an increase in income during that period are those earning over $200,000 a year. Further, as one percent of the nation controls eighty percent of the resources, there is a polarization of wealth in this country. Ms. Friedan encouraged the members of the women's movement for equality, the civil rights movement, the labor movement, everyone—to develop a new vision of community and come to a new sense that concerns itself with the social well-being of women and men, and young and old, and Blacks and Whites.

Thus, something more is needed than education by itself. Something more is needed than politics by itself. Something more is needed than economics by itself. Family or group support and sense of belonging are conditions precedent to all but the most self-actualized in a Maslowian sense. African American women have achieved before in spite of great odds against them (Giddings 1985).

Althea Gibson was the first African American to win the Wimbledon tennis championship, in 1957 and 1958. In track, Alice Coachman was the first Black woman to win a gold medal in the high-jump competition, and Jackie Joyner-Kersee became the first woman to win back-to-back gold medals in the heptathlon in 1988 and 1992.

African American women such as Patricia Roberts Harris (Carter administration) and Hazel O'Leary (Clinton administration)—as well as Jocelyn Elders (formerly of the Clinton administration)—have held high-level and cabinet positions. However, while former Surgeon General Jocelyn Elders was being summarily dismissed for remarks portrayed as imperious, several other members of the Clinton cabinet including the Secretaries of Commerce, Housing and Transportation (the Secretary of Agriculture had already resigned under fire) were under active investigations for alleged misconduct.[17] Nevertheless, they were allowed to remain pending the outcome of the investigation into their various predicaments. There is much less tolerance in the political world for any deviation, large or small, on the part of the Black woman, even globally.[18] Rarely are her activities deemed to require protection, and her removal during times of political expediency is easily effectuated.

Strategies must be developed to increase the level of functioning of the masses of African American women. Such strategies, based on the theoretical and factual findings presented in this book, must include approaches that influence the political environment of the global economy[19] of the New World Order. The only other way would be to amass vast amounts of economic resources. Given the infeasibility of the latter, the former is a more likely strategy for success. Further, such strategies are likely to need considerable focus, discipline and persistence, because the degree of provincialism, nepotism, regionalism and xenophobia will increase proportionate to the decrease in resources likely to occur with the expansion of the New World Order and its accompanying restrictive policies. As goods and services become more scarce, those not within the immediate mantle of New World Order power will experience a mean-spiritedness that will make the apartheid of South Africa at its zenith seem mild. When efforts by "minority" groups to countermand exclusion and suppression by majority groups are decried as fostering "stereotyping, balkanization and deepening polarization," as Supreme Court Justice Anthony Kennedy did in *Miller v. Johnson*,[20] institutionalized racial relationships are frozen and minorities remain "minor."

As the groups designated as "minorities" become more numerous in U.S. society, the power elite will become more and more repressive in efforts to solidify and make their lock on the world's resources that much more formidable. Any strategies which might be effective in offsetting this result unfortunately are rhetorically limited by the relative access of the Black woman to such prerequisites as education, mass communication, money and power. But it is no answer to say that she cannot get power because she does not have power. One uses what one does have. This statement is illustrated by the different reactions that Black professionals from various disciplines had to the New World Order agenda as it developed during the last decade of the twentieth century. Many of the lawyers looked desperately for legal loopholes in the devastating cases as they came out one by one. It was presumed that the right legal "theory" could offset the impending decimation of civil rights for minorities and women. Even though the intent became less subtle, many of the lawyers still could find possible answers and solutions within the context of their law books—keeping the faith in the system as members of their profession had in the almost sixty years between the *Plessy v. Ferguson* case and *Brown v. Topeka Board of Education.*

Medical professionals preferred more patient-responsive health insurance programs. Educators recommended greater resources for more effective educational curriculums. Social workers strove to retain some vestiges of a needs-based welfare system. There were some lawyers who followed the tradition of some of the community activist-style people. Blacks in the social organization arena advocated letter writing to public officials and voter registration campaigns. Community awareness drives and grassroots mobilization are important features of this reaction. The problem is that the youth who were a cornerstone to this approach were different from the youth of the 1960s. Much of the coordination that following a community of interest strategy would have reaped was no longer feasible. The Black community had not been saturated with dope and stripped of hope in the sixties. Like the python, the New World Order had strangled its victims before it swallowed them—that way they were easier to digest and let "nature" take its course—which conceivably could include the elimination process.

Further, as many of the problems that made walking ghost towns out of many Black neighborhoods have had a universal effect,[21] African American women and other Afrogeneric peoples must join with those from the poor and working classes who are Euro- and Asiogeneric.[22] Otherwise, the world will degenerate into a state of petty ethnic squabbles of people such as those from the former Yugoslavia,[23] to those from Somalia,[24] and those in the United States[25] who will be unable to live together. With this scenario, ultimately, the postindustrial period of this Information Age[26] will go the way of other past grandiose civilizations and nation-states which have become too parochial to be.

In the midst of all these New World Order changes, the Black woman is particularly vulnerable. Knowing that the changes hit her the hardest, she has to stand up against the brutally heedless imposition of the New World Order. As Dorothy (Chapter 3) told the author, "The only thing worth dying for is living."

NOTES

1. See also, Letter to the Editor by Howard M. Halpern, Former President of the American Academy of Psychotherapists, "How Hate Speech Leads Readily to Violence," *New York Times*, May 5, 1995, p. A14.

2. John Kifner, "At Least 21 Are Dead, Scores Are Missing After Car Bomb Attack in Oklahoma City Wrecks 9–Story Federal Office Building: 17 Victims Were Children in 2d-Floor Day-Care Center," *New York Times*, April 20, 1995, pp. A 1, A 11.

3. Rick Bragg, "In Shock, Loathing, Denial: 'This Doesn't Happen Here.' " *New York Times*, April 20, 1995, pp. A 1, A 13.

4. Bev Smith (Talk Show Host of BET's (Black Entertainment Television) Weekly Series "Our Voices"), "Toward Communities That Value Diversity, Education and the University's Role Revisited," Keynote Presentation at the Twenty-Second Annual Black Aspirations Celebration, Cleveland State University, April 24, 1995 at 6:00 p.m.

5. Peter Applebome, "The Extremists—Radical Right's Fury Boiling Over: Virulence of Anti-Government Groups Is Rising, Experts Say," *New York Times*, April 23, 1995, p. A 13; H. T. Smith, "NAACP Needs Black Legal Warriors Now," Preamble, *NBA: National Bar Association Magazine*, Vol. 9, No. 3, May/June, 1995, p. 1.

6. Todd S. Purdum, "Army Veteran Held in Oklahoma Bombing; Toll Hits 65 as Hope for Survivors Fades: 2 More Questioned—Officials Suspect Links to Armed Rightists Based in Michigan," *New York Times*, April 22, 1995, pp. A 1, A 8.

7. Editorial, "The Perils of Haste: Terrorism Endangers More Than Life; the Larger Threat May Be to Liberty," *The Plain Dealer*, April 23, 1995, p. 2–C; Jim Nichols, "Aftershock: In the Wake of the Oklahoma City Bombing Will Americans Overreact, Sacrificing Freedom and Judgment on the Altar of Fear?", *Plain Dealer*, April 23, 1995, p. 1–C, 5–C; Elisa Ben-Rafael, "Bury the Dead, Abandon Fear and Hate," *Plain Dealer*, April 23, 1995, pp. 1–C, 3–C.

8. James C. McKinley Jr., "Question in Bombing Trials: Can Two Masterminds Exist?", *New York Times*, April 15, 1995, pp. A 1, A 6 in which it is stated "Ever since Ramzi Ahmed Yousef was arrested in Pakistan two months ago on charges that he engineered the World Trade Center explosion, Federal prosecutors have found themselves in a predicament in their efforts to prosecute Sheik Omar Abdel Rahman and 10 others in a related terrorism case."

9. H. T. Smith, "NAACP Needs Black Legal Warriors Now," Preamble, *NBA: National Bar Association Magazine*, Vol. 9, No. 3, May/June, 1995, p. 1.

10. Tim Weiner, "F.B.I. Hunts 2d Bombing Suspect and Seeks Links to Far Right; Rain Stalls Search of Rubble; Focus on Arizona—Investigators Searching for Evidence of a Broader Plot," *New York Times*, April 23, 1995, pp. A 1, A 12.

11. Cf. James Brook, "Amid Islam's Growth in the U.S., Muslims Face a Surge in Attacks; Survey of Mosques Documents the Hate Crimes," *New York Times*, August 28, 1995, A1, A9.

12. Robert D. McFadden, "Bomb Scare Shuts 3 Major Airports in New York Area," *New York Times*, August 29, 1995, A1, A12 quoting Linda Hall Dashle, deputy administrator of the Federal Aviation Administration in Washington, who stated, "[I]n these uncertain times, you can understand the need for our facilities to be extra cautious. It's always better to be safe than sorry" and also quoting a delayed passenger, Tony Tripodi, dean of the College of Social Work at Ohio State University, who likewise stated, "With everything that's going on, we'd rather be safe than sorry."

13. Peter T. Kilborn, "Backlog of Cases Is Overwhelming Jobs-Bias Agency: Some Workers Giving Up—As Classes of Protected People Expand, Tight Budgets Are Forcing Cuts in Staff," *New York Times*, November 26, 1994, A1, A8.

14. Betty Friedan, "Beyond Polarization: A New Paradigm," Presentation at the 90th Annual Meeting of the American Sociological Association, Washington, D.C., August 22, 1995.

15. Cf. Keith Bradsher, "Skilled Workers Watch Their Jobs Migrate Overseas: A Blow to the Middle Class; College-Educated Foreigners Are Doing High-Technology Tasks for Far Less Pay," *New York Times*, August 28, 1995, A1, C6. The article notes that "Some American workers have trained their foreign replacements [in fields such as computer programming and engineering—fields that traditionally are non-union]."

16. But also see, Saul Hansell, "Chase and Chemical Agree to Merge in $10 Billion Deal Creating Largest U.S. Bank: Deposing Citicorp; 12,000 Job Cuts Seen, Many in New York, as Branches are Shut," *New York Times*, August 29, 1995, A1, C4 and Floyd Norris, "As More Banks Vanish, Wall St. Cheers," *New York Times*, August 29, 1995, C1, C8 in which it was stated that "[I]nvestors have been betting that many banks will disappear, being acquired at a premium. And those banks that remain are expected to become more efficient—largely by dismissing people and closing branches—and thus keep *profits* [italics added] high."

17. Stewart M. Powell, "Clinton Cabinet Supplies Barbs for Political Foes," *Plain Dealer*, March 15, 1995, p. 7–A; David Johnston, "Concluding That Cisneros Lied, Reno Urges a Special Prosecutor," *New York Times*, March 15, 1995, pp. A 1, A 12.

18. Bill Keller, "Winnie Mandela's Fortunes Buffeted Anew by Graft Case," *New York Times*, March 2, 1995, pp. A 1, A 6.

19. Joe McDonald, "Mrs. Clinton Urges Better Lives for Women," *Plain Dealer*, March 15, 1995, p. 5–A.

20. 91 S. Ct. 160 (1995).

21. Victor Perlo, *Economics of Racism U.S.A.: Roots of Black Inequality*, New York: International Publishers, 1975, p. 259.

22. Cf., Barbara Crossette, "U.S. to Help Girls in Poor Lands Stay in School," *New York Times*, March 8, 1995, p. A 9; but, also see, Steven Erlanger, "Accord Reached for I.M.F. to Lend Russia $6 Billion," *New York Times*, March 11, 1995, p. A 4.

23. Roger Cohen, "C.I.A. Report Finds Serbs Guilty in Majority of Bosnia War Crimes," *New York Times*, March 9, 1995, A 1, A 6; Alan Cowell, "New Croat-Bosnian Link Worries U.N.," *New York Times*, March 8, 1995, p. A 4; Editorial, "Balkan Brinkmanship," *New York Times*, March 10, 1995, p. A 14.

24. Donatella Lorch, "Gunmen Race for the Spoils in Mogadishu," *New York Times*, March 2, 1995, pp. A 1, A 4; Donatella Lorch, "Last U.S. Marines Quit Somalia as Escorts for the U.N.," *New York Times*, March 3, 1995, p. A 3; Barbara Crossette, "U.N. Chief Ponders Future of Peacekeepers: As Troops Leave Somalia and Then Bosnia, It's Time to Take Stock," *New York Times*, March 3, 1995, p. A 3.

25. E.g., Todd S. Purdum, "Broad Group Visits President on Affirmative Action's Future: He Says He Fears Issue Will Splinter the Nation," *New York Times*, March 15, 1995, pp. A 1, A 13.

26. But see also, Marc Gunther, "Trying to Bring Journalism With Capital 'J' to Cyberspace," *New York Times*, August 28, 1995, C7 in which it is noted that "Allison Davis [a Black woman], a former producer for 'Today,' is leading an NBC News venture that is distributed on, and underwritten by the Microsoft Network;" and Laurie Flynn, "Permanent Task of Office Temps: Learning to Use New Software [Windows 95]," *New York Times*, August 28, 1995, C3 stating, "Not preparing for Windows 95 could seriously limit job opportunities."

Bibliography

Adler, Freda. *Sisters in Crime: The Rise of the New Female Criminal*. New York: McGraw-Hill, 1975.

———, and Rita James Simon. *The Criminology of Deviant Women*. Boston: Houghton Mifflin, 1979.

Akbar, Na'im. *Chains and Images of Psychological Slavery*. Jersey City, N.J.: New Mind Productions, 1984.

Aldridge, Delores P. *Focusing: Black Male-Female Relationships*. Chicago: Third World Press, 1991.

———. "Toward an Understanding of Black Male/Female Relationships." In *Black Studies: Theory, Method, and Cultural Perspectives*, edited by Talmadge Anderson. Pullman, Washington: Washington State University Press, 1990.

Aldridge, Delores P., and LaFrancis Rodgers-Rose. *The Politics of Black Women's Health*. Newark, N.J.: Traces Institute, 1993.

Allen, Robert L. *Black Awakening in Capitalist America*. Garden City, New York: Anchor Books, Doubleday & Company, 1970.

Amaker, Norman. *Civil Rights and the Reagan Administration*. Washington, D.C.: Urban Institute Press, 1988.

Anderson, Talmadge. *Black Studies: Theory, Method, and Cultural Perspectives*. Pullman, Washington: Washington State University Press, 1990.

Asante, Molefi Kete. "International/Intercultural Relations." In *Contemporary Black Thought*, edited by M. Asante & A. Vandi. Beverly Hills: Sage, 1980, 15–28.

———. *The Afrocentric Idea*. Philadelphia: Temple University Press, 1987.

———. *Kemet, Afrocentricity and Knowledge*. Trenton, New Jersey: Africa World Press, 1990.

Bazelon, David L. "The Hidden Politics of American Criminology." In *The Evolution of Criminal Justice: A Guide for Practical Criminologists*. Beverly Hills, Calif.: Sage, 1978.

Beale, Frances. "Double Jeopardy: To Be Black and Female." In *The Black Woman: An Anthology*, editor Toni Cade Bambara, 90–100. New York: Signet, 1970, 90–100.

Beckman, Bjorn. "Empowerment or Repression? The World Bank and the Politics of African Adjustment." In *Authoritarianism, Democracy and Adjustment: The Politics of Economic Reform in Africa*, edited by Peter Gibbon, Yusaf Bangura, and Arne Ofstad. Uppsala, Sweden: Nordiska Afrikainstituet, 1992, 83–105.

Bell-Scott, Patricia and Beverly Guy-Sheftall. *Double Stitch: Black Women Write About Mothers & Daughters*. New York, N.Y.: Harper-Perennial, 1993.

Bernard, Jessie. *Marriage and Family Among Negroes*. Englewood Cliffs, N.J.: Prentice-Hall, 1966.

Billingsley, Andrew. *Black Families in White America*. Englewood Cliffs, N.J.: Prentice-Hall, 1968.

_____. *Climbing Jacob's Ladder: The Enduring Legacy of African-American Families*. New York, N.Y.: Simon & Schuster, 1992.

Blackwell, James E. *The Black Community: Diversity and Unity*. New York: Dodd, Mead & Company, 1975.

_____. *The Black Community: Diversity and Unity 3rd ed*. New York: HarperCollins Publishers, 1991.

Bullard, Robert. *Confronting Environmental Racism: Voices From the Grassroots*. Boston, Mass.: South End Press, 1993.

_____. *Unequal Protection: Environmental Justice and Communities of Color*. San Francisco: Sierra Club Books, 1994.

Bureau of Justice Statistics, Special Report. *Survey of State Prison Inmates, 1991, Women in Prison*, U.S. Department of Justice, Wash., D.C.: GPO, 1991.

Bynum, Victoria. *Unruly Women: The Politics of Social and Sexual Control in the Old South*. Chapel Hill, N.C.: The University of North Carolina Press, 1991.

Chambliss, William J., and Robert B. Seidman. *Law, Order and Power*. Reading, Mass.: Addison-Wesley Pub. Co., 1971.

Cleaver, Eldridge. *Soul on Ice*. New York: Dell, 1968.

Cloward, Richard A. and Lloyd E. Ohlin. *Delinquency and Opportunity: A Theory of Delinquent Gangs*. Glencoe, Ill.: Free Press, 1960.

Cooley, Charles Horton. *Human Nature and the Social Order* [microform]. New York: C. Scribner's Sons, 1902.

Coser, Lewis. *The Functions of Social Conflict*. Glencoe, Ill.: The Free Press, 1956.

Cressey, Donald, and David A Ward. *Delinquency, Crime and Social Process*. New York: Harper and Row, 1969.

Cruse, Harold. *The Crisis of the Negro Intellectual*. New York: Morrow, 1967.

Dahl, Robert. *Who Governs? Democracy and Power in an American City*. New Haven, Conn.: Yale University Press, 1962.

Dahl, Robert, and C.E. Lindbloom. *Politics, Economics, and Welfare: Planning and Politico-economic Systems Resolved into Basic Social Processes*. New York: Harper, 1953.

Dahrendorf, Ralf. *Class and Class Conflict in Industrial Society*. Stanford, California: Stanford University Press, 1959.

Davis, Angela Y. *Women, Race and Class*. New York: Vintage Books—A Division of Random House, 1983.

DeFleur, Melvin L., William V. D'Antonio, and Lois B. DeFleur. *Sociology: Man in Society*. Glenview, Illinois: Scott, Foresman and Company, 1971.

Diallo, Yaya and Mitchell Hall. *The Healing Drum: African Wisdom Teachings*. Rochester, Vermont: Destiny Books, 1989.

Dickerson, Bette J. *African American Single Mothers*. Thousand Oaks, California: Sage Publications, 1995.

Diop, Cheikh Anta. *Civilization or Barbarism: An Authentic Anthropology* (trans. from the French by Yaa-Lengi Meema Ngemi), edited by Harold J. Salemson and Marjoliun de Jager. Brooklyn, N.Y.: Lawrence Hill Books, 1991.

Drake, St. Clair and Horace R. Cayton. *Black Metropolis Volume 2: A Study of Negro Life in a Northern City*. New York: A Harbinger Book—Harcourt, Brace & World, Inc., 1945.

Du Bois, W. E. B. (1903). *The Souls of Black Folk*. U.S.A.: The Avon Discuss Series of 1968.

Durkheim, Emile, *Durkheim and the Law*, editors Steven Lukes and Andrew Scull. New York: St. Martin, 1983.

Elliott, Rogers. *Litigating Intelligence: IQ Tests, Special Education and Social Science in the Courtroom*. Dover, Mass.: Auburn House Publishing Company, 1987.

Ellul, Jacques. *Propaganda: The Formation of Men's Attitudes*. New York: Vintage Books, A Division of Random House, 1965.

Epperson, A. Ralph. *The New World Order*. Tucson, Arizona: Publius Press, 1990.

Etzioni, Amitai. *The Active Society: A Theory of Societal and Political Processes*. New York, N.Y.: The Free Press, 1968.

Fanon, Frantz. *The Wretched of the Earth*. New York: Grove Press, 1965.

Freire, Paulo. *Pedagogy of the Oppressed*. New York: Continuum, 1993.

Gary, Lawrence E., and Lee P. Brown. *Crime and Its Impact Upon the Black Community*. Washington, D.C.: The Howard University Press, 1975.

Giddings, Paula. *When and Where I Enter: The Impact of Black Women on Race and Sex in America*. New York: Bantam Books, 1985.

Glaser, Daniel. *Adult Crime and Social Policy*. Englewood Cliffs, N.J.: Prentice-Hall, 1972.

Glasgow, Douglas G. *The Black Underclass*. New York: Vintage Books, 1981.

Glueck, Sheldon. *The Welfare State and the National Welfare*. Cambridge, Mass.: Addison-Wesley Press, 1952.

Goffman, Erving. *Stigma*. Englewood Cliffs, N.J.: Prentice-Hall, 1963.

Gresson III, Aaron David. *The Recovery of Race In America*. Minneapolis, Minn.: University of Minnesota, 1995.

Hale, Janice. *Black Children: Their Roots, Culture and Learning Styles*. Provo, Utah: Brigham Young University Press, 1982.

Hare, Nathan, and Julia Hare. *The Endangered Black Family*. San Francisco: Black Think Tank, 1984.

Harrington, Michael. *The New American Poverty*. New York: Penguin Books, 1986.

Hemmons, Willa Mae. "From the Halls of Hough and Halsted: A Comparison of Black Students on Predominantly White and Predominantly Black Campuses," *Journal of Black Studies*, 12, 4 (1982): 383–402.

Henderson, Lenneal L. "Empowerment Through Enterprise: African American Business Development," *The State of Black America 1993*, edited by John Jacob. New York: National Urban League, 1993.

Hill, Robert Bernard. *Research on the African-American Family: A Holistic Perspective*. Westport, Conn.: Auburn House, 1993.

Hill, Robert B. *The Strengths of Black Families*. New York: National Urban League, 1972.

Hill-Collins, Patricia. "The Afro-American Work/Family Nexus: An Exploratory Analysis." In *Black Studies: Theory, Method, and Cultural Perspectives*, edited by Talmadge Anderson. Pullman, Washington: Washington State University Press, 1990: 98–109.

Hill Collins, Patricia. *Black Feminist Thought: Knowledge, Consciousness, and the Politics of Empowerment*. New York, N.Y.: Routledge, Chapman and Hall, Inc., 1991.

Hornsby, Jr., Alton. *Chronology of African American History: Significant Events and People from 1619 to the Present*. Detroit, Mich.: Gale Research, Inc., 1991.

Horowitz, Donald L. *The Courts and Social Policy*. Washington D.C.: The Brookings Institution, 1977.

Horowitz, Ruth. *Teen Mothers: Citizens or Dependents?* Chicago: University of Chicago Press, 1995.

Hutchinson, Earl. *The Mugging of Black America*. Chicago: African-American Images, 1990.

Inkeles, Alex. *What Is Sociology?* Englewood Cliffs, New Jersey: Prentice-Hall, 1964.

James, George G.M. *Stolen Legacy: Greek Philosophy Is Stolen Egyptian Philosophy*. Trenton, New Jersey: Africa World Press, 1992.

Jewel, K. Sue. *Survival of the Black Family*. Westport, Conn.: Greenwood Press, 1988.

Karenga, Maulana. *Introduction to Black Studies*. Los Angeles: University of Sankore Press, 1993.

Karenga, Maulana, and Jacob H. Carruthers (Association for the Study of Classical African Civilizations). *African Worldview: Research, Rescue, and Restoration*. Los Angeles: University of Sankore Press, 1986.

Kershaw, Terry. "The Emerging Paradigm in Black Studies," edited by Talmadge Anderson. *Black Studies: Theory, Method, and Cultural Perspectives*. Pullman, Washington: Washington State University Press, 1990.

Kitson, Gay C., and William M. Holmes. *Portrait of Divorce: Adjustment to Marital Breakdown*. New York: Guilford Press, 1992.

Kunjufu, Jawanza. *Developing Positive Self Images and Discipline*. Chicago, Illinois: African-American Images, 1984.

Ladner, Joyce A. *The Death of White Sociology*. New York: Random House, 1973.

Liebow, Elliot. *Tally's Corner: A Study of Negro Streetcorner Men*. Boston: Little, Brown, 1967.

Lusane, Clarence. *Pipe Dream Blues: Racism and the War on Drugs*. Boston, Mass: South End Press, 1991.

McAdoo, Harriette Pipes. *Black Families*. Beverly Hills, Calif.: Sage Publications, 1981.

McAdoo, Harriette Pipes. "Strategies Used by Black Single Mothers Against Stress." In *Review of Black Political Economy* 14 (no. 2/3 1985): 153–66.

McClain, Paula, and Albert K. Karnig. *Urban Minority Administrators: Politics, Policy and Style*. New York: Greenwood Press, 1988.

Madhubuti, Haki R. *The Black Male, Obsolete, Single, or Endangered?* Chicago: Third World Press, 1990.

Marable, Manning. *How Capitalism Underdeveloped Black America*. Boston: South End Press, 1983.

Martin, Elmer P., and Joanne Mitchell Martin. *The Black Extended Family*. Chicago: University of Chicago Press, 1978.

Merton, Robert King. *On the Shoulders of Giants; A Shandean Postcript*. New York: Free Press, 1965.

Merton, Robert K. *Social Theory and Social Structure*. Glencoe, Ill.: The Free Press, 1954.

Mills, C. W. *The Power Elite*. New York: Oxford University Press (Paper), 1959.

Myrdal, Gunnar with the assistance of Richard Sterner and Arnold Rose, *An American Dilemma: The Negro Problem and Modern Democracy*. New York: Harper and Brothers, 1944.

Myers, Lena Wright. *Black Women, Do They Cope Better?* Englewood Cliffs, N.J.: Prentice-Hall, 1980.

Neely, Richard. *How Courts Govern America*. New Haven, Conn.: Yale University Press, 1981.

Nobles, Wade W. "Extended Self: Rethinking the So-Called Negro Self Concept." In *Black Psychology* (2nd ed.) R.L. Jones (Ed.). New York: Harper and Row, 1980.

Noblit, George W. *Schooling in Social Context: Qualitative Studies*. Norwood, N.J.: Ablex Pub. Corp., 1987.

Parsons, Talcott. *The Social System*. New York: The Free Press, 1951.

_____. *American Sociology: Perspectives, Problems, Methods*. New York: Basic Books, 1968.

Perlo, Victor. *Economics of Racism U.S.A.: Roots of Black Inequality*. New York, N.Y.: International Publishers, 1975.

Phillips, Llad and Harold L. Votey, Jr. *Economic Analysis of Pressing Social Problems*. Chicago: Rand McNally College Pub. Co., 1974.

Piven, Frances Fox, and Richard Cloward. *Regulating the Poor: The Functions of Public Welfare*. New York: Random House, 1971.

_____. "Poor People's Movements: Why They Succeed, How They Fail." *Rural Sociology* 45, 1 (Spring 1980): 171–173.

_____. *The New Class War: Reagan's Attack on the Welfare State and Its Consequences*. New York: Pantheon, 1982.

Prestage, Jewell L. "Political Behavior of American Black Women: An Overview." In *The Black Woman*, edited by LaFrances Rose. Beverly Hills, Calif.: Sage, 1980, 233–50.

Quinney, Richard. *Class, State and Crime: On the Theory and Function of Criminal Justice*. New York, N.Y.: David McKay Company, 1977.

_____. *Criminology: Analysis and Critique of Crime in America*. Boston: Little, Brown and Co., 1975.

Rainwater, Lee and William Yancey. *The Moynihan Report and the Politics of Controversy*. Cambridge, Mass.: MIT Press, 1967.

Rank, Mark Robert. *Living on the Edge: The Realities of Welfare in America*. New York: Columbia University Press, 1994.

Rodgers-Rose, LaFrances, and James T. Rodgers. *Strategies for Resolving Conflict in Black Male and Female Relationships*. Newark, N.J.: Traces Institute Publications, 1985.

Rose, LaFrances. *The Black Woman*. Beverly Hills, Calif.: Sage, 1980.

Rose, Peter I. *They and We: Racial and Ethnic Relations in the United States*, Second Ed. New York: Random House, 1974.

Ryan, William. *Blaming the Victim*. New York, N.Y.: Vintage Press, 1972.

Scheingold, Stuart A. *The Politics of Law and Order: Street Crime and Public Policy*. New York: Longman, 1984.

Sennett, Richard, and Jonathan Cobb. *The Hidden Injuries of Class*. New York, N.Y:. Vintage Books, 1973.

Shakur, Assata. *Assata: An Autobiography*. London: Zed Books Ltd., 1987.

Silberman, Charles E. *Criminal Violence, Criminal Justice*. New York: Vintage Press, 1976.

Skolnick, Arlene. *Family in Transition: Rethinking Marriage, Sexuality, Child Rearing and Family Organization*, 3rd Ed. Boston: Little, Brown, 1980.

Skolnick, Jerome H. *Justice Without Trial: Law Enforcement in a Democratic Society*. New York: Wiley, 1966.

Smith, David A., and József Böröcz. *A New World Order? Global Transformations in the Late Twentieth Century*. Westport, Connecticut: Praeger Publishers, 1995.

Spencer, Herbert. *Herbert Spencer: Structure, Function and Evolution*. Edited by Stanislav Andreski. New York: Scribner, 1971.

Stack, Carol. *All Our Kin: Strategies for Survival*. New York: Harper and Row, 1981.

Staples, Robert. *The Black Woman in America: Sex, Marriage and the Family*. Chicago: Nelson-Hall, 1973.

Staples, Robert. *The World of Black Singles: Changing Patterns of Male/Female Relations*. Westport, Conn.: Greenwood Press, 1981.

Steffensmeir, D., and J. H. Kramer. "Sex-Based Differences in the Sentencing of Adult Criminal Defendants: An Empirical Test and Theoretical Overview." *Sociology and Social Research* 66 (April, 1982): 289–304.

Sutherland, Edwin H. *White Collar Crime*. New York: Holt, Rinehart and Winston, 1961.

_____, and Donald Cressey. *Criminology*. Philadelphia: Lippincott, 1974.

Swinton, David. H. "The Economic Status of African Americans," edited by John Jacob. In *The State of Black America 1993*. New York: National Urban League, 1993.

Taylor, Ronald L. "The Study of Black People: A Survey of Empirical and Theoretical Models." In *Black Studies: Theory, Method, and Cultural Perspectives*, edited by Talmadge Anderson. Pullman, Washington: Washington State University Press, 1990.

Taylor, Steve. *Durkheim and the Study of Suicide*. New York: St. Martin's Press, 1982.

Thomas, W. I. *The Unadjusted Girl*. Boston, Mass.: Little, Brown, 1931.

Thomas, W. I., and Florian Znaniecki. *The Polish Peasant in Europe and America, Vol. I-IV*. Chicago, Ill.: University of Chicago Press, 1918.

Tonnies, Ferdinand (C.P. Loomis, trans.). *Fundamental Concepts of Sociology*. New York, N.Y.: American Book, 1940.

United States. Civil Rights Act of 1964, 42 U.S.C. 2000, et al.

_____. Civil Rights Restoration Act of 1991, 42 U.S.C. 1981 as amended; 42 U.S.C. 2000e as amended.

Vold, George B. *Theoretical Criminology*. New York: Oxford University Press, 1985.

Walters, Ronald W. *Black Presidential Politics in America: A Strategic Approach.* Albany, N.Y.: State University of New York Press, 1988.

Walton, Jr., Hanes. *Black Politics: A Theoretical and Structural Analysis.* Philadelphia, Penn: J.B. Lippincott Co., 1972.

Warfield-Coppock, Nsenga. *Afrocentric Theory and Applications, Volume I: Adolescent Rites of Passage.* Washington, D.C.: Baobab Associates, 1990.

Watson, Wilbur H. *The Village: An Oral Historical and Ethnographic Study of a Black Community.* Atlanta, Ga.: Village Vanguard, 1989.

West, Cornel. *Race Matters.* Boston: Beacon Press, 1993.

Whyte, William F. *Street Corner Society, the Social Structure of an Italian Slum.* Chicago, Ill.: University of Chicago Press, 1943.

Wilhelm, Sidney. *Who Needs the Negro?* Cambridge, Mass.: Schenkman Pub. Co., 1970.

Wilkinson, Doris Y. "Afro-American Women and Their Families." *Marriage and Family Review* 7, 3–4 1984: 125–42.

Williams, Evelyn. *Inadmissible Evidence: The Story of the African-American Trial Lawyer Who Defended the Black Liberation Army.* Brooklyn, New York: Lawrence Hill Books, 1993.

Williams, Juan. *Eyes on the Prize: America's Civil Rights Years, 1954–1965.* New York: Penguin Books USA, 1987.

Wirth, Louis. *The Ghetto.* Chicago: University of Chicago Press, 1929.

Woodson, Carter G. *The Mis-Education of the Negro.* Trenton, New Jersey: Africa World Press (1990 edition first published by Associated Publishers, 1933).

X, Malcolm and Alex Haley. *The Autobiography of Malcolm X.* New York: Grove Press, 1965.

Yochelson, Samuel and Stanton E. Samenow. *The Criminal Personality.* New York: J. Aronson, 1976.

Index

About the Author

WILLA MAE HEMMONS is a lawyer and sociologist. She received her PhD in Sociology from Case Western Reserve University and her JD from the University of Illinois School of Law. She is a practicing attorney in the areas of criminal law, domestic relations and contracts, and is also a Professor in the Department of Social Work at Cleveland State University.